A People's History of the Portuguese Revolution

People's History

History tends to be viewed from the perspective of the rich and powerful, where the actions of small numbers are seen to dictate the course of world affairs. But this perspective conceals the role of ordinary women and men, as individuals or as parts of collective organisations, in shaping the course of history. The People's History series puts ordinary people and mass movements centre stage and looks at the great moments of the past from the bottom up.

The People's History series was founded and edited by William A. Pelz (1951–2017).

Also available:

Long Road to Harpers Ferry
The Rise of the First American Left
Mark A. Lause

A People's History of the
German Revolution, 1918–19
William A. Pelz
Foreword by Mario Kessler

A People's History of the Portuguese Revolution

Raquel Varela

Edited by Peter Robinson
Translated by Sean Purdy

First published by Bertrand Editora as *História do Povo na Revolução Portuguesa 1974–75*

English language edition first published 2019 by Pluto Press
345 Archway Road, London N6 5AA

www.plutobooks.com

British Library Cataloguing in Publication Data
A catalogue record for this book is available from the British Library

ISBN   978 0 7453 3858 3   Hardback
ISBN   978 0 7453 3857 6   Paperback
ISBN   978 1 7868 0357 3   PDF eBook
ISBN   978 1 7868 0359 7   Kindle eBook
ISBN   978 1 7868 0358 0   EPUB eBook

This book is printed on paper suitable for recycling and made from fully managed and
sustained forest sources. Logging, pulping and manufacturing processes are expected to
conform to the environmental standards of the country of origin.

Typeset by Stanford DTP Services, Northampton, England

Simultaneously printed in the United Kingdom and United States of America

I dedicate this book to the historian Valério Arcary from whom I learned the centrality of theory in the history of revolutions. I also learned from him not to be afraid when the empirical evidence forces us to start over again. His intellectual courage is an example for me.

I also want to dedicate this book to Peter Robinson, who did an extraordinary editing job, adding various notes, ideas and texts from his pen that made the book much better. His gentleness and passion for the revolution that helped build 44 years ago is still evident today.

Finally, I want to thank William Pelz (1951–2017), who introduced me to Pluto Press. Born in a working-class district on the south side of Chicago, Bill liked to refer in his biography to his initial hope of pursuing a career as a bus driver, explaining that he later lowered his expectations and became an academic historian instead. Bill never got to drive buses, but was a brilliant historian and author of important works dedicated to the study of the working class.

Contents

Photographs, Figures and Tables

Photographs

Figures

Tables

Acknowledgements

This book would not have been possible in the first place without the aid of Alejandro Lora, my Erasmus student, who did an exhaustive, months-long search of social conflicts in the Portuguese Revolution. The researcher Joana Alcântara systematised this collection in a detailed project that listed the strikes, demonstrations, workers' and social movements during the 19 months of the Portuguese Revolution. I want to thank all those colleagues who have aided me with articles, references, data and, sometimes, criticism. Essential, in particular, but not in any special order were: Miguel Pérez, Jorge Fontes, Marcelo Badaró Mattos, Alberto Carrillo-Linares, Encarnación Lemus, Ángeles González, Marcel van der Linden, Felipe Abranches Demier, Renato Guedes, Ana Rajado, Carlos Pratas, Sara Granemann, Cleusa Santos, Antonio Louçã, Rivânia Moura, José Babiano, Rui Bebiano, Natércia Coimbra and Giulia Strippoli.

I would also like to thank the precious help of those interviewed for my research whose names are mentioned throughout the book. I appreciated the accessibility of the following institutions: the Hemeroteca Municipal de Lisboa, the Arquivo Rádio e Televisão de Portugal (RTP), the historical archives of the CCOO (Fundação 1 de Mayo, Madrid), the archives of the Centro de Documentação 25 de April, the archives of the Centro de Intervenção para o Desenvolvimento Amílcar Cabral and the International Archive of Social History (Amsterdam).

Travel expenses to access files were supported by the projects 'Transición La Ibérica. Portugal y España. El Interés International por la Liberalización Peninsular (1968–1978)' (HAR2011-27 460) and 'History of Industrial Relations in Portugal and the Lusophone World' (PTDC// EPH-HIS/3701/2012).

Special thanks to my outstanding editors, Eduardo Boavida and João Santos, as well as the whole team at Bertrand. Finally, thanks to the Instituto de História Contemporânea, Faculdade de Ciências Sociais e Humanas, Universidade Nova de Lisboa and the International Institute of Social History where I conducted all my research. Thank you for the dedication and commitment of the entire Pluto team.

I also wish to thank my family and Guida Jorge who lovingly helped take care of Manuel and David allowing them to earn even more affection and education than was available from their sometimes-absent mother.

Editor's note on the English edition

Note by the English editor, Peter Robinson. As we cannot take it for granted that the English-speaking reader will be familiar with aspects that people in Portugal know about, more background information has been spliced in, for example relating to the geography and history. Some phrases and sentences have been drawn directly from a little booklet I wrote, called *Portugal 1974–75 The Forgotten Dream*. I wrote the section on the links with Britain and the International Left in Chapter 17.

I was in Portugal for some of the time as a political organiser for the British International Socialists and subsequently interviewed and wrote about these amazing events. I completed a M Phil thesis in 1999, called *Workers' Councils in Portugal 1974–1975*, and it took me ten years because life got in the way. I studied in depth, four studies of embryonic workers' councils. They were:

- the Inter-Empresas (May 74–March 75)
- the Revolutionary Councils of Workers, Soldiers and Sailors (CRTSMs) (April 75–June 75)
- the Popular Assemblies (July 75–November 75)
- the Setubal committee of Struggle (October 75–November 75)

We have spliced in examples from all four organisations into the English edition.

The reader may like to refer to the further reading section, which is only of books in English.

I would like to thank Martin Sear and Justin Gutmann for their help in my editing. I want to also thank David Castle from Pluto Press for his patience. Thanks to *Socialist Worker* and Jose Reis who supplied most of the photos for this edition.

List of Abbreviations

ADUs   Assembleas Democraticas de Unidade – Democratic Unit
            Assemblies
AOC   Aliança Operário-Camponesa – Workers' and Peasants'
            Alliance
CDS   Centro Democrático Social – Democratic and Social
            Centre party
CDR   Comités da Defesa da Revolução – Committees to Defend
            the Revolution
CGTP   Confederação Geral dos Trabalhadores Portugueses –
            General Confederation of Portuguese Workers
CM   Comissão de Moradaores – Resident's Commission
COPCON   Comando Operacional do Continente – Continental
            Operations Command
CRTSMs   Conselhos Revolucionários de Trabalhadores, Soldados
            e Marinheiros – Revolutionary Councils of Workers,
            Soldiers and Sailors
CT   Comissão de Trabalhadores – Workers' Commission
CTT   Correios, Telégrafos e Telefones – Post, Telegraphs and
            Telephones
Efacec   Empresa Fabril Ateliers de Constructions Electriques de
            Charleroi
EPAM   Escola Prática de Administração Militar
EPC   Escola Prática de Cavalaria – Practical School of the
            Calvary
EPI   Escola Prática de Infantaria – Practical School of Infantry
FRELIMO   Frente de Libertação de Moçambique – the Mozambique
            Liberation Front
FSP   Frente Socialista Popular – Popular Socialist Front
FUP   Frente de Unidade Popular – Popular United Front
FUR   Frente de Unidade Revolucionária – United Revolutionary
            Front
GNR   Guarda Nacional Republicana – Republican National
            Guard. A para-military police force
JOC   Juventude Operária Católica

JSN	Junta de Salvação Nacional – Junta for National Salvation
LCI	Liga Comunista Internacionalista – Internationalist Communist League
LUAR	Liga de Unidade e Acção Revolucionária – League of Revolutionary Unity and Action
MDP/CDE	Movimento Democrático Português/Comissão Democrática Eleitoral – Popular Democratic Movement/ Democratic and Social Centre party
MES	Movimento de Esquerda Socialista – Movement of Left Socialists
MFA	Movimento das Forças Armadas – Movement of the Armed Forces
MLM	Movimento de Libertação da Mulher – Womens' Democratic Movement
MPLA	Movimento Popular de Libertação de Angola Angolan Popular Liberation Movement
MRPP	Movimento Reorganizativo do Partido do Proletariado – Movement for the Reorganisation of the Party of the Proletariat
OGMA	Oficinas Gerais de Material Aeronáutico
PAIGC	Partido Africano para a Independência da Guiné e Cabo Verde – African Party for the Independence of Guinea and Cape Verde
PCP	Partido Comunista Português – Portuguese Comnunist Party
PIDE/DGS	Polícia Internacional e de Defesa do Estado/Direcção Geral de Segurança – International and State Defence Police
PM	Polícia Militar – Military Police
PPD	Partido Popular Democrático – Popular Democratic Party
PRP/BR	Partido Revolucionário do Proletariado /Brigadas Revolucionárias – Revolutionary Proletarian Party/ Revolutionary Brigades
PRT	Partido Revolucionário dos Trabalhadores – Revolutionary Worker's Party
PS	Partido Socialista – Socialist Party
PSP	Polícia de Segurança Pública – Public Security Police
RAL 1	Regimento de Artilharia Ligeira 1 – First Light Artillery Regiment. Later renamed RALIS

RALIS	Regimento de Artilharia Ligeira de Lisboa – Light Artillery Regiment of Lisbon
RIOQ	Regimento de Infantaria Operacional de Queluz
RPM	Regimento de Polícia Militar – Military Police Regiment, see PM
RR	Rádio Renascença – Radio Renascenca
SAAL	Serviço de Apoio Ambulatório Local – Mobile Service for Local Support
SUV	Soldados Unidos Vencerão! – Soldiers United Will Win!
TAP	Transportes Aéreos Portugueses – Portuguese Air Transport
TLP	Telefones de Lisboa e Porto – Lisbon and Porto Telephones
UDP	União Democrática Popular – Popular Democratic Unity

I

Introduction

For those who want to overthrow the system that oppresses them, it helps to learn and remember and to be inspired by others who have tried to do the same.

A revolution took place in Portugal. We can date this precisely: between 25 April 1974 and 25 November 1975. The revolution was the most profound to have taken place in Europe since the Second World War. During those 19 months, hundreds of thousands of workers went on strike, hundreds of workplaces were occupied sometimes for months and perhaps almost 3 million people took part in demonstrations, occupations and commissions. A great many workplaces were taken over and run by the workers. Land in much of southern and central Portugal was taken over by the workers themselves. Women won, almost overnight, a host of concessions and made massive strides towards equal pay and equality. (Strikes towards equal pay were also made by men in favour of women – it was a class approach not just gender.) Thousands of houses were occupied. Tens of thousands of soldiers rebelled. Nobody predicted that so many would try quickly to learn and put into practice the ideas that explode from those who are exploited when they try to take control of their own destiny. Portugal 1974–1975 was not an illusion. We have to remember, celebrate and learn from Portugal. That is why this book has been written.

This is not the first book which tries to capture and celebrate our achievements. I am deeply indebted to some of the work and research that has been done already.

The history of the Portuguese Revolution, as with the history of any revolution, is the history of the State, which could no longer govern as before and the history of those who were no longer willing to be governed in the same way. This book deals with a part of the construction of an alternative, of those who were no longer 'willing to be governed' as they had been before.

People changed. They changed because they refused to fight in the war, because they demanded a say in where the crèche was located or in the accounts of the companies. They changed because they learned the meaning of direct democracy in many forms: possibly because of direct person-to-person and face-to-face democracy, or the vote of a raised hand in the residents' commissions, committees of struggle, occupied lands, workers' commissions, soldiers' assemblies, and general meetings of workers or students.

New forms of democracy were forged, as they always are when people become engaged in struggles. Democracy becomes our weapon. It is far more than merely putting a cross on a ballot paper once in a while.

Never before in the history of Portugal did workers have such a consciousness of being workers and of being proud of it: 'There is only serious freedom when there is peace, bread, housing,' they sang.'

The revolution profoundly changed Portugal. But the revolution did not change the relations of production in a lasting way. The State recovered, the regime stabilised itself and governments operated without the involvement of the masses of people who had helped make the events in 1974–1975.

The revolution was defeated. It was not crushed like that in Chile the year before or the uprisings in Hungary in 1956. As always, the victors write and rewrite history. The scale and magnificence of the struggles below and the capacity to involve is overwritten and lost. Some have likened it to a hallucinogenic dream, others a forgotten dream and yet others an impossible dream. It is almost as if nothing really happened – as if we have nothing to learn.

Photo 1 The community of an occupied farm holds a meeting to decide how the work of picking the olives should be shared out. (*Socialist Worker*)

Most of the accounts that appeared at the time – and since – have been top-down, often written by 'personalities' focusing perhaps on themselves, or upon the army and senior military personnel and bourgeois machinations and almost never on the *povo*, that is, the people. Where the working class is referred to, for example, 'the threat of labour unrest', it is as seen from the outside as a problem rather than the solution.

The rewrites have marginalised the working class, and I mean this in the broadest sense. The leaders of the Portuguese Revolution were those who lived from their work, their children and families: intellectual and manual workers, men and women, skilled and unskilled.[2] This included ordinary soldiers, who came from the ranks of the working class, and who were immensely politicised by the struggles of their brothers and sisters.

The revolution has been marginalised in many other ways; but actually, Portugal had been marginalised before the revolution, as being a backward fascist corner, not as an outpost of capital. I prefer not to use the word fascism to describe the autocratic dictatorship but I respect the rights and sense of those who suffered under the dictatorship to call it fascist. The fact is that Portuguese capitalism was locked into international capitalism. The Portuguese empire became one of the pillars of the free world, a founder member of NATO (1949), and recipient of modern arms and expert advice on techniques of repression. Capital was investing in the shipyards and large modern factories in the industrial belt of Lisbon. The African wars could not have continued for very long without NATO weaponry and equipment. International capital was benefitting from the supply of raw materials for Angola and the sourcing of cheap labour for South Africa.

Hence, Portugal cannot be isolated from the international financial crisis – one symptom being the 1973 oil crisis and the collapse of the Gold Standard.[3] Portugal was also an echo of political turbulence. One might recall May 1968 France with student riots and a nationwide general strike and the Italian 'hot autumn' of 1969, strike waves in Germany and Britain in the early 1970s, and the struggle against military rule in Greece in 1973–1974.

In charting the chronology of the revolution, the focus is first and foremost on strikes, demonstrations and occupations of factories, businesses and homes. This is distinct from the existing historical literature which emphasises the dates of the coups and changes of provisional governments and the role of the armed forces. My angle shifts from that of institutions to the social field. The coups of 28 September 1974 and 11 March 1975 came about because of the struggles in workplaces and communities, and the coups were defeated because of these very forces. I advance the hypothesis that 11

March 1975 was the result of the extension – detailed throughout this book – of workers' control. The fall of the Fifth Provisional Government at the end of August 1975 was not the end of the revolution, but merely the maturing of the revolutionary crisis, that is, the moment when the political parties, namely, the Popular Democratic Party (PPD),[4] the Socialist Party (PS)[5] and the Portuguese Communist Party (PCP)[6] at the top of society and the Armed Forces Movement (MFA), allied together or not were no longer 'able to govern' and those from below were 'no longer willing to be governed'.

Despite the pretensions of the Socialist and Communist Parties, state and revolution drifted apart in 1974–1975. Indeed, the revolution was constructed *against* the State.

So this is a people's history. In the last decade, *people's histories* have widely surfaced as a genre after the unexpected success of Howard Zinn's *A People's History of the United States*.[7] They are different from conventional historical accounts, representing more closely 'History from Below' to use Hobsbawm's phrase. Howard Zinn said that histories of the people are the voice of those who had no voice. Chris Harman, author of *A People's History of the World*,[8] called them the 'scaffolding of society'.

Photo 2 Workers and Soldiers Demonstration, 16 July 1975. Armed soldiers (and tanks) support a demonstration in Lisbon called by Inter-Commissions (federation of shanty town neighbourhood committees). (*Socialist Worker*)

In *A People's History of the Portuguese Revolution*, readers will find a history of resistance, of the 'voiceless', those who have been habitually absent in history books, buried by decrees, diplomatic statements, back-room deals and conventional political struggles. You will not find here a history of colonial war, but the history of resistance to forced labour in the colonies or a history of anti-war resistance. You will not discover the history of the fall of the provisional governments, but the history of workers' control which led to the fall of various coalitions that tried to rule the *strange ungovernable people of Iberia* – people who learned for the first time how to govern themselves. You will not read here the indispensable history of political parties, but that of the working class in its widest sense. Nor will the reader find a history of the intense diplomatic relations of the period, yet there will be references to solidarity movements between countries by those from 'below'.

The authors who have dedicated their research to people's histories have clearly distinguished themselves from those who see the people as a spontaneous and disorganised crowd. This book is inspired by a broad concept of the working class; it highlights the history of grass-roots workers' organisations that were often closely linked to political leaders and parties from the far-left. While not exhaustively studied in this book, the political groups are fundamental in explaining the dynamics of the revolutionary process. But I would like to suggest that many activities were spontaneous – well not quite spontaneous.

A total history, desired by all, is not only the history of resistance. But it cannot be accomplished without the history of resistance: those who did not accept orders without first contesting, discussing and voting on them.

Raquel Varela,
November 2018

2

The Seeds of Change

People make their own histories, but not in circumstances of their own choosing.
Karl Marx: 'The Eighteenth Brumaire of Louis Bonaparte'[1]

Whose Power?

While there were many momentous moments, probably the moment in which the Portuguese Revolution came closest to insurrection, that is, the moment in a revolution where the conquest of the State under the leadership of workers takes place,[2] was to be found at São Bento on 13 November 1975. São Bento, in Lisbon, was the seat of the Portuguese parliament. It was here that the Constituent Assembly and the Government were being held hostage, surrounded by a mass of almost 100,000 people, the majority of whom were construction workers. The scenario was almost unreal: it was Europe, in sunny Lisbon, the disproportionately large capital of Portugal, and the capital of the last colonial empire in history. If it were not for the helicopters, the hostages in the São Bento Palace, including the prime minister, would not even have received food or blankets. Outside there was a gigantic demonstration of workers who elbowed each other and literally stood on top of each other on the palace steps with red flags and banners, yelling slogans.

Suddenly, a cement truck entered the square and crossed the mass of demonstrators who surrounded the Assembly and, with smiles and raised fists, they moved aside to let it pass. On top, there were two men. One of them wore jeans and an open shirt, had a cigarette in his mouth and smiled triumphantly at the crowd. With one hand on the cement mixer and the other raised as a clenched fist he yelled along with the other demonstrators: 'We are the people! We are the people! We are the people!'[3]

Later, Prime Minister Admiral Pinheiro de Azevedo asked the commandos to come and rescue him and his ministers. They refused. He then requested a helicopter to rescue just a few of them. The Military Police overheard the request, alerted the building workers and the helicopter was prevented from landing.

After 36 hours, the prime minister conceded all the building workers' demands with effect from 27 November.

When he decided to suspend government functions on 20 November 1975, one week after the siege of the Constituent Assembly, Prime Minister de Azevedo of the Sixth Provisional Government – at the end of nearly 19 months of revolution, five governments had already fallen – confessed in his forthright and indiscrete style that the very state had been destabilised. Visibly irritated, he responded to a journalist's question on the military situation: 'The situation, as far as I know, is the same: first, plenários [democratic meetings of the soldiers] are held and afterwards orders are given [to the Government]!'[4]

The paralysis of formal government was so total that, on 20 November, the government actually declared it was not going to do anything 'political'. In fact, the government announced: 'we are on strike, everybody is on strike, the government is also on strike'. It would merely act in an administrative capacity until the resolution of the power conflict. The government threatened to set itself up in exile in Porto, while the peasants and farmers in the North threatened to cut off food supplies to the 'red commune' of Lisbon.

The undermining of state and political power was symbolised by the physical siege of the government buildings, and the Constituent Assembly within, by tens of thousands civil construction workers. This was a classic power confrontation – those at the top 'could no longer continue as before' and those below 'no longer wanted to'.

The occupation of São Bento in Lisbon was recorded by Robert Kramer for the film, *Scenes of the Class Struggle*. Kramer came to Portugal in 1975 to see and experience the revolution, as did thousands of young activists from all leftist political tendencies, including Maoists and followers of Che Guevara:

The Revolution! This was a revolution that would be accomplished without deaths in the metropole and for this reason it infatuated the world. 'I know that you are celebrating, man' sang Chico Buarque, one of the most famous artists of Música Popular Brasileira (Brazilian Popular Music, MPB) in a Brazil which still lived under the boots of military dictatorship. This 'celebration' led many, precipitously, to speak afterwards of a 'revolution without deaths' forgetting that the 'party' in the metropole came at the price of 13 years of horror in the colonies. The empire strikes back.[5]

Let us not forget these horrors in the colonies. The Portuguese Revolution began in Africa. Portugal, having acquired the first of the European colonial empires, clung to its empire long after other nations had relinquished theirs. Typically, the wars are described as guerrilla uprisings but it is important to emphasise the part played by workers. Freedom struggles began with a strike, which escalated into urban uprising in 1959, which took place in Pidjiguiti, Guinea-Bissau, a Portuguese colony on the coast of West Africa. The Portuguese authorities responded to the strike with brutal repression, as the Franciscan priest Pinto Rema reported:

> The insubordinates had paddles, sticks, iron bars, stones and spears. The two sides in confrontation did not cede, did not talk. In the first encounter, two police chiefs, Assunção and Dimas, were savagely attacked after they had fired in the air. Seventeen guards were wounded in this skirmish. The police lost their self-control and began to shoot to kill in force without any consideration. In the end, there were 13 to 15 dead spread out on the docks of Pidjiguiti. More bodies of sailors and stevedores were dragged away by the waters of the Geba river, we don't know how many.[6]

The historian Dalila Cabrita Mateus recounts that the brutal response to the strike heavily influenced the Partido Africano da Independência da Guiné e Cabo Verde (the African Party for the Independence of Guinea and Cape Verde, PAIGC), which decided to adopt an armed struggle strategy based on the peasantry:

> A confidential report from this meeting, the 'most decisive' in the history of the PAIGC according to Cabral [a key guerilla leader], shows that the passage from nationalist agitation to a strategy of struggle for national liberation was prepared here, adopting three important deliberations: first, the shift of activity to the country, mobilising the peasants; second, preparation for the armed struggle; third, the transfer of a part of the party leadership to the exterior.[7]

On the other side of Africa, in Mozambique, members of a mutual association for the Makonde people insisted, during the midnight hours of 11 June 1960, that they wanted to speak with the Portuguese authorities to negotiate the return of Makondes[8] to Mozambique from Tanganyika. They desired 'uhulu that is the power to live in freedom without forced labour'.[9] The war which drove the Portuguese out of Mozambique was launched from the Makonde homeland of the Mueda Plateau and this revolutionary movement was to be known as the Frente de Libertação de Moçambique (Mozambique Liberation Front, FRELIMO).

It is worth emphasising that almost 60 per cent of the salary of the Makondes, who were forced to work in the gold mines of South Africa, was directly delivered in gold to the Portuguese state. The State paid a part of the salaries of the workers in local money with the remainder going directly into the coffers of the metropolitan state.[10]

The Angolan Civil War was triggered on 4 January 1961, as an uprising against forced cotton cultivation. In February 1961, the Portuguese Army reacted to a strike of cotton workers in Lower Cassanje by napalm bombing of the population. Situated in the north of Angola, this area was a cotton monoculture exploited in monopoly fashion by Cotonang, a company financed by Portuguese and Belgian capital:

> The revolt was openly declared on January 4 when the foremen of Cotonang were held captive in the area controlled by the traditional regional authority Quivota about 10km from the post of Milando ... it was followed by a threat from the population that they would attack anyone who forced them to work in the cotton fields and state services or pay the annual tax. Production was stopped for one month.[11]
>
> Constituting numerous groups, the rebels assaulted official and private installations, damaged roads, bridges and rafts, and destroyed a Portuguese flagstaff, but did not kill any Europeans. In more distant areas, such as in the posts of Luremo, Cuango and Longo, there were multiple instances of burned cotton seed hummocks, ripped-up registers of the native population and other signs of hostility. Gatherings of the population not only became more frequent, but more threatening. This was despite Cotonang showing its apprehension with the development of the revolt and European merchants making multiple calls for armed intervention to end the uprising ...[12]

Many authors position the beginning of the colonial war in Angola on 4 February 1961 when the Movimento Popular de Libertação de Angola (the People's Movement for the Liberation of Angola, MPLA) attacked the prisons in Luanda. But 4 February cannot be explained without studying the January massacre in Lower Cassanje that Dalila Mateus classifies as a 'general rehearsal for the colonial war.[13]

In the Lower Cassanje massacre, 10,000–20,000 peasants were killed. From then on, nothing would be as it was before. Portugal would confront a 13-year war of resistance that began at this moment.

Forced Labour

Portugal was the empire that used various forms of forced labour in the most systematic way and for the longest time. Widely denounced in the press and by international agencies,[14] forced labour brought with it all the ailments of the society of which it was part: poverty, non-existence of social mobility, family break-ups, mere subsistence agriculture, extreme income inequality (see Table 2.1) and racist political police. As Dalila Cabrita Mateus stresses: 'The Polícia Internacional e de Defesa do Estado (International and State Defence Police, PIDE) in the colonies did not hassle whites; it only hassled blacks.'[15] This polarisation contributed to transforming the majority of the peasant population into avid supporters of the liberation movements.

Table 2.1   Mozambique: Salaries in 1969

Industrial Salaries (daily)	Agricultural Salaries (annual)
Whites: 100 escudos minimum	Whites: 47,723 escudos
Mulattos: 70 escudos maximum	Mulattos: 23,269 escudos
Africans (semi-skilled): 30 escudos	Africans (citizens): 5,478 escudos
Africans (unskilled): 5 escudos	Africans (non-citizens): 1,404 escudos

Source: *Anuário Estatístico*, Vol. II, 1970, cited in CFMAG Topics, 1975.

Forced labour in the Portuguese Empire would last until 1974. As the workers were rooted to the land and labour was scarce, the only way to make people work in the mines of Mozambique, or the cotton plantations in Angola, was to make it compulsory. 'Without gold there would be no South Africa and without Mozambique there would be no gold', the historian Perry Anderson has aptly written. Without forced labour, I might add, there would be no Estado Novo (New State) in Portugal.[16] Basil Davidson notes that there was a total of 2,094,000 forced labourers in the Portuguese Empire.[17]

Accumulation through forced labour could not exist without a dictatorship able to generate a workforce and impede production stoppages or the struggle for wage increases. It was the 'primitive accumulation of capital' in the words of Karl Marx in one of the best-known chapters of *Capital*.[18] It was a typical process of the dispossession of the peasants, forcibly torn from their lands and driven to work, mainly in the mines. And the accumulation (in gold!) was directly transferred to the vaults of the metropole and ended up financing the large conglomerates that were at the forefront of the modernising march of Portuguese capital, accomplished under the yoke of the Salazar dictatorship. Although this modernisation was delayed, in comparison to other capitalist countries, the proletariat had already developed sufficiently to contest modernisation and engage in bitter social conflicts.[19] In short, the dictatorship was necessary to harness the workforce in order to accumulate capital.

By early 1974, the PAIGC in Guinea was on the verge of victory and FRELIMO – the front for the liberation of Mozambique – had opened a new offensive. There was no prospect of winning the wars in Africa. The number of Portuguese dead, an estimated 9,000, was greater than in any conflict since the Napoleonic wars and the army was being blamed for these failures. Some officers were ashamed of wearing their uniforms in the streets of Lisbon. A crisis had been developing in the middle ranks of the army. In 13 years, nearly 200,000 men failed to report for enlistment and 8,000 deserted.[20]

Introducing the MFA

The story of the Portuguese Revolution often starts, incorrectly, with the *Movimento das Forças Armadas* (MFA) – the Armed Forces Movement. One should start with anti-colonial revolution in 1961, however, it was the MFA who opened up the gates of revolution. On Sunday 9 September 1973, amid stringent security precautions, 136 officers, none more senior than captain, met deep in the countryside ostensibly for a 'special farmhouse barbecue'. They were drawn together by self-interest; they resented diluting their ranks with conscript officers who had briefly attended the military academy. By April 1974, the MFA had built a network of 200 supporting officers from all three services and had drafted its first programme calling for 'Democracy, Development and Decolonialisation'. Europe's oldest dictatorship needed to reorganise and modernise its industry. The MFA wanted a democratic modern 'mixed economy' on the Western European pattern and refused to accept blame for colonial reverses. At that time, none of the officers would identify themselves as 'socialist'.[21]

Internal Migrations

The new factories needed workers and they were pulled in from the countryside. The migrants were among the poorest people in Portugal.

They were from Beiras, the North and Alentejo – a huge mass of people expelled from the countryside in the 1960s by hunger, backwardness and the strength of the gradually modernising forces of capitalism. They were driven to the cities where they lived, almost like animals, in shanty towns in Lisbon, Setúbal and Porto. Once again one is reminded of Marx's phrase[22] – the primitive accumulation of capital – and his account in which peasants were forced off their land and sucked into the towns through the centuries, in Britain. The separation of the peasantry from the land was a necessary condition for the development of capitalism, in that it created the conditions in which there was a pliable and abundant proletariat.[23]

My great-grandfather, César Sabino Dias owned a small grocery store in Garvão, near Ourique in Alentejo, where the family lived comfortably. In the 1960s, news was heard that there was work in Lisbon and the possibilities of ending the anguish of seasonal work in the fields. Many people from the village departed for Lisbon and the Garvão grocery store went bankrupt. Already fairly old, César, always a supporter of the Communist Party, obtained employment as a porter in the metallurgical factory Luso-Italiana in Moscavide, a workers' neighbourhood that spread in these years as others did in Porto, Setúbal, Barreiro, Almada, Vila Franca and throughout the great outskirts of Lisbon. César's grandson, Fernando, my uncle, was an excellent student who juggled seasonal work and scholarships and was able to study to become an agricultural engineer.

Another uncle, Hermelindo Cardeira Mariano (otherwise known as 'Lim') was the fourth of five children born in Fanhais, a village of resin collectors near Alcobaça. His mother owned a tiny plot of land, and things were made worse by a price freeze on crops. She was unable to provide work for all the brothers. More than half of the village emigrated to France in the 1960s. The government called up men for the war and Hermelindo was mobilised to Guinea.

When 'Lim' was in Guinea, the César family, including grandparents and parents and their two children lived in an old apartment of 40 square metres in Moscavide. Sometimes cousins and nephews came from Garvão to study in Lisbon and stayed there as well. The small house 'smelled like pork'.

The mass entry of women into the labour market from the 1960s onwards led children to be educated – 'created' as it was then called – by their grandparents, most of whom were domestic workers or rural labourers, in their home.

Such stories are true of the many Portuguese families who left the fields in the 1960s – due to agricultural mechanisation – and migrated to Lisbon, Porto and Setúbal, where the Lisnave cranes rose and the smell of rubber from Mabor infested the air. They came to live in cramped shanties or small, damp and very precarious apartments. They helped create a new working class. It is these people who made 25 April and conquered the welfare state for their children. This giant leap was one of hope for an entire generation, inside and outside Portugal.

Overview

Thanks to the collapse of a British-made deckchair in September 1968, the long-serving dictator Salazar suffered a stroke and severe brain damage.[24] His withdrawal from politics encouraged those who were attempting to reform the system from above.

By the late 1960s, Portugal was the least developed country in Western Europe. It had a large peasantry in the North, landed estates in the South and relatively small, concentrated industrial centres around Lisbon and along the North Coast in the Porto region. Migration statistics reveal the consequences of this deplorable situation. Between 1960 and 1973, over 1.5 million Portuguese left the country for French and German factories,[25] working like robots, or migrated to the colonies to be a small boss where life would supposedly be easier. In addition to the onerous costs of leaving Europe, however, the new settlers in Africa would also have to collude with and participate in a barbaric regime, where only a minority of whites managed to retain the basic humanity necessary to recognise blacks as equal to them. It is clear that PIDE informers, who were despised in the homeland, were 'lords' in the colonies, and were received by the colonists with bows when they entered hotels.[26]

Anachronistic, suffering from a brutal colonial war and the freezing of social mobility, the country could offer little to its youth. The population actually declined at the end of the 1960s. Social provisions were archaic. Portugal's rates of infant mortality, infectious disease and illiteracy matched those of Turkey.

One commentator opined that Portugal at the time was a type of an 'Atlantic Albania' where:

Divorce was suppressed, where (many) books, films and songs were prohibited, where the arts were censured, where social communication was muzzled, where many children walked around shoeless, where the majority of the population did not have a refrigerator, telephone or bathtub, where you could not tell jokes about the authorities or criticise the powerful, where you did not have the right to demonstrate or strike, where you needed a license to own a lighter or a transistor radio, where agriculture was operated by medieval ploughs and animal traction, where road traffic was crawling with wagons and ox carts, where ready-to-wear clothes were almost non-existent, where Coca-Cola was contraband, where the political police used torture in prisons, where there were no highways nor ... elections.[27]

Europe's oldest dictatorship needed to reorganise and modernise its industry. Portugal, on the edge of Europe geographically and politically, became a semi-colony of the advanced Western imperialist countries. New developments like the gigantic shipyard complexes of Lisnave and Setenave were financed with the help of foreign capital. In search of cheap labour and a friendly regime, the multinationals such as Timex, Plessey, Ford, General Motors, ITT and Philips set up large modern plants, mostly in the Lisbon industrial belt. The urban working class grew along with the shanty towns. Foreign capital accounted for 52.2 per cent of Portugal's total manufacturing investment by 1968.

The most backward capitalism in Europe was likely to be hardest hit by the developing world crisis:

In 1971, the USA dealt the final blow to the 'economic order' drawn up in 1945. Most currencies became floating currencies and it was only with the Smithsonian agreement, held in Washington on 18 December 1971, that a devaluation of the dollar of 7.89 per cent was formalised, fixing the price of an ounce of gold at $38. This decision brought about a general currency readjustment, while the fluctuation margins, fixed at 1 per cent under the Bretton Woods accords, rose to 2.25 per cent. The dollar became inconvertible; the portion of the USA's gold reserves fell to 28 per cent of world reserves and its balance of payments deficit reached $23.5 billion. Like any crisis of great magnitude, the one that shook the world in the first half of the 1970s was generated by multiple factors: the petroleum shortage, terrible monetary circulation, trade war, heated class struggle, etc ...'[28]

Michel Beaud remembers: 'The crisis is there, with all its parade of consequences, uncontrollable and indomitable. Weakened growth, rising unemployment, higher inflation, lower spending power for workers'.[29] 'In 1974, United States production had fallen 10.4 per cent and unemployment was at 9 per cent'.[30] The annual growth rate of the Gross Domestic Product of the USA went from 4.7 per cent in 1970–1973 to 2.4 per cent in 1973–1978; in Great Britain, it went from 4.3 per cent to 0.9 per cent; in Japan, it went from 8.1 per cent to 3.7 per cent; and the number of unemployed tripled in Great Britain and in the German Federal Republic between 1973 and 1977, to cite some examples.[31] The greatest crisis of the post-war era began in the United States of America.

Public opinion in the Western World doesn't seem to have been aware of this crisis except in October 1973, after the price of petroleum quadrupled. Memory is short.

After Salazar's death, reforms were attempted. Salazar's successor, Marcello Caetano, introduced the so-called primavera, the 'spring' of liberalisation. Censorship was relaxed – slightly. Political prisoners were allowed exile and some exiles were allowed to return home. A student movement emerged, encouraged by liberalisation and inspired by the students in Europe and the United States. The movement identified with the anti-colonial struggle in Africa. Students who failed their exams could be conscripted into the armed forces. This helped to spread radical ideas into the military.

Unable to reform itself, the regime almost collapsed from the rot in its backbone – the armed forces. The Portuguese bourgeoisie were on the verge of losing the State; it had not yet fallen, but it was in severe crisis.

So by 25 April, we see the convergence of a numbers of factors, the external changes in the world political economy, the collapse of the Portuguese empire, the demographic move from the countryside, the sclerotic nature of the ruling elite and the rise of the MFA. The collapse of the ossified ruling order resulted in the most important social rupture in post-war European history. The social explosion that followed the coup by the junior officers of the Armed Forces Movement (MFA) on 25 April 1974 was so deep and lasting that until today historians have been unable to completely account for how many mobilisations there were in the first week in the workplaces and the neighbourhoods – hundreds, maybe thousands, surfaced.[32] These formations powered the new forms of democracy and the drive towards workers' control. Indeed, they powered the revolution.

3

25 April 1974:
'The People are no Longer Afraid'

The command post of the Armed Forces Movement notes that the civilian population is not respecting the appeal made several times already to stay at home.

MFA Communiqué, April 1974[1]

The massive crowd that followed behind the armoured column of Captain Salgueiro Maia blatantly ignored the many MFA (Armed Forces Movement) broadcasts on television and radio that told people to stay at home. They climbed the steep streets of Lisbon to the headquarters of the GNR (Republican National Guard) in Carmo Square, where the dictator Marcelo Caetano begged them to let him deliver power to a general. The longest European dictatorship of the twentieth century collapsed in complete humiliation.

On 24 April 1974, at around 10pm, Otelo Saraiva de Carvalho arrived at the Command Post of the MFA, a prefabricated shed situated in the north of Lisbon in the First Engineering Regiment of Pontinha. The small windows were covered with grey blankets so that the lights would not raise suspicions. The scenario was sparse: there were four wooden desks, a few telephones and a map with the position of military units. There were also seven military officers: the Lieutenant Colonels Nuno Fisher, Lopes Pires and Garcia dos Santos; the Majors Otelo Saraiva de Carvalho, Sanches Osório; Lieutenant Captain Hugo dos Santos Vítor Crespo and Captain Luís Macedo. Their plan for a military coup was, above all, based on army units[2] with the national territory divided in two areas: north of the River Douro would be under the command of Eurico Corvacho and the 'rest of the country' under the command of Otelo. The tension was high in the Command Post. The month before a frustrated coup attempt had led to the imprisoning of fellow MFA officers. After all this dictatorial 'long night'[3] had survived 48 years.

At 12.20am, the password for the beginning of the revolt was broadcast: it was the song *Grândola, Vila Morena*[4] by the well-known folk and political musician José Afonso, who was commonly known as Zeca, on the Rádio Renascença programme *Limite*. This song would become the musical symbol of the revolution, among other reasons, for its lyrical allusion to 'fraternity', 'equality' and the land 'where it is the people who give the orders'. At 3am, when there was almost no transportation on the roads, the military columns began to move. Soon after, the MFA took control of RTP (Rádio e Televisão de Portugal), the public service broadcasting organisation (Rádio Clube Português), the headquarters of the Military Region of Lisbon and the headquarters of the Military Region of Porto.

At around 3am, the Command Post intercepted the following conversation between the Minister of the Army, Alberto de Andrade e Silva, and the Minister of Defence, Silva Cunha. Andrade e Silva told Cunha: 'I ask that you do not worry since everything is fine and there is no problem at any point in the country'.[5] Andrade e Silva was obviously as removed from reality as the Russian Czarina in 1915: when the Duma was dissolved, she limited herself to only write in her diary of the 'delicious swims in the sea', the hunts and the taste of her tea.[6] Or as distant as the editorial in the French newspaper *Le Monde* on the eve of May 1968 that proclaimed: 'France is boring!'[7]

The last objective of the MFA was control of the airport – this took longer than expected since the forces of the Escola Prática de Infantaria (Practical School of Infantry, EPI) of Mafra, a town one hour outside of Lisbon, had got lost on the way. Yet Captain Costa Martins had already successfully bluffed the forces at the First Aerodrome Base that they were surrounded, stopping all traffic in Portuguese air space at 4.20am.

The best-known armoured column of the military coup was commanded by Captain Salgueiro Maia. His function was not to take over military units but, above all, to assemble the units loyal to the regime at the Terreiro do Paço (Palace Square, also known as Commercial Square) on the banks of the Tagus River, near the centre of Lisbon. At a little after 1am, Salgueiro Maia woke up his troops in the Escola Prática da Cavalaria (Practical School of the Calvary, EPC) in Santarém and ordered them to assemble. There, he gave a speech, which has since become famous:

> There are various forms of states: the socialist states, the capitalist states and the state we are in. Now, on this solemn night, we are going to end this state. So, anyone who wants to come with me, we'll go to Lisbon and finish it. This is voluntary. Those who do not want to leave are not obliged and can stay here.[8]

Every soldier volunteered and 240 could set off to Lisbon, a little before 6am. The column entered Lisbon and took up position at the Terreiro do Paço. A platoon of the Seventh Calvary Regiment, and two from the Second Lancers Regiment, which had been sent to defend the Ministry of the Army, put themselves under the command of Captain Salgueiro Maia. At around 9am, the frigate *Almirante Gago Coutinho* (under NATO command) positioned itself in the Tagus River near the aforementioned Terreiro do Paço, threatening the forces of Salgueiro Maia. Across the river on the hill where the statue of Christ the King (inaugurated in 1959) was located, an artillery battery prepared to fire on the frigate. The commander of the frigate backed down, but the reports were contradictory – some have said that the commander gave orders to shoot, but the sailors refused while others claimed that the commander had been persuaded by the head of the navy, Vítor Crespo, to retreat.

Soon afterwards, the most well-known military event of 25 April occurred. The loyalist Brigadier Junqueira advanced on Ribeira das Naus Avenue, heading towards the Tagus River. Salgueiro Maia addressed Junqueira and his soldiers with a white handkerchief in his hand. The nervous Brigadier ordered Captain Maia to join his troops in the rearguard. Salgueiro Maia then asked to speak to Junqueira's troops at a point midway between the two opposing columns. Exasperated, the brigadier ordered his aide Sottomayer to open fire, but he refused and was arrested: 'The same order was then given to the soldiers in the tanks who also refused. Isolated, Junqueira moved to Rua do Arsenal where the rest of his column was positioned and quickly retreated. Those who remained joined Maia's troops.'[9]

The political instincts of the junior armed forces officers were underestimated. The MFA challenge to the generals created a conflict in the army between the old guard and the comparatively junior officers but in so doing unleashed the frustrations and energies of people, including rank-and-file soldiers. The junior officers' challenge led, unwittingly, to challenging of the State itself.

Please Stay at Home!

The rebels released more than a dozen communiqués on the first day of the revolution with almost all of them asking the population to stay at home. Before 4am, the first MFA communiqué was aired on the radio followed by Bobby Scott's song *A Life on the Ocean Wave*, which would afterwards become known as the 'anthem of the MFA'. The communiqué proclaimed:

'This is the Command Post of the Armed Forces Movement. The Portuguese armed forces appeal to residents of the city of Lisbon to go to their homes and remain in the utmost calm.'[10] At 7.30am, a new statement was released:

> As has been widely divulged, the Armed Forces unleashed at dawn a series of actions that liberated the country from a regime that has long dominated it. In its communiqués, the armed forces have called for the non-intervention of police forces in order to avoid bloodshed. Although this desire remains firm, they will not hesitate to respond in a decided and unyielding manner to any opposition that manifests itself. Aware that it interprets the true feelings of the nation, the Armed Forces Movement will continue with its liberating action and appeals to the population to remain calm and withdraw to its homes. Long live Portugal!'[11]

Yet the people refused to sit at home, on the sidelines. At 10.30am, the MFA read a new statement: 'The Command Post of the Armed Forces Movement notes that the civilian population does not respect the appeal already made several times to stay at home'.[12] Indeed, young people rode piggy-back on the military convoys and surrounded the headquarters of the GNR (Republican National Guard) in Carmo Square shouting 'Victory!' and 'Death to fascism!'.

Salgueiro Maia celebrated this day:

> When we went from Terreiro do Paço to Carmo, I saw the largest celebration I had ever seen, and that probably won't ever be repeated, where people cried and hugged each other. It was in exaltation that we arrived at Rossio [square]. When I got there, there was a crowd formed on top of the tanks, that I did not expect, and there was a jeep in front of the column where a captain came out. I turned to him and asked 'so what are you doing here?' He says: 'The government sent me here, but I'm with you,' and I told him to join up behind us.
>
> When we were immersed in something that people did not fully understand what was going to happen, [but] when they found out that we all were on the same side, we started to be approached by two or three newspaper boys who began to distribute newspapers that had just recently been freed from censorship. In front there were flower sellers. The flowers that were available at that time were white and red carnations. They grabbed the bouquets and gave them to us and all kinds of people began to offer us things, including a man with a ham and a knife.

In this context, since red stands for the left and has a certain meaning, photographers begin to appreciate photos of the red carnations; but the reality is that they were red and white, those that were available for sale, as well as some lilies, but these did not have the same meaning; if there were four bouquets of carnations there was only one of lilies. They were the flowers that were available for sale at the time; afterwards the photos began to highlight the reds.[13]

The ordinary people, who spontaneously socialised with the military, brought them carnations, sausages and hot soup. The following conversation between a couple and three soldiers were overheard on the military radio:

[Female voice] 'Go up on the elevator and buzz the first on the left. The soup is already warm'.

[One of the soldiers] 'Thank you, my lady. We will have to go one at a time because we are working'.

On 25 April, military radios still intercepted the pleas of the GNR (Republican National Guard). At around 1pm, for instance, guardsmen complained that: 'Students and boys are stoning our forces ... We urgently need to take action'. At 3.35pm they pleaded: 'We are completely surrounded ... They have given us an ultimatum of 10 minutes'.[14]

Meanwhile at Carmo, the scene was directly filmed by a RTP journalist, showing the somewhat surreal mix of students and other people mixing with armed soldiers:

[Voice of the journalist, Adelino Gomes] Salgueiro Maia ordered his forces to aim at the building. He just gave an ultimatum to the commanding colonel that if they do not leave he will destroy the headquarters. So, we are in an extremely important moment, even frightening, and I think we have reached the end of this siege around Carmo Headquarters ... No one leaves, the doors remain tightly closed, the tank manoeuvres in front of the doors of the Carmo Headquarters ... The retreat begins now. They will now take up position. I think we will continue here ... to observe all this.[15]

The RTP television report was interrupted and machine gun fire is heard and pigeons are seen fleeing into the trees. Yet the people did not flee the area. Bullet holes in the wall are shown. In the midst of intense background noise, the reporter continued:

> We still hear bursts of machine guns; we do not know what is actually happening. 'They should come out with a white flag, hands in the air and unarmed', Captain Maia ordered. Let's see if we can register the moment the doors open, or if they will remain closed as in the last three hours. [Voice heard from a megaphone] 'We do not want blood! We will fire with tanks, it will destroy the building'. And so ... they will fire. The Carmo Headquarters continues to resist and resists with no answer! The answer is to keep the doors closed. Dr. Feytor Pinto [the government's Communications Director] now addresses the commander of the forces [The scene shows that the square is completely occupied with people].
>
> However, the people who are here have occupied the tanks of the troops and are standing on top of them. They are clinging in various areas, on multiple floors of the several buildings here, the alleyways ... I think someone is coming, possibly General Spínola ... [The loud noise blocks out the reporters' voice and a flood of people moves toward Spínola's car] ... the soldiers were unable to contain the people ...
>
> Oh, look, now a window has opened on the first floor and Captain Maia speaks. 'Gentlemen, I ask that you please withdraw from the area so that we may gather our forces, organise the column. There will be many opportunities to rejoice'. [He is interrupted by shouts] ...
>
> We will talk now with Captain Maia, who says that, despite the will of the people who are here to see General Spínola, he is worried since they have information that the PIDE have snipers in the windows, so it would be quite risky if this happened. So he asked some people who were once members of the Portuguese democratic opposition in 1969 to try to convince the people to disperse, to leave so that the rebellious security forces can take the surrounded members of the Government and the other individuals who are inside.
>
> [Voice of Francisco Sousa Tavares]: 'Portuguese people. We are living an historic moment that no one has seen since 1640.[16] It is the liberation of the homeland!' [He is interrupted at this point by the crowd].[17]

The film shows the tanks leaving with members of the overthrown government inside. One of the soldiers in the car made the V for Victory sign and waved to the population. The people hurled themselves against the tanks in celebration.

The tanks left Carmo, surrounded by people on the street elatedly applauding from the windows. The now euphoric journalist continued: 'It is an historic time, even though it is too recent to begin writing history three minutes after it happened ... The words of a man are nothing before the historic image that we are witnessing.'[18]

People immediately directed their anger against other symbols of the regime: the censorship services, the offices of the only legal political party, Acção Nacional Popular (National Popular Action, ANP), the dreaded headquarters of the political police, the PIDE-Direcção-Geral de Segurança (General Security Directorate, PIDE-DGS), the office of the regime's newspaper, *The Age* and the prisons, where they demanded the release of political prisoners.

The PIDE

The MFA had not taken over the PIDE headquarters. Apparently, the commander Jaime Neves thought it would be risky with such few men at his disposal. Nevertheless, on this day, at António Maria Cardoso Street, in the central Lisbon neighbourhood of Chiado, members of the political police indiscriminately shot protestors.

The PIDE killed: Fernando Luís Barreiros dos Reis, 24, a native of Lisbon and soldier of the First Company of Penamacor who was on leave; Francisco Carvalho Gesteiro, 18, an office worker and native of Montalegre; the Azorean José Guilherme Rego Arruda, 20, a student in Lisbon; and Joseph James Harteley Barnetto, 37, from Vendas Novas. The angry population, who besieged the PIDE headquarters, clearly surpassed the MFA in this respect. It remains to be asked why the political police headquarters was not considered a strategic target in such a well-prepared and implemented plan. In almost all dictatorships that fall because of the fury of the people, the symbols of repression are the first to be attacked.

The agents and informers of the PIDE – 'snitches' as they were disparagingly called – were hounded throughout the country in schools, universities, towns, workplaces and in companies. This comes as no surprise since 'Political and social repression was the great stigma of dictatorship ... In the emerging political culture of the revolution, the police and repression were considered equal to fascism'.[19] On the first day of the revolution, at the entrance to the offices of the newspaper *República*, three agents were 'beaten' by protestors screaming 'kill, kill' and 'murderers, murderers'.[20]

At 9.30am on 26 April, the PIDE unconditionally surrendered. Eduardo Gajeiro, a photographer at the time for the newspaper *O Século*, famously captured the moment that a soldier removed a portrait of the ex-dictator Salazar from a wall inside the PIDE headquarters. Even more brutal and humiliating was the photo of a surrendering PIDE agent wearing only his underwear with his arms in the air. Three hours later, the facilities of the Comissão de Exame Prévio (the Preliminary Examination Commission, that is, the censorship offices) were publicly looted by demonstrators.[21]

Political Prisoners

Families and friends of political prisoners responded immediately. They went to the prisons of Caxias and Peniche to release their loved ones. The situation in Caxias was somewhat unusual. Late in the morning of 26 April, most of the 81 political prisoners were liberated amidst great excitement. Family members, prisoners and soldiers cried and hugged each other. However, an order from the Junta de Salvação Nacional (Junta of National Salvation, JSN) stipulated that political prisoners who were also involved in 'blood crimes' should remain in jail:

> In the presence of astonished journalists ... the prisoners returned to their prospective cells so that they could ascertain who would stay and who would leave. Thus, Palma Inácio, who was amongst the first to be freed, declared 'this does not mean only freedom for us, but for all the Portuguese people', returned to cell number three in which he had spent six months.[22]

Popular pressure from the leftist political parties and the prisoners themselves forced the JSN to backtrack and by 27 April all political prisoners had been freed.

Moreover, on 30 April, all the political prisoners in the Tarrafal concentration camp in the Portuguese colony of Cape Verde in Africa were released. A Lisbon newspaper reported:

> The release of prisoners and their reunions with family, friends, and the people that awaited them at the exit was an emotional moment ... the population of the provincial capital, where yesterday some groups damaged police cars and beat some people regarded as informers of the extinct DGS, awaited the arrival of the motorcade from Tarrafal to the city of Praia.[23]

On 1 May, over 500 political prisoners were freed from the central jail of Machava in southern Mozambique: 'Men with bed rolls on their shoulders and their belongings in old suitcases [left prison and were] received with great emotion by family, friends and many others.'[24]

Euphoria

On 26 April, the second edition of the newspaper *República* was awe-inspiring. The front page headline, in bold letters, announced: 'This newspaper was not targeted by any censorship commission'. It was a 'long night', the newspaper wrote, referring to the 48 years of dictatorship and remembering those who had resisted the New State from the demonstrations against famine in the Second World War to the dead in the Tarrafal concentration camp where political prisoners were sent. On the front page of the 26 April 1974 edition, addressing those who had not 'seen yesterday', the *República* newspaper declared: 'The euphoria of the people of Lisbon is a referendum'.

There were few people, however, who had not 'seen yesterday'. The people took to the streets that day and even 'forgot' to go to work. At the beginning of May, the Sindicato dos Profissionais de Escritórios de Lisboa (Union of Office Professionals of Lisbon) threatened to act against all companies that 'refuse to pay 25 April to all workers who did not show up to work that day'.[25]

The 26 April 1974 edition of *República*, tells us that in Porto, the second largest city of the country, the afternoon of 25 April was marked by a 'students and workers' celebration of the fall of the regime and popular persecution of elements from the PIDE and the Polícia de Segurança Pública (Public Security Police, PSP). There were clashes in front of Porto City Hall, which injured 17 people. '[Protesters] stoned the premises of the South Africa consulate, Fiat, Ford, Abreu Agency and the Ministry of Finance on Aliados Avenue. During the night, on the same avenue, a large crowd fraternised with soldiers whose vehicles were followed by cars, honking rhythmically while some trucks filled with soldiers mixed with kids from the poor neighbourhoods.'[26]

In Coimbra, soldiers, workers and students with a '1968 look' (bell-bottom pants, shirts with open collars and long hair) organised a massive demonstration that marched throughout the city.

The MFA had organised a successful coup, a nigh perfect operation, and immediately purged the armed forces of the supporters of the former regime, compulsorily retiring most of the generals. It had a minimum programme to end the colonial war and initiate the democratisation of the country, even though the contours of the process were still imprecise.

Nevertheless, the mobilisations of the people outshone the Armed Forces. The coup opened the doors to a social and political situation that immediately exceeded the objectives of the MFA. For example, south of Porto, in Coimbra:

Thousands and thousands of people gathered at the vast Republic Square ... When the entire audience was already in the [University] stadium area a minute of silence was held for the victims of fascism in Portugal and, afterwards, several speakers, workers and intellectuals, referred, among other things, to the excellent prospects opened up to the country on the path of democracy, stressing the need to end the colonial war, the high cost of living and the corporate regime as well as the urgency to recognise workers' right to strike and the forty-hour work week.

Finally there was a proposal to immediately take over the Municipal government ... After this proposal was adopted by acclamation, all those present headed to May 8 Square (here, at the City Hall, the keys to the city were given to a commission of 'democrats') ... A new procession was then organised to General Headquarters where the commander of the military region was informed of what had happened.[27]

The PIDE-DGS was abolished. Not so for the tarnished forces of the riot police (PSP) and the national guard (GNR). They would be required to 'hibernate' in the following months before they were replaced, especially in Lisbon, by organs created by the MFA itself, namely, the Comando Operacional do Continente (Operational Command of the Mainland, COPCON).[28] The commander was Major Otelo Saraiva de Carvalho, who was often referred to simply as Otelo. The aim was to enforce the new conditions created by the Carnation Revolution. It was a conglomeration of special military forces including commandos, military police, paratroopers, marines, Queluz Infantry and the Lisbon Artillery Regiment (Regimento de Artilharia Ligeira de Lisboa, RALIS).

The former regime strongmen Marcelo Caetano and Américo Tomás were dispatched from the Carmo Headquarters to the Pontinha Barracks and then to the city of Funchal in the Madeira Islands. The *Diário Popular* reported that:

More than 20,000 people celebrated in this city yesterday, the May 1 cel-ebration. Protesters left Municipal Square and marched through various streets, demanding the departure of the members of the old Madeira government who were in the São Lourenço Palace ... At one point, an effigy of Salazar was thrown from a window of the Town Hall symbolising the fall of fascism.[29]

The effigy fell from the window, but Marcelo Caetano and Américo Tomás, guilty of war crimes and torture, were to be exiled without being tried, to Brazil, with the connivance of the MFA. This would soon provoke protests from the left-wing opposition, including some, but not all, of the Communist Party.[30]

The days before May Day became a permanent 'festival of the oppressed'.[31] Even the prostitutes of Lisbon organised and campaigned to sack their pimps. Those members of the armed forces who were below the ranks of lieutenant would only be charged half price.[32]

This is how the eminent Portuguese poet, Sophia de Mello Breyner Andresen, celebrated 25 April:

This is the dawn I waited for
The new day clean and whole
When we emerge from night and silence
To freely inhabit the substance of time.[33]

Most of the symbols of the dictatorship were dismantled in a few days. The Portuguese Revolution, which would be the most radical social revolution in Europe in the previous 30-year period, began as a democratic revolution. Freedom was its initial objective: 'In every corner, Freedom writes and sings its name', the front page of *Diário Popular* exclaimed.[34]

On the day of the coup, only one factory was actually on strike – the Mague metallurgical factory, with 2,000 workers. Their demand for 6,000 escudos (£100) as a monthly minimum was immediately conceded by the management, who feared the consequences of being branded as fascists by Portugal's new rulers. Naturally, the military Junta, which the MFA had helped set up, was unhappy about this victory and declared that the new pay deal was an example, which should not be followed.[35]

We can see what began on 25 April as a democratic political revolution fermented the seeds of social revolution. Phil Mailer captures the brilliance:

Perhaps the most beautiful thing is the sense of confidence, growing daily. There is nothing but goodwill for the working class throughout the world. People are discussing the situation in France, England, Argentina and Brazil as if they'd been professors of politics all their lives. My neighbour has changed beyond recognition, as she wonders ecstatically if the workers can win. She says she 'doesn't understand much about politics'. But after months of silence, forced respectability and fear, her open happiness and excitement are unbelievably refreshing.[36]

In this case, the dictatorship was replaced by a group of discontented officers committed to fostering a democratic regime, which opened the doors for a more profound revolution, struggling for grass-roots power and social equality. These foundations were constructed by 'ordinary' people – the working class including those in army uniforms, popular sectors and students – in the slipstream of the army, who therefore acted with little fear, but who would soon enter into history themselves. They soon became the vanguard of the revolution, leaving the MFA to constitute the central pillars of the State.

Power did not 'fall onto the street'[37] in 1974–1975. It was buttressed by the MFA along with the parties with a working-class base (the Communist Party and Socialist Party). It was an unusual metamorphosis: the generals fled and the captains entered. The bourgeoisie tried to govern and avoid the collapse of the State propping up a disaffected section of its own class – the junior officers of the MFA. It discovered early on that the coup did not stop the clock; it actually accelerated it. History, some have joked, knows how to start, but not how to end.

The MFA would be surprisingly predictable in the sense of failing to develop political autonomy and it often took the lead from sections of the bourgeoisie – but not always.

It was, first of all, the struggle for freedom that brought people onto the streets. And, once in the streets, they collectively entrusted the possibility of winning the fight for equality. The appeals for 'normality' and 'freedom in responsibility'[38] and slogans such as 'it's urgent to govern',[39] printed in bold letters on the pages of some newspapers, were in vain, suggesting that it was at least as difficult and complex to take people off the street as it was to put them on it.

Colonel Cruz Oliveira, a doctor in the Air Force, stated in an interview that when the Revolution broke out on 25 April, he was placed on the Coordinating Commission of the MFA and in the first days before being appointed to the healthcare area, he did not have a clear mission: '[I] did a lot, went to grocery stores where the employees did not let the boss enter, I searched for Legionnaires' disease in Docapesca [the fishers' wharf in

Lisbon]. They told me this: 'Hey man! You're going to deal with this' and each of us did what we could.[40]

On 28 April, the residents of the Boavista district of Lisbon occupied vacant homes and refused to leave, although they were urged to do so by the military and the police. Immediately, the JSN (Junta de Salvação Nacional) reacted and sent word that no more 'abusive' occupations of houses would be allowed.[41] Over the next two weeks, another 1,500 to 2,000 occupations took place in Lisbon, and others around the rest of the country. These were mainly of vacant government-owned housing. On 11 May, the government published a decree to legalise the occupations that had already taken place.[42]

Due to the 'the rising cost of living, greatly affected by the speculative madness in housing', rents were frozen. Incredibly, the freeze on rents stayed in place in Portuguese cities until 14 August 2012. Little did residents know that in just a few months the Junta would no longer exist and that the residents' commissions would become the alternative power at the municipal level. It would be the case that residents' commissions, in partnership with the local military, decided which houses and companies would be occupied and where schools, crèches, cultural associations and the headquarters of political parties would be located.

From 29 April onwards, bank workers began to control the outflow of capital and mounted pickets at bank entrances. They would meet eight months later in a plenary assembly to demand the nationalisation of banks, which would be implemented one year after the fall of the old regime.[43]

Returning to 28 April 1974, office clerks occupied their union offices and drove out the leadership. On 29 April, 10,000 students met in plenary at the Higher Technical Institute and civil construction workers dismissed the union leadership and occupied union offices. Workers at Transul, a transport company, went on strike. On 19 April, workers from several trade unions organised a demonstration against the Ministry of Corporations and Social Security, which would soon become the Ministry of Labour. Cruz Oliveira, one of the MFA leaders, explained how Pereira de Moura[44] and Victor Wengorovius[45] tried to calm the spirits of the people that threatened to invade the Ministry, something the MFA wanted to avoid:

The huge crowd, it was a huge crowd, with their Lisnave helmets and all that, heard Pereira de Moura talk, [they responded] 'yes sir, it's all very well, ok. But we're going in!' I thought I had to say something. I announced that we were going to transform it into the Ministry of Labour. Wengorovius went upstairs to paint a sign saying Ministry of Labour and put it in the window. Then I told the crowd 'a proof that we are with the revolution is if we all go down the road and shout that this is now the Ministry of Labour. And so it was, everybody went joined in'.[46]

Throughout the country, many street names were changed. In Algés, a group of residents changed the name of the football stadium to Liberty Stadium. In Guarda, a demonstration was organised where, according to *Diário Popular*, 'The people passed a motion destined to alter the topography of the city.'[47] In Barreiro, Salazar Park would become Catarina Eufémia Park, named after a harvester in Alentejo murdered by the GNR after a strike by salaried agricultural workers. The imposing suspension bridge Oliveira Salazar, which spanned the two margins of the Tejo estuary in Lisbon, became the April 25 Bridge.

Furthermore, the exiled leaders of the banned political parties immediately rushed back to the country. Mário Soares, leader of the newly formed Socialist Party, supported by German social democracy,[48] and Álvaro Cunhal, leader of the pro-Soviet Communist Party vied to see who would arrive first. The arrival of both was widely acclaimed. Furthermore, there were dozens of exiles, both anonymous and known, who arrived by plane, train or car, literally 'taking to the highway' to return to Portugal. As the newspaper *Diário Popular* reported: 'On arrival in Portuguese territory, many had tears in their eyes. The encounters of the refugees with families, friends and comrades were very emotional moments.'[49]

May Day

Medeiros Ferreira estimated that two million people across the country celebrated the first legal May Day in over 48 years.[50] The *República* newspaper reported: 'Kilometres and kilometres of people. Happy people.'[51] Ana Mónica Fonseca wrote: 'The people are no longer afraid. This amazing and emotional discovery dominated the gigantic May 1 demonstrations yesterday, assuming national proportions. A former political exile who returned from France told us in tears: "Tell your newspaper that this was more beautiful and splendid than the liberation of Paris which I witnessed".'[52]

There were demonstrations all over the country, for example, in Lisbon, Porto, Setúbal, Barreiro, Beja, Faro, Leiria and Bragança. Newspaper editors, the Bar Association, teachers, factories and businesses, musicians, film-makers and actors all signed letters endorsing the May Day demonstrations. In Lisbon, there were two demonstrations: the first, which assembled close to half a million people in the stadium of the Federação Nacional da

Alegria no Trabalho (National Federation of Happiness at Work), soon to be renamed the May 1 Stadium, was called by the unions, the Communist Party and the Socialist Party. The second, the 'Red May Day' was organised by the Maoist-inspired Movimento Reorganizativo do Partido do Proletariado (Reorganised Movement of the Party of the Proletariat, MRPP) at Rossio Square and attracted, 40,000 people, according to *Diário de Notícias*.[53]

In fact, the newspapers declared that it was not possible to say exactly how many people participated since it attracted 'unprecedented huge crowd[s]'.[54] One group of protestors held a large placard that said: 'Our destiny will be made with our hands'. Another man held a banner saying: 'Nobody paid us, we came freely',[55] in reference to the recruitment of people for the (rare) 'popular' demonstrations during the Salazar regime.[56]

At the 1 May stadium demonstration, the slogans on placards included words such as 'death' and 'shooting'. Other demands included the democratisation of institutions, mingling with socio-economic demands such as wage increases and the establishment of a minimum wage of 4,000 escudos. In the demonstration called by the MRPP, the focus was on the immediate return of the troops and the end of the colonial war.

May Day demonstrations took place all over the country. Spaniards from the frontier region of Galicia flocked across the border to Minho in the north of Portugal to celebrate. Soldiers also celebrated International Workers' Day – the *2.0 Grupo de Companhias de Administração Militar* (Second Group of Military Administration) were given free entrance to an evening show with the guitarists Carlos Paredes and Fernando Alvim, as well as the actor Mario Viegas.

Snapshots

Dozens of film-makers from around the world travelled to Portugal in 1974 to film the revolution. In many cases, they recorded images: workers with cheap and frugal clothes, sometimes without teeth or semi or completely illiterate, who were also leaders of the most advanced, festive and egalitarian social struggle happening in the world at that time. Among the enthusiasts of this 'other country', a favourite expression of the film director Sérgio Tréfault, were thousands of workers who in the 1960s had constructed '*bairros de lata*' (shanty towns) in Lisbon, Porto and Setúbal.

Glauber Rocha, the influential Brazilian film-maker, captured this well in his film *The Arms and the People*.[57] He was in the Rossio in the middle of a crowd to interview a 16-year old when a passing worker says:

– If you are a worker, speak. Here is a worker. What is your name?
– Francisco José Catarino.
– How old are you?
– 46.
– You work in what industry?
– Construction.
– What do you think about what has happened in Portugal?
– It was a wonderful thing!
– Did you expect it or was it a surprise?
– I expected this for a long time and only now it has happened.

In another scene shot in the middle of a shanty town, a poor woman in a head scarf, Maria Luisa Gameiro Madruga, doggedly explains:

I have five children, all with great need. We all sleep together in one bed, parents, children, we don't distinguish. A man who wants to satisfy his needs [an allusion to sex] has to hide from his child, a woman who wants to satisfy her needs has to hide from her child. I think ... this is already enough to say.[58]

4

Who Governs?

Our destiny will be made with our own hands.

1 May demonstrators, 1974[1]

Plenários

People met and celebrated and talked everywhere. The Portuguese have a rather lovely word for this: the *plenário*. But let us focus, for the moment, on meetings in places of work. 'Why do workers always, independently and apparently "spontaneously", adopt the same mass meetings-based, delegate-generating, committee-constructed form for their most powerful expressions of resistance? The answer is simple, because the form is simple; the form is constructed from the requirements of the situation, not plucked from thin air.'[2]

The following declaration by workers from Efacec-Inel, an electrical components manufacturer, when they called for a meeting, on 21 May 1974, captures the spirit well:

> We decided to translate the feeling of all of us that it is time to reclaim the rights granted to us by our condition as workers in this awakening from a long night. We are happy to know that every day comrades from other companies have seen their legitimate aspirations satisfied ...
>
> A general meeting is absolutely necessary to allow us to carry out these points and solidify our ideas ...
>
> Comrade!
>
> Go to the general meeting!
>
> Don't miss it!
>
> Don't think that if you are not there, others will think and speak for you. This is what they did to you for 48 years.
>
> Don't let anyone else do it for you!
>
> To talk and think now is not only a right.
>
> Thinking and talking is a duty now.[3]

Workers' Commissions

What is most impressive from the point of view of social and workers' movements in the Portuguese Revolution is not the number of meetings, which is, of course, relevant, but the emergence of what were generally called the *Comissão de Trabalhadores* (workers' commission). Meetings considered the questions and issues of the day, but the workers' commissions became the backbone of the organisation (almost universally) in the workplaces. The workers at Efacec, for example, would hold meetings of the workers' commission 'every Friday at 7pm' and with meetings of the Cultural Commission on Saturdays and Wednesdays. Democracy had truly arrived in the factories.

This dynamic shook the very foundations of the industrial hierarchy. The strikes were mostly 'wildcat', agreed in democratic workers' assemblies and led, in most cases, by workers' commissions, which arose spontaneously in the vacuum created by over 48 years of dictatorship in which workers' organisations were banned. Moreover, they were formed outside the Communist Party and the Socialist Party – both of which were manoeuvring to be part of the First Provisional Government – and in general, the trade unions, played no part in these early days. The lack of a relationship with the unions is covered in Chapter 6. It must be stressed that this type of organisation, the workers' commission,[4] would feature as a 'thorn in the side' of successive governments. This was true whether they were involved in defending the country from right-wing coup attempts (as on 28 September 1974 and 11 March 1975) or fighting the government's policy of 'national production and sacrifice'.[5] In the first week of May, the newspapers dedicated entire pages to the positions taken by the workers' collectives. Workers' commissions spread like wildfire across the country in the first weeks after the coup.

Strikes and Occupations

Strikes can show workers that they have the powers to change society. There were plenty of protests and riots and marches but strikes necessitated workers acting as a collective, which is far more threatening, a more apparent and direct expression of the contradiction between capital and labour. They question who is in control of the company, the workers or the bosses.[6] Table 4.1, based on the research of Santos, de Lurdes, Lima, Ferreira and Matias[7] shows the types of industrial actions, including strikes that occurred between 25 April and 1 June 1974. In these five weeks, there were 97 strikes and 15 threats to strike, more than had occurred in any previous one-year period including the peak year of 1969, in which there were 100 strikes or threats to strike over the whole year. The majority, 58 strikes, occurred in industry and there were also occupations of workplaces. Occupations began, for example, at Timex (more on this soon), the Firestone tyre factories across the country and at Lisnave shipyards. Brian Parkin, a comrade visiting from the UK, recalls: 'crossing the Tagus on the (now collectivised) ferry and walking into the Lisnave shipyard. We were met, not by security staff, but by workers with red armbands and being taken to the boardroom. Because [although] managers were running technical aspects of the yard, the workers were running it. Things like that were a massive shock.'[8]

In four of the strikes, there were kidnappings of bosses or confiscation of equipment.

Table 4.1   Strikes in Portugal between 25 April and 1 June 1974

	Threats to Strike	Strikes	Forms of Struggle Workplace Occupations	Kidnapping of Bosses or Confiscation of Equipment
Industry	8	42	26	4
Gas, Electricity, Water, Transport, Commercial and Communications	6	15	8	
Banks, Insurance, Services	1	1	1	
TOTAL	15	58	35	4

Source: Maria de Lurdes Santos, Marinús Pires de Lima, and Vítor Matias Ferreira, *O 25 de abril e as Lutas Sociais nas Empresas*. (Porto: Afrontamento, 1976), Vol. 1.

The research by Santos *et al.* establishes that the majority of demands in these strikes revolved around wage increases, minimum wages, participation in company profits and the right to 13 and 14 month salaries.[9] In 40 per cent of the cases, aspects of control of the company were demanded. In almost half of the strikes studied, there were calls for *saneomento*, that is, the firing of bosses, managers and administrators with links to the fascist regime (more on this further on in this chapter).

Maria Luísa Cristovam published a comparative study of strike demands in 1979 – after the end of the revolution – and in the 1974 and 1975 strikes. She concluded that during the two years of the revolution, between 15 and 22.7 per cent of strike demands were related to control and power in the workplace, while in 1979, only 3.7 per cent of strikes focused on management questions.[10]

Moreover, in 1974–1975, 39.8 per cent of strikes were of a profoundly egalitarian character, including demands for equal pay increases for all workers, abolition of privileges, reduction in the range of salary levels and constitution of a national minimum wage.[11] Such demands indicate that this was a period of enormous upheaval.

Examples of strike processes vary. In 1974, José Manuel de Mello, head of the powerful industrial CUF conglomerate (Companhia União Fabril), contacted Joaquim Aguiar, an economist and consultant for the Mello Group. This is what Joaquim told the author:

> José Manuel de Mello called me to the 6th floor of Infante Santo [CUF headquarters] and says to me: 'There are 4,000 workers surrounding the management, what do we do?' We were in May 1974, the 7, 6 or 9 May, I don't know. ... I grabbed my briefcase – I was wearing a brown shirt – and left. What was I going to do with 4,000 workers surrounding management? I don't perform miracles! Well, I came back. Let's see then what we can do? So that's when, for the first time, management distributed a statement to the workers. But as no one had the courage to deliver the [printed] statement to the employees, it remained in a pile and the wind ended up distributing it. This was to show that the management reacted, that it was not in a panic, about to flee. This attitude, despite everything, continued for years.[12]

The Timex dispute captured headlines. This involved 2,000 workers, mainly women, at the American watch factory, located on the southern margin of the Tejo River. They:

> felt the need to organise the struggle in the factory and deepen and strengthen the list of demands elaborated during a strike held at the end of the first week of February [before 25 April], decided to convene an assembly of all Timex workers. This assembly elected a workers' commission composed of thirty members representing all sectors of the factory.[13]

The workers' commission, which met on Monday 6 May, presented 23 demands that included, among others, paid holidays, reduction of the workday, compensation for sickness and abolition of any type of performance bonus. They ended their list of demands with the following:

22. The maximum salary for all workers [including managers] at Timex will be 16,000 escudos. All salaries higher than this figure will be frozen until they are affected by the current [salary] grade.

23. There will be a general increase in salaries when the workers and the [Workers'] Commission decide it is necessary according to rises in the cost of living and the level of inflation.

Note: The workers also wish to demand a daycare centre ...

The measures presented will take effect from 9am on 27 May 1974.

When the deadline is reached, if these measures mentioned in the 23 points have not been enacted, the workers at Timex reserve the right to respond with collective, dignified and civic reaction.[14]

The Timex workers, who had warned management that they reserved the 'right to respond', duly responded by going on strike and stopping the production of watches. Their actions echoed the pattern of many other protests: demanding labour rights and the removal of bosses linked to the New State.

The workers' commissions may have lacked formal organisation but the level of struggle forced them to meet and consult frequently. They were highly democratic. The commission at Plessey included 118 workers – all of whom insisted on going to the first meeting with the management.[15]

Another case, which had its hilarious moments, occurred in the Telefones de Lisboa e Porto (Telephones of Lisbon and Porto). This is commonly known as the TLP. The TLP had been formed in 1968 and was responsible for telecommunications services in the metropolitan areas of Lisbon and Porto. (Outside the two cities the CTT – Correios, Telégrafos e Telefones – Post, Telegraphs and Telephones – maintained telecommunications and postal services.) The following scene was filmed in its entirety by RTP, the public television network. Surrounded by many spirited workers who circled the administrative building, a manager, facing the insults and foul language of the crowd, tried to give an interview, but was interrupted by a moustachioed worker, visually typical of the 1970s, who told the reporter: '"Interviews given by these fascist sirs are very dubious". The manager responded determinedly, but quietly that this "was the first time that they called me such a thing". Another manager haughtily said to the cameras, that "he hoped he could leave after the end of another day of work".'[16]

In the first statement of what they stressed was the 'democratically elected' workers' commission of EFACEC-Inel on 21 May 1974, the commission stated that it was 'simply limited to hear and transmit to all the workers' decisions'. These first decisions included a large list of demands related to working conditions. A few days later, after the management's refusal to accept all the demands, the workers gathered in a general assembly, the fifth in less than a month, and voted to:

1. Strike with the immediate and permanent occupation of workplaces by the workers of these premises.

2. Deny access to managers of any of EFACEC-Inel's facilities in Lisbon unless they accept the proposals of the Commission.[17]

The strike would last 21 days but the workers did not win all their demands. This was not uncommon: in the sectors and companies with the most radicalised struggles (Timex, Lisnave, Carris, trucking, refineries, bakeries and the Lisbon subway, among others), the full list of demands would be achieved not immediately but over the course of the revolution; for every strike and occupation generated stories and a new-born confidence.

Here is rather dramatic anecdote by a British docker, about his visit, in May, to the Lisnave shipyards:

On my first trip four or five weeks into the revolution I went along to the giant Lisnave shipyard which I knew was under workers' occupation. Immediately the guys on the picket line realised that I was English I was the object of much excitement and I was led further and further into the massive shipworks. There on a nearly completed bulk carrier a group of British contract spot welders had continued to work and the strike committee tasked me with trying to persuade them to join the occupation. I clambered down the ship's ladder deep into the main hold and I did my best to reason with these Brit scabs. But they were on loads a money fixed contracts and didn't give a fuck about the Portuguese or their occupation. So I climbed back up. The strike committee went into a huddle and then asked me to try again but this time they gave me a written message and a small parcel wrapped in an oilcloth. I climbed back down, to be met with derision – but this time I told the scabs that the workers' committee wanted them to know that they had imprisoned their management in their offices. And just in case the seriousness of the strike committee's determination was in any doubt, I unwrapped the oilcloth parcel to reveal a large pistol. I have never been sure whether the gun was loaded – but the bold scabs got the message and pissed off back home.[18]

Solidarity Actions

Secondary actions, in other words solidarity strikes were spawned. They emerged in companies in the same corporation or in the same economic sector such as the press, transportation and civil construction. An example of this was in May 1974 when 350 metal and concrete workers at the shipyards of Alverca-Intento in the industrial zone in Vila Franca de Xira, north of Lisbon, began a strike against their employer. Soon after, their fellow administrative workers in the Lisbon, Revim, Porto and Portimão offices downed tools, increasing the total number of workers on strike to 700. The strikers declared in solidarity: 'No return to work if the company does not meet [our colleagues'] desire for a salary increase'.[19]

On the very same day, fare collectors and bus drivers in the João Belo company in the south of the country stopped collecting tickets in 'virtue of the firm not respecting until midnight last night demands for monthly salary increases to 8,000 and 7,000 escudos respectively'.[20]

The government hated to see strikes infecting other workers and it would prohibit solidarity strikes in the Strike Law of August 1974, alleging the defence of the 'national economy' (we will look at the reaction to this in Chapter 6).

It is also important to stress that the poorest and most oppressed sectors of the working class also participated in these strike movements. In the Miraflores Industrial Park, 800 construction workers, half of whom were African immigrants from Cape Verde, went on strike on 14 May 1974. Their demands included: 'Minimum monthly salary of 6,000 escudos, 40 hours of work in a five-day week, 30 days of 100 per cent paid holidays, the right to strike, Christmas bonus paid eight days before, registration of all employees with the obligation to immediately integrate them into the union as effective members.'[21]

In this company, construction workers earned 2,600 escudos per month before the strike. It is worth noting that they were also explicitly 'inspired by the process of the workers of Torralta (in Troia, south of Setúbal) and that they aimed 'to spread the strike movement to other companies in the sector, notably in the Algés zone'.[22]

Saneomento

Many strikes and workplace conflicts, and indeed occupations, began with the demand for the resignation of managers linked to the old regime. Workers just hated working with those managers who had denounced them to the political police. This came before economic demands. In Portuguese, this was known as *saneomento*. This does not literally refer to a purge, but has positive connotations related to hygiene, health and cleanliness.

One can suggest that this was pursued purely on moral grounds, but the issue is extremely political in the way it focuses upon who does the managing and even leading to questioning of ownership.

The majority of *saneomentos* after 25 April 1974 were decided by workers' and/or residents' commissions, in general assemblies of students or schools and in most cases were voted on in open plenaries. Almost all those evicted had links to the regime and were often police informants, the famous *bufos* (snitches), who were easily and clearly identifiable. In the great majority of these cases, the government and the company administrations reacted quickly to ratify the decisions of the workers. The same workers who showed themselves willing to negotiate complex agreements, even, for example, salary increases that fell short of demands, always remained intransigent in not accepting the existence of *bufos* in the places where they worked, lived or studied.

Saneomento occurred not only in companies that constituted the mainstay of the Portuguese labour movement: shipbuilding, air transportation and communications (Lisnave, TAP, CTT and TLP) but also in hundreds of small businesses, such as workshops, laundries, sewing and alterations shops, etc. In February 1975, less than a year after the April coup, official sources showed that 12,000 people had been removed or suspended from their previous positions by legal or illegal means despite calls for moderation by both the Socialist Party and the Communist Party.[23] Formulated by workers' commissions in the majority of cases, similar demands multiplied throughout various social sectors with the strongest presence in the universities and schools.

The following example, from the postal and communications sector, is indicative:

For more than an hour, in the front of the administrative building of the CTT, on Rua de S. José, employees of this public company demonstrated in mass yesterday demanding the firing of the administrative corps from the old regime. Hiding themselves in the interior of the building, the administrators only left after a military force came to get them.[24]

In a strike at the worker-occupied Messa in Mem-Martins in suburban Lisbon, in addition to the improvement of working conditions, as reported in *Diário de Lisboa*, the workers demanded that: 'The company eliminates all the dictators who always restricted the aspirations of workers in their professional development, imposed unjust punishments, used inappropriate words for bosses to subordinates or vice versa, protected snitches, sheltered shoe polishers [bootlickers], who are usually the least competent.'[25]

Note the rich choice of words. The tenor of the disputing parties is worth exploring. It is, of course, a subjective evaluation. The differences between social classes may be seen not only in clothing, health, height and in general physical development, but also in body language. Probably, these differences are all the more noticeable to the naked eye, the greater the inequality in a country and lack of access to education and healthy food. It is no coincidence that we associate the image of the bourgeois man as haughty and arrogant, who speaks determinedly with a low voice; we do not imagine workers speaking like this since the body language of the working classes is more servile as seen, for instance, in the shyness of his/her look with the head a little less upright and the shoulders drooped. Without entering here into stereotypes, the revolution also subverted these bodily gestures.

The Faculty of Pharmacy declared itself self-managed by majority vote. Doctors at the Santo António General Hospital in Porto 'Gathered in a general assembly' demanding, among other measures, the 'immediate cessation of all functions of the director of the Santa Casa da Misericórdia [a private Catholic charity] as chairman of the board of this hospital'.[26] The Bar Association met in a plenary session demanding 'the resignation and trial of magistrates who collaborated with PIDE'.[27]

The actions of workers at the Ribeira market were symptomatic of the general *saneomento* movement. The workers at the most popular market in Lisbon, located at the Cais do Sodre on the city's waterfront, assembled and released the following statement:

Workers at the Lisbon Fruit Supply Market (Cais do Sodre) freed the facilities of technical, inspection and administrative services yesterday from the fascist rule of the Junta Nacionalde Frutas (National Fruit Board), forcing all its employees to abandon their posts ... [We will] not uphold from now on any impositions that we were subjugated to such as the extortion of taxes from producers ...

We demand:

1. Immediate withdrawal of all useless employees from the Market.

2. Immediate refund of the security deposit that was imposed on us for the possible charges of debts to this agency which were never verified ... [to the contrary we are] creditors of the long years of freedom that were taken from us ...[28]

The settling of scores with the old regime also resulted in the welcoming back of those who were politically persecuted and sacked from work during the dictatorship. In May, a plenary meeting of the bank workers demanded the readmission of 'fired bank workers'.[29]

Less than a week later, various plenaries at the universities – where the far-left constituted a vanguard and counted on thousands of activists and sympathisers – promoted the readmission of professors and students expelled during the fascist regime. On 29 April 1974, a meeting of The Council of the Faculty of Letters presided over by the most distinguished Portuguese geographer, Professor Orlando Ribeiro, decided 'to propose the immediate cancellation of all pending disciplinary processes and the reintegration of all students affected by such sanctions'.[30]

The government and senior managers of the TLP and other companies quickly realised, especially in the case of the Lisnave shipyards where the directors rebuffed the attempt to evict a manager, that such refusal to evict accomplices of the regime had a disruptive effect not only on the whole company or public service but also appeared to question fundamental assumptions about ownership and even power. No wonder Governments wanted to settle such issues as quickly as possible, making it safer to accept demands than to perpetuate conflicts.

Table 4.2   Political Purges in the Revolution (private and public sectors)[31]

Total Number of Persons Suspended or Fired (by legal and illegal means)	
April 1974 to February 1975	12,000
March 1975 to November 1975	8,000
By sector	
Armed Forces (April–September 1974)	60 generals, 103 Navy officers, 300 other officers of various ranks
Public Sector Workers (April–December 1974)	4,300
Ministry of Justice (April 1975–middle 1975)	42 judges
Ministry of Education	Setting for the majority of spontaneous purges. All university rectors and directors were fired by the JSN.

The Army on the Side of the People?

The MFA was loathe to wield force, which is what armies do traditionally. This army had mutinied and sought a social base to legitimise its position. It needed mass support. This was expressed in terms of collaboration across the classes. Although the military was to be used against workers, on and off throughout the process, but even in the early days, we see examples of soldiers siding with those in struggle.

A good example of interventions took place at the Ribeira Market. The workers sent their demands to the City Hall, refusing to recognise the authority of the National Fruit Board. The letter ended with the salutation, 'Long Live the Armed Forces Movement!', who actually had nothing to do with the conflict. The MFA arrived, this time in the person of Captain Alfredo Horta, who went to the market, where he 'recognised and gave support to the workers' decisions'[32] and assigned five soldiers to supervise. Cruz Oliveira, one of the MFA leaders, emphasises that the majority of the MFA interventions which appeared supportive also served to arbitrate, fitting within the framework of a state structure that intended to nullify, in a mediated and negotiated manner, any threats to state power.

Here is another incident involving soldiers. In a scene at TLP filmed by RTP and already referred to, the thin, short and moustachioed worker was visibly angry, speaking loudly and with conviction. He interrupted the managers. At first, both of them maintained an arrogant pose with paused speech, but then they began to babble and their words trembled, as they are visibly harassed by the crowd outside that is heard shouting 'thieves'. While the screams continued and the words are barely audible, a worker approached the cameras again and pointed to one of the directors, saying: 'This man is a bad man for trying to boycott the work of the company. Moreover, he refuses to resign ...' The worker could not finish the sentence because the gates of the headquarters of the TLP suddenly opened and a group of MFA soldiers entered, to escort the managers out under protection. Now, with the doors open, the cries from the street were more clearly heard. Inside and out, working men and women jostled each other shouting 'Victory, Victory, Victory'.[33]

There were to be many similar interventions. Workers and the people (*povo*) in general, loved the army. In the first week of May, the Grupo de Música Contemporâneo de Lisboa (Contemporary Music Group of Lisbon) sent salutations to the Armed Forces Movement (MFA). The Liceu Camões (Camões School) General Assembly of Teachers declared its support for the JSN and the Democratas do Montijo (Democrats of Montijo) decided to collectively adhere to the programme of the JSN and demanded for street names to be changed to 'April 25' and 'Armed Forces Street'. A meeting of the Teatro da Cornucópia (Cornucópia Theatre) decided to collaborate 'in the course of the military revolution, which they vibrantly salute, towards a total social transformation'.[34]

The slogan 'the MFA is with the people, the people are with the MFA' soon gained enormous popularity. People were to have many hopes, and illusions, in the armed forces. We will see, as we cover the narrative up until 25 November 1975, a number of amazing acts of solidarity between members of the armed forces and the *povo*. These illusions in the MFA were to have dire consequences.

The Press

Saneomento affected all sectors, albeit unevenly. What happened in the newspapers was significant especially because it impacted upon the content of the news; the papers, freed of their shackles, were now more than ready to report the happenings in the workplaces and on the streets. Hundreds of workers at the Empresa Nacional de Publicidade (National Advertising Company), the owner of the *Diário de Notícias* and a series of other publications,[35] met in an assembly immediately after 25 April, demanding the 'immediate termination of the functions of all managers'.[36]

In the same week that the management of the *Diário de Notícias* was evicted, the editorial board of *O Século* elected five representatives by direct and universal vote, requiring that the head editor of the newspaper be subject to them and not to management. The *Diário de Lisboa* also elected a new editorial board in order 'to maintain a pluralistic and independent orientation'. In Porto, a branch of the censorship office (*Exame Prévio*), located in a building in D. João I Square, was occupied by journalists with the 'intention of using the same building for the headquarters of the National Union of Journalists'. Of monumental importance, but often forgotten, was the fact that in this case 'it was decided to deliver all the archives [of the censors] to the union'.[37] The journalists of *O Primeiro de Janeiro* elected a new editorial board with quite unexpected intentions and presented:

a document to the director of the newspaper tomorrow, clearly reflecting that the editorial board has decided that the newspaper will be for general information, active and open to all democratic and progressive currents, rejecting any form of internal censorship or interference and recognising that every journalist has the right to intervene in everything that concerns the newspaper's political line, to ensure the guiding principles to which it is obliged.[38]

Indeed, the press in Portugal underwent rapid and far-reaching changes. In a mere week, the entire propaganda structure of the New State collapsed, to be replaced by another highlight of the revolutionary process: a strong, confrontational, polemical and engaged media.

Residents' Commissions

The 25 April coup occurred in the context of a vacuum of organisation which allowed the mushrooming of rank-and-file organisations. Workers' commissions (*comissão de trabalhadores*) and residents' commissions (*comissão de moraderes*) emerged simultaneously.[39] It may be that they inspired one another. Residents' commissions were born with the primary need to ensure decent housing for the most impoverished sectors. As we have seen in Chapter 3, it seems the first occupation movement occurred in the Boavista neighbourhood in Porto, where the houses were unoccupied despite repeated requests to the municipalities, which until 25 April 1974 had distributed housing based on loyalty to the regime and bribes. The movement spread to Lisbon, in the neighbourhoods of Chelas, Relógio, Casalinho, Curraleira and Caxias in the municipality of Oeiras, among many other places. Many of them formed alliances with workers' commissions. The movement also took hold in Setúbal and Porto neighbourhoods. Maria das Dores, a street vendor, was one of the occupiers in the Chelas district: 'If you saw the dunghill of the shack where I lived with the water and the mud at the entrance ... We need at least a house to live, we will not live all our lives like pigs in the pen. Is it right that my children sleep in the same bed as me? Is this misery, right?'[40]

The government responded with threats that were published in some papers with capital letters: 'THE JUNTA OF NATIONAL SALVATION WILL NO LONGER TOLERATE THE ABUSIVE OCCUPATION OF HOUSES'.[41] The population disobeyed. A representative of the residents of a Lisbon district near the Catholic University, who had lived in a 400-shack community for 15 years without water or electricity, delivered the following letter to the JSN:

The people who occupied the neighbourhood of the Salazar Foundation consider this occupation an act of justice, for every worker should be entitled to housing and to not live in miserable shacks, while those who do not work live in luxury and opulence ... That construction of houses be resumed by contractors ... That the Municipality initiate the building of sewage drains, water mains and finally, in order of priority, the installation of electricity by the company.[42]

The social and workers' movements proceeded in this manner: house to house; factory to factory; company to company.

The First Provisional Government

The social explosions were of great concern to those who were trying to form a government. Hence Mário Soares on 2 May 1974, argued for the need for the Communist Party to enter the government to contain the outbreak of widespread political activity from below. The generals António de Spínola and Francisco da Costa Gomes also invited the Communist Party to form part of the government as a way of establishing order.

The First Provisional Government took office on 16 May 1974 with little ability to govern a country, while alternative centres of power were emerging and multiplying. It was for this reason that it would be the first of six such governments during the 19 months of the revolution. As Ramalho Eanes, leader of the counter-revolutionary coup of 25 November 1975, asserted many years later, the conditions for the stability of the State, national unity and industrial peace were decidedly not assured.

The First Provisional Government was composed of parties from the right to the left, two seats each for the Socialist Party (PS), the Portuguese Communist Party (PCP) and the Popular Democratic Party (PPD). The Socialist Party had reformed in 1973, but in 1974 it was still an embryonic party, with its cadre largely from the petty bourgeoisie, almost all of whom were in exile.

The Communist Party, the largest political organisation in Portugal and by the end of the 1960s and beginning of the 1970s the only force that effectively resisted fascism, with an important group of clandestine members many of whom were in prison, had no more than 3,000 militants, some of them employed as rural salaried workers in the south of Portugal. (One year after the revolution, the Communist Party grew to 100,000 members.)[43] Chameleon-like, the PPD was an embryo of a liberal party that would display social democrat colours during the revolution.

The CDE – the Democratic Electoral Commissions – emerged as an electoral front during the tightly controlled elections, which were held in October 1969. The electoral front consisted of communists, radical Catholics and prominent 'left' intellectuals. The CDE had been an important forum for anyone who opposed the regime, but its influence waned as the other parties gathered momentum.

The second half of May was marked by the radicalisation of social conflicts. Despite successive appeals by the Communist Party for the working class to support the new government, nothing seemed to quench the explosion of social conflicts. A government decision on 24 May to approve a minimum monthly wage of 3,300 escudos, the equivalent of £55 in those days, which fell well short of that demanded by workers, provoked the eruptions of even more strikes and workplace occupations. The majority of the workers' movement demanded minimum wages above 4,000 or even 6,000 escudos.[44]

We have already referred to the waves of strikes and occupations but they plagued the government in its first few weeks, and there were a lot more.

Between 15 and 30 May, strikes broke out among the following groups of workers and companies: fishers, woolworkers, bakers, oil workers, the CTT, Carris, the Lisbon Metro, pharmaceutical laboratories, cork workers and the Viana do Castelo shipyards. On 13 May, Pfizer, Firestone and the Borralha mine workers began work stoppages. On 14 May, workers at Bayer Pharmaceuticals, the national book club company Círculo de Leitores and Simões & Cia, went on strike. On 15 May, it was the turn of workers at CIBA-Geigy Portuguese, National Margarine Factory, Beechman-Bencard in Grão-Pará, in the construction and wool sectors, the Estoril Company (refused to collect fares), public transport (refused to collect fares), a partial strike of sellers at Salvador Caetano, a strike with the kidnapping of a manager for one day at Lisnave and another one-day strike at Vitrohm. On 16 May, work stoppages began at refineries, at Messa in Habitat, at Philips, in the glass industry, insurance companies, banks and ITT. On the same day, 20,000 woolworkers paralysed production. At Lisnave, sectors of the company went on strike, demanding:

A minimum wage of 7,800 escudos; increased subsidy for night shifts; 40-hour working week with overtime limited to a maximum of 16 hours per month and increasing remuneration; 100 per cent sick and accident pay; right to a two-hour assembly in the company every fortnight and other demands around safety standards, welfare, discipline, and the sanitation of personnel with the dismissal of legionnaires [state-organised militias] and informers for the former PIDE-DGS.[45]

On 17 May, an intermittent strike began at Renault and workers stopped production at the Luso-Belga, Pereira, Brito, ENI and ACP companies. Textile and woolworkers demonstrated at the Ministry of Labour.

Between 22 and 25 May, there were also strikes in Berliet, Ulysseia Movies, Flama, Melka, Tecnivega and an 'exam' strike by secondary school students. On 26 May, the workers of Covilhã, many of them women, ended their two-week strike, when employers retreated and negotiated wage increases. On that same day, various regions of the country also approved the 'English week', that is, the right to rest on Saturday afternoons and Sundays. On 27 May, bakery workers – contrary to their union instructions – went on strike.

In this phase, workers at Carris in Lisbon went on strike, demanding parity with the Metro workers even though their union was against the work stoppage. CTT workers at Terreiro do Paço also began strike action. Lisbon, the capital of the last European empire, woke upon 28 May with no buses, electric trams or bread. Most of the strikes in May were won by the workers, much to the consternation of the Provisional Government, which had assumed office only in the middle of May.

The Postal Workers Strike

One of the most radical struggles at that time was the CTT strike,[46] which also evolved from a workers' commission:

> Over a thousand postmen and as many employees invaded the administration building, on San José Street in Lisbon, demanding that chief postmaster and the board of directors of the CTT be arrested, and, after obtaining the support of all the [workers in the] services of the Restauradores, Terreiro do Paço, D. Luis, 24 de Julho and Conde de Óbidos [public buildings and squares in central Lisbon], marched together to the Cova da Moura [the armed forces' headquarters] to show their support for the MFA.
>
> Held by workers in an office, the postmaster, Carlos Ribeiro, and the administrators Luis de Athayde and Valle Guimarães, were taken under custody to [the Ministry of] National Defence.
>
> By the time the workers were concentrated in front of the building on S. José Street, management ordered that the iron gates be shut, but this did not stop some protesters who climbed the railings and opened it from the inside.[47]

Bob Light, a visitor from the UK, tells us he joined the demonstration by striking postal workers:

> The first surprise for me was that our seeming destination was an army barracks; my second surprise was that there were several tanks parked in the road – with their guns pointed inwards at the barracks; my final surprise was that, despite the tanks on the lawn, leaning out of every single window in the barrack block there were uniformed soldiers giving the clenched fist salute and waving red carnations.[48]

Peter Robinson writes:

> This was amongst the first of many occasions when the rank and file workers came into conflict with the military. On 19 June the government gave the order to call in the army against 1,000 postal workers employed by CTT who had gone on strike. Faced with this threat the strike committee called off the strike and secured desultory gains. A number of Communist Party members tore up their party cards in disgust and joined the rapidly expanding revolutionary left. By contrast with the Communist Party, the Socialist Party had conspicuously supported the strike and stressed the democratic (i.e. non-PCP) nature of the strike organisation. By doing so it enhanced its reputation as 'democratic' and 'left wing' – which proved important later.[49]

The postal workers' dispute was an isolated victory for the First Provisional Government, and the MFA discovered that the tap of revolution, once turned on, was difficult to turn off.

The Far-Left Thrive

So far, we haven't said that much about the revolutionaries; far-left groups had been very active in supporting the postal workers and organised a demonstration in support of two army cadets who had been imprisoned for refusing to participate in the mobilisation against the CTT strikers.

Many camps emerged from splits inside the Communist Party, in particular over the Sino-Soviet conflict there were also Maoist organisations and, to a lesser extent, Guevarists and Trotskyists.

Culturally, these latter groups were an uneven combination, inspired by May 1968, Che Guevara and Woodstock: selfless and even somewhat fanatically militant, they fought for a release from the shackles of conservatism and Fordist exploitation, that is, a highly regimented high-volume manu-facturing system, designed to churn out standardised, low-cost goods. The factory was even viewed, by some, as a type of concentration camp.

The far-left organisations, especially the Maoists but also the Partido Revolucionário do Proletariado-Brigadas Revolucionários (Revolutionary Party of the Proletariat – Revolutionary Brigades, PRP-BR) and the Movimento de Esquerda Socialista (Movement of Left Socialists, MES) exercised influence in some workplaces. The Communist Party, who had the honour of having some of its most militant members in Salazar's prisons, contemptuously referred to them as 'adventurous' and 'boys from the cafés on Roma Avenue'. Labelled as 'far-left' and 'petty bourgeois', such groups were complex, divided and imaginative yet succeeded in fracturing the hegemony of either pro-Soviet or social democratic parties in workplace organisation.

Summing Up

In the first two weeks of May, workers' commissions, general assemblies of workers and widespread demands for improvements in wages and working conditions multiplied. In addition to Timex, in the first half of May 1974 there were strikes of construction workers in Torralta, in the chemical plants of the Companhia União Fabril in Barreiro, in the woolworks of Covilhã, in the J.J. Gonçalves company, in the A.C. Santos supermarkets and the Panasqueira mines.

Just looking at some actions on 6 May, for example, we see at the airline company TAP (Transportes Aéreos Portugueses) worker demands would begin a course of action that would lead to self-management. On that very same day general assemblies were held throughout the country: for example at the Carris public transportation company, Sacor petroleum conglomerate, rail workers, miners, Lisbon drivers, hospital workers in Coimbra, radio and television workers in Porto, metal workers in Porto and Matosinhos and TLP employees in Lisbon and Bragança. At the Oficinas Gerais de Material Aeronáutico (General Aeronautical Workshops, OGMA) workers demanded wage increases. On the same day, officers in the navy elected a representative committee and presented a series of demands. Workers at Siderurgia (the National Iron and Steel Company) threatened to strike and Lisnave workers abolished the internal company manager/worker committee, striking at the company on 10 May for a day.

The Portuguese Revolution was characterised by highly radical-ised social conflicts (strikes, demonstrations and occupations) involving students, workers in the new industries, employees in the informal sector, women, sections of the middle class and the rank and file of the armed forces. Munoz recorded 958 separate industrial conflicts in companies and factories, 300 of which occurred between May and June 1974.[50] With the exception of July and August 1974, every month in these two years saw at least 100 conflicts. Yet this is clearly an underestimate since Muñoz relied solely on just two newspapers sources. As we will see time and time again the revolution was marked by the centrality of a resilient social movement which affected all sectors of Portuguese society, not only the working class. Figure 4.1 tries to show this graphically:

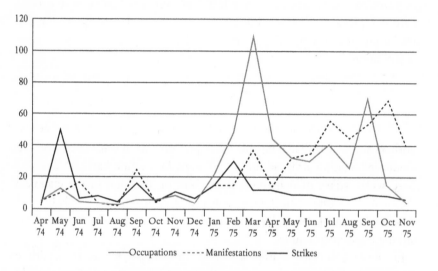

Figure 4.1   Social Struggles Surged Following the Events of 25 April 1974

Source: Varela, R. et al. (2014) *Relações laborais em Portugal e no Mundo Lusófono. História e Demografia.* Lisbon: Colibri.

The main political parties were vainly trying to govern the country by maintaining production, which meant respecting private property and the hierarchy of the functioning of companies. From the outset, the workers' commissions and the embryonic residents' organisations challenged the fragile establishment. Chapter 6 will examine the role of the unions and their inter-relationships with workers' commissions, and with the governments.

From the government's perspective, the endless number of strikes rendered the social and political situation uncontrollable. Figure 4.2 gives an overview of the number of strikes up to November 1975.

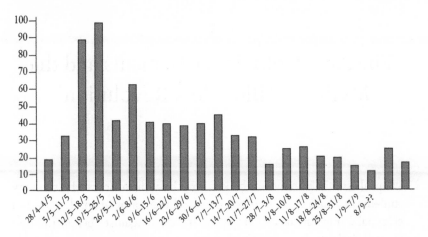

Figure 4.2   Strikes during the 1974–1975 Revolution

Source: Miguel Pérez, 'A mobilizacao operaria anticapitalista na Revolucao de 1974–75', I Congresso de Historia do Movimento Operario e dos Movimentos Sociais, 15–17 March 2013, Lisbon, FCSH-UNL, 6.

The insistence of workers in the metropole and the liberation movements in Africa created a political situation provoking the fall of the First Provisional Government, which did not even last two months. Now it is time for us to return to Africa.

5

The Anti-Colonial Movements and the Myth of a 'Bloodless Revolution'

I appeal especially to those who know me best, the officers who were my students in Mafra ... I speak to you to tell you, once again, that this is a criminal war in which you participate. It is a war against a people fighting for their independence and freedom.[1]

Fernando Cardeira, an official deserter who lived in Sweden, speaking to PAIGC Radio during the dictatorship.

Protests

Pedro Rodriguez Peralta, a short dark-skinned man, was a captain in the Cuban armed forces who was captured and wounded by the Portuguese military in Guinea-Bissau in 1969. He was brought to Lisbon and imprisoned. In May 1974, five years later, the demand for his release was the watchword for one of the huge anti-colonial demonstrations organised by the far-left.

This took place at 5pm on the evening of 25 May, at the front gates of the Principal Military Hospital. According to Phil Mailer 'two thousand young demonstrators sat on the steps of the church opposite and carried out a 20-hour vigil, halting traffic and singing anti-colonial songs.'[2] It was impossible to predict what would happen. This was an authentic grass-roots mobilisation that faced a strong repressive apparatus, with policing by the Guarda Nacional Republicana (Republican National Guard, GNR) on horseback and the forces of the Polícia de Segurança Pública (Public Security Police, PSP). Among others, Maoist militants of the MRPP and Trotskyists from the International Communist League (ICL) hoisted placards with anti-colonial slogans, such as 'Immediate independence for the colonies'.[3] They were joined by workers from Cape Verde, who lived nearby.

The release of Captain Peralta would not be accomplished on the day; he would be finally freed at the end of September 1974, in the tumultuous political context that led to the resignation of President Spínola.

During these months, many other anti-colonial protests arose through general assemblies, demonstrations, occupations and protests against soldiers embarking Portugal to fight in Africa. They were essentially protests led by far-left groups and students, aptly captured in the following newspaper report of events at the University of Lisbon:

> After successive preliminary assemblies and a final meeting yesterday afternoon at the Faculty of Sciences, attended by Angolans and others from the colonies who live in Lisbon, as well as numerous progressive young students, participants of the meeting went to the House of Angola [a government colonial office], whose premises were occupied. Later a military force arrived and after learning of the reasons for the occupation, withdrew. United in general assembly, the Angolans elected a provisional leadership commission and approved a motion of support for their brothers, who with arms in their hands, were fighting colonialism, associating this salutation, not only with the MPLA, but with all movements in the colonies fighting for independence.[4]

The independence of the colonies was eventually achieved through the combination of various factors that included the crisis in the army, reflected in the divisions among generals, the refusal of officials to continue the war and the demoralisation of the soldiers, whose deaths continued to occur after 25 April in areas where the war continued. The political crisis fed the military crisis and vice versa. There was a combination of social conflicts in the metropolis, such as the strikes that weakened the government that were not directly related to the colonial wars, and the protests that directly questioned the colonial war, largely organised by students and the extreme left.

The Hidden Carnage

The Belém Tower is a fortified tower, built in the early sixteenth century and is located near the mouth of the Tagus River. It is in the shape of an arrow pointing to Africa, celebrating the Portuguese maritime discoveries and the formation of the Portuguese Empire. Immediately next to it is the national monument to the Portuguese fighters killed in the colonies. The national holiday that takes place on 10 June celebrates the Day of Portugal. Tellingly, this used to be known as the 'Day of the Portuguese Race' but is now a commemoration dedicated to the sixteenth-century poet, Camões (generally considered Portugal's greatest) and the Portuguese People. Every year on

10 June, ex-combatants meet at the monument and, with the support of state institutions and the conservative parties, pay homage to those killed in combat in the colonial war – to the Portuguese felled, not the Africans.

The Colonial War by Aniceto Afonso and Carlos de Matos Gomes,[5] a most authoritative source, unpacks the death toll in the Portuguese Army and the brutality of their actions, such as the use of napalm on civilians.[6] According to the General Staff of the Army, 8,300 Portuguese soldiers died in service in Guinea, Angola and Mozambique.[7] It is not surprising that it is much more difficult to estimate the number of dead on the side of the liberation movements, the number of guerrillas and civilians, because this work has not been done by historians of Africa. According to international studies directed by Ruth Sivard,[8] three to five times as many guerrillas died than Portuguese soldiers and ten times as many civilians. So the most conservative estimates for the total number of victims exceed 100,000 dead.

We also know very little about the accompanying 'destruction and dislocation of the material and symbolic structures of African societies'.[9] It would be inappropriate to ascribe the lack of references to the number of victims as merely a symptom of statistical uncertainties. The failure to question the values of the rulers of the empire has traditionally been accompanied by assumptions that the colonial war was a 'less intense' war, with few deaths, a supposedly 'low cost conflict'.[10] This omission contributes to the spread of the myth, still prevalent in sections of Portuguese society, that the Portuguese built a revolution 'without deaths', 'peaceful', almost an extension, though not direct, of the country of 'kind customs' that the propaganda of the Salazar government promoted.

Such research artificially separates the revolution from its main cause and airbrushes the dead who fought the Portuguese Army, leading to the construction of a false memory, one that underplays the history of war and liberation.

The Liberation Struggles

The book we have just referred to, *The Colonial War* by Aniceto Afonso and Carlos de Matos Gomes, was published in the year 2000. In the 1970s, it was common to refer to the struggle of the colonial peoples as 'anti-colonial revolutions' as all the liberation struggles of the post-war period were called. This terminology has now been marginalised in favour of 'colonial war'. This shift devalues the mass peasant and popular mobilisations against the Portuguese colonial empire. The guerrilla support base was a peasant and dispersed population. In some cases, the guerrillas' own villages were destroyed by napalm and their populations relocated in villages controlled by the army. Consequently, there was widespread peasant support for the guerrillas, similar to what happened in China, Cuba, Vietnam, Indonesia and even in the anti-Nazi resistance in France or Yugoslavia, without which the guerrillas would not have survived.

Working against the current, one of the historians who stresses the qualitative importance of anti-colonial resistance, is Dalila Cabrita Mateus in her book, *A PIDE-DGS e a Guerra Colonial* (*The PIDE-DGA and the Colonial War*).[11] For example, in Mozambique, the political police acknowledged that subversive networks had reached an 'impressive vastness' and that, in spite of this, it was 'impossible to root out an evil whose genesis is a population brainwashed in favour of subversion'.[12]

From a study of the evolution of the political police in the colonies as well as using African sources and a number of interviews with guerrillas, Dalila Mateus has demonstrated the brutality of the crackdown on the guerrillas. Her study of the PIDE in the metropolis shows that they were ineffective, despite the strong repression against members of the Communist Party. In the colonies the PIDE was brutal, arresting and torturing thousands of combatants with broad support among the white settlers, aided by a network of information with close links to the military command. It was, above all, extremely effective.

It is also necessary to stress the impact of the strikes and work stoppages in Angola and Mozambique during this period, which are so often forgotten in the histories, and which inspired other workers in the region, including in South Africa.

A wave of strikes arose in May 1974 in companies and sectors of public administration in Angola and Mozambique in the cities of Luanda, Lobito, Lourenço Marques, Beira and Vila Pery.

> Rail traffic on the Benguela line from Lobito to the border is completely paralysed ... The Railway Workers' Union ordered a strike of all employees of the Benguela Railway Company in order to force the achievement of a collective bargaining agreement for which the railway workers have fought for a long time.
>
> This strike, in addition to affecting the Angolan economy also equally affects neighbouring countries, in particular Zaire and Zambia.[13]

The legendary Benguela railway, the brainchild of Cecil Rhodes, linked the port of Lobito on the Atlantic Ocean to the interior of the country. It proved to be very profitable since it was the shortest way to bring the mineral wealth of the Congo within the African continent to the Atlantic and then through the maritime trade routes to Europe.

Strikes were not confined to the transport sector. On 15 May 1974, in Lourenço Marques, Mozambique the workers of the daily newspaper *O Diário* also went on strike and suburban transport workers threatened to stop transportation, if the 'immediate resignation of the management' was not undertaken.[14] Two days later, the city faced a general strike. The tugboat workers from the port at Lourenço Marques, who worked up to 24-hour shifts without overtime pay, went on strike on 17 May 1974. Workers at the Machava cashew factory refused a salary increase from 37 to 45 escudos; they demanded 200. At the Fábrica Colonial de Borracha (Colonial Rubber Factory), where average salaries were 800 escudos, the workers demanded an increase to 2,500. On the same day, the railway lines between South Africa, Rhodesia and Swaziland were closed due to a strike by 3,000 railway workers.[15]

In Lobito, the workers at the Sorefame Company went on strike but remained in the workplace, demanding 'better wages and better working conditions'.[16] *Luanda* also seemed 'to be on fire'. Rosa Coutinho, the newly appointed president of the Governing Board of Angola, took some time to appreciate the extent and source of the violent unrest: 'The first reaction that I found in Luanda was the expulsion of the canteen owners from the slums. Luanda looked like it was on fire. Houses were burned. The revolt of the people against the small merchants created problems later because they no longer had supplies.'[17]

Deserters

The struggles of the emerging liberation movement in the colonies exacerbated other long-standing strains on the regime in Portugal in relation to the anti-colonial revolutions. The most obvious impact was the refusal by young conscripts to go to war.

The number of Portuguese military personnel in the colonial wars was only surpassed per capita by the Israeli armed forces. Yet in 13 years, nearly 200,000 men failed to report for enlistment. In a study by the Estado-Maior do Exército (General Staff of the Army), desertion from military service was massive and growing: in 1961, the percentage of absentees was 11.6 per cent; from 1962, it grew steadily so that by 1972, it had reached 21 per cent.[18]

The main reason for desertion was the outright refusal to fight. Although often for personal reasons, it was seen as political. The war resistors' movement during the New State arrived late and gradually,[19] but eventually resulted in a fearless opposition.

The historian Rui Bebiano has traced the general history of resistance to war and the tardy and ambiguous positions of all the opposition sectors on the question of the independence of the colonies. From the late 1950s and throughout the 1960s, first the Communist Party (since 1957), then progressive Catholics, the Social Democrats of Acção Socialista Portuguesa (Portuguese Socialist Action, ASP) and a number of armed struggle groups adopted a position in favour of independence with varying nuances depending on the organisation. Opposition positions on the colonial war ranged from the nationalist argument that the colonial war negatively affected state finances and internationally brought the country into disrepute, embraced by the Communist Party and social democratic sectors, to the voluntarism of the extreme left, who raised the principle of self-determination. In any case, the regime would gradually become increasingly isolated with respect to the war.

Rui Bebiano recounted what he witnessed in 1970 during the screening of the militaristic film *The Green Berets* with John Wayne: the movie-goers united in a cry of 'Down with the colonial war'. He also remembered: 'The huge ovation for the bassist Charlie Haden at the Cascais Jazz Festival in 1971 when he dedicated the "Song for Che" to the struggle for the independence of the colonies from Portugal, something which incidentally earned Charlie Haden an immediate expulsion from the country.'[20] Charlie Haden was a famous American bassist, known for his melodic bass lines, and who founded the Liberation Music Orchestra (LMO) with Carla Bley in 1971. Their first album dealt with the Spanish Civil War.

Here is an extract from the *Song of the Deserter* by Luís Cilia:

> Oh sea! Oh sea!
> That kisses the earth,
> Tell my mother,
> I'm not going to war.

> Tell my mother, oh sea,
> I don't want to kill
> Deep down, who goes to war
> Is not the one who makes it.

> I will sing to freedom,
> For my beloved homeland,
> And for the sad, black mother
> Who lives in chains.

> But the voice of our people,
> On judgement day,
> Will say to you, oh sea,
> From wind to wind,
>
> Who are the traitors,
> Is it the ones who steal our bread?
> Or is it we the deserters
> Who say no to the war.[21]

The Road to Sweden

The desertion of seven officers, who ended up in Sweden in 1970, became an inspiration to the generation who refused to go to war. It is worthwhile recounting this since it was both exceptional and yet typical of young people's resistance to the war. Youth, desertion, courage, fear, fraternity, vows of love – all these elements were present in the fascinating story of these seven Portuguese officers, who defected and became symbolic of a whole generation of students inspired by May 1968, by military officers horrified by the colonial slaughter, by young people who aimed to break the shackles of authoritarianism and the immense cultural and intellectual prison that was Salazar's Portugal.

The defection had a wide impact on the Salazar regime and at the international level. Traitors to the motherland in Portugal and heroes in Sweden, the officers linked their defection directly to the struggle against the colonial war. Amílcar Cabral wrote to thank them and their anti-colonial statements were heard by the guerrillas in the middle of the bush in Guinea, Angola and Mozambique.

The story begins with the imminent posting of the lieutenants through Service Order no. 105 on 5 May 1970 from the Fifth Infantry Regiment in Caldas da Rainha (just north of Lisbon) to Guinea and to Mozambique. When the orders arrived the seven officers had already decided to disobey.

They had entered the Military Academy at 18 years of age in 1961, the very year that the war broke out, unaware that the war would be long and difficult and believing that they would never serve since the engineering course they enrolled in would last at least seven years. The choice of the Military Academy was more of a desire for social mobility, an opportunity to study and to leave the provinces behind, rather than the ambition for a military career.

During the first years of the war, they were shocked by what they heard. Fernando Cardeira remembers that once while drinking: 'the officers who came from the war spoke proudly of imprisoning, torturing and killing ... I remember known "heroes" of war, decorated by Salazar, such as Lieutenant Robles and others, who bragged of the atrocities they committed, of the massacres that they did there.'[22]

In 1965, they began to study at the Technical Institute in civilian clothes and were free to attend the student meetings of the Reunião Inter-Associações (Inter-Associative Meetings, RIAS), assemblies, politicised and improvised music gatherings and street demonstrations. The experiences at the Technical Institute were crucial in consolidating their opposition to the colonial war. It also brought them in contact with leftist ideas. Fernando Cardeira, perhaps the most politicised of the group, remembers that during these years most students read more Marx, Engels and Lenin than engineering books.

Luck also played a part in their life. In 1968, some of them were finalists in a competition at the Technical Institute, winning a trip around Europe. This was a pivotal moment. They visited Paris in April 1968, a city already bedecked with posters of the revolutionaries Rosa Luxemburg and Che Guevara. Daniel Cohn-Bendit and Alain Krivine led demonstrations at the time. When they returned to Portugal, some asked for a discharge from the Military Academy. This was not an easy option: besides the shock that it caused for parents and other family members, the regime required them to pay 34,000 escudos to be discharged, an exorbitant amount for those who had a monthly salary of just over 2,000 escudos. Many had to borrow money or managed to save the required amount. They were required to bide their time in the barracks for a year before they could officially leave.

After they had taken the decision to desert, the question of how to do it still remained. One option was to procure documents and cross the border. The first plan was to go with militants of the Communist Party who they knew, even though they themselves were not members. They were, in fact, already very critical of the Communist Party for its position against the May 1968 uprisings and their support for the Soviet invasion of Prague. The Communist Party said that they were not willing to help them because they were against defections. The Party line was explicit; politicised soldiers should go to war and then publicise their opposition and organise subversion.

The deserters were composed mainly of lieutenants who had left the Military Academy (they were joined by another soldier who had not been a student with them). At the time, they were 26 or 27 years old, almost all were married and some had young children. The decision to desert was therefore a family decision relying on the unconditional support of their wives, who would join them after a few weeks in Sweden.

The group of six of them left for Gerês, crossing the border in broad daylight at 4pm on 23 August 1970. They still keep photographs of themselves on the border at Gerês, near the Portela do Homem mountain pass, where they appear smiling and relaxed on a beautiful sunny day. They each paid the *coyote* (the people smuggler) just over 1,500 escudos, a 'bargain' since the usual cost was up to 10,000 with the risk of being cheated. The 1,500 escudos included the bus fair to Paris and a night in an inn in Ourense, Spain.

After many scares and adventures, they arrived in Paris and wandered the city for two weeks making friends and encountering solidarity. They slept here and there among the many other Portuguese exiles they came across in the esplanades of the Latin Quarter. They wandered about not knowing what to do next until they met a Portuguese comrade exiled in Sweden who was on holiday in France. The comrade was Fernando Beijinha, a political activist very close to the PAIGC, the liberation organisation of Guinea-Bissau. He suggested they go to Sweden, where there were already several hundred Portuguese emigrants and deserters. They would not be officially recognised as political refugees, but the Swedish government would do everything necessary in practice for them to have equivalent status.

They were greeted warmly on their arrival in Sweden. The newspaper *Uppsala Nya Tidning* devoted its entire front page to the arrival of the deserters: 'Six Portuguese officers ask for political asylum in Uppsala'. The government gave them political asylum, housing, some money and offers of scholarship for everyone to learn Swedish.

A few months after arriving in Sweden, they met Palma Inácio, a leader of the armed-struggle group Liga de Unidade e Acção Revolucionária (League of Revolutionary Unity and Action, LUAR), who sought them out there to invite them to join his organisation and go to Portugal to make the revolution. One of them, Fernando Cardeira refused, recalling that:

We were unenlightened politically, but we did not want to return to Portugal to participate in a revolutionary 'project' that had no consistency ... The 1968 trip had opened up new horizons for us, we had seen the films we couldn't see in Portugal, read the books that we couldn't read, seeing things as mundane as the window display of a sex shop.[23]

Even before arriving in Sweden, the group had decided to make their desertion a political act against the war. In Paris, they sent hundreds of postcards denouncing the war and colonialism – a plan already prepared in Portugal – to their former Army trainees, former university and Military Academy colleagues, friends and family. In Stockholm, on 17 September, they organised a press conference that had reverberated in the Swedish media. Cardeira remembers going to Stockholm in 1970 to participate in demonstrations against the war in Vietnam, where he met deserters from that war. The news of his defection also reached newspapers in France, Germany, Italy, Norway and Denmark. He did an interview, which was broadcast by the Portuguese section of the BBC.

There were no mobile phones, but there was a military transmission system and the news quickly spread to Portugal and the colonies. In September 1970, the PAIGC newspaper, *Actualités*, published a photo of the deserters on the front page with the headline '6 Portuguese Lieutenants, 4 Intended for our Country, Refused to Fight in the Colonial War'. Next to the photo, they placed the lieutenants' statement: 'We wholeheartedly support the men who, with guns in their hand, fight against the Portuguese colonial army in Africa'.

The following message was broadcast by Radio Conakry in Guinea:

Here speaks Militia Lieutenant Cardeira … I speak mainly to those who know me best, the officers who were my fellow students in Mafra in the 3rd term of COM[24] in 1969, the lance-corporals that I met in the first and second terms of CSM[25] in 1970 in Caldas da Rainha, to the soldiers who met me in Leiria and Évora. I speak to you to tell you, once again, that this is a criminal war in which you participate. It is a war against a people fighting for their independence and freedom. It is a war that will impoverish our Portugal that sacrifices her children for the benefit of the great masters of international capitalism. In the Portuguese army there are only two correct positions: either sabotage or defect. We all know that is impossible to sabotage the colonial war when you are in the field. There, it is a fight for survival … Those who send you to the front count on this … They know you do not go willingly but have to defend yourselves and thus defend their interests. So when sabotage is not possible, we can only desert. And don't let it scare you! We came in a group of seven all at once and we were well received everywhere. And I can assure you that you may also defect because you will be well received by the PAIGC, who will send you to the country of your choice.[26]

On 31 December 1970, the Minister of National Defence and the Army, Sá Viana Rebelo, launched a fierce political attack against the deserters, who were considered to be traitors to the motherland. In his statement, published in the *Diário de Notícias*, the minister sought to hide the fact that these men had served in the Army and highlighted the danger of the politicisation of the universities:

> The commands responsible have lately voiced their apprehension about the state of the trainees coming to the Officers' and Militia Sergeants' courses from the universities, high schools and technical schools ... In several such establishments no one is able to teach competently. They are truly centres of subversion ... Their actions are so harmful that just a few months ago six militia lieutenants, ex-students of Engineering at the Military Academy, deserted to Sweden ... Under the law until recently in force, [these students] had to attend the last three years of civil engineering school in Lisbon and at this [university] received enough inspiration to betray the motherland and conduct a vile campaign abroad against their country and against their comrades in the Army, in which they never effectively served.[27]

The revolution was defined by the overlap of anti-colonial struggles and the eruption of struggles in the 'mother' country. The situation in Portugal reinforced the legitimacy of the liberation movements in the colonies and precipitated their independence in a short time. (Within 19 months, all the former colonies would become independent.)

Political Oppositions

Various 'Marxist/Leninists' (commonly known as 'Maoists'), Castroist and Trotskyist sects were opposed to the wars. They were inspired by the Cuban and Chinese revolutions, May 1968 in France and Mexico, the Italian 'Hot Autumn' in 1969 and in the principle of the self-determination of peoples, they viewed the fight against the war as a defence of the anti-colonial revolution. This was in contrast to other denunciations against the war that focused on the credibility of the country, the influence on the duration of the dictatorship and international isolation. The radical left groups were, of course, inspired by the anti-colonial leaders Simón Bolívar, Ho Chi Minh and Che Guevara (and his famous speech 'Create one, two, three, many Vietnams') and would influence anti-colonial demonstrations organised in Portugal in the last years of the regime and after it fell.

Anti-colonial opposition groups germinated within Portugal, such as the Comités de Luta Anticolonial e Anti-Imperialista (Committees of Anticolonial and Anti-Imperialist Struggle, CLACs) linked to the Organização Comunista Marxista-Leninista Portuguesa (Portuguese Marxist-Leninist Communist Organisation, OCMLP) and the Movimento Popular Anti-Colonial (Popular Anti-Colonial Movement) connected to the MRPP.

Outside the country, in France, the Netherlands and Sweden, there were deserters' committees or support groups including the Angola Comité (Angola Committee, Netherlands), Comités de Desertores Portugueses (Portuguese Defectors' Committees linked to the O Communista newspaper of the OCMLP, Sweden) and the Associação Resistência e Trabalho (Association Resistance and Work, Netherlands).

Differences over Africa leading to the fall of the First Provisional Government

The Captains' Movement arose from divisions within the ruling classes of the New State and the prolongation of the war, within the context of the 1973 international oil crisis. Yet the attention of Portuguese business was beginning to turn away from Portugal's African empire, and towards Europe. The political strategies favoured in ruling class circles increasingly reflected this emphasis.

We have already covered, albeit all too briefly, the combination of factors that led to the 25 April 1974 coup by the MFA. Having seized control of critical institutions, they left the command of the economic sector to the Portuguese elite, represented by General Spínola.

Nowadays, it is hard to believe that General António de Spínola, with his monocle and swagger-stick, was seen by rebellious officers in the Portuguese Army as the lynchpin in the overthrow of a fascist dictatorship.[28] Spínola fought for Franco in the Spanish Civil War and had been the military governor of Guinea, one of Portugal's African colonies. He was also a director of the Champalimaud group, one of two huge native conglomerates (the other was CUF), which had enjoyed state protection against foreign competition; even Coca-Cola was prohibited.

General Spínolo had published a famous book Portugal and the Future[29] a year earlier, where he advised a political solution to the war. When the Portuguese Prime Minister Caetano read it, he understood 'that the military coup, which I could sense had been coming, was now inevitable'. From the outset, Spínola was known as an advocate of a federalist solution for the colonies.[30] After he tried to impose changes to the MFA programme during preparations for the coup – and was forced to retreat – he said in his first communiqué to the country that the first task of the JSN immediately was 'to ensure the survival of the nation as a sovereign country and also including the whole empire'. The following day, the MFA's programme was published, stating that the 'overseas policy of the Provisional Government recognises that the solution to the wars overseas is political and not military'.

Just one day after the coup, the country became aware that there were disagreements on the issues of how to end the war and resolve the colonial question.[31] The MFA, regardless of the fragile political experience of its members, was in fact against the war; it was exactly this that had motivated the middle-level officers to undertake the coup.

In July 1974, the revolution in the homeland of the colonial empire, the refusal of soldiers to fight in the colonies and a worsening crisis of leadership in the State, led the government to cave in and support independence for the colonies.

Thus, on 9 July, Palma Carlos resigned as prime minister and the First Provisional Government fell. Palma Carlos was replaced by Vasco Gonçalves, a member of the MFA close to the Communist Party, who was called up directly to try to contain the crisis of the State.

On 27 July 1974, António de Spínola, now the President of the Republic, was forced to change tack; he solemnly recognised the rights 'of the peoples of the Portuguese overseas territories to self-determination'. Acclaimed at the Carmo military headquarters during the coup two months before, he was now a defeated general with a failed political project. A large and jubilant demonstration was organised at the Belém Palace, Spínola's presidential office, to support the self-determination decision, which Spínola himself was against. Despite dissenting from Spínola's position on the question, the government parties would launch a joint statement praising the decision of the President of the Republic.

Ruy Luís Gomes,[32] a sympathiser of the Portuguese Communist Party and a member of the Council of State, declared at the demonstration that: 'Today, after 50 years, General Spínola and all of us, the Portuguese people, thank the people of Guinea, Angola, Mozambique for becoming independent'. In the same speech, he noted that this recognition 'represents a new April 25'.[33]

It would not be the first – nor the last – time during the revolutionary process when workers or the public would thank others for what they themselves had done. We will see other similar occasions in which, for example, workers were grateful for government intervention in companies, when the occupation of companies left no other alternative; the same would apply to the MFA and land occupations. The State was 'legalising' situations, which created social legitimacy for it, thus ensuring that its power was not devastated by the ongoing conflicts.

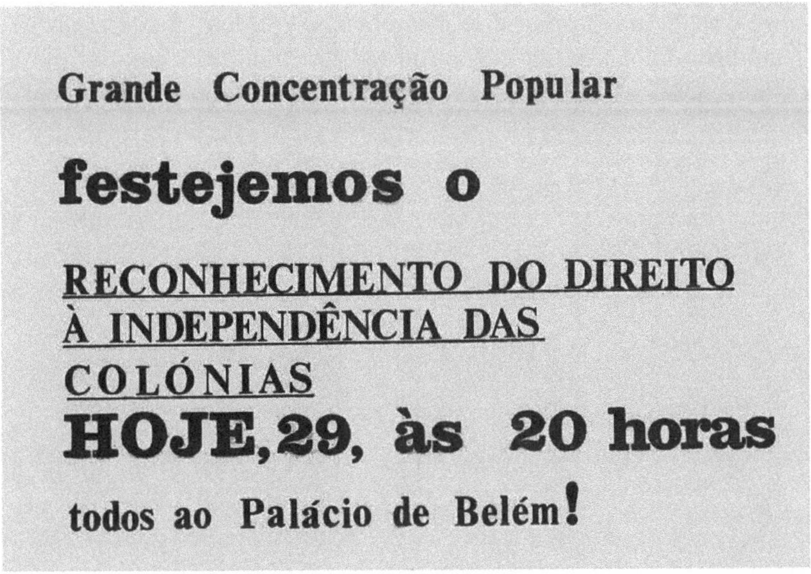

Figure 5.1   Anti-colonial demonstration leaflet. The text reads: 'Great Popular Concentration. We celebrate the recognition of the right to independence of the colonies. Today, the 29, 20hrs, everybody to the Belém Palace!

The regime lost the war by a combination of factors that go far beyond the number of rifles and the theatre of war itself.

Indeed, the main causes for the defeat of the regime were the support of the majority of the peasant and urban population of the colonies for the independence struggle, coupled with the struggle of the workers in the 'mother' country. The officials stopped believing in military victory and the demoralised soldiers, who were in the colonies after April 1974, refused to fight. We have seen that young people deserted and some became activists against the war. The crisis in the army was of such a size that it was the mid-level officers who prevented the State from collapsing and 'falling into the street'.

In the midst of this complex chessboard, the famous image of the carnation in the muzzle of the gun was not merely symbolic; it reflected the profound disruption of the military hierarchy. Vera Lagoon, one of the most controversial journalists of the period, described in a column titled 'Gossip', this reversal of military values under the impact of the revolution:

> We passed a soldier entirely covered with flowers: from the back to the chin: white flower pots at his waist; and jasmine in the muzzles of rifles ... We were already accustomed to the floral soldiers. Since 25 April, we have been accustomed to many things. Freedom, for example. Yet uniformed police in dark blue and red carnations still surprise us. Yet Republican guards with red carnations still surprise us.[34]

6

Strikes and their Reverberations

We fight actively against the 'strike law' because it is a deep blow to the freedoms of workers.

Statement of Lisnave shipyard workers[1]

Unions and the Intersindical

Government-controlled national unions, created under fascism, were discredited as governing structures by the labour movement. In most cases, the unions were empty façades, a creation from above. The post-Salazar regime – sometimes called the 'new spring' or 'The New State' – allowed the trade unions to run internal elections without first submitting lists of candidates to the secret police (PIDE). In 1969 and 1970, elections took place in five unions. Fresh blood was brought in. The textile union, for example, appointed a student militant as its organiser. By October 1970, there were 20 or so unions with independent elected leaderships who convened a semi-legal federation called the Intersindical. This was led by the Communist Party and progressive Catholics (the Catholics were sympathetic to MES – Movement of Left Socialists).

By 25 April, the Intersindical comprised a loose conglomeration of only 20 relatively independent unions. After the coup, the Communist Party put its resources not into the workplaces but into the Intersindical. Within weeks of the coup, the number of affiliated unions rose from 22 to 200, transforming the Intersindical almost overnight into the national trade union umbrella organisation. Over the next 19 months, a smaller national rival emerged, led by the Socialist Party.

The rise of the student and workers' movement, the drain of the colonial wars and economic crises combined to alarm the regime. By the early 1970s, Caetano had returned to traditional conservatism and repression. There was no room for reforms when a war was being fought and when nearly half of central budget expenditure went on the armed forces. But the workers' movement could not be simply pushed back. Caetano had introduced a Law of Collective Contracts, which resulted in an annual round of wage negotiations. As a result, in the textile industry, there was a strike every year from 1970–1973. Short-lived, spontaneous strikes also took place in a number of sectors. A new strike wave broke out in the last three months of 1973.

Many workers felt they had to do something about the unions linked to the old regime. As early as 28 April, there were occupations of the headquarters of the Bus Drivers' Union, the Union of Office Workers of Porto and of the Bakers' Union, also in Porto. On 29 April, office workers occupied their union, in Lisbon, and expelled its board of directors. And on 30 April, the civil construction workers dismissed the board of directors of their union, occupying its headquarters as well.

Of the 158 companies which experienced labour disputes between 25 April and 1 June 1974, the negotiation of conflicts was, in 61 cases, handled by the commission of workers, by the works' committee in six and by national or regional unions in ten instances.[2] None of the fascist unions were involved and they were left totally discredited.

Table 6.1   The growth of the Intersindical (1970–1975)

15 December 1970	12 unions/ 172,000 workers (Catholic progressive initiative, PCP influence grows)
18 January 1971	190,000 workers
16 June 1973	160,000 (fewer active after the repression of 1972)
11 May 1974	54 unions
1975	2 million workers (according to the PCP)

Source: The author.

'The Unions Lag Behind the Workers'

Those unions which had some life organised after the coup. An outstanding example was the metal workers union. Shortly after 25 April 1974, the metal workers, through their union, demanded a minimum salary of 6,000 escudos and also called for the cancellation of the 20 per cent reduction of salaries of women metal workers, one month's vacation, a month and half of holiday pay, a 13-month salary, the abolition of the Ministry of Corporations and the creation of a Ministry of Labour. Significantly, they demanded equal pay. The demands were not met by the Metalworkers Employers Federation; it conceded 4,400 escudos in an agreement signed between the Federation and the Ministry, on 12 June 1974.

This generated discontent and criticism in some of the factories (and also from the Metalworkers of Lisbon, led by a MES member, Jerónimo Franco). In fact, in most large factories and companies – and not just the metal workers sector – the workers' independent actions meant that union demands were far exceeded, and considerably higher wage gains were achieved. Many workers at large metal factories gained in excess of 7,000 escudos.

Overturning the corporatist legacy of the New State, the metal workers union opposed the separation of work from larger social issues, refusing class collaboration and they suggested a decisive break from management in the factories and companies.

Even the moderate newspapers did not hesitate to publish headlines such as 'THE UNIONS HAVE BEEN OVERTAKEN BY EVENTS' in bold capital letters. One journalist wrote that the public transport strike had been called for midnight on 27 May, but against the wishes of union leaders the workers went on strike one day earlier at midnight on 26 May, leaving Lisbon 'totally bottlenecked'. Union delegates even went to the Santo Amaro and Arco do Cego tram depots, trying to convince workers to begin the strike on 27 May, but 'workers eventually stopped listening to the union delegates and joined the movement'.

In an interview one of the union delegates, after impetuously suggesting that the strike could have been organised by elements connected to reaction and perhaps even by those who are still PIDE informants, ultimately admitted that this new working class was beyond the control of union leaders and that: 'It was probably not a far-right or far-left movement. There are lots of new people, mainly in Cabo Ruivo, who do not accept things with the same thoughtful consideration as those more experienced and politicised.'[3]

'No Strikes for the Sake of Strikes'

We have already mentioned how the generals Spínola and Costa Gomes, along with Mário Soares, the leader of the PS, had invited the Communist Party to form part of the government, as a way of containing the social explosion. The Communist Party joined and helped 'manage' the unrest. All those, including the Communist Party, feared 'the anarchic strikes'. They had to be stopped.

On 30 April, probably inspired by the Communist Party, the unions occupied the Ministry of Corporations and Social Security (in Lisbon), renaming it the Ministry of Labour. The first Minister of Labour in the First Provisional Government was a Communist Party militant.

The Communist Party appealed for a policy of 'national reconstruction' and even led a demonstration in Lisbon on 1 June 1974, organised by Intersindical, with the motto 'no strikes for the sake of strikes'. The Communist Party paper *Avante!* warned workers to avoid 'reactionary manoeuvres to promote industrial unrest'.[4] The 1 June demonstration was a disaster – Phil Mailer claims less than 500 people attended,[5] although the paper of the Communist Party *Avante!* claimed there were 10,000.

Thus, the party denounced strikes as 'adventurist', the work of 'provocateurs', potentially responsible for the 'return to fascism', and 'acts of sabotage'.[6] There were many statements such as: 'The strike weapon – which is now a conquered right – cannot be used lightly. In the current political context, all other forms of struggle must be exhausted, such as negotiating with employers to obtain just demands and only then – and always with eyes on what is essential and what is secondary.'[7]

Pressure was put upon the unions to contain the strikes and demands. The role of the unions, like that of the MFA, was ambivalent. To put it mildly: to both support the workers and to tame them.

The Communist Party, Unions and the Workers' Commissions

The history of trade unions in the Portuguese Revolution has not yet been written.

What exists is very fragmented and general. There is no history, for example, of Intersindical in the Carnation Revolution. The Communist Party was putting its resources into an alternative power base – the unions and a national trade union confederation, the Intersindical. The Communist Party were dominant in it but the influence of the revolutionary left, in particular that of MES had been important, particularly in the metal and textile unions. By 25 November, the Intersindical claimed around 1 million members.

On the other hand, histories of the workers' commissions are not lacking, with many empirical studies that provide us with a solid basis for analysis, even if there is still much to be analysed. These studies demonstrate that there was a tense and difficult relationship between unions and workers' commissions.

Although the unions had now been legalised and it was possible to transform or manipulate them, they had, in general, insufficient authority within the workplaces. Very occasionally, for example, in some textile factories, workers belonged to a single union and the union committee was in effect the workers' commission. Otherwise, in a factory of 150 workers, there could be members of as many as 20 unions. In response to the proliferation of the workers' commissions, the Communist Party promoted Commissions of Union Delegates, coordinated by the different unions in the workplaces. As a result of this, in many workplaces, there was a crucial clash of organisations, between the workers' commissions elected by the workers in the assemblies and the union delegates. In a number of cases, the union delegates were not elected by the workers, or indeed may not even have worked in the factories.

Communist Party statements at the time accused the workers' commissions of being 'ultra-left', of 'playing the game of the right', and of being 'lackeys of the bosses'. This position of the Communist Party was inseparable from the policy of alliances that advocated participation in a national unity government with sectors of the Portuguese bourgeoisie. Consequently, many leading activists in the workers' commissions left the Communist Party. Swamped by the spontaneous militancy of the rank and file, the Communist Party for a time lost much of its influence in the workers' struggles. Those places where the party had influence were characteristically less militant.

The takeover of unions was often achieved in collaboration with the Ministry of Labour. Unions did not have money to pay officials. Communist Party militants went to work full time in them. Some had been recently released from prison and were looking for work, others went on indefinite holiday from work and many were paid by the party. Most of the leaderships of these unions were not elected but established by those who had occupied the union offices.

The Communist Party and most of the union leaders considered workers' commissions 'primitive forms of organisation, instruments of patronage and "divisiveness"'.[8] The 17 May edition of *Avante!* declared that the Communist Party is the organisation that warned the Intersindical not to 'deviate from its "principle objectives", pitting the party against workers' commissions: "it is not the structures that should be great, but the resistance".'

On 13 and 14 July 1974, a General Assembly of the Intersindical was held and pronounced: 'that the current unions do not have the capacity to respond and coordinate the situations created by the demands due to its [the union] structure, which, in the majority of cases, is professional in scope.'[9]

The Inter-Empresas

A new period of strikes emerged at the end of August 1974. It resulted from a combination of political and economic factors, inspired by the promise for independence for the colonies and the fracturing within the bourgeoisie. There was also the deepening economic crisis,[10] which witnessed dozens of employers responding with lay-offs and the closing of factories and businesses. There were many strikes but three strikes in particular stand out: the Portuguese Airline (TAP), the *Jornal do Comércio* and the Lisnave strike. The strike at Lisnave was not about wages and conditions but explicitly political, against the attempt by the frustrated government trying to impose an extremely restrictive law, curtailing the right to strike.

We will see how such tumult helped bring about the coup attempt of 28 September. But before immersing ourselves in strike waves again, we need to turn the spotlight onto the inter-factory (inter-empresa) organisation that was emerging in Lisbon. This was not dissimilar to workers' councils, which emerged in other countries in revolutionary periods. Fernanda worked at the Plessey site on the south bank of the Tagus Estuary and she was a member of the first workers' committee. She told Peter Robinson:

It was said 'why should we be on our own if other people across the road had the same problems?' Then we decided to join, and to discuss things in general. Workers from practically all the factories of the Margem SUL – (South Lisbon conurbation, on the far side of the Tagus Estuary) – were there. The meetings were a place, a way, for people to meet and discuss. The main purpose of these meetings was to defend the revolution![11]

Immediately after 25 April, links among workplaces were rapidly established. The key workforce, employing 10,000 people, was the Lisnave ship repair yards, the most modern and second-largest in Europe. Artur Palácio worked at Lisnave for many years and had been a member of the Lisnave workers' commission since its inception. He recalled the inter-workplace meetings:

I attended some fifteen or twenty meetings but cannot recall how often they met. They were not regular meetings but occurred whenever the need arose. I believe that the initiative to form the Inter-Empresas came from Lisnave itself but am not sure ... The first meeting had more than two hundred people; it was held at Lisnave during the period of the May strike ... That first meeting in May had the character of support for strikers. Twenty-five contos (25,000 escudos – nearly £500 in 1974) was collected for the workers of Sorefame.

... There were many people experienced in workers' struggles, including some from CUF, Parry & Son, S.R.N., Olho de Boi (a naval base shipyard), Cergal, Applied Magnetics, and Sogantal. Some of the factories had not even a workers' commission then, just workers who came from the factories.[12]

The meetings were informal, 'a place for people to meet and discuss'. In the early days, the network was known by a variety of names; Palácio used the term 'inter-comissões'.

In addition to organising collections, the inter-empresas helped to organise demonstrations in defence of workers who were under attack by the government, sometimes by the armed forces, not to mention the Communist Party and the Intersindical.

After 28 September, the workers' commissions consolidated their power and the name Inter-Empresas started being used with capital letters. The meetings were very open; more people were being delegated by their commissions. An official bulletin was published, and the meetings settled down into a once-a-week pattern. We will return to them in Chapter 10 when, on 7 February 1975, they ruptured the alliance between the major political parties and the MFA.

Jornal do Comércio

In the months after 25 April 1974, there were struggles in all the newspapers. The workers at the *Diário de Notícias* were active in demanding the resignation of management. At *O Século* conflicts would lead to the shutdown of all services at the printer, the Sociedade Nacional de Tipografia. In many cases, the fight spread to other publications in a particular group.

On 22 August 1974, 300 workers at the *Jornal do Comércio* went on strike and occupied company facilities demanding the resignation of the director Carlos Machado and equal pay with the workers of the *Diário do Povo*. They demanded freedom of the press and accused the newspaper of having a 'right-wing political line' and forcing workers to follow that line. Management refused to dismiss the director Carlos Machado and refused to negotiate. The workers proceeded with their strike and published a strike newspaper. They rejected the company policy of not providing training for employees to use the new offset press, which would involve redundancies because 'others from outside will come to work the new machines'.[13]

The government responded once again with force. The matter was under the jurisdiction of COPCON. On the night of 26 August, the riot police (the PSP) and a detachment from the RAL 1 (Artillery Regiment) surrounded the facilities.

At 5pm, on 27 August 1974, the workers demonstrated in front of the Ministry of Labour. This was supposedly the most left-wing ministry in the government. The First Provisional Government had appointed Avelino Gonçalves, a Communist Party member, to be the Minister of Labour. He was confronted at the door of the ministry by angry workers. They had lived through the censorship before 25 April, had now been radicalised, and were fervently involved in the 'battle for the control of information'.

On 28 August, the military vacated the premises and sealed the entrance to prevent the further output of the strike newspaper.

This case generated a wave of solidarity from all the press. On 27 August, workers at the *Diário do Povo* published a statement of 'solidarity with their comrades at the *Diário do Comércio*'.[14] On 29 August, the Sindicato de Jornalistas (Journalists' Union) sympathised with the protest; on 3 September, an assembly convened by the journalist union and the unions in graphic arts, editors and newspaper and interestingly the union for sellers of lottery tickets, convened a national 24-hour strike. On 4 September, only two newspapers, *O Século* and the *Diário de Lisbon*, were able to publish.

The strike at the *Diário de Comércio* would last 46 days and only ended on 28 September when an arrest warrant was issued for Carlos Machado, accused of participating in the coup attempt.

The battles for a free press were particularly significant, and those at *República* and Rádio Renascença played a part in the summer and autumn of 1975.

The Strike Law

On 27 August 1974, the Second Provisional Government, backed by the Communists but not the Socialists, passed an 'anti-strike' law. They officially legalised strikes for the first time. Strikes, as stipulated by law, would be decided by trade union commissions and, in their absence, could be decided by workers' assemblies, provided such decisions were submitted to a vote, had a 50 per cent majority of the votes and a representative of the Ministry of Labour was present at the polls.[15]

The law banned political stoppages and sympathy strikes. A 37-day cooling off period was introduced. Strikes by the military and militarised forces, fire fighters, police forces and judges were prohibited. Employers were assured the right to lock out workers.

The Strike Law was opposed by the strikers at TAP and the *Diário de Comércio* and notably, as we shall see, by the Lisnave shipyard workers. In effect, it was not applied during the revolution, ignored by the workers – and in practice the workers' commissions exercised their power to strike.[16] This law was passed, it should be remembered, by a government with the participation of communists and socialists, reflecting the lack of control that the Communist Party and the remaining components of the interim government, including the military, had over the working class.

Lisnave

The Lisnave shipyard was located on the south bank of the Tagus River, amidst a bastion of workers' neighbourhoods. The shipyard was economically strategic for the country.

A handful of revolutionaries, mainly Maoists, from the shipyard, set out to organise an 'illegal' one-day strike and demonstration against the legislation. On 7 September, a plenary of 2,000 workers ratified the proposal for a demonstration to terminate at the Ministry of Labour, in the centre of Lisbon. Lisnave workers demanded the purging of management and rejected the Strike Law (which they called in their press releases the 'Anti-Strike Law'):

We are not with the government when it promulgates anti-worker laws, restricting the struggle of workers against capitalist exploitation. We will actively fight against the 'strike law' because it is a deep blow to the freedoms of workers. We reject the rights that employers have to put thousands of workers in misery since the lock-out law is a law against workers and a protection for capitalists.[17]

The Government, through the Ministry of Internal Affairs, outlawed demonstrations on 11 September, fearing that they would spread struggles to other companies. On the morning of the 12 September, a MFA delegation went to Lisnave to try to convince the workers to delay the demonstration until Saturday. This was in vain. On 12 September, the workers gathered inside the shipyard, sanctioned the event, with only 25 votes against.

On the 12 [September] at 9am, a delegation from the MFA, consisting of one major and three captains, arrived with delegates from the workers' commission. They brought with them a statement from the Liga Comunista Internacional (International Communist League, LCI) and another from the Communist Party with a plan for the demonstration, but they did not bring the statement of the workers. They came in search of those responsible, but were told that no such thing existed because all decisions had been taken by workers. So they were all responsible.[18]

Outside, the COPCON forces, in a large military operation, surrounded the shipyard. But the marines refused to suppress the demonstration, which began at 5.20pm and lasted for six hours, marching through the main avenues of Lisbon. A worker described the event:

At 5.20 this afternoon, we began the demonstration and in the middle of the yard we encountered a Marine company and three 'chaimites' [armoured cars] barring the way. We shouted: 'Soldiers are children of the people,' 'Soldiers are or will be workers'. At that moment, some Marines started to cry and the commander, faced with this, opened up the passage.[19]

Despite inflamed feelings, the demonstration, from the shipyards to the Ministry of Labour, finished peacefully. A soldier recalled:

Before lunch the rumour circulated that we were going out and we soon guessed it was to Lisnave ... the commander told us that he'd received a telephone call about a demonstration at Lisnave, led by a minority of leftist agitators and that our job was to prevent it from taking place. We were armed as we had never been before with G3s and 4 magazines ... The demo began and a human torrent advanced with shouts of 'the soldiers are the sons of the workers', 'tomorrow the soldiers will be workers' and 'the arms of soldiers must not be turned against the workers'. The commander soon saw that we weren't going to follow his orders, so he shut up. Our arms hung down by our side and some comrades were crying ... The following day, in the barracks, things were livelier. Before morning assembly many comrades were up and shouting the slogans of the demo, 'the soldiers are sons of the workers', 'down with capitalist exploitation'.[20]

The radicalisation at TAP on 17 September was not oblivious to the impact of the demonstration of Lisnave workers five days before, that had forced the retreat of the soldiers sent to repress the demonstration.

TAP

The most vicious example of the use of military in strikes (that is, in the metropolis) was against the employees who worked for the national airline, TAP (Transportes Aéreos Portugueses). It just so happens that troops had been heavily deployed against TAP workers before 25 April. One reason for the heavy-handed intervention then was that TAP strikes impacted upon the operations in the colonies. Another reason was that TAP had an international profile and the regime didn't want to be seen tolerating the breakdown of law.

On 2 May 1974, the trade union commission of TAP, which represented the TAP unions and was not directly elected by the shop floor, had presented a document to the Junta of National Salvation (JSN) with a series of substantial pay demands including 'cleansing' of managers linked to the fascists, and reorganisation leading to self-management. They also insisted on the readmission of all those dismissed without cause during the New State dictatorship. This document was approved at a general meeting of the workers in one of the largest halls in Lisbon, the Lisbon Coliseum. The demand for the dismissal of management accused of repression in 1973 was quickly ceded by the JSN. This was despite the fact that the document approved in the Assembly was only that the 'workers require' rather than the 'workers demand' the resignation.[21]

In an attempt to reconcile the interests of the parties in conflict, an Administrative Council was created. This comprised three representatives of the workers and three officers appointed by the JSN. It was chaired by Colonel Moura Pinto, who soon proved not only unable to mediate conflicts, but was offensive and therefore compounded tensions. The Administrative Council would continue to be a source of conflict, fermenting the radicalisation of workers. The Administrative Council threatened redundancies.[22]

The trade union committee commission responded by saying that they did not trust the calculations submitted to justify the redundancies and threatened there would be 'confrontation with the workers', if the redundancies proceeded.

The Administrative Council responded with a declaration of war. It was one of the most famous statements of management aggression in this period, revealing a total inability to understand the impact that the change of the political situation had made, in a few weeks, on the culture of workplace relations. This was despite concessions by the workers who had accepted, 'sacrifices' and, in some cases, even retreated from their demands. Yet the Administrative Council declared:

Currently, TAP employees are divided into two major groups:

One, composed by those responsible, idle and mediocre that, perfectly aware of their limitations, adopt the path where everything is easy and all they do is destroy.

Another, more numerous, formed by passive, cowardly and indifferent workers, who apolitically watch their own destruction.

The first group refuses to collaborate with the administrative commission, which is perfectly consistent with the doctrine that it advocates; the second, by its attitude of permanent abstention, achieves exactly the same result.[23]

The response was almost immediate. The Trade Union Commission met, rejecting the insults and declaring it had no political confidence of the Administrative Council. The TAP workers' commissions went even further, releasing a document that considered the Workers' Council itself compromised by collaboration with the Administrative Council. They accused the Trade Union Commission, who had not been elected directly, of favouring the staff unions and ignoring the most disadvantaged workers (the wage differences between employees ranged from 5,000 to 52,000 escudos). They rejected any talk of self-management (considering that this 'cannot exist in a capitalist society') and sent a tough message, especially to the communist and socialist parties, which, in the Government, had advocated reconciliation:

> We will not be intimidated by manoeuvres that aim to make us give up our struggle, particularly by those who raise the scarecrow of economic chaos. Economic chaos has always existed and will continue to exist. Economic chaos is production not geared to meet the needs of the majority, but is orientated for the maximum profit of a minority. ... this chaos will only end when our struggle achieves final victory, capitalism is overthrown and we, the workers, control the whole society aiming to achieve a society without classes, without exploiters nor exploited.[24]

It is not easy to ignore the revolutionary tone. Revolutionaries, in particular MES, the MRPP and the PRP had a presence in TAP. The most prominent workers' leader was Santos Junior, from MES. In many cases, the radicalisation of struggle and the presence of leaders from the radical left, though few in number, was not a mere coincidence. They related to the struggles, unlike the Communist Party. Far-left leaders in the workplaces were always a greater problem for the Communist Party than the existence of these far-left leaders in the universities.

On 25 July, the Maintenance and Engineering Division workers called a strike for 26 August, if the following demands were not satisfied:

a) saneomento,

b) wage revision,

c) immediate application of work schedules already agreed in the A.C.T. negotiation,

d) prosecution of the criminals who on 12 July 1973, at the time of the invasion of TAP facilities by repressive forces (riot police), tried to boycott the just struggle of the workers,

e) the non-recognition and non-acceptance of unfair dismissal,

f) punishment of those responsible for redundancies made before 25 April.[25]

The demands were not met so, on August 26, the maintenance workers went on strike. The government responded by sending in the army and on 28 August, workers were placed under military rule. The Communist Party cell accused their fellow workers of being an adventurous minority and for having blocked the return of soldiers from Guinea and thus undermining the anti-colonial struggle. The newspapers, however, noted that 3,000–4,000 workers attended the strike plenaries. The newspaper *Revolução* published a statement from a 'workers' commission', on the army operation:

These shock troops, fully armed as if they were entering immediately in combat, were composed of a complete company of commandos, a para-trooper company, equipped with camouflage, four bandoliers for every man, machetes, armed with G-3 machine guns 7.62 calibre with retractable butt stocks. Five Chaimite armoured cars with machine gun nests facing the workers and equipped with their respective crews were ready to intervene. It was no surprise that there were also friendly 'German shepherds' there.[26]

The media was forbidden to enter TAP. The strike continued on the 29 August with workers picketing, with arms crossed, at the entrances. Under threat and surrounded by the military, the workers drifted back little by little. But on 17 September, they released a statement regarding 'intolerable militarisation', already in its fourth week, and convened a plenary meeting in the renowned Voz do Operário (Workers' Voice) meeting hall. There they decided to begin a strike on 24 September and approved a proposal to depose the union committee and conduct rank-and-file elections for a workers' commission to replace it. For their part, the trade unions of the various sectors of TAP disassociated themselves from the proposed strike called for 24 September and refused to 'recognise the validity' of the plenary.

The workers of Sidurgia, the National Steel Corporation, demanded an 'Immediate end to the military occupation of TAP and the re-establishment of workers' freedoms'. The government did not have sufficient strength to maintain the situation for much longer.

The strike began on 24 September, commencing again with the maintenance services, which together comprised some 2,000 workers, paralysing the entire airport. The military seized eight workers and took them for questioning at the Sapadores Barracks in Graça. This triggered a demonstration of workers to free them. The demonstrators twice marched around the Ministry of Labour. With megaphones, workers proclaimed their support for the strike. The detained workers would be released around midnight, but on the condition that they return to the barracks on the next day.

In the morning, the General Directorate of Information announced the sacking of 200 workers, all from hangar six. The newspapers reported that the situation was unprecedented and would 'aggravate the situation in an important company at the national level'.[27] There were debates about which unions were in favour and against the strike and about the possible dissolution of TAP. There was a climate of panic in the press.

On 25 September, a demonstration of 5,000 workers and supporters took place at the São Bento palace. On the following day, the leadership of the Chemical Workers Union broke from the Intersindical over this, disagreeing with its failure to support the TAP workforce.

Several thousand TAP employees went on strike on 27 September and organised a demonstration; the inter-empresas network played a major role in organising the support of delegations from other workplaces and in planning a bigger demonstration for Saturday, 29 September. The industrial sociologist Fátima Patriarca recalled the meeting of 27 September:

> Every organisation was having meetings. Their messengers were running from one meeting to another to keep contact. All the key activists were at the Inter-Empresas meeting. It was the intervention from the Lisnave delegate, a member of the PRP, which settled the issue of the demonstration. He wasn't a delegate in the fullest sense ... The Intersindical

neither supported nor condemned it. Also there were practical reasons for refraining from demonstrating.[28]

In the end, there was a demonstration of about 40,000 people on the 28 September, which was certainly not large by the standards of the time. But there was a distraction; hence Fátima's reference to 'practical reasons', namely, the failed coup attempt of 28 September, which we will describe in more detail shortly.

As a result of the collapse of the coup, the strike ended, the Military Detachment was dissolved and the workers were readmitted, most of them almost immediately. 'In short,' Miguel Pérez says in his study of workers' commissions, 'repression did not hinder the combativeness of the workers of Maintenance and Engineering Division of TAP.'[29]

28 September

The independence for the colonies and the growing militancy in the workplaces resulted in a sector of the Portuguese bourgeoisie supporting an extremist solution. As Kenneth Maxwell stresses, what occurred in Lisbon, Luanda and Maputo was inseparable:

The crises which moved Portugal decisively to the left also moved Portuguese Africa equally decisively toward independence. They appeared as a series of sometimes lengthy struggles in which political tensions in Portugal, developments in Africa, and external pressures combined to force major confrontations. During these crises, the most politically sophisticated Portuguese were well aware of their underlying causes. But also these never did surface in the Portuguese press, and even when they did it was mostly by insinuation. Only when the crises were over and the consequences patent – the resignation of Premier Palma Carlos on June 9 and the appointment of General Coronel Vasco Gonçalves in his place; the resignation of General Spinola on September 30 and his replacement by General Costa Gomes – were any of these crises publicly discussed by outsiders. No one involved, however, ever doubted that the shape and content of the political future of Portugal and the achievement of independence in the colonies were intimately linked. The outcome of the struggle in one sphere would help to consolidate victory or bring defeat in the other.[30]

By September 1974, the industrialists who had welcomed 25 April now began to denounce the Second Provisional Government in the bitterest of terms. They had little faith in the government, which was generally regarded as favourably disposed towards 'communists'. They were worried that the troops could no longer be trusted and longed for 'law and order'. Many factory owners and foreign investors were withdrawing entirely from Portugal.

The TAP, Lisnave and newspaper strikes, particularly at the *Jornal do Comércio*, generated fear among the ruling coalition. Strikes created situations of ungovernability, testing the power structure in above key areas creating a national impact and highlighting the degree of politicisation and the knock-on effects on other sectors. In my opinion, this is central to understanding the origins of the attempted 28 September coup in 1974.

Sections of the bourgeoisie now drew the conclusion that the use of armed force was becoming necessary and urgent. Leading industrialists met with President Spínola and a few of the generals. They claimed they had a mandate from the population, the so-called 'silent majority'. Spínola called on the 'silent majority' to mobilise, culminating in a march on 28 September 1974, which was intended to be 300,000 strong. Arms were supplied to fascists, who would foster enough disorder to give the generals an excuse to intervene, attack the left and re-establish 'order'.

Their calculations did not take account of the reaction of the people. Workers mobilised in the country through road barricades, cutting off the means of transport. Working people responded magnificently. Within hours of the attack, barricades were set up along the main roads, sometimes using expropriated bulldozers, lorries and cement mixers. Soldiers fraternised openly with workers manning the barricades and handed over arms. Armed workers searched cars, and strikers at Rádio Renascença went back to work and occupied the radio station in order to 'defend the revolution'. Many papers printed second editions or special broadsheets, including the workers' committee of the big Lisbon daily *O Século*. This reported how the Porto section of the union of bank employees commanded its members to 'Close the banks immediately. Don't make any payments. Set up pickets at the doors to check entrances and exits. Watch the telex and the telephones.'

This mobilisation was an extraordinary success and led to the immediate defeat of the coup. The demonstration of the 'silent majority' never took place and the debacle led to the resignation of Spínola, and the strengthening of the left.[31]

7

Self-Management and the
Struggle Against Redundancies

In the boss's time, we didn't even feel like working because he was always
screaming at us and a person didn't even feel like working, we just felt like
beating him up and things like that.

Young worker at Sousa Abreu, an occupied textile factory[1]

Overview

This chapter starts by looking at the economic crisis – global and
Portuguese – which meant that for many owners, Portugal was not a good
investment and, rather than face the wrath of an unruly workforce, it was
easier to abandon ship. Many fled to Brazil. Self-management assumed two
forms: self-managed firms and cooperatives. The Portuguese word for
self-managed firm is *autogestão*; this is where the firm is run by the workers,
but they do not own them legally. We will look at some well-known, and
rightly celebrated, examples of where workers took over their firms.

We will briefly touch upon some other difficulties of self-management
and point out that self-management is not the same as workers' control. We
will return to the issue of workers' control in a later chapter.

The Slump in the Portuguese Economy

The importance of the wars in Africa and the Captain's Movement cannot
eclipse the impact of the world economic crisis. It was the largest crisis
since the Second World War, beginning in 1970–1971 and continuing until
1973, only showing signs of recovery on a global level towards the end of
1975.

The construction of a political-institutional narrative, which *almost*
disregarded economic factors, means that even today the global crisis of
1973 is absent from most of the works about the Portuguese Revolution,
forgetting that it is the recessionary measures in response to the crisis that

closed the businesses, and that workers occupied the factories in response to this, and not the other way around.

According to Eugénio Rosa, between January and December 1974, unemployment doubled; the areas of Lisbon, Porto and Setúbal being the most affected in terms of absolute numbers, and Alentejo and Algarve, in terms of the proportional impact.

From 1961 to 1974, the country had almost full employment, the fruit of a war economy (that mobilised workers and turned them into soldiers). War production had a stimulating effect on some sectors of the private economy. This was coupled with the massive emigration of the 1960s (and the respective remittances from the emigrants) and an impetus to transform into a definitively modern and industrial country (albeit uneven and combined) remembering, at the same time, the extreme drain on public accounts due to the costs of the war.

In March 1974, when the old regime was still in place, the *Sindicato dos Caixeiros de Lisboa* published a bulletin against the high cost of living, defending the struggle of workers whose salaries had been literally swallowed by inflation. In six months, between October 1973 and March 1974, prices of cod rose by 113 per cent, potatoes rose by 80 per cent, gasoline rose by 66 per cent.

The Explosion of Occupations

The international economic crisis hit 'Portugal severely', wrote Silva Lopes, then Minister of Economics.[2] Silva Lopes noted the extraordinary impact of unemployment and the underinvestment of businesses on the self-management processes:

> With the explosion of social conflicts in the first months after 25 April, the workers in many companies kicked out the bosses or their representatives, citing arguments about economic sabotage, collaborating with the dictatorship regime, repression on the job, etc. At the same time, the deterioration of the economic conditions of the companies was pushing many of them towards unsustainable situations of lack of liquidity or solvency and led many owners to abandon them.[3]

The discussion of why workers fight, what sets off a process of struggle and how it radicalises is a fascinating question, one of the most difficult to answer for students of social conflicts. Factory takeovers opened up new ways of considering the very structures of society. In the early days, many of the occupations and seizures came about because of the dislike of the managers and owners, who were intrinsically tainted by being sympathetic to the fascist regime. Servility was forsaken. We will see some charming exchanges between bosses and workers. Here is an example from the textile sector: 'The women had voted that all supervisors – who were men – would have to retrain to get proper management qualifications. In the meantime, they would run the factory themselves. I remember them laughing about how easy it was – the sudden realisation you don't need bosses.'[4]

The following interchange at a company attests to the atmosphere at the time. At the entrance, there were several workers in a picket. The boss's brother approaches them:

Worker, shouting: 'You have been coming here for 8 days to provoke us and this has to stop. The workers have decided! You must respect the will of the workers! The workers want to continue with the firm operating and you don't want to let us, you come here to provoke the workers. The workers want you to hit the road, that you continue the process of sanitation, and later we will let you know what we've decided …

… And look, one question, has the State also recognized that your brother took thousands, embezzled thousands, out of the country?'

Boss's brother: 'This is a ridiculous claim that you're making'.

(Is interrupted)

Worker (shouting): 'They're not ridiculous claims! The Judicial Police arrested him and they didn't arrest him for nothing, see?'[5]

In the above description, we saw that the boss ran away with the money. In other instances, bosses just gave up. As mentioned before, a number fled to Brazil.

According to a survey carried out by the *Confederação da Indústria Portuguesa* (Portuguese Confederation of Industry, CIP) and analysed by the historian Miguel Pérez, 'there were 24 company occupations registered in the last third of 1974, and 83 from January to April 1975, 55 from May to August, and 14 from September to the end of 1975'.[6] These numbers should be treated with some caution and do not represent all of the companies occupied (many of which were quite small, with 5, 12, 20 workers, and were not registered with the CIP), but the number of occupations grew considerably from July 1974 to March and April 1975.

According to Nancy Bermeo, approximately 60 per cent of all the worker-managed firms were abandoned before they were taken over.[7] The RTP television channel ran a series on the process of self-management and the diverse histories of the role of workers' commissions in factories and companies. It dedicated an episode to the story of Auto-Rali and Auto-Sol, which were under self-management. The two companies in the auto-mechanic sector located in the Lisbon region comprised four different workplaces and there was an elected workers' commission in each one. Since October 1974, when management fired 36 workers, they had been self-managed and they were absolutely clear that the companies would have folded otherwise. An Auto-Rali worker was interviewed:

Journalist: Tell us, please, what has your experience been at Auto-Rali?

Worker: I begin by saying that if we had not taken this attitude, this workplace would be bankrupted, it wouldn't exist. We took this attitude …There is no doubt that I always worked and there was never a boss who gave me anything; it was always the value of my work.

Another worker: When I was learning the craft, I earned 25 *tostoés* [pennies] per day.

Journalist: And before the 25th of April, how much did you earn?

Worker: 3,800 escudos.

Journalist: You did this [work]?

Worker: Yes, yes, sir, the same.

Journalist: And now how much do you earn?

Worker. Now I earn 7,100 escudos.[8]

Not only did the salaries increase. In addition to improved access to education, health care and social security (all forms of a social or indirect salary), there were other forms of salary in kind in this period that became significant: 'Now along with his work, the workers already have a cafeteria serving in the order of 70 to 80 meals, they eat for lower prices, lately around 23, 24, 25 escudos'. Smiling to the camera one of the workers explained that 'the [new] head of the workshop remains calm and is a good fellow and we 'work more easily, as he [our own boss] agrees with us.[9]

Pérez reminds us:

The company becomes a space of struggle between the workers and the private capitalists, who always exercise an uncontested authority inside the companies. Now, the workers feel they have the right to dispute the decisions of the owner and to call them into question, and they turn to radical forms of struggle to do this: occupation is the second most frequent form of struggle (35 out of 159, according to the numbers from GIS)[10] and it has become common for workers to unilaterally enforce their will in the company in questions of hours and sanitations. The workers' commissions affirm themselves as the essential structure of workers' organisation in the companies'.[11]

Sogantal

Visitors were inspired by workers' control 'in practice'. One of the most celebrated occupations followed by self-management occurred at the Sogantal factory. It was a French company which manufactured tracksuits.

The material for the tracksuits came from France all cut. Once assembled and sewn in Portugal, they were sent back to the mother factory in France which was responsible for marketing them. Thus it was cheaper to pay the Portuguese workers less and transport the material here and there than to have to meet the wage rates of French workers![12]

The owners 'benefited from the meagre salaries and the absence of union pressure before 25 April' and where there was 'a very repressive work environment, with elements of paternalism'.[13] The occupation began in May 1974. The women workers, begin to 'slow the rhythms of work' as a form of pressure to win the demands they had made on the company: one month of paid vacation, a 13-month salary, and a drive towards equal pay that can be found in many sectors, a general raise of 1,200 escudos for all, equally. The management reacted at the end of May by closing the business. Miguel Pérez tells us:

On 13 July, the Management and its Portuguese representative abandoned the facilities. The factory is in the hands of the workers and will continue to sell the available reserves to pay wages. They are receiving solidarity from far-left parties and groups such as MES and MRPP, but also from the local section of PS, as well as the support of the Sindicato dos Têxteis e Vestuário do Sul. The solidarity sale of tracksuits is being organised in schools and factories. The first sales will serve to pay part of the quantities owed to the workers, who receive the solidarity and support of the musician José Afonso.[14]

It was a total surprise when, in the early hours between 23 and 24 August, Pierre Lardet, the boss, with a group of two dozen men, forcibly entered the factory and tried to seize the machines. The workers and people remonstrated furiously. The Republican National Guard (GNR) had difficulty controlling the angry population. 'The manager flees the company protected by troops in the middle of jeers and insults from the people'. The workforce took over the management:

> From that point on (24 August) we began to sleep in the factory. ... We carried out pickets, while some of the workers stayed in the factory others went to sell the output to many companies and offices in various parts of the country. We took statements with us to publicise our struggle and, in this way, we were supported by various unions. It generated such solidarity that, despite not needing the tracksuits, many people bought the product just to support us. And this money all together served to pay our salaries. We managed to maintain the factory for more than a year and, in this time, the idea arose of self-management, that is, other companies would give us work and we would use the factory to produce it.[15]

The workers developed demands on the ministry, calling for nationalisation and the payment of wages by the State.

Sousa Abreu

The public television channel RTP had daily news programmes which depicted strikes and demonstrations, with interviews with the workers on prime-time shows, like 'Temas e Problemas' (Themes and Problems) or 'Artes e Ofícios' (Arts and Crafts), that were dedicated to the occupied factories or to agrarian reform – social concerns were increasingly reflected in the television programming.

There are plenty of other examples where workers took over running their workplaces, such as the small wool processing plant Sousa Abreu. On 30 July 1975, the RTP reporters went to see how the factory was being self-managed.[16] A sign on the factory door read: 'Work is not a commodity, it is a right. We want to work to live and not live to work. To the capitalist, the worker is a machine. The capitalists are only interested in the workers when they produce profit ... Against exploitation, for the right to work!'[17]

Looking at the interview, one can see a worker, pudgy, beaming, her hair pulled back, wearing a work coat, with a strong northern accent, explaining to the camera how she works, where the wool thread came from, etc. 'I work here in the *canileiro* [part of a loom that spins wool into threads],' she said with an open smile, but seemingly embarrassed to be filmed. Mr

Ribeiro, another worker, said that the idea to occupy the factory came from the union: 'the president of the union, knowing that the factory was going to close, told us to occupy the facilities because otherwise the boss would take the raw materials and not even pay our overdue wages or indemnities.'[18]

Their story began on 8 September 1974. The workers learned of the threat of redundancies. A general meeting of the workers took place on 15 September, which elected a workers' commission comprising three members. Clara, a worker, told her story: 'In the beginning, it was complicated [pause]. There were few of us, on the first night there really were very few of us. Later people began to join us even from other factories. We occupied the factory on 8 September and we began to work beginning on the 16th.'[19]

The journalist wanted to know the details of the occupation:

Journalist: 'This committee was chosen by everybody in the General Meeting of Workers?'

Quitéria: 'Yes'.

Journalist: 'Does this commission have any time-frame?'

Quitéria: [doesn't understand the question, appears to be surprised]

Journalist: 'That is, could it be replaced if they are not satisfied with you?' [Silence].

Quitéria is calm but doesn't understand the question. She responds: 'I mean, I think our co-workers are satisfied with us'.

Journalist: 'Yes, but that isn't what I was saying. I know that they are satisfied now. But if they weren't, could you be replaced?'

Quitéria: 'Ah! Yes, yes'.

Journalist: 'Mr Ribeiro, how did you convince the other people?'

Mr Ribeiro: 'It wasn't necessary, they saw that the boss would never open the factory and it was they themselves who started to come'.

Journalist: 'How many looms were there operating before with the boss, previously, when it was on the verge of closing?'

Mr Ribeiro: 'There were five'.

Journalist: 'And now?'

Mr Ribeiro: 'Twenty-five, twenty-six, up to thirty'.

Journalist: 'What is the biggest difference you see between working for the boss and in the system you have now?'

Mr Ribeiro: 'The difference is that now we are more at ease, we can go to the bathroom, we can talk freely and we work more. In the boss's time, we didn't work as much. Now we work more because the profit is for us'.

Other worker: 'I enjoy the work more now, we work more at ease, with more pleasure. The old boss was our friend, but the one who left robbed us of our sweat. Now I have more pleasure in life, at work, I don't feel sad about anything'.[20]

The perception of injustice goes beyond anxieties of directly experienced exploitation. The interviews filmed in the heat of the moment also spoke volumes about humiliations such as being followed, pursued, controlled in basic issues like going to the bathroom or having 'the boss bothering them'.

As one of the workers in Sousa Abreu poignantly said: 'That period was very fruitful, however. Liberty, solidarity, poetry were in the streets. And not by decree, there weren't the cultural programmes of today, but rather a new project of society. There was no fear of walking in the street; there was a less selfish society. The only danger was for the right wing and those from the old regime.'[21]

Jean-Paul Sartre

The philosopher Jean-Paul Sartre was very impressed by the workers' management at Sousa Abreu and the functioning of the workers' committee. He wrote in March 1975:

The [thing] that most interested me was certainly seeing the self-managed factory Sousa Abreu. It's a factory with around 30 workers in the textile industry. The workers were abandoned by the boss some six months ago and most of the factory equipment, except for the machines, was taken by the boss to build a factory at another site.

Therefore, they were alone, and they decided to continue the work managing themselves. And they did it. They continued the jobs they were doing before and continued to have the same staff that was working before, except for the secretaries and, evidently, the boss and some workers who left of their own free will. Even so, they increased production compared to the time of the previous ownership, because the factory was in crisis and full of debt.

They created a group of three to six workers for general decisions. These decisions are made in the following way: the less important decisions are made by the group in question; the more important decisions are made by the whole factory assembly, which meets and is consulted about the decisions to make.[22]

Sartre had lived through the experience of May 1968, in France, where the revolution had been profound, with solidarity between students and workers, with a peak in the general strike of 1 million people. It was, however, an extremely short revolutionary situation. In France, where the experience was brief, self-management did not develop in the factories.[23]

Problems of Self-Management

The quote is from the world-famous author, García Márquez, Lisbon said in early May 1974: 'If anything can stop this revolution it's going to be the light bill.'[24] He had a point. The backdrop of the self-management processes was the economic crisis and not the 'chaos' provoked by the lack of control of production. The fall in productivity in 1974–1975 was much more tied to the actual lack of orders than to any decline in the quality of management, according to the 1976 report by Massachusetts Institute of Technology, commissioned by the Banco de Portugal.

It seems that most of the firms which were taken over fell into the hands of workers like 'rotten fruit from an old tree'. The task was enormous. Workers had to take on all the difficulties faced by any company in the middle of an economic crisis with the aggravating factor of having to learn to manage production.

Vitorino Santos, a fashion designer from the Sousa Abreu textile factory, gave an interview, after the revolution, where he recalled that: 'Self-management also has its problems. The contradiction between capital and labour disappeared, but problems arose between the workers' commission and the workers. There were those who raised themselves up or tried to raise themselves up as bosses ... I witnessed situations like this in practice.'[25]

Somebody needs to take over from the managers; there was a vacuum. Sometimes technicians tried to fill the vacuum. But it was not 'the beginning of a socialist society'.

An article by Tony Cliff and Robin Peterson, written just after 25 November, is worth quoting at length:

On some workers' commissions and in some factories the technicians are more than advisors. Their claim to be technicians, servants of knowledge and neutral, probably means that workers are less resistant than to the obvious administrative lackeys of management. For instance, at OTIS elevators where a combined workers' commission and administration runs the factory the technicians play a dominant role in the new management. It is no accident that the gap between the workers' commission and the workers is growing here.

In May 1975 [OTIS] management abandoned its plant at Alverce on the grounds that pouring money into the plant would be subsidising socialism. The workers' commission was not just in a position of controlling what happened on the shop floor but also in a position of managing Otis's Portuguese operation in all respects including advertising and financing.

Although only seven of the 16 members of the workers' commission are from the offices and administration, they play a dominant role, with the plant workers only looking on.

But to compete successfully on the capital market and to make the needed investments the workers' commission will have to rethink its policy of no dismissals. This will undercut the unity of the workers. Nationalisation should then be a prime target. The role of the technical advisor was more than merely advisory, and there was some gap between the administration and the workers.

The administrators and the technicians will lead the charge of the scared and make coherent doubts which may be stewing in other people's minds. The same people who will be talking about greater efficiency will be talking about the need to make greater sacrifices. They won't be touching the real problem, that we live in a system that judges efficiency in terms of profit and that never dares look in the face the anarchy and waste created by its own system.[26]

No wonder one of the workers in Sousa Abreu confessed that: 'if I had a proper boss I would prefer to work for the boss than for myself ... If a boss appeared like that [who cared about us] ... because today there are hardly any like that.'[27]

Crying out for Government Intervention

In the sections dedicated to labour in the pages of the daily newspapers, there were entire columns about the 'The Struggle Against Redundancies'.

In February 1975, the workers in the enamel products factory, Esmaltal, in the north of the country started a strike against unemployment. This workers' press release demands government support:

> Considering that the bosses have reached the point of preventing us from selling the only thing that we have our labour-power;
>
> Considering that only the organised struggle of the working class is capable of making the bourgeoisie retreat;
>
> We, the workers of Esmaltal, have occupied the facilities with permanent pickets, without stopping work, as a measure to defend our legitimate rights. We demand governmental intervention in the company and its nationalisation.[28]

Between 1974 and 1975, firms were in the first place taken over by the workers and then this was legally ratified:

> Many companies were hit with a situation of economic and social rupture with the departure, voluntary or involuntary, of the employer and the beginning of a management led by the workers, through a committee designated in a plenary. The third parties that entered into relations with this committee (suppliers, clients, official entities) had a practical need to recognise its acts, which led to an intervention by the public authorities through an official declaration certifying the committee to represent the company. The credentials were given out mainly by the Ministry of Labour.[29]

The call for government intervention became common. Consequently, from the end of 1974, the Ministry of Labour became involved in many of these occupations. Silva Lopes tells how workers demanded support from the State to keep them in activity'.[30] As a result, the reaction of the Third Provisional Government, then in office, was to approve a decree of state intervention in businesses. Decree-Law no. 660/74, stipulated that the State should intervene in businesses in case of abandonment, disinvestment, deliberate non-payment of suppliers and fiscal fraud. Notwithstanding all of this, ownership was not changed.

After 25 April, between 1974 and 1975, the self-management project represented 626 self-managed companies and 319 collectives.[31] Self-management was also adopted in the social pact and was written into the

Portuguese constitution. By 1975, around 300 companies had been taken over by the State.

But in 1974 and 1975, it was the workplaces struggles that led the way; the State lacked the means to impose its power. The State was thus obliged to take on the role of:

1. Protecting the companies which had been taken over financially in some way – which meant allocating public money to support employment *de facto* because it avoided the destruction of wealth – as a counter-cyclical measure, that is, as a measure to recover the rate of profit.

2. Sending repressive forces that were tolerated by the workers, commonly COPCON, in extreme situations when there was physical conflict between workers and bosses, especially when some of these bosses attempted to remove the machines or important documentation.

3. Trying to ensure the economic management process (and this policy was carried out both by the Socialist Party and by the Communist Party)[32] which avoided political struggle, with strict coordination between the workers, the unions in formation, and the Ministry of Labour (which was heavily influenced by the Communist Party).

The Term Workers' Control was used Indiscriminately

In January 1975, the question 'Who needs bosses?' was commonplace. It would have been heretical nine months before.[33] The idea that the management of factories or businesses could be replaced by workers' self-management would have seemed, even to the workers themselves, perhaps especially to them, an impossibility before the revolution.

Initially, many of the takeovers were motivated by the 'sanitation' of officials close to the old regime. However, at Sousa Abreu, the determining factor would be the redundancies and the surging unemployment rate, and this appears to be the principal reason for the occupations that began in October, as many of the people linked to the old regime had already been removed. The history of the Sousa Abreu occupation is very similar to other occupations from this period.

Figure 7.1 illustrates the process.

In 1974 and 1975, in Portugal, the term workers' control was used indiscriminately for 'participation in management', 'publication of accounts', and 'control over production', and political organisations and unions imbued the term with a meaning that accorded with their particular political

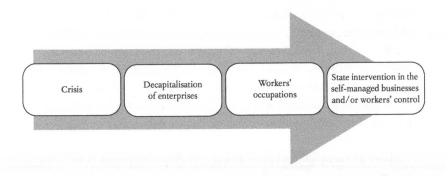

Figure 7.1 Workplace occupations and self-management

strategy. During that period, the concepts became intertwined and toppled over one another, reflecting the diversity of the evolution of the struggles in the factories and companies. Almost daily, workers in the companies were passing from the stage of democratic conflict (e.g. persecution of PIDE informers) to one of occupation. The State would intervene in a company and shortly afterwards it would enter into a regime of self-management or sometimes the self-management began even before the state intervention. Sooner or later, the question of workers' control would arise and following that, or before, it would evolve into a proposal for an embryonic form of connection of the control of that factory with the control of others in the same manufacturing line or sector.

The concept of workers' control is indiscriminately used to describe things that are quite different from one another. More than anything else, it is confused with self-management.

Tony Cliff and Robin Peterson put it this way:

The root cause of the number of workers ready to accept the return of former owners is that workers' control has been tried at factory level, while there has not been workers' power at state level, and this has led to an inevitable cul-de-sac. ...

From workers' control without workers' power it is only a short step to the workers returning control to the old bosses in despair. Many workers who were confused are now disillusioned with 'socialism' or 'workers' control', and instead of becoming revolutionaries, are listening to, and turning to, the Right.

Empty stomachs may lead to rebellion, but they can also lead to submission. With unemployment running at 20 per cent, and inflation raging, many workers listen to the siren-calls of the Right which say the old days were better ...

As a militant from Setenave shipyard put it: 'Even at Setenave we don't have workers' control. How can we if we don't control the banks. Our attitude is that we want to know everything ... We want to control decisions but we do not take responsibility. We don't believe that we can have workers' control alone'. The militant is completely correct – and a revolutionary.

Many workers fell into the illusion that they could exist as an island of socialism in a sea of capitalism.[34]

Workers' control, in the case of the Portuguese Revolution, is also confused with co-administration, state intervention in companies, the occupation of factories and companies, union-based demand processes, industrial democracy, and even with the administration of the State itself.

Nancy Bermeo tells us that worker management encompassed fewer than 3 per cent of all industrial firms and included less than 6 per cent of all industrial workers. She goes on to say that: 'Ironically, worker managed industrial firms warrant attention not because they are numerous, but because they are not numerous. They are not a critical part of that transition to socialism that was never made.'[35]

But the: 'Socialists had been the only major party to consistently champion workers' control in its programs and public statements. Embracing the idea of "self-managing socialism", the party program of 1974 envisioned a society wherein the means of production would "naturally be social property", managed democratically by collectives of workers.'[36]

The Communist Party favoured nationalisation and state management in the industrial sector and, reluctantly, supported the takeovers and self-management in the rural sectors.

Workers' control is a process of dual power that consists of the organisation of workers in the production level – whether formalised or not – with a view to taking political power. It is a *situation* in the process of a struggle in the midst of the revolutionary process and not a structure or an institution. This specific phenomenon is quite distinct from self-management (a form whereby the workers become their own bosses) and from co-administration (whereby, normally, the workers through their unions, manage the factories or companies in a partnership arrangement with the bosses / owners and/ or with the State).

I believe that the government was much more worried about workers' control than self-management, and the proof of this is that 80 per cent of the interventions in companies (a reform measure) only took place after April 1975, when workers' control (a revolutionary form of the social process) occurred in large businesses, particularly the metal-mechanic sector and the businesses that would be nationalised. This is further explored in Chapter 12. Decree 222-B/75 was a tentative instrument for the State to contain the conflicts that reached production after April 1975.

This protection was further embodied in 1976 in Article 61 – (Cooperatives and self-management) of the Decree of Approval of the Constitution no. CRP 1976, 4 October 1976, which ensured:

1. All have the right to construct cooperatives, the State having the duty, in accordance with the Plan, to stimulate and support initiatives to this end.

2. Experiences of self-management shall be supported by the State.

8

Women in a Democracy are Not Mere Decoration: Social Reproduction and Private Life in the Revolution

The 'decolonization of women' is a necessity.

Simone de Beauvoir, June 1975,
Lisbon Faculty of Language and Literature[1]

'Men in the square and women at home' was a common saying, popularised during the New State regime. That truism, as seemingly solid as the military and legal force of the dictatorship, vanished into thin air. The question of equality, including the question of equal pay was advanced by women during the revolution. This was not on the MFA agenda or that of government; while not opposing equal pay and better rights for women, in reality they only responded to the pressure generated by women activists. Feminist movements that sprang up in the revolution or were boosted by it, Women's Democratic Movement,[2] Women's Liberation Movement[3] and the Union of Antifascist Revolutionary Women[4] did have some influence, however, the participation of women in the revolution as a whole was far more important than any other groups such as these. Participation was massive. Housewives came out in 1975 into the streets to protest against the high cost of living and demonstrated at the entrances to the supermarkets against the increase in food prices. Women agricultural workers took the lead in the call for agrarian reform. Women industrial workers, living in shacks, demanded decent living conditions. This participation went far beyond the gesture of poking carnations into the muzzles of the MFA men's guns on the morning of 25 April.

As Manuela Tavares recalls, women's participation in the workers struggles had fairly recent precedents in the form of the 'down tools' strikes of 1969,[5] in favour of better working conditions and also in the demonstrations against the colonial war.

The Three Marias

In 1971, while still under the rule of the fascist Salazar regime, three brave Portuguese women, the 'three Marias', wrote a collaborative work *Novas Cartas Portuguesas*, in which they condemned oppression, discussed sex and criticised the colonial war. Their writing is 'lyrical, fierce, intelligent, passionate, erotic, and often strikingly beautiful and powerful.' After the book was published, the authors were charged by the regime with obscenity and abuse of freedom of the press. A long and ugly trial ensued that dragged on for years and made international headlines.

Soon after the coup, on 7 May 1974, the 'three Marias' were spectacularly acquitted.

The Role of Women in the Old Regime

Salazar proclaimed, in one of his decrees designed to educate the work force, that: 'There was never a good housewife that did not have plenty to do'.[6] In 1970, in Portugal, 68 per cent of housewives in the 20 to 54 age group were officially registered as such.[7] The corporatist regime exploited the differences between the sexes as a way of disciplining the workforce.[8] Women guaranteed the 'work of reproduction', took care of the home and the children up until the 1960s, helping keep unemployment levels down to 'acceptable' levels. This all changed as a consequence of the wave of foreign investment, generating a demand for more women workers. The 'feminisation' of the labour market in Portugal was reflected in the evolution of the female economic activity index, which went up from 13.1 per cent in 1960 to 42.2 per cent in 1996 and up a little further to 42.7 per cent in 2001.[9] Out of the total number of women working in 1960, 28.4 per cent and 44.3 per cent were employed in industry and in the services sectors, respectively. By 1970, the percentages of women in those two sectors had increased to 30.8 per cent and 47.2 per cent.[10]

The subjugation of women was furthered by a meshwork of laws that were in force that socially and legally disqualified women; for example, they were forbidden to leave the country, without permission from their husbands. They did not have the right to vote (except when they were the head of a family) and they had very limited access to civil service positions.

After 25 April

The *Obra das Mães pela Educação Nacional* (Mothers Task Force for National Education) and the *Mocidade Portuguesa Feminina* (Portuguese

Female Youth –MPF) created back in 1936 and 1937 were shut down[11] by the MFA immediately after the coup of 25 April. Women started having access to administrative, diplomatic and judiciary careers; they acquired the right to vote and were granted equality in the eyes of the law which meant, for example, an end to the legal provisions that reduced sentences of men for crimes that were committed against their own wives or children. The equality achieved in 1974 was finally formalised in the 1976 constitution. This included the abolition of the man's right to open his wife's correspondence!

At a meeting of the Movimento de Libertação da Mulher, held in June 1974, one case was reported of a language teacher whose husband refused to authorise her to travel abroad with their eight-year-old son and she declared she could not go alone because 'the child was too small to be left in the charge of the father'. *Diário Popular* reported that the question of housewife's rights was raised. Another woman testified: 'I am a frustrated person, all that I know to do is wash clothes; I have never had any contacts or a chance to study. When I go out with my husband, I only watch cowboy films or bawdy revues and I cannot go alone because it would look bad; I have to content myself with whatever he likes.'[12]

At a demonstration held on 17 July attended by a huge turnout of men and women alike, placards were waved with the slogans 'Divorce, yes; illegitimate children, no!' and 'Democracy without Divorce; a farce'.

At a political rally in Lisbon on 21 June 1974, 10,000 people crowded into the former Sports Pavilion to hear a woman, with a broad smile, speaking in favour of the right to divorce and against the 'the stigmatising branding of the illegitimate child'. She received a huge round of applause. At the heart of the demands was precisely the need to revoke the *Concordata* Article, which hindered divorce among Catholic couples, and to abolish the idea of the 'illegitimacy' of the children. The law regulating the dissolution of marriages was passed in February 1975.

The Movimento Democratico das Mulheres, closely aligned with the Communist Party, issued a frank communication proposing the replacement of:

the oppressive and humiliating, petty domestic economy that binds women to the kitchen and the children's bedroom, obliging them to dispense their energies in tasks that are largely unproductive, enervating and depressing, by the collectivisation or socialisation of all such tasks, establishing collective canteens, laundries with reasonable process, domestic appliances at accessible prices and broad networks of crèches and kindergartens throughout the country.[13]

Photo 3   To fight against their bosses' lock-out, the dry-cleaning workers at Tinturaria Portugal decided, at a Plenary Meeting on 18 November 1974, to continue occupying their workplace. (Jose Reis)

Gender Equality in the Workplace

The entrance of women in the labour market had a direct impact on narrowing wage differentials and also on the opening of crèches. Women began to be able/to be obliged to work full time, just like men. Not only that, they began to participate in the workers' commissions and the social conflicts.

Class struggles and gender struggles were profoundly linked. Women were the central characters in the occupation of the Salazar Foundation neighbourhood in Ajuda, Lisbon, on 2 May. They played a central role in residents' struggles throughout the revolution, because of the responsibility they had in administering their homes. 2,000 workers, mainly women, occupied the Timex Company on 6 May and they were followed by the workers of Sogantal and of Messa. On 14 May, the Cintideal workers came out on strike with a list of demands that included the 'abolition of control over visits to the toilets', while at the same time, in the newspaper industry, a struggle was on course to claim the right to two months' maternity leave.

At Ciba-Geigy, there was a ten-day strike demanding the presence 'of women in positions of command'.

On 24 June, the Mafalda shirt factory workers held the American boss hostage for refusing to pay their wages. During the year of 1974:

> The women of Madeira came out on the streets against the colony's regime in the cane field fights for the occupation of the sugar mills, and foremost among them were the women of Calheta, Ponta do Sol and Machico. In that same year, the first woman ever to take office as a minister of government, Maria de Lurdes Pintassilgo, headed the Ministry of Social Affairs, albeit in the first free elections only 8 per cent of the elected representatives were women.[14]

International Women's Day, on 8 March 1975, was freely celebrated all over the country. Again throughout the country, from February 1975, there was a huge increase in social struggles; workers of the Tomar spinning factory occupied the installations to prevent sabotage (shortage of materials, closure of the bathrooms and the refectory). Prior to that, on 5 January 1975, 200 Plessey company workers, once again mainly women, held a demonstration in front of the Ministry of Labour. In Porto, workers occupied the Plessey plant that the boss was trying to close and at the end of that month women workers of Applied Magnetics marched to the Ministry of Labour to demonstrate for 'payment of overdue wages and the re-opening or nationalisation of the company'.[15] On 11 March, at the Antar factory in Porto, workers took over the management; in the same city, 650 Rolsol workers began a fight to defend their jobs. In the great demonstration of 17 May 1975, under the banner of '*Casas sim, barracas não!*' (Houses, yes; Shacks, no), women were at the forefront.

Candidinha Fashion Atelier

The occupation of the Candidinha Fashion Atelier building, right on the Avenida da República, one of Lisbon's main thoroughfares, was a magnificent illustration of how preventing the stripping of company assets and how the struggles for better working conditions was intrinsically linked to the question of reproductive/domestic labour (looking after the home and the children).

According to investigative journalists from the RTP, the Candidinha Atelier was part of: 'The decadence of a highly over-privileged class which when faced with the revolt of those it exploits, reneges on its responsibility ... and flees! The clientele flees! Two of the proprietors fled after not paying wages since April and failing to attend meetings with the workers' commissions.'[16]

The Atelier building was covered with posters with workers' demands, signed by the MDP or the MFA or simply anonymous. Some of the women had been working in the Atelier for 17 years: 'The workers occupied the Atelier and organised a provisional regime of self-administration. They met in plenary sessions in which for the first time they openly discussed and made peer decisions regarding the problems of exploitation they were the victims of and the best way to overcome the situation of the moment. They decided to form picket lines.'[17]

One of the workers spoke of how they found out that the boss filmed their conversations. The RTP television recording shows the boss's bureau and on top of it are two wooden desk ornaments one bearing the warning *Cuidado. Estou maldisposto.* (Watch out. I am in a bad mood) and the other read, in English, 'Danger. Explosive boss'.

It is worthwhile examining the eyewitness accounts. One woman worker recalled:

We were already in a bad situation because, prior to 25 April, the situation of the High Fashion trade was declining ... They brought us all together in the work space in the fitting room and Mr Miguel told us a lot of stuff, how bad we were, how we had to make ready-to-wear clothing, how they did not have this that or the other ... and they put us on a four-day week right away in May and I went up to him and told him he could not do that [here she raised her voice] and he just laughed. Cristovão sat himself down in the big chair [she sits down in imitation] and I had not even gone beyond the office door and he said, 'I didn't know you had so many children', still mocking us.[18]

Another worker with a broad smile who took part in the pickets (which were maintained day and night for fear that the employers would take the sewing machines away) gleefully recalled:

We always had to enter by the tradesman's entrance. The front door was only for the showroom ladies. We had to enter by the back door. They made us get used to not having a refectory for our meals because the refectory there could only accommodate 20 people and there were 70 of us. So we had to eat in the Atelier and they always tore a strip off us, if any of the work got soiled. Once we are all together eating in a huddle like animals ... I was around 28 at the time and I had never experienced such situations, there were words used that I did not even know existed or what they meant but I got to know them here in the firm ... I am married and I have a three-year-old girl and there are times when I have to make sacrifices for her and ask for baby-sitters and quarrel with my husband but I hope that in the end all this will bring us better times.[19]

Another very young worker said:

I get on very well with my work colleagues but I had to tell them at home that I had to come and take part in the pickets; I am young and they did not want me to spend a night away from home in any circumstances ... There is that vexation associated with sleeping away from home staying out all night, and my mother could get no sleep, but a short while ago my brother got back after being away from home and he persuaded them that I had to remain in the pickets ... I really enjoy talking to my colleagues, especially about things that we [at home] have never discussed. After 25 April, I got to know about lots of horrible things like the situation of the political prisoners as I never imagined there were any ...[20]

Again, the testimony of a woman worker who was very excited with everything that happened:

I have had a lot of issues with my boyfriend. It so happens that I had a problem just now, last Friday. But we cannot take everything to heart and we have to show our will and support our colleagues in this struggle. My boyfriend thinks that the struggle is good but some days are worse. His birthday is on Friday and he wants me to not come here to the action but instead spend his birthday with him, so I asked my colleagues and we exchanged turns in the pickets. But if it had not been possible to change my turn, I would have been obliged to come and take my place in the struggle.[21]

Another woman worker stated:

I have no mother, my brother is in the forces, my father is sick and the 14-year-old girl at home cannot take on the responsibility for the housework as yet. I always stay here one night a week in the picket line but I cannot be here on weekends. I have to prepare the food at night after work, I have to clean the house and put my brother's clothes in order because he always comes at weekends and it is I who have to do all the work ...[22]

A young female worker gave witness:

I take part in the picket on the night from Sunday to Monday; I asked the committee for that. I come at 9pm and go through to 9 in the morning when I carry on at work. My parents took a dim view of my spending the night out like that ... I work every day, then I go to school and from school I come to the picket; two days and a night with no rest [smile]. Well now, I very much like being here and now I have to go to the showroom. Before, I used to be afraid to go there. I was always running [laughter]. I was more afraid of a certain man that circulated there, Mr Alves, he always looked at me like this ... I was very scared of him. The employers never spoke to us in the street, not so much as a good morning.[23]

The demands that emerged from those heady forays were mostly the same and shared by a broad set of workers – better wages, better working conditions – but many others were introduced specifically by the day-to-day experiences of women at work stemming from women's long connection with the management of the home. There were calls for paying overtime when children were being assisted, the abolition of control over the visits to the toilets at work, equal wages for equal work, the expansion of crèches and improvements in the sanitary conditions of housing. Basic rights were won such as prenatal maternity leave of seven weeks and post-natal leave of seven weeks and 'free care services of a doctor or a midwife at the time of birth'.[24] All this contributed to reversing the terrible maternal-infant health figures.

Changes in Legislation

The broadest and most visible changes of the revolution were those affecting women's lives. In the sphere of family life, those who were formally subordinate shone, not only women but also to children and to old people without economic autonomy as well as those 'who lived in families that were inconsonant with the traditional model.'[25] As early as May 1974, in response to social pressure, the Family Allowance had been increased to 240 escudos for all children. Whole chapters of the Civil Code were altered putting an end to the distinction between legitimate and illegitimate children. In addition to crèches, schools were opened for children with disabilities. In 1974 and 1975, there was a drop in the average age for the first marriage, which may have been due to factors such as wage increases, freedom to choose a partner, more intense social life and greater sexual freedom. Those aspects have not been sufficiently researched, as yet.

The old divorce law was annulled and women were granted access to diplomatic careers, starting in 1975. The constitution defined the new relations between the family, as an institution, and the State. The family became the object of special protection afforded by the State which took on responsibility for publicising and disseminating family planning methods, for developing a national network of maternal-infant assistance and for cooperating with parents in the education of their children and, further-more, for fostering the social and economic independence of additional household members.[26]

The Church

Criticism of the Church was not at the heart of the social movement, although it has to be emphasised that the Church played a fundamental role in mobilising and consolidating the counter-revolution and indeed its opposition ensured that the law permitting unrestricted abortion in Portugal was only enacted in the twenty-first century. Nevertheless, 25 April set in motion a process that made Portugal an increasingly lay society, as was mirrored in the question of the role of women, in intra-family relations and in the sphere of sexuality.

Exposure

When the political women prisoners were released from the Caxias prison, some talked about what had been done to their bodies. Teresa Libano Monteiro tells us:

On 26 April 1974, the political prisoners held in the Caxias prison were released. From that day forth, Portuguese society had to face up to the reports of those who had been imprisoned and tortured. Among such reports were those of women who publicly described, on television and in the newspapers, the atrocities they had been submitted to. For the very first time, aspects related to the body, the sexuality and the intimacy of those women who had been the victims of torture were exposed in the media; that is, publicly. Things that had never been spoken about in public before were then being discussed.[27]

The public disclosures of the naked female body began to acquire legitimacy. In front of the cinemas, long queues formed to watch films with erotic scenes such as *The Last Tango in Paris* and *Emmanuelle*. Pornography, which up until then had been prohibited (it is important to remember that the majority of the books seized by the New State were pornographic and not political) suddenly became unrestricted. The awakening, the liberation of sexuality was accompanied by a new fashion constructing the 'attractive being'.

Teresa Torga

In 1975, Teresa Torga was an artiste performing in revues. On 6 May, at 4 in the afternoon, she took off all her clothes in a Lisbon street:

> Some passers-by, visibly surprised upon seeing such an uncommon sight, went up to the woman with the intention of protecting her from the eyes of other passers-by and persuade her to get dressed and go away. In the middle of the confusion, the reporter Antonio Capela appeared and started taking photographs. The people around were furious at what they considered to be a 'moral depravity', surrounding, shoving and hitting him and only the intervention of a local shopkeeper prevented the crowd from destroying his camera ... Meanwhile the woman had been led to the doorkeeper's lodge of a nearby building.[28]

Zeca Afonso, one the most influential folk and political musicians in Portuguese history and the composer of *Grândola, Vila Morena*, immortalised Teresa Torga in a song that also became an icon of the fight for women's equality:

> In the middle of the crossroads
> Where the street meets the Avenue
> Lost to the world, at four, there
> Was a woman dancing bare-naked
> Passers-by seeing the strange scene
> Hurried quickly towards her
> Anxious to put all her clothes on
> But there was Antonio Capela

Making the most of the hubbub
Eager to capture her picture
In a democracy, the women
Are not just a mere decoration
They say her name is Teresa
Works in a Benfica nightclub
Bares with the fun-loving crowd there
Living in poor rented rooms now
She was once star of the show though
Now she's a model unwilling
Antonio Capela can say so
Teresa Torga, Teresa Torga
Beaten in the fierce forge of life
No banner flies without fighting
There's always a battle in strife[29]

In the field of everyday behaviour, it should be remembered that an immense change took place in the homes, in the schools, in the bars. Politics was discussed everywhere. People ceased being subservient. They became actors in their workplaces and homes and the resulting socialisation created new cultural and social spaces.

9
Artists and the Revolution

Lisbon is the biggest village in the world. When I get back I will tell you all about this revolution.

Gabriel García Márquez, summer 1975.[1]

The Brick Wall Press

The censorship during the dictatorship had shut men's mouths and suppressed freedom of artistic expression. Now everything was new, everything was in some way a space for art, for creation and creativity. It was an art that was highly and openly engaged. The social explosion created a cultural brew that was reflected immediately in many sectors: books, music, plays, comic strips, painting and photography.

During the first strikes in May and June 1974, José Marques wandered around Lisbon with a camera in his hand capturing the 'graffiti' on the walls, fondly referred to at the time as the 'brick wall press'. The tight corset of censorship had burst apart. Typical slogans of the left-wing parties were 'Armed Forces + the People = Free Portugal', 'For the Organisation of the Proletariat', 'Long live the freed prisoners', 'Long Live Communism', 'Neither Marcelo nor Spínola! All power to the working class', 'Democracy for the People; Dictatorship for the Bourgeoisie', 'The People's Revolution. The People in Arms cannot be defeated', 'Amnesty for the Deserters', 'Not one more soldier for the colonies'. Anarchist influences could be detected in slogans such as 'No God, No Boss' and 'Power to the Barcelos Rooster'.[2] On the pillars of the bridge, one could see evidence of a dispute to rename it. On one side was painted 'The April 25 Bridge' and on the other 'The Red Bridge'.[3]

Apart from the graffiti or developing out of the graffiti, wall paintings blossomed. The people expressed there what had been forbidden to them. The paintings came from the people, and they were an immediate, brilliant and direct way to celebrate and propagandise. They were much more immediate than other forms of artistic output; anybody who could lay their hands on gloss paint could have their say. It would help if they had a modicum of artistic talent.

> The wall paintings, were for sure one of the richest and fruitful achievements of April ...
> One can say that everything was written on the walls of this country after the 25 April. So the richness of creativity, thematic or pictorial, was transposed to the walls, with the goal of freeing the freedom, of suffocating the hidden fire. The graffiti, either a mere party source, either telling individual experiences, of a region or a people, are one of the most beautiful moments of the great boom of freedom brought by the 25 April.[4]

The mural art of the Carnation Revolution can only be compared to that of the Mexican Revolution. But there was an exceptional difference: those in Mexico were painted as part of Government initiatives. Well-known artists, such as Diego Riviera, were commissioned. Those in Portugal bloomed from below.

> anyone could go out, day or night, with paint cans and paint away to their heart's content, which helped the mural movement to flourish. It was quite a unique popular painting movement, more akin to South America than Europe. The movement started quickly in May '74 and by the summer of '75 there was hardly an unpainted wall anywhere in Lisbon or in the rural towns across the country. Generally political groups respected the murals of others, there was an informal protocol that implied that if a group got to a wall first then they had the right to keep it and rework it.[5]

There were exceptional artists and authors associated with the propaganda of that period, as for example João Abel Manta, and his magnificent drawings. Thousands of posters and paintings filed the walls with joy.

Ever since August 1970, the Acre Group (Alfredo Queirós Ribeiro, Clara Meneres, Lima Carvalho) had been surprising the Lisbon inhabitants by painting abstract designs in streets and paths.[6] The murals of April were painted by the hands of artists like those of the Acre Group, but also many of the paintings which graced the walls with gladness in those days were by complete unknowns, young people, adults and old people. This took place throughout the country, from the big cities to the smallest hamlets.

Here are some descriptions, but of course, a wall painting is worth a million words. In Laranjeiro, a characteristic but catching a 'power of the people' a mural was painted in red and green; in Campolide, one of the murals depicted a large ship entering a river with a factory to one side, the 25 April bridge with a big demonstration and a carnation in the middle underneath the word 'socialism' in red letters. In Belas, Sintra, a MDP/CDE mural showed a child holding a carnation meeting a worker. In Covilhã, a mural in modernist style displayed a clenched fist and a political prisoner, which symbolised the end of imprisonment in the form of a dove painted by a child. In the fields of the south, there were murals taking up agrarian reform issues, such as 'Land for those who work it', showing an agricultural labourers, perhaps a little too muscular but undoubtedly happy, and with clenched fists raised. Thus, neorealist aesthetics, essentially simple and agitational motifs, appeared side by side with more highly elaborated murals, some of them with surrealist aspects and full of humour, corrosive humour, such as was frequently found in the paintings of the anarchists. Phil Mailer makes a slightly derogatory comment but then describes a moment of true subversion:

Unfortunately many of these 'political' murals lacked both imagination and humor. The messages were ideological to the extreme, with a complete lack of irony, just giant but bland statements and aspirations of unity and of successful class struggle. There were exceptions, however. One bright graffitist intervened in the doctrinaire messaging, painting the words 'Taxi, Taxi!' in a word bubble coming from the image of Maoist leader Arnaldo Matos as he addressed tens of thousands of workers. It made the whole thing seem ridiculous, a moment of true subversion.[7]

Sometimes the whole front or side of a building was taken up by a mural as was the case with the mural 'The World of Work' that the MRPP painted in Santa Maria das Olivais. Another mural was 'Let the rich pay for the crisis. No to the Social Pact' done by UDP supporters. In Viana do Castelo, the Communist Party painted a eulogy to work with a reference to the shipyard workers of Viana. Bread, Peace, Land, Liberty, Socialism and the portraits of Marx, Lenin and Mao Tse-tung were dominant themes.

The destruction of those murals was an act that destroyed an artistic heritage of inestimable value. Supporters of 'law and order' felt it was incumbent upon them to wipe out the memory of times when the people 'were no longer afraid'; in which they, the people, had taken part of their political destiny into their own hands in an exemplary manner. That reminder of direct democracy, which hung heavy over the process of democratic 'normalisation' like bars of steel, had resulted in the destruction of one of the most fertile exponents of grass-roots art in our history. Fortunately, many of these have been photographed and have been captured in the book *As Paredes na Revolução*[8] and one can also see a magnificent testimony on the website for the Centro de Documentação 25 de Abril.

Posters

The streets became plastered with posters and placards. On the initiative of the far-left-wing organisations, the Communist Party and various associations of artists that were formed on 10 June, Portugal Day was celebrated by a recently created association, the *Movimento Democrático de Artistas Plasticos* (The Democratic Movement of Plastic Arts Practitioners, MDAP), with a large painted panel in the Belém Gallery celebrating freedom. In addition to the MDAP, a group was created by artists linked to the Sociedade Nacional de Belas Artes-SNBA (National Fine Arts Association) and the Círculode Artes Plásticas (Plastic Arts Circle) in Coimbra and Acre emerged, and in 1975, the Associação Portuguesa de Artistas Plásticos (Portuguese Association of Plastic Arts Practitioners), popularly known as the 'papas',[9] was set up.

At the beginning of May, in the Praça de Londres (London Square) in Lisbon, someone was trying to peel off one of the posters of the *Acção Popular Nacional* (National People's Action) party, the former single party of the dictatorship. It was hard to get off because it was well stuck on and only came off in pieces. A passer-by saw the scene and called out 'Hell, it's harder to pull down a poster than a whole government at once!'[10]

The posters of the old regime were replaced by new ones, full of colour and vivacity in total contrast with those of the regime which young people considered to be grey and emasculating – just as stifling as the monotonous voices of the dictators Salazar and Caetano. During the election of 1975, as 'parties were not allowed to flypost on top of one another's posters it became necessary to carry longer and longer ladders to reach bits of unposted wall'. Instead of the sombre New State motto typically inscribed at the entrance to the schools 'If you knew how hard it is to command you would prefer lifelong obedience', alternatives appeared such as 'Flowers, Freedom, Fire, Imagination, Force, Unity, Art, Revolution' in letters of red and green.[11]

Politically, the posters mirrored the myriad groupings that came into existence in the early days of the revolution. The themes were still dominated by the idea of liberation: white doves, red carnations, soldiers with carnations pinned to their chests.[12] Others were already beginning to contest the capitalist system – a cartoon published on 11 May 1974 depicts, on one side an old man is standing with the part of the Portuguese flag that has the shield on it, the green part in his hand and on the other side a youth gleefully running off with the rest of the flag; the red part.[13]

In April 2009, José Gualberto de Freitas brought them all together in a book titled *A Guerra dos Cartazes* (The War of the Posters),[14] exemplifying the political atmosphere being experienced at the time.

Paintings

The most famous painting of the revolution *Poetry is in the Street* by Vieira da Silva, is a modernist portrayal of a demonstration by people with carnations in their hands thronging the streets of old Lisbon.

The impact of the revolution would later make itself felt in the works of Júlio Pomar, António Pedro and Júlio Resende, which were to be shown in exhibitions in the course of 1976 and 1977. Some of them caused a public scandal, like the exhibition 'Eroticism in Portuguese Modern Art', which was prohibited in Estoril in 1977 but was eventually held in the School of Fine Arts, with the support of the then State Secretary for Culture, David Mourão-Ferreira.

Like everything else in the revolution, art was the stage for scenes of conflict and the expression of tensions, which, on the face of it, were evidence of hopes for the future.

Writers

On May Day 1974, some of the most outstanding Portuguese writers of the day signed a petition[15] demanding the replacement of those responsible for the television and radio networks: 'The systematic political and cultural repression that was exercised for decades by the Radio Televisao Portuguesa and the Emissora Nacional de Radiodifusao ... is still vivid in the Memories of the Portuguese people. Those who were responsible in the past for the deliberate lies and falsification cannot possibly honestly communicate the authenticity of the present'.[16]

Another writer, Urban Tavares Rodrigues, gives us an amazing description of life in the capital during those days in which even the rain was a source of happiness:

The city is vibrant, hope lives everywhere between the blue skies and the showers of these days in which everything is exceptional ... A short while ago, near the street where I live there appeared a demonstration of bakery workers swept by the new wind that is blowing and learning how to chant 'The people, united, will never be defeated. There is not one youth in blue jeans to be seen. It is the people, the real people, the people of that bleak country of desistance which it was until yesterday ...

... there is the hunt for the PIDE (Political police agents). There is a persistent misgiving that the thousands of criminals and torturers that are at large may dream up and carry out sinister actions. It is the people now who are taking on the task of vigilance.[17]

In summer 1975, one of the world's greatest writers, Gabriel García Márquez, visited Lisbon and spent 15 days in Portugal writing a series of reports to be published in Colombia by the *Alternativa*[18] review, which he had founded with other left-wing intellectuals in 1974. 'He met with writers and poets and was greatly moved by the revolutionary process'.[19] The meetings he organised during his stay in Lisbon were attended by the well-known writers Maria Velho da Costa, Luis de Sttau Monteiro,[20] José Gomes Ferreira, José Cardoso Pires and Saramago (who won the Nobel Prize for Literature in 1998). Almost 35 years later, the journalist Ricardo Rodrigues told us:

García Márquez landed at the Portela airport off a flight from Rome on the first day of June in 1975 on a visit to Lisbon. He said, 'I had the feeling of living once more the experience of a first arrival from my childhood. Not only because of the very early summer that year in Portugal and the smell of shellfish on the breeze but also because of other breezes; because of breathing in the air of a new freedom that was everywhere.[21]

One such article, titled 'Portugal, território livre da Europa' ('Portugal, Europe's Land of Liberty') is pure reporting, immersed in descriptions of the ambience, the smells, the experiences in the streets. Another, 'O Socialismo ao alcance dos militares' ('Socialism within the Grasp of the Military'), is an essay on the Portuguese Revolution and the fact that the Armed Forces had organised the coup without wishing to take power themselves. Yet another article describes the political chequerboard of the revolutionary period, the European and American pressures, and the grass-roots movements organised by the ordinary people. The title of that article embodies a question, which to this day goes unanswered: 'Pero qué carajo piensa el pueblo?' ('But what the hell do the people think?').[22]

García Márquez describes a Lisbon, which, in his words is 'the biggest village in the world' because of the intense social and socialising life that people were living – a militant city that never slept:

Everyone talks and no one sleeps; at four o'clock in the morning, there was not a free cab to be found anywhere. Most of the people work without a timetable and without a break, even though the Portuguese have the lowest wages in the whole of Europe. Meetings are scheduled late at night, office lights stay on until the small hours of the morning. If anything can stop this revolution, it's going to be the light bill.[23]

The Spaniard Manuel Vázquez Montalbán was in Lisbon when the coup took place – at the time he was a leading journalist and subsequently became a world famous writer. He wrote articles for the *TeleExpress* of Barcelona at a time when Spain was still in the dark night of Francoism.

Paco Ibanez, Patxi Andion and the new Catalonian song are on the radio and television and the same can be said of the democratic Spanish intellectuals and politicians who are flocking into Portugal moved by the idea that 'This is the first revolution we can get to by car'. While tourism had been one of the top foreign currency earners for fascist Portugal, in democratic Portugal, it is destined to be replaced by political tourism ... the hotels are filling up with voyeurs of freedom.[24]

Many other committed writers visited or passed through Lisbon: Michel Foucault, Jean-Paul Sartre, Simone de Beauvoir, Louis Althusser, Raymond Aron, Marguerite Duras, Sebastião Salgado. Revolutionary leaders like Tariq Ali, Basil Davidson, Hugo Blanco and Ernest Mandel paid their respects. Salvador Allende's widow, Hortensia Allende came to see the revolution as did the Cuban dancer Alicia Alonso and the American film director Robert Kramer. Valentina Terechkova, the Russian astronaut, flew in to the revolutionary capital and was acclaimed as a heroine by the people of Lisbon.

Flamarion Maués counted the impressive number of 145 publishers, who during the period from 1968 to 1982 published books with a political content 'especially works associated to left-wing thinking'.[25] It was a time when more works were published and more copies printed of essays, novels and political theory of critical, Marxist, anarchist, socialist and social-democratic thinking than at any other time.

Theatre

New theatrical groups were formed, many of them in the form of actors' cooperatives. Crowds filled the Comuna, Barraca and Cornucopia theatres to watch independent plays addressing social themes and the question of freedom. Plays by the German revolutionary playwright Brecht were produced along with many other plays by authors of the *engagé* theatre. Regular commercial theatre entered into decline; during those years, it was replaced by the vigour of independent theatre. Public funds began to be allocated to finance cultural activities, including the theatre. The general political climate along with intense union engagement led to discussions and disputes around actors' working conditions.[26] On stage, the themes addressed were socialism, the 'new man', and the classless society free from the exploitation of one man by another. Culture reached the smaller cities in the interior. Mário Barradas, founder of the Centro Cultural de Évora – CCE (Évora Culture Centre) told researcher Micael de Oliveira how the adventure of the CCE began:

> We went to four cities: Coimbra, Leiria, Viseu and Évora. In Coimbra, the Gil Vicente Theatre was in the hands of the university; in Leiria, the José Lucio da Silva theatre was in complete disrepair at that time; in Viseu, what is the Viriato theatre today was then a warehouse for storing potatoes. After that I went to Évora and the local council said to me 'Do you want the theatre?' 'Yes, I do,' I said. 'Well then here are the keys. The theatre is yours'.[27]

Censorship

The television broadcast of the celebrations of Portugal Day, on 10 June, was censored, towards the end the programme, by the government because the group from the Commune theatre was caricaturing leaders of the deposed regime. An exhibition of the works of artists of the period that was about to go on exhibition to countries behind the Iron Curtain was prohibited. In Viseu, as part of the culture-stimulating campaigns, which almost always brought with them the PCP's policy of 'The People-MFA Alliance', a group of artists tried to paint a mural. They got a frankly hostile reception from the local people but, as time went by, first the children joined in and finally the adults did too and the mural became a collective experience of socialisation.[28]

Music

José Mário Branco, Zeca Afonso, Francisco Fanhais, Sérgio Godinho, Luís Cília and many hundreds of other musicians, who were never well known to the general public formed the 'protest music' movement, whose roots can be found in the song that came into being in Coimbra during the 1960s, nurtured by the academic crises and the student affrays. The song 'Trova do Vento que Passa' ('Ballad of the Wind that Passes') became popular within the student resistance against the Salazar regime, much as Bob Dylan's 'Blowing' in the Wind' would in the US Civil Rights Movement. The song was by Adriano Correia de Oliveira, a singer associated with the Coimbra fado, and was based almost entirely on the poems of Manoel Alegre, who wrote 'Trova' in 1963. He had been imprisoned by the PIDE for his political views. Another protest song that was taken up by the movement was 'Os Vampíros' (The Vampires) by Zeca Afonso, 1971 in the Zip-Zap programme. Readers may recall that it was the playing of another song by Zeca Afonso – Grândola, Vila Morena – on Rádio Renascença, which was the signal for the 25 April coup.

Another memorable song was 'Mudam-se os Tempos, Mudam-se as Vontades' ('Times Change, Inclinations Change') by José Mário Branco. The great concert of 29 March in the Coliseu dos Recreios was another spin-off of a musical movement that 'emerges with the characteristic of imparting cultural dynamism and which takes on a social-political role in arousing awareness and in the struggle against the dictatorship'.[29] Music was also driven by the struggle against the colonial war and the demand for civic and political freedoms. Many singers and musicians followed the more radical proposals, accompanying the development of the social movement – it was no longer just a struggle for civil liberties and an end to the colonial war, but much more for an end to exploitation, poverty and the lack of social justice. 'True freedom can only exist when there is peace and bread, good housing, good health, education; when what people produce belongs to the people' sang Sérgio Godinho, in his song called 'Freedom':

> We bear the burden of the past and its seed
> The longer the wait the greater the need
> Only a torrent can assuage such a thirst
> Only a torrent can assuage such a thirst
> After so many years of furtively whispering

It is those who have nothing that can yearn to have everything
Only lives of stagnation really yearn for full living
Only lives of stagnation really yearn for full living
True freedom can only exist when people have
Peace and bread, good housing, good health, education
True freedom can only exist when people have
Freedom to change and decide
When what people produce belongs to the people
When what people produce belongs to the people.

The song captures the spirit well.

Before 1974, culture was controlled by the State and the press muzzled by censorship. Despite this, there was a clandestine artistic movement, which helped nurture imaginations and sow seeds of discontent. The revolution opened up the gates of art to the people, not just an artistic elite. Never in the history of Portugal had workers been so aware of their condition of workers or so proud of it. And now, they had the accompanying music. There was an immense response at street level, literally with 'brick wallpress' and posters. Popular music was opened up and adapted. Communal and political theatre opened up. There was a proliferation of literature, although much of it was in the form of artistically boring political tracts. But writers were inspired and their works were enriched as a result. Maybe painting and sculpture did not produce another Picasso nor did drama produce another Brecht, but it is certain that artistic creativity was stretched and enhanced by the revolution, and it maybe, possibly, that some of it has faded away — like the paintings on the walls in the streets.

10

Workers' Commissions and Unions

The Inter-Empresas Demonstration of 7 February

By January 1975, battles against redundancies were coming to the forefront. Self-management of workplaces was but one response. Another type of reaction came from the 1,000 workers in the Lisbon branches of the electrical engineering group, Efacec-Inel. They called upon the Inter-Empresas to organise a great demonstration.[1] A TAP worker recalled the Inter-Empresas planning meeting of 2 February 1975: 'the biggest meeting, I can remember was in the "Voz do Operário" ... there were about 1,000 people. It was the meeting to plan the demonstration. The support of Lisnave workers was decisive.'[2]

At the time, 37 or 38 workers' commissions (accounts vary) were involved. The manifesto called for the destruction of capitalism, a system in which redundancies are considered inevitable and proposed the right to refuse overtime work. The lead banner was to read: 'Unemployment is an inevitable consequence of capitalism. That is why workers want to destroy it and build a new world'.

The NATO military manoeuvres on the outskirts of Lisbon, seen as a provocation, coincided with the demonstration, which was scheduled for 7 February, a weekday night, ending at 10pm in London Square. At the last minute, another slogan was added: 'NATO out, national independence!'

Intersindical, the Communist Party and Socialist Party condemned the demonstration. The coalition government went further and banned all demonstrations between 7 and 12 February 1975. The demonstration was supported by MES, PRP, UDP, LUAR, LCI, Communist Party (m-1) and Base-FUT.

On 4 February the Communist Party issued a statement from the Central Committee in which it defended Portugal's part in the military alliance under present conditions, and denounced the protest as provocative.[3]

The Communist Party concluded that any 'clash with NATO troops would favour the interests of reaction'. Octávio Pato, from the Communist

Party, even went on television and advised people to give flowers to the marines of the NATO fleet. Unsurprisingly, regardless of the opposition, the Inter-Empresas decided to go ahead with the demonstration. Interestingly the MFA still had to consider its position. The French weekly *Libération* commented:

> By coincidence, the monthly delegate assembly of the MFA was taking place on the Thursday. It was expected that it would ban the demo ... On the Friday morning members of the Commissions (i.e. the Inter-Empresas) went to see COPCON (the newly created internal security force). At the end of this meeting, it was announced that MFA did not object to the demo.[4]

According to the description of the *Diário Popular*, 80,000 workers participated, filling Rossio and Marquês de Pombal Squares and marching to London Square to the Ministry of Labour, where they arrived at 10pm. The slogans included 'No to dismissals, down with capitalism'; 'Against redundancies' – 'unity of the working class'; 'Strike yes, lock-out no'; 'Overtime no, reduction of working time yes'; 'Part-time work no, all workers permanent'. During the demonstration, inflammatory speeches were made against the government and the Communist Party, the 'Battle for Production' and Civic Student Service. The Intersindical was accused of being 'yellow' and 'reformist'.[5]

The most newsworthy moment of the demonstration was when the military cordon joined in, chanting the demonstration slogans against NATO, to the enthusiastic applause of the demonstrators.

Palácio from Lisnave tells his part of the story:

> The demonstration met police and military officers all along the way. They wanted to discourage or divert us. The demonstration never stopped in spite of different attempts to stop it. The army blocked the streets leading to the American Embassy ... I asked the people through the megaphone whether or not they should advance ... the people would not let themselves be fooled or impeded. So I went to talk to an officer and told him 'the people of the demonstration want to pass'. And so we moved on. ... As the demonstrators went past, the commandos turned their backs on the demonstration, turned their weapons on the building and joined the people in the chanting.[6]

Libération reported that 'people were crying with joy' and that 'such a scene helps you understand Portugal today'. The demonstration eroded the PCP–MFA bond and opened the way for future MFA–People Power developments. The MFA had disagreed with the Communist Party and favoured the expression of autonomous workers' power.

This was, up until this moment in the revolution, the most powerful expression of dual power. It came out of a workers' council structure, a form that emerges in revolutionary processes. Sheila Cohen writes:

> The term 'Workers' Councils' can perhaps stand as a catchall title for an unpremeditated, quasi-spontaneous, 'groundup' organisational form reproduced over many periods and across many countries by groups of workers previously unaware of such a structure or of its historical precedents. Its highest form the Soviet, its 'lowest' the simple workplace representatives' committee, this formation recurs time and again in situations of major class struggle and even everyday industrial conflict.
>
> ... Fully-fledged workers' councils exist, almost by definition, at times of heightened class struggle, times which generate not only these formations but all the vehicles of class struggle: mass strikes, occupations, sometimes riots.[7]

These types of organisations have threatened the status quo and posed an alternative power, a dual power. Most of this has been hidden from history and at the time people related to the more recent, geographically closer experiences of France in 1968.[8]

It is significant that this massive demonstration against redundancies, along with that against the strike law that authorised lock-outs, provoked so much opposition from the State and the trade unions and, at the same time, united so many workers. The Inter-Empresas were viciously attacked by the Communist Party and the Intersindical. Many of the revolutionaries of the far-left were vigorous in their counter-attacks, and political sectarianism was an endemic and negative feature. As *Diário Popular* noted:

> There were no incidents in the demonstration against unemployment that, prohibited by the Civil Government of Lisbon, was maintained by the organisers gathering tens of thousands of people ... Pickets of Steel, Efacec, TLP, Petroquimica, Tecnividro, Applied, Fabrica Portugal, Bertrand, Nitratos de Portugal, and other workers ensured the orderly nature of events ... Finally, in Plaza de Londres, in front of the Ministry of Labour, 'Long live the working class' and other slogans were chanted,

many against Intersindical, which they dubbed 'yellow'. 'Down with yellow syndicates' was an expression used several times and widely applauded.[9]

The Marxist-Leninists were extremely hostile to the existing union leadership; those unions which had not responded sufficiently to 25 April were considered relics of fascism, while those under the Communist Party were branded as social-fascist. It was not clear whether the intention was to replace the unions, bypass them or complement them. But in practice, the unions were also making headway, addressing 'bread and butter' demands.

The demonstration was the most significant single action organised by the *Inter-Empresas*. It was also its last major action. There were a number of reasons for this. One facet was the relations with the union movement, a second being the shift by the Communist Party in its relationship to the workers' commissions and a third being the sectarianism of the Maoists within the *Inter-Empresas*; this was driven by the view that the need for 'The Party' was paramount, thereby leaving no oxygen for independent autonomous organisation.[10]

The Role of the Intersindical

The struggle of the Communist Party for a single united union movement (*unicidade*) was one of the most difficult battles the party would fight during the revolution, and from autumn 1974, the Communist Party would invest a great deal of its energies in this process. They had created the mythology that the Communist Party was at the centre of the post-25 April 'broad anti-fascist unity' popular uprising.[11] Their interpretation of 25 April has exaggerated the wave of strikes unfolding in 1973, a process on which Intersindical did exert an important influence but it should not be conflated, with the workplace militancy post-25 April. This continuum is pure myth; there is a clear difference between struggles before 1974 and after.

The Intersindical, before 1974, was an embryonic organisation. The strength of the strike movement since the end of the 1960s does not allow us to conclude that there was a continuum between the pre-revolution and post-25 April struggles. Its scope was reduced in relation to the impact of the workers' movement – before the revolution, the Intersindical meetings represented a maximum of 170,000 workers. This narrative of the strike movement omits the workers' commissions and qualitative leap that the revolutionary situation underwent, sparked by the coup of 25 April 1974.

Notwithstanding this large number of people who were joining the Trade movement, by winter 1975, the Intersindical had around one million members.

Even in the heady days just before 25 November, the workers' commissions were more powerful than the unions, even when the unions acted together.

As a member of the workers' commission of Setenave remarked to the film-director Daniel Edinger on the national structure of the workers' commissions, whoever dominates such a structure effectively dominates the country.[12] Between October 1974 and January 1975, the Communists invested a great deal of effort into the establishment of a single trade union confederation (the Intersindical), which they saw as a counterweight to the workers commissions. This culminated in a massive demonstration, an 'immense sea of people' on 14 January 1975; the demands were against unemployment and the cost of living, and against the monopolies and the *latifúndios* (the large landowners).

The call for unity was extremely powerful. The Communist Party sought to convince the workers of the need for union unity through a single union federation, (*unicidade*). In effect, this federation was the Intersindical.[13] There were many examples of this policy in *Avante!* The same is true of *Alavanca*, the press agency of Intersindical, run for a time by Avelino Gonçalves himself (a member of the Communist Party and Minister of Labour of the Interim Government). The first issue of the *Alavanca* came out in December 1974, focusing precisely on the battle for unity: 'Peace and Unity of Union', 'There is no place in the context of the Portuguese Society for Union Pluralism', 'More Power to Unity', 'If it's not the Union, dismiss them as dogs'.[14]

On 16 January 1975, another important counter-demonstration in defence of unions took place but this was for *unicity* – and against a single monopolistic union structure. The prime organisers were the Socialist Party, who had a presence within some unions, often accompanied by the virulent anti-Stalinist MRPP party. The Socialist Party advocated union pluralism, that is, the existence of more than one central union. (The UGT, which was established in 1978, would also in fact be a Socialist Party transmission belt.)

The argument for unity, 'united we will win – divided we fall', is often presented as something to be had at all costs and was often used by both the Communist Party and the Socialist Party, but to different ends. In certain contexts, it acted as a lowest common denominator; it was used to blunt the struggles of the most militant sectors. The Union Associations Act – which provided for *unicidade* – was approved by the Council of the Revolution on 30 April 1975. Despite the danger of neo-corporatism, in this case of imposing a form of organisation of workers through the State, *unicidade* was widely supported by workers as it was part of the consciousness of the workers. For this reason, many of the workers' commissions either had no stance against *unicidade* and a united trade union federation, or they even supported it.

This was despite the fact that the Intersindical often acted against the interests of those who were leading day-to-day struggles. Workers' commissions were not a nationally organised alternative, although often in factories they were a force that nullified that of the central trade union, as we have pointed out. There was a colossal difference between their power, widespread in companies and factories, with much greater penetration than that of Intersindical, and the embryonic and 'beardless' union organisation. However, the Intersindical did mature, partly because it had brought together many experienced militants: at the national level, it developed an infrastructure with delegates, headquarters, staff and funds.

At the Congress of Trade Unions held on 25–27 July 1975, the majority of the attendees[15] approved the National Intersindical Statutes, which prohibited the right of tendency (in other words, to have organised factions), which made it almost impossible to resolve internal leadership disputes, and ultimately tied the unions to government policy. Congress decided to support a political programme for the unions that accepted the 'sacrifices of the workers', as long as they also combated 'economic sabotage', fighting for the extension of social rights and defended the 'Battle for Production'.[16]

The Workers' Commissions and the Communist Party

I have already suggested that after 7 February the Inter-Empresas had been losing ground – with the emergence of the unions being one factor. As important, or possibly more important, was the change of tack by the Communist Party towards workers' commissions. After the victory of *unicidade*, formalised with the statement of 14 January 1975, the Communist Party changed its policy: it began to both recognise the importance of the workers' commissions and to dispute the leadership of the workers' commissions locally in workplaces. The Communist Party was able to coordinate nationally as well. The decision was made to convene the First National Unitary Conference of Workers, held on 2 February 1975, at the Instituto Superior Técnico. This was ostensibly a 'non-party' conference and was attended by 191 workers' commissions from the whole country.

One outcome was the creation of a National Commission for the defence of workplaces, 'considering that in its objectives it intends to maintain relations with the worker's commission and conduct studies of situations on a case-by-case basis, to propose adequate solutions'.[17] The hitherto bellicose tone towards the commissions was replaced by appeals to unity.[18]

In connection with this theme, Eduardo Pires, leader of a Maoist organisation, the UDP, questioned the strength of the revolutionaries in the shipyards of Lisnave in 1974 and asks why they lost that influence in 1975. He points out, among other reasons, that by 25 April 1974, many of the best cadres of the Communist Party in Lisnave, had been persecuted in the repression of 1972–1973 and had been sacked. After 25 April, they gradually returned, often from exile, and were to be reintegrated into the company. There was another factor to be considered. The far-left, clung to the idea put forward by the Communist Party that fascism was still a threat, and it maintained semi-clandestine recruitment structures, whereas 'the Communist Party set up recruiting tents at the entrance to the shipyards in broad daylight.'[19] Interestingly, the potential threat of 'reaction' – of the return of 'fascism – was used as an argument throughout the period of the revolution' – and to obtain support for the governments (and the MFA in particular). It suited the MFA to play up the wickedness of the old regime and to label it as being fascist.[20]

Above all, the Communist Party had developed a strategy of fighting from within and attempting to win over the workers' commissions: 'In this period the Communist Party took control of the workers' commissions in various enterprises such as Lisnave, Siderurgia, Efacec (but this took a long time) and Sorefame. It had the majority of factories. When it took control, it allied the workers' commissions with the Intersindical.'[21]

Carlos Nunes, a PRP militant and a delegate to the 'ad hoc' workers' commission of Lisnave in May/June 1974, describes how the Communist Party gained control at Lisnave:

The Communist Party had stepped up its level of aggression and repression in factories, even resorting to physical means … meetings being manipulated so that only Communist Party members or people on their side were permitted to speak. They went around with lists of those to be supported, nudging people which way to vote.

So a new secretariat was elected comprising six members of the Communist Party, four from the Socialist Party and one or two of the revolutionary left.[22]

Workers' commissions affirm themselves as the essential structure of workers' organisation. Arising in the heat of struggle, assembling processes and presenting demands, they appear as the natural way to win wage and working condition conflicts and are an essential part of the repertoire of the working class's forms of struggle. Looking at the struggles, we see that the unions had a very limited role, acting as the vanguard of the struggles in just two sectors. These were the woolworkers and the metalworkers, two sectors with trade unions from a strong tradition of struggle and with oppositionist leadership, which had the confidence of the workers.[23]

Miguel Pérez, a scholar of workers' commissions, states that in 1976, the only reliable study carried out by the Communist Party on the number of commissions was quoted by Álvaro Cunhal in the report to the Eighth Congress of the Party.[24] Excluding Braga and Bragança there were around 1,250 workers' commissions throughout the country in 1976, about half in the district of Lisbon. According to this data, the Communist Party line would predominate with 56 per cent and unitary proposals with the participation of the Communist Party with 26 per cent. Other authors (Peter Robinson, Phil Mailer) show higher numbers, ranging from 2,500 to 4,000, probably because they refer to events prior to 25 November 1975, but they do not indicate the sources for the numbers we have quoted here.[25]

Table 10.1   Number of workers' commissions in Portugal

Source	Number	Geographic terrain
Álvaro Cunhal 1976	1,250	About half in the district of Lisbon (with the exception of the districts of Braga and Bragança).
Peter Robinson 1974–75	2,500	The whole country
Phil Mailer 1974–75	4,000	The whole country

During March, April and May 1975, the Communist Party's policy of the Battle for Production to avoid workers' control alienated it from the influence of the workers' commissions, which in the metalworking sector began to be organised by sector – this would disrupt the stability of the Fourth Government, which could not resist despite the efforts of all parties to limit or prevent workers' control. The government fell. The organisation of workers' commissions and workers' control developed considerably in this period[26] (see Chapter 12, on Workers' Control and 11 March).

Table 10.2   The Communist Party, the Workers' Commissions and the Intersindical

25–29 April	Military coup; negotiation at the entrance to the PCP in the First Provisional Government.
29 April–February 1975	Construction of Intersindical, attempt to erase the workers' commissions.
February 1975–May 1975	(inconclusive data). Unitary Conference of Workers, attempt to pull in the direction of the workers commissions.
May 1975	Opposition to workers' control, struggle for the Battle for Production, loss of influence in the workers commissions.

Workers' control and the resulting labour conflicts would have an impact on the elections that took place in various unions in summer 1975. The Socialist Party teamed up with sectors of the revolutionaries (mainly AOC and MRPP) in several firms and managed to win elections and make gains from the Communist Party. This included some highly significant sectors, such as the Lisbon Banking Union (which would become central to the formation of an alternative trade union centre, the UGT, in the post-revolution period). Similar electoral gains took place in the high school and university student associations.[27] The Communist Party would admit, as early as October 1975, in *O Militante*:

> In recent months, there has been witnessed the temporary passage of several trade unions into the hands of the enemy of the unitary trade union movement.
>
> In the same vein as the sabotaging incidents of unitary labour in the trade unions and the strengthening of workers' unity, capitalist and reactionary forces with left-wing or ultra-leftist affiliation have now targeted the bankers (after the chemical, the hotel, the metal industries) to foment the division ...[28]

'Here is the Nursery' – Urban Struggles and Residents' Commissions

The canteen, which up until now served poor children, as if it were a charity, had to end and begin to serve everyone.

Lavradio-Barreiro[1]

Dirt, potholes, children playing in the street, shacks squeezed shoulder to shoulder. The scene is of Quinta das Fonsecas, but it could be in any other slum in Greater Lisbon or Porto. The industrialisation of the 1950s and especially the 1960s, required a proletariat and generated a movement from the countryside to the city (partly prompted by agricultural mechanisation).[2] The increase in the working population changed the shape of the cities through the growth of large areas of poor working-class neighbourhoods – the so-called neighbourhoods of shacks or slums – where the population would 'never feel comfortable'. And even before 25 April, this exposure of poverty to the eyes of everyone – how many of these neighbourhoods weren't in central parts of the cities? – had a political impact. It was a 'little hell of solitude, discomfort, poor hygiene – in sum, abandonment,'[3] as an RTP host would later say in a visit to Quinta das Fonsecas, after 25 April 1974.

According to various sources, only about 40 per cent of homes in the country have access to running water and sewage systems, while in the outskirts of Lisbon and Setúbal, slums are proliferating without the most elementary conditions. The precariousness of these areas of shack housing was cruelly laid bare in the floods of 25 November 1967, which caused hundreds of deaths. In Porto, the example of precarious housing *par excellence* was the 'islands', a traditional form of accommodation for poor families that has existed since the earliest times of the city's industrialisation.[4]

Essentially, all of the sources tell of a degraded housing stock for one-quarter of the population in working-class, and even some middle-class neighbourhoods. There were reports of streets to be paved, deficient sewers and a lack of basic services like pharmacies. There was an industry around property and 'subleasing', which speculated on a basic necessity of the population, the right to live in a decent space. All this became the target of anger and popular protests in 1974–1975.

Since 1965[5] there had been a new market, a market for land, which was privately developed. Until 1965 the difference in valuation between an agricultural/rural/undeveloped plot and an urban one was regulated by the State. With the transfer of large populations from the countryside to the city, the Salazar government opened up space for a new private sector.[6] This made the cost of housing skyrocket. It was not just the cost of construction that rose considerably, but also the ground rent.

Profits were checked during the revolution by one of the processes of dual power that first emerged and spread quickly: the housing occupations. The occupations, which spanned the entire country, led to a historic decline in the value of land property. A reduction of housing costs meant that in effect workers' wages increased indirectly in this period.

Just three days after the 25 April coup, residents of the neighbourhood of Boavista, in Lisbon, occupied a housing estate and refused to leave, despite being intimidated by the MFA. In Porto, it began in Bairro São João de Deus, with a plenary on 27 April 1974. In the Ajuda area of Lisbon, Bairro Salazar was renamed Bairro 2 May, in reference to the date of that occupation. In the capital, between 1,500 and 2,000 units of public housing were occupied in the first ten days.[7] These would be the first of hundreds of housing occupations, to be followed by an urban movement of a social and political nature, which evolved from demands linked to the question of housing and mobility conditions, hygiene and childcare (nurseries, etc.), into the political questioning of state housing options and property, and even into a confrontation with the very notion of local government boundaries and authority, which accelerated in the second half of 1975.

In Nova Oeiras, in the suburban outskirts of Lisbon, the population decried the lack of nurseries. Those that existed cost 1,500 escudos per month, completely incompatible with a worker's salary. They decided, therefore, to occupy a vacant house where: 'we began our struggle for this nursery in order to serve the people ... in just two days 23 children were signed up, with ages between one month and six years'.[8]

In Chelas, one young man explained how one occupation took place:

The occupation began last Saturday, at 7 in the afternoon. We entered into the buildings and broke down two, three doors, that weren't open, which we promised to pay for. Two buildings were occupied with seven stories each with three homes on each floor. There are 23 families. They also occupied the storage, the porter's house, because the need for housing is so bad that nothing escaped [laughter]. After that we informed COPCON, they guaranteed that they wouldn't interfere, we know that the builder had gone to them, but COPCON didn't intervene. On Sunday he came with the police, we talked, but we didn't come to any conclusion.[9]

Dows tells us that:

A special problem arose when an occupied house belonged to an emigrant worker, or was the main source of income for an elderly person; in such cases occupiers were sometimes evicted, and it became accepted practice not to touch the house. This practice was made easier when COPCON began to keep a list of such houses: when someone wanted to occupy a house, they checked the list; if the house was unlisted, the occupation took place and was registered.[10]

Replacing City Councils

We touched upon the *comissão de moraderes* – residents' commissions – in Chapter 3. It must be stressed that these were authentic 'organs of local decision-making'. The residents' commissions arose almost immediately as a structure for making local decisions:

The formation of a particular Residents' Committee normally involves holding an assembly or plenary with residents of the area in question, almost always on the initiative of residents who are more politicised or linked to left groups. These first meetings elect a committee, with various shapes and sizes, and approve a document in which they state the people's most pressing demands.[11]

As the revolution proceeded, they acted as a parallel power in the face of the reorganisation of city councils. The city councils had largely been dominated by cadres aligned with the Communist Party and the MDP/CDE (which was generally considered to be Communist Party front). The Communist Party in fact would continue to resist holding elections during the entire process, despite pressure from the Socialist Party.[12] The city councils had little power when it came to the question of housing (accommodations, cultural spaces) and there were strong tensions between many of these processes. In the end, the city councils served more as an arm of the state apparatus – and as a source of cadres and financing for the main parties (especially, at the time, for the Socialist Party and Communist Party), than as organs of local management. Local management was taken on by the residents' commissions bypassing local authority structures and often in direct contact with the MFA. Hence, there are many stories of the residents' commissions occupying a building and simply getting the MFA to endorse the act. At other times, the occupation was accomplished with members of the armed forces accompanying the members from the residents' commission.

The residents' commissions, organising in various ways, emerged in parallel with the workers' commissions. These two forms of organisation were the first bodies to present and develop an alternative power.[13] Like all phenomena of dual power in a revolutionary process, they were largely spontaneous, but they were also influenced by political struggles, and it was often the case that their leaders were associated with political parties. The idea that the residents' commission was political, but non-party political, was 'a hard fought for and staunchly defended position. Thus, militants or sympathisers of different parties – left, right, or centre – and the majority without party allegiance could work together, united by their acts, instead of being divided by their words'.[14]

Some of the established local government administrative structures were opposed to the demands from the radical commissions that questioned land property ownership. Pedro Ramos Pinto[15] calculated that roughly one-third of the residents' commissions in Lisbon had a more radical stance.

Most of the demands faced by the residents' commissions were emergencies such as: the right to housing (keeping the population in the same location or neighbourhood); nurseries and daycare; and basic sanitation. The commissions were organised by neighbourhood – and not necessarily administrative divisions, as in the case of parishes[16] – and therefore they had a dimension that generated solidarity and harnessed conflicts, in the area of communal life outside the workplace.

The occupations began in the council housing, where the scarce distribution of houses had been a target for corruption. But beginning in the middle of 1975, the occupations spread to the vacant houses around the country and they began to question the cost of rent, imposing limits based on the average worker's wage. Between January and March 1975, due to the increase in occupations and the growing crisis of the State, the first coordinating bodies emerged. Among them were the Central Committee of residents' commissions of Council-Housing Neighbourhoods of Porto, created on 14 December 1974; the inter-commissions of poor neighbourhoods and slums of Lisbon, created in January 1975, which had 18-member residents' commissions; the inter-commissions of the neighbourhoods of shanty towns in Setúbal, in February 1975. In March 1975, there were 57 residents' commissions in Lisbon, capable of mobilising thousands of residents.

Government Responses

The Provisional Government attempted to react, first by trying to prohibit the occupations. It released dozens of statements and issued threats in the press during the first months, trying to prevent the housing occupations. In one statement, the Ministry of Social Communication published a note declaring: 'It was found yesterday in Lisbon that some families living in precarious conditions, having been misinformed, have wrongfully occupied vacant housing, convinced that they were allowed to do this ... Disobedience may bring about grave consequences.'[17]

They did not happen. On the contrary, threats were to be in vain – even generating, in some cases, a growing opposition to the government. Government then changed tack. It created an emergency programme to try to resolve the most pressing problems in the slums and maintain a more structured link between the residents' commissions and the State.

Thus, the SAAL (Serviço de Apoio Ambulatório Local) programme was created.[18] SAAL was funded through an order from the Ministries of Internal Administration and Social Welfare and the Environment, on 4 August 1974. It was primarily aimed at helping through 'the City Councils' the initiatives of poorly housed populations, in the sense of contributing to the transformation of their own neighbourhoods'. The idea underlying the formation of SAAL was based on the experiences in Latin America, which utilised processes of self-construction. Although this was not its objective, the SAAL Project also tried to tackle the question of unemployment by using volunteer labour, since unemployment had been created as a counter-cyclical measure against the crisis of 1973 (laying off workers or closing factories completely in order to reverse the fall in the average rate of profit). This aspect of unpaid volunteers was the target of biting criticisms from various residents' committees, while others saw it as a means to involve residents in their own social process. SAAL included different dimensions such as cultural, associative and political revitalisation.

SAAL would be very connected to various residents' committees, although it was a controversial programme that received many criticisms from certain political quarters, as one of its founders and creators, Nuno Portas recalls.[19] While residents could enjoy the financial and technical support of SAAL, the underlying political dynamic of SAAL was to suppress the formal self-organisation of residents and thus quench a vital component of dual power. Although the figures are not clear, it is worth noting that the majority of residents' commissions were not affected by SAAL.

One thing that stands out during SAAL was the formal recognition, under the auspices of the programme, of 131 residents' associations; around 40 hectares of land acquired and 4,000 houses delivered to residents. It is important to highlight – because the memory of a post-revolutionary nation, created mainly by the victors of the counter-revolutionary coup of democratic-parliamentary stabilisation, continues to associate the revolution with 'chaos' – that an audit of SAAL's accounts carried out years later detected no irregularities 'with respect to the management of monies given by the government to the cooperatives and residents' associations'.[20]

In his post-revolutionary assessment of SAAL, the architect Nuno Portas argued that, among the various causes of SAAL's problems, one was the short period that the revolutionary process lasted. This did not allow a great number of the houses that were planned to be built. During the Estado Novo, the average time between the decision of the Fundo de Fomento and the completion of the house was seven years and, writes Nuno Portas, even if this time were reduced, it could never have been less than two years.[21] Effectively, Portugal at the time was building about one-third of homes needed. This scarcity was due to the dependence of the construction sector on 'cyclical crises in the civil construction sector, almost always characterised by bankruptcies and business mergers'.[22]

February 1975 Onwards

The government had no way to resolve, physically, the problem of giving homes to the population through social housing because of the time and resources that this would require. They understand this because they saw 'so many people without homes and so many homes without people'. Those who lived for so long in shacks and now had the strength and optimism of a revolution would not wait. From February 1975, the housing occupations spread to vacant houses (small and medium properties), the price of rents began to be questioned, and the government did not know what to do.

I suggest that this process, together with the process of workplace occupations/workers' control is what precipitated the desperate failed right-wing coup of 11 March 1975. The post-11 March social reforms were not an offer from the Revolutionary Council, as some histories would have it, especially as constructed by the Communist Party. On the contrary, the coup was the result of the social revolution that took place in workplaces and neighbourhoods. The defeat of reaction on 11 March 1975 only gave more impetus to a process that had begun before and it was with great difficulty that the Revolutionary Council tried to hold it back, not with prohibitions and police measures, but with concessions in the area of social rights and with a call from worker-controlled businesses for nationalisation.

The occupations of vacant houses became more systematic. Note the account of a resident in February 1975: 'The people took over the house, and the neighborhood discussed in an organised way which families would go, meeting two criteria: first, not being afraid, second, being in need, because there were those who needed it but wouldn't risk it.'[23]

Many property owners reacted individually, renting the houses at very low prices to prevent them from being occupied. The government reacted as well, deeming occupations unacceptable: 'The Military Police of the Military Region of Porto has visited the occupied houses to inform that within days appropriate legislation will be passed, it being anticipated that, in many cases, these occupations will not be permitted to occur.'[24]

Therein was the crisis of the State. Properties were occupied, the cost of rent consequently fell, the State sent in the Military Police to 'inform' the owners, the authorisation is written retrospectively, and the 'authorities' were unable, in many cases, to suspend the occupations. Many commissions began to organise alternative popular tribunals where they decided, regardless of the State, the justice of these occupations: 'In the face of the government attack, the participants strengthen their positions. In July (1975) the first case against a participant (in Setúbal) is brought before the tribunal. A demonstration is organised against the judgment which culminates in solidarity from the workers in the Tribunal, including the judge.'[25]

In March 1975, the government tried to accommodate the occupations of vacant houses with legislation that allowed such occupations under certain conditions (social emergency, abandonment of the house, but everything carried out jointly with the ministries). In some zones, they asked the residents' commissions to take a survey of the empty houses and give it to the respective parish board.[26]

In Setúbal, the City Council was overtaken by a particular political event. On 7 March, there was a PPD rally and a counter-demonstration with a few hundred people. The PSP – the public security police – opened fire and killed a worker, wounding others. The people reacted immediately, forming a large demonstration surrounding the PSP offices. The army closed the station and replaced its garrison, but it could not prevent this case from having a political impact throughout the city, because the use of repression meant that the civil authorities had lost legitimacy. This had a knock-on effect upon the occupation of properties. '[After March 7] one could walk on the street and see families with bundles on their back in search of a house to enter'.[27] The Fifth Division, (which was a wing of the MFA responsible for 'cultural dynamisation' and generally close to views of the Communist Party) called for a meeting where it condemned what it considered to be the 'savage housing occupations', but it lacked the social force to reverse them. The Government would be forced to pass a decree suspending the evictions and legalising the occupations that had already taken place.

In Porto, a crisis occurred in the management of the City Council, thanks to a strike of municipal workers and the residents' protests, which led to the dismissal of the council's Administrative Commission. The same city council had been surrounded by the people immediately after 25 April because the police, fleeing the protests, had taken refuge there. On 5 April 1975, a grand plenary of residents' commissions was held in the Crystal Palace.[28]

In Setúbal, a campaign spread after May 1975 calling for a rent cap of 500 escudos per bedroom (the minimum wage at the time was 4,400 escudos per month). This struggle reached more than 1,500 families and from it, a Residents' Council emerged that placed a programme on the agenda calling private property into question.

Chip Dows, based on the study that he conducted for the city of Setúbal, located the origins of the housing problem to the price of land. In Setúbal, there were 1,152 shacks, but in addition 520 houses were completed and more than 3,000 nearing completion (many only lacked a habitation license). In addition, there were vacant houses that maintained the high rents – because if they were placed on the market, they would make housing prices fall. The rents in the city of Setúbal, between 1970 and 1975, rose between 130 per cent and 140 per cent. Therefore, concludes the author, 'the development of civil construction did not resolve the housing question, because the price of the houses that were constructed did not allow more than 30 per cent of the population to have access to them'.[29]

Table 11.1   Rental market in Setúbal 1970–1975

	1970	*1975*	*percentage increase*
T2	1,130 escudos	3,160 escudos	137.6
T3	1,540 escudos	3,730 escudos	142.2
T4	1,870 escudos	4,500 escudos	140.6
Average per bedroom	–	–	142.9

Source: Chip Dows, *Os Moradores à Conquista da Cidade* (Lisbon: Armazém das Letras, 1978).

Local power effectively existed as a parallel power to the State, and this is a vital facet of a revolution, as Charles Tilly reminds us.[30] The inevitability of the need to take power into ones' own hands is illustrated well in an interview with the Residents' Committee of the 25 April Cooperative in Lisbon, where a resident admitted in September 1975 to the cameras:

> Thanks to stalling by the governments, city councils, boards, there has been a demobilisation because the people start not to see their problems resolved (in the most elementary things like water or energy), since the city council gives us absolutely no solutions at all. Either there aren't enough workers, or there isn't enough money ... We solved the problem, resolving things through the unemployed brigades. But the city council tries everything not to move forward with the fair aspirations of the people.

> Journalist: What is your plan? Naturally, all these areas with under-installation will require a profound conversion.

> In our booklet of demands, two of the demands we made on the government, and they are really fundamental, were the construction of houses, which is reflected in two ways: either though the cooperatives and associations or by demanding public housing. This is only being followed in public housing, not through the cooperatives, because the government either doesn't give us the funding or doesn't give us the loans.[31]

It is the extent of this dual power – organic or inorganic, embryonic or organised or even nationally coordinated/organised – that is under discussion, and not whether it existed or not. The biggest question is how far it went and what forms it took on, what shape this parallel power to the State had – in other words, what was the extent of the State's incapacity to impose its power.

Extending Local Power

The crisis of the State itself – exacerbated by the existence of this dual power over the management of community life and the housing stock – would give more force to the phenomenon of local forms of power. This was reflected between March and July 1975 in the formation of 66 new residents' commissions in Lisbon. Also, as a result of this situation, a new organisation of commissions involved in occupations was formed, in Lisbon and Porto, called CRAMO (Comissões Revolucionárias Autónomas de Moradores, or Autonomous Revolutionary Residents' Committees). The PRP and UDP were heavily involved. The CRAMOs, with the support of SAAL commissions in Lisbon and Porto, began to organise a simultaneous demonstration for 17 May 1975.[32]

These demonstrations, which called for the rejection of the Decree 198 A-75, which condemned the occupation of houses, allowing the occupiers to be expelled, as well as the imprisonment of the future ones were enormous (considered one of the largest demonstrations of the entire period) and united thousands of people with demands for housing. On the placards were slogans against subleasing – a phenomenon in which one dwelling held several families, houses that were over-occupied and lacked hygiene – but there were also placards against self-construction (and the unpaid labour associated with it) and for lower rents.

Another woman from Quinta da Calçada, chubby, in a smock, was interviewed on camera and she talks about:

> The bureaucracy that we've run into! Since the beginning of the inter-committees, we've run into every obstacle. One time it's because there's nobody who wants to work, another time it's because there's no money, another time it's because the money is frozen. I've already told them that if the money didn't get unfrozen now in the summer, it'll be even worse in the winter, it starts to get cold, then it'll be even more frozen.[33]

Dows documents later attempts to form a more general type of coordinating body representing all the residents of the city, and capable of dealing with many problems. Two such residents' councils were formed in June 1975 – one in Setúbal and one in Porto – but in neither city was this project alone enough to sustain the coordination.[34]

In June, there were already residents' commissions that, beyond being sites of struggle for housing and accommodation, considered themselves 'schools of revolution', who called for unity with sailors and soldiers. Other organisational infrastructures uniting residents' commissions with other types of organisation emerged. One model was for residents' commissions to come together with workers' commissions and the local barracks, and we will see later how this was articulated through the Popular Assemblies, in particular that from the Pontinha barracks. Pontinha happened to be the same barracks, which was Otelo's operational base for the 25 April coup.

12

Workers' Control, 11 March and Nationalisations

There will not be workers' control if we merely intend to run the bosses' businesses.[1]

Shipyard worker, Lisnave shipyards, Margueira, 1975

Workers' Control

Workers' control is one of the most interesting but least studied phenomena of Portugal's revolutionary period. That is obviously a paradox because the existence of workers' control is one of the criteria for defining a period as being revolutionary.

In the social fracas, starting from 25 April 1974, battles for workers' control existed in the form of radical protests (strikes, kidnappings and occupations). Such conflict, which is not the same thing as trade union demands (better wages, etc.), was at its sharpest, above all, in the sphere of combat that forced the sackings (*saneomento*) of managers and foremen. Initially, the focus was still on personnel and company structure and not the political power of the State, nor gaining of total control over production.[2]

A new period of strikes was registered from February 1975 onwards, reflecting the process of the radicalisation of the revolution in which there were growing social conflicts in general.[3] This period is marked by the proliferation of organs of dual power[4] (at this stage, mainly workers' and residents' commissions[5]), by the development of land occupations in the South from February 1975 onwards and the demand for nationalisation of the financial system led by the bank workers. This last demand was also echoed by workers in the largest companies, including the important CUF corporate group. In this period, there were strikes in dozens of factories and businesses. Strikes at TAP, in chemical companies and a general strike in the high schools that continued for nearly a month were particularly noteworthy.[6] The conflict at Rádio Renascença, with successive shutdowns and occupations by the workers, also began in this period.[7]

From April 1974 to February 1975, the conflicts taking place in the companies, in essence focused upon demands and reorganisation inside the workplaces. Workers' control demands were being formulated, emerging from the more militant workplaces. They were sometimes restricted to certain sections of a company as was the case with TAP. In other places, it reached across the whole works (Lisnave, *Jornal do Comércio*). Even then, it was quite limited in terms of the national panorama.

11 March

In March 1975, as in September 1974, sections of the ruling class saw a military coup as the necessary response to radicalisation. The 11 March coup was a desperate and vigorous attempt on the part of the bourgeoisie to overthrow the revolution precisely because the threat of workers power was on the increase, especially in the schools (with the February strike in higher secondary education), in the neighbourhoods, with the explosion of residents' movements starting in February 1975, and with the flourishing of workers' takeovers and control itself.

The March conspirators included the businessman Miguel Champalimaud (of the conglomerate by that name) and several high-ranking military officers who had connections with Spínola. On 11 March two Harvard T-6 trainer planes and three helicopter gunships from the Tancos airbase strafed the RAL-1 barracks in Lisbon, killing one soldier (Soldado Luís) and wounding 14 others. Paratroopers surrounded the barracks but could not be persuaded to fire. Fierce discussions broke out between the two camps and, within hours, the paratroopers were explaining to the RAL-1 soldiers 'we are no fascists – we are your comrades'.

The organisation of military resistance to the coup attempt of 11 March was led by COPCON, which had some forewarning and was on the alert. Working people responded magnificently. Within hours of the attack, barricades were set up along the main roads, sometimes using expropriated bulldozers, lorries and cement mixers. Soldiers fraternised openly with workers manning the barricades and handed over arms. Armed workers searched cars, and strikers at Rádio Renascença went back to work and occupied the radio station in order to 'defend the revolution'. Many papers printed second editions or special broadsheets, including the workers' committee of the big Lisbon daily *O Século*. This reported how the Porto section of the union of bank employees commanded its members to 'Close the banks immediately. Don't make any payments. Set up pickets at the doors to check entrances and exits. Watch the telex and the telephones.' (On the following day, the MFA Revolutionary Council was set up and it immediately announced the nationalisation of the banks with the exception of foreign banks.)

Although 11 March was an amateurish and a rather desperate affair, it succeeded brilliantly in cementing the alliance between soldiers and workers. After the failure of the coup, right-wing generals and some company directors were arrested. The former President Spínola and others were whisked off to Spain 'by the helicopters of reaction'.

The coup exacerbated the crisis of the State, opening the way for even fiercer debates about workers' control in all the country's major companies. It was not the political crisis of 11 March that gave rise to workers' control; it was the struggle in the factories and companies which precipitated the botched coup.

The acceleration of the wider political struggle led, in turn, to increased militancy in the workplaces. The demands often emerged out of occupations, which took place all over and everywhere.

After 11 March, workers' control became a major topic of debate in all the major companies as shown by Fátima Patriarca's research of the documents of some of those companies, registering workers' plenary discussions and those of the workers' commissions. Here are two examples.

SAPEC

Prior to 25 April, there had already been some incidents of strife and even 'sackings due to intervention of the PIDE' at the Belgian-owned fertiliser company SAPEC, which employed 1,000 people. After 25 April, the first demands were for wage increases and 'standardisation of social benefits'. There was a protest, a workers' commission was elected and the workers opposed the distribution of dividends. The workplace was occupied on 25 June. One of the reasons for this confrontation was that the company administration wanted to transfer a massive amount (11 million escudos) to its headquarters in Brussels supposedly to pay out dividends; a withdrawal that would put the workers payments at risk.

In front of the television cameras, one worker with thick hair and large spectacles that were the fashion at the time, recalled that one of the most important points had been the demand to purge Dr Manuel Sanchez Ingles Esquivel, former civil governor of Setúbal, because: 'He was an individual linked to the fascist regime and so he had acquired capital because of his good relations with that government'.[8]

At SAPEC, the workers opposed the refusal of the 'administration to cut down on superfluous spending' and were against the salary increases for service managers, which the workers alleged were precisely an example of such 'superfluous spending'. They proudly remembered how throughout the occupation the company never stopped production. It was the second most important in the country in fertiliser production and the first in pesticides and it produced and sold animal feeds, fruit tree seedlings and seeds and offered crop spraying services.[9]

Finally, the reporter asked the worker what the result of their recent meeting with the government had been and he came out with this succinct retort 'We won, it is not the least bit surprising that we won'.[10]

The Lisbon International Fair

In summer 1975, the *Feira Internacional de Lisboa* (Lisbon International Fair, FIL), a centre *par excellence* of the country's business activity, was in the hands of the workers.

This year, the FIL workers, by taking the organisation of the fair into their own hands and occupying the respective installations, rescued it from a situation that could have jeopardised its specific function even further, given the country's economic context. The fair brought in more revenue than the year before and its stands were visited by around 260,000 people.[11]

The impetus of the social struggle that questioned capital accumulation and turnover and the pressure in favour of the Battle for Production were two contradictory positions, nevertheless, they were subjectively assimilated by most of the workers. The case of the FIL is a good illustration of that phenomenon. The workers occupied the FIL but maintained their spirit of production-ism taking pride in the tremendous effort with which they had 'set up the Fair in just one and a half months whereas previously it had taken two and a half months'. The spirit was clearly visible throughout the Fair, which was full of machinery, many metallurgy and metalworking exhibits and agricultural implements.

A young worker spoke before the RTP television cameras. She was attractive and sure of herself, which in itself was unusual. It was common practice for the television channels to interview many very poor people, illiterate or uneducated people, who would timidly utter poorly articulated phrases. Teresa said:

Our fight had been going on since before 25 April because part of the Associação Industrial Portuguesa [Portuguese Industrial Association] had set up a form of protection for the big economic groups in the Fair that we could not willingly accept because some were sons and others step-children. We put up a big fight but we were never listened to. After 25 April though, we could really speak out! On 25 April, there was a list of claims and demands regarding the types of wages and the definition of the FIL itself. That was one of the things we requested from the Association, our employer; that they should define, once and for all, what the goal of the FIL was and what direction it should take. It was a question that had always hung in the air and never been answered. Meanwhile there was the ongoing struggle of the workers here and accordingly there appeared this occupation of the Lisbon International Fair. ... The occupation took place because, apart from the problem of wages, there were loads of other internal problems, including those in the social aspect; there were no worker amenities, workers had to eat their meals alongside the toilets, I can tell you, (expression of shame) together with the rubbish, in short, a miserable situation. So on 9 May we occupied part of the exhibitors' area as a refectory.[12]

At that juncture, another worker joined in the conversation, leading the discussion to a more strategic field, which was something quite normal. In other words, apart from discussions of labour relations aspects, the objectives of the work being done was also questioned:

There is the aspect of Labour–Capital relations but there is also another fundamental problem which is not altogether dissociated from the first one and that is regarding the purpose of the Fair itself. We can see that the pavilions and stands belong to the AIP but the land belongs to the Council and it has a concession contract arrangement with the Association. Quite simply it must be seen that the workers increasingly felt the events that were held here, were not fulfilling the true purpose for which the installations were made. The FIL should be an event with promotional objectives alright, but those should not be disconnected from the revolutionary process the country is undergoing.[13]

Evolution of Workers' Control

We have already seen that there were a number of occupations which led to self-management. Sometimes this came about without an occupation, simply because the owners had abandoned the factories and farms. Hence, the proprietorship of the companies (maybe not legally) went into the hands of the workers themselves. Acts such as these were celebrated by the movement.[14] I have already suggested that self-management is not the same as workers' control. To quote a worker from the Lisnave Margueira shipyard: 'There will not be workers' control if we merely intend to run the bosses' businesses'[15] and that:

> If workers' control at the factory floor level is the working class's first step towards controlling the boss's administration, workers' control at the level of all shipyards, then at the level of the metalworking and mechanical branches and lastly at the level of all the workers' commissions throughout the country, are the second, third and fourth step that the class will take and that it needs to take to ensure that the bosses do not play cat and mouse with us.[16]

In her study of workers' control, Fátima Patriarca gives dozens of examples of communications issued by factory and company assemblies that rejected the Battle for Production proposal and argued in favour of workers' control, as a way of developing the workers' movement by creating leaders and class awareness and eventually abolishing the system of capitalist relations altogether. Lisnave's Conselho de Defesa dos Trabalhadores (Workers' Defence Council) rejected measures that it said were 'inserted in an economic battle that did not merely mean producing more'.

In May 1975, workers at the Sacor company, in the north, proposed that gas and fuel should be supplied to companies with economic problems where the bosses had fled and they defended the idea that workers' control could only be meaningful, if it 'leads to increased awareness (on the part of the workers), that is to say, if it enables them to increasingly see where their real interests lie and leads them on to the fundamental issue: the conquest of power'.[17]

Workers' control emerged in the companies to be nationalised, in the main metalworking and mechanical industrial companies and even in some other sectors. This went beyond the mere self-management, which had been established in some smaller companies and often included companies that had serious financial or production problems.

At the Sociedade Central de Cervejas, in May 1975, the workers made it clear:

> that the bosses continue to be fully accountable and paid for the work of administration. Workers' control is not going to solve all the workers' problems. It does not solve the workers' bread, wages or employment

problems. Other forms of organisation are needed that will lead the workers to take power. Workers' control will enable the workers to:

a) Take steps to thwart economic sabotage attempts.
b) Become progressively more prepared to take over political power.[18]

At the Iberonica company, in September 1975, 'workers demanded access to the accounts books and access to workers' control'.[19] A RTP reporter described the company's situation in front of the cameras:

We are here at the Iberonica, a small electronics company with just 12 workers and all the specific problems of small- and medium-sized companies. For a long time now, there has been a struggle between the 12 workers and the bosses represented by the managing partner of the company. In a few moments, the workers' commission will tell us briefly just what that struggle against reactionary bosses has been like.

One of the workers said:

Essentially, it can be summed up as follows. Already, before 25 April, the workers were considered to be agitators and communists, especially two members of the workers' commission and one female comrade. Later that became more acute with the advent of 25 April which he [the boss] could never accept. He started taking out massive amounts of money and doing crazy stuff in what was a genuine attempt to prevent the possibility of maintaining the workers in the company. He started off by sacking 20 workers ... And it got worse in December [1974] when he dismissed a female worker ... We went to the Ministry of Labour and those workers had to get their jobs back. This individual continued to make things worse and, in May, he tried to steal material for a friend of his. We went to the Ministry again and we began to exercise control in the company which we believed was workers' control but with the scaling up of the class war in Portugal, we realised that we were being deceived. As we were being deluded the boss did not even bother to show up at the company anymore; we suffered a total boycott of the boss, he stopped taking responsibility for anything, started to shout out loud that he was a reactionary fascist, took out more money, failed to attend a meeting at the Ministry of Labour on 18 August, that is, last month, so we decided to occupy the installations. Then he finally showed up at a meeting on 22 August. Our only demand is that the company should designate a manager to handle all this – we do not want to take over the management of the company or take possession of it; we just want that manager to run the company in complete agreement with the workers. A workers' commission taking genuine control over production, ... that is something he really does not want.

With few exceptions, it is possible to create a portrayal of workers' control in the revolution which it is divided essentially into three major periods: 1) atomised forms; 2) workers' control coordinated by sectors; and 3) workers' control disseminated at the national level and coordinated in an embryonic form at district and national levels.[20]

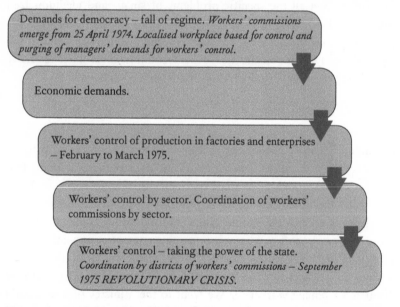

Figure 12.1   Evolution of Workers' Control in the Carnation Revolution.
Source: Fátima Patriarca charts the development of the debates around workers' control.

The Portuguese version of the 'biennio rosso' was one of the uncommon circumstances in the history of post-war twentieth century in which workers, and workers' control vied for power. We have suggested how worker self-management formulations, – whereby the workers become totally or partially their own bosses – may not take up the issue of State Power. Gramsci warned workers against the illusion that a simple factory occupation could solve the problem of power. He urged the workers to form 'a loyal armed force, ready for any eventuality' and an anonymous editorial (probably written by Gramsci) cautions readers:

A permanent establishment of the workers in the factories as self-governing producers rather than wage-earners is not possible unless other forces enter into play, forces which will completely displace the focus of the present struggle, which will carry the battle into other sectors, direct the workers' power against the real centres of the capitalist system: the means of communication, the banks, the armed forces, the state.[21]

Table 12.1 Illustration of the Workers' Control Debate in the Major Companies

Company	Source date	Objectives	Organisation and form of production control
Sorefame	4 March 1975	Purges, dismissals and demands.	
CT Socel	5–6 May 1975	Battle for Production. Control of Management.	
Ministry of Labour	7 May 1975	National productivity and reconstruction.	Co-management (unions).
State Department of Industry	7 May 1975	Socialism, education for workers to manage production directly.	Workers' control (workers' commissions and restructuring commissions). Critical of self-management.
Sacor (Workers Group)	May 1975	Socialism, workers' power/ dual power. Production to meet needs. Workers' control. Critical of self-management.	Workers' commissions.
Sociedade Central de Cervejas (workers group)	June/July 1975	Socialism, workers' power/ dual power. Production to meet needs. Workers' control. Critical of self-management.	Workers' commissions.
CDT Lisnave	14 July 1975	Socialism, workers' power/ dual power. Production to meet needs. Workers' control.	(National control commissions for the shipbuilding industry made up of workers' commissions delegates.)
CDT Lisnave	15 July 1975	Education for workers to manage production directly. Workers' control.	No references regarding organisation.
Lisnave (Margueira Group workers)	July 1975	National independence. Workers' control.	Rejection of co-management.
Textiles trade union leaders	30–31 July 1975	Power duality. Rejection of the Battle for Production, rejection of self- and co-management.	Union and workers' commissions.

continued

Company	Source date	Objectives	Organisation and form of production control
Ministry of Labour	August 1975	Production and management control articulated with the MFA's Programme/Government Planning. Guarantee austerity measures.	Production control commissions with workers' commissions and unions. Uncoordinated control factory by factory.
CCP Sorefame	September 1975	Education for workers to manage production directly.	
Ministry of Industry	Sixth Provisional Government (no date)	Government planning. Guarantee austerity measures.	Organisation yet to be defined. Uncoordinated factory-by-factory control.
National Congress of Workers' Commissions	27–28 September 1975	Socialism, Workers' control over all production extended to include all companies. Control factory by factory refused.	National coordination of all workers' commissions.
EFACEC	November 1975	Control over production to ensure production to meet needs.	No references.
CT of the Lisbon Industrial Belt	8 November 1975	Detailed control of all aspects of production without the aim of altering company proprietorship.	Workers' commissions with unions.
EFACEC	9 November 1975	Political control over production.	Control of all workers, rejection of self-management.
Constitution	April 1976	Control of management.	Workers' commissions.

Source: Fátima Patriarca, 'Controlo Operário em Portugal (I)', *Análise Social* 12(3) (1976): 765–816; and 'Controlo Operário em Portugal (II)', *Análise Social* 12(4) (1976): 1056–1057.

The Communist Party and Workers' Control

The Communist Party definition of workers' control was that it was a form of co-management organisation, possibly incorporating workers in all kinds of associative bodies – unions, associations, cooperatives, peasants leagues, residents' commissions and others, with a view to defending the revolution and ensuring the Battle for Production, 'the main battle front of the working class'.[22] It meant that such organisations participated (not controlled) alongside the unions in establishing the companies' plans, process, salary issues, etc.,[23] all strictly bound up with the overriding objective of the Battle for Production. The Communist Party relied heavily on the Intersindical to spread this message.

Thus, 'workers' control' was subservient to the Battle for Production. There was another policy attached to the latter, which was to curb what the Communist Party described as 'unrealistic demands' made by workers. At a Communist Party rally held on 18 May 1975 in Vila Franca de Xira, the general-secretary Álvaro Cunhal declared that: 'the great task of the moment was the "Battle for Production"' and it had to put an end to 'unrealistic demands' and the strikes. At another rally held on 28 June at Campo Pequeno, Veiga de Oliveira, communist Minister of Transport and Telecommunications in the Fourth Government, reminded people of the victories achieved with the nationalisation of the railways, of TAP, marine transport and dozens of road transport companies, and he criticised the wave of demands and strikes being called in those companies, which he said were 'sabotage' and 'reactionary'.[24]

That policy achieved a broad consensus in both the coalition and the Revolutionary Council in the MFA. The Socialist Party and the PPD declared that the difficult situation called for the contention of demands and claims;[25] Costa Gomes stated that work was 'a way of being with the revolution'.[26] Ramiro Correia announced that: 'political power necessarily involves the "Battle for Production"'.[27] Vasco Gonçalves's speech on Labour Day was perfectly in tune with Communist Party policy:

> At this moment, our economic crisis is the most important obstacle to overcome. It is our greatest difficulty, and the time we have to overcome it is limited. Or we recuperate, by ourselves, with our own effort, or we will seriously jeopardise the march of our revolutionary process and the future of our 'mother' country. Then we would see the return of fascism, of economic dependence, and the loss of liberties. Our fight is decisive. I hereby call on all workers, on all patriots, to engage in the Battle for Production because the future of the revolution depends on our victory in that battle. The Battle for Production is a necessary stage in overcoming the economic crisis and creating conditions for the future development of the economy along the road to socialism.[28]

The State and Workers' Control

In an effort to stem workers' control, the State Secretary for Labour Carlos Carvalhas put forward two draft bills designed to tighten control over the workers that would dispel the effects of real forms of workers' control.

In practice, the measures never came fully into effect. The first draft bill presented in May 1975 proposed the official constitution of control of production commissions that were to participate in company planning and 'foster the normal development and the qualitative and quantitative improvement of production'.[29] Article 5 of the second draft bill establishes that: 'the commissions' activities must never be directed against the global interests of the economy and consequently must never, in any circumstances, contribute to any paralysis of the company's regular production process'. The bill also stipulated that it was the production control commission's responsibility to 'ensure the fulfilment of the government programme for the sector'.[30] The Communist Party paper *Avante!* underscored that policy, announcing the creation of control commissions designed to guarantee the 'victory of the "Battle for Production"'.[31] The Socialist Party and the PPD also came out in favour, stating that the difficult situation required that the claims[32] should be curbed and that 'the way to political power is through the "Battle for Production"'.[33]

Some of the newly elected parliamentary representatives were against that strategy. A debate sprang up. A working document of the Fourth Provisional Government's State Department for Industry and Technology elaborated by João Martins Pereira opposed Carvalhas's arguments stating that:

> Control of production cannot be considered an end in itself but rather as a means, among others, to putting the socialist revolution into practice, or rather, to achieving it in the shortest possible time, while at the same time avoiding the well-known inconveniences of a 'nationalisation process' of the top-down type. Such an intervention is vital to 'oppose the pragmatic motivations of 'National Reconstruction' which postpone the revolution until such time as reconstruction has been completed (as was the case in Western European countries after the war).[34]

Nationalisations

The first nationalisation following the revolution took place just one month after the fall of the regime. On 21 May 1974, the workers at the *Companhia das Águas* (Water Company) occupied the company's offices and demanded that it should be nationalised. The name was changed to *Empresa Pública das Águas de Lisboa* (Lisbon Public Water Company, EPAL). Nationalisations, however, only started again after the victory of the enactment of the Law of Colonial Independence in summer 1974.

In September 1974, Decrees 450, 451 and 452/7 decreed the nationalisation of the *Banco de Portugal* (Bank of Portugal), *Banco de Angola* (Bank of Angola) and the *Banco Nacional Ultramarino* (National Overseas Bank) which, according to Medeiros Ferreira was 'the first step for the State to occupy the only place on the Portuguese side in the management of the financial consequences of decolonisation that had come about with the enactment of Law 7/74, dated 26 July'.[35]

Decolonisation had forced Portuguese capitalism to take refuge in centralisation to save as much as possible of its capital tied up in the colonies. One should not underestimate the role played by the revolutionary struggle in the metropolis in enforcing those measures; first, the very decolonisation process itself was determined by the revolutionary dynamics in the metropolis in the period after 25 April; then again, the bank workers' union had been involved in vigorous struggles since 25 April 1974 and in the aftermath of the defeat of the right-wing coup headed by general António de Spínola on 28 September 1974, the State increased its powers of inspection of credit institutions with the issuing of Decree540-A/74, dated 12 October 1974.

Most of the nationalisations were carried out between 11 March and May 1975. On 11 March 1975, bank workers occupying bank installations demanded the nationalisation of the banks. As we have already seen, on the next day, 12 March, the Revolutionary Council, which had been set up that very day, announced the nationalisation of the banks with the exception of foreign banks and on 24 March, it was the turn of the insurance companies. On 14 April, there were massive demonstrations in Porto and Lisbon in support of the bank nationalisations.[36] On 15 April, the Fourth Provisional Government decided to nationalise dozens of companies belonging to the expropriated financial groups, including companies in basic sectors like petroleum, electricity, gas, tobacco, breweries, steelworks, cement, marine transport, shipbuilding and repair, trucking, and urban and suburban collective transport. As we have mentioned, many of such companies were linked to the big economic groups that had grown extremely rich during the New State such as CUF, the Champalimaud group, the Espirito Santo Group, etc.

The nationalisation of the banks was not restricted to a mere nationalisation but was more of an expropriation because it was carried out without there being any compensation. It was a policy forcefully imposed on the political parties and the MFA by the workers who, in the dynamics of the revolution, obliged the Revolutionary Council and the Fourth Provisional Government to implement it by decree. It was the revolution that placed the nationalisations at the heart of Portuguese history. Neither the Communist Party nor the Socialist Party nor the MFA supported nationalisation as one of their strategies in the two-year period of 1974–1975. A fierce social struggle on the part of workers in the companies (among them, Central de Cervejas and Lisnave) broke out in an effort to achieve their nationalisation. The recession continued: inflation, galloping increases in food prices and transport fares and, above all, the presence of unemployment, which reached its height in that period, were vital factors.

The history of the nationalisations is fairly complex because they seem to have actually strengthened State power, while apparently taking it away from the companies. It has Bonapartist[37] aspects but they are contradictory insofar as the outcome of the nationalisations was the State's taking control of the companies with the double result of rescuing, in economic terms, companies that were in the middle of an economic recession, but at the same time safeguarding the property that objectively was about to be targeted by the workers who wanted workers' control. A political struggle broke out inside the companies, especially after March 1975. On the one hand, there were those who organised themselves in an endeavour to control production (and profits and wages as well) with the intention of 'the workers taking power'. (This position was strongly represented or was dominant in many factories.) Other groups of workers, influenced by the Communist Party and government thinking, took a defensive stance of favouring co-management involving combinations of administrators, workers and the State, and they tended to emphasise the defence of the 'national economy' and the 'Battle for Production' and to reject wage control, for example, and the nationalisation of foreign capital companies.

At the moment when the nationalisations took place, they represented the victory of the workers and a defeat for the capitalist system – a heightening of the class struggle that directly targeted private property. From then on, the history of the Revolution was to be the history of the extraordinary self-confidence that the workers and some parts of the intermediate sectors of society acquired, starting on 11 March 1975 – the day the right-wing coup was defeated and which led to the development of embryonic dual power bases. It was the confidence that they could win, that they could question the private ownership of the means of production and that confidence was to spread like wildfire throughout the country and was at the root of the crisis that began in July, the so-called Hot Summer.

A number of companies, including some reasonably large ones, managed to escape the wave of nationalisations, among them the cork processing, sugar refining, textiles and wine exporting industries, most of them located in the north of the country. (It was precisely through those companies that nucleuses of the new private groups, such as Américo Amorim, subsequently emerged.) The *Sector Empresarial do Estado* (State Business Sector, SEE) experienced a vigorous development after 11 March 1975, as Silva Lopes has recorded, with the State holding the positions of command or influence in the fields of transport, refineries, electricity, banking, etc.[38] It is estimated that, prior to the nationalisations, companies linked to the public sector employed two-thirds of the workforce that the SEE came to employ after the nationalisations. In the first year after the 1975 nationalisations, the SEE employed around 300,000 workers, equivalent to 8 per cent of the active population, and generated gross added value of somewhere between 20 and 25 per cent of the GNP. As Silva Lopes notes, Portugal ended up with one of the biggest corporate sectors in Western Europe, achieving a situation that was not unlike those of France, Italy, the United Kingdom and Germany. In those countries, the public sector employed, on average, 10 per cent of the workforce.[39]

The nationalisations were carried out in the context of a generalised, worldwide crisis of capital accumulation and to some extent the way they were carried out, without workers' control, suggests that the Portuguese bourgeoisie used the nationalisations as an expedient to 'lose the ring but save the fingers'. It was a way of putting an end to social conflicts inside the companies and rescue the companies from a financial crisis. That is confirmed by the rhetoric of the parties forming the government coalition who, without exception, appealed for an end to the struggles inside the nationalised companies, using the argument that the companies then belonged to the Portuguese people but omitting the fact that the State was still capitalist and so were the companies that it administered. Medeiros Ferreira, for example, argues that the nationalisations made it possible for the military to take control of the financial system[40] and Silva Lopes points out the effects that had on the economic situation.[41]

As mentioned above, in 1975, the nationalised companies employed 8 per cent of the active population. The nationalisations were made under pressure from the workers, who often came together in large meetings occupying the company installations and demanding their nationalisation. Other extraordinary workers' victories accompanied the nationalisations such as considerable wage increases in a period of high inflation rates (20–30 per cent) and other social benefits. Also, the nationalisations were made without any compensation payments. Mirroring the acute critical stage of the class struggle, many capitalists, among them some of Portugal's wealthiest individuals were either arrested after the coup of 11 March and/

or fled the country, mostly going to Brazil. They would only return to Portugal at the end of the 1970s, when the governments began a process of compensation or of handing back the companies. The compensation values were determined by the terms of Act 80/77 dated 26 October.[42]

Many workers supported the Government's nationalisation policy even in important factories like Sorefame.[43] The militants wanted the nationalisations to be under workers' control. Conversely, the Government saw this as a way to deflect the demand for workers' control, indeed a way to divert the revolution. The importance of the nationalisations carried out during the revolution does not essentially lie in their economic impact or the eventual design of an economy with a socialist aspect – because the economy and the State both continued to be capitalist and the foreign companies and banks continued to be exempt from interventions.

The expansion of workers' control and the growing crisis in both the government coalition and the MFA was accompanied by a social atmosphere that not only mirrored the crises but contributed towards intensifying matters. The social situation was becoming highly polarised.

Actually the nationalisations of some companies were carried out to avoid the exodus of capital and the bankruptcy of the country – a form of control over investments – as much as to avoid the flourishing of workers' control.

After the counter-revolution, it took a decade to hand back the nationalised banks and companies to the private sector.

13

The Birth of the Welfare State

All people have the right to work. Social Security is the right of all.
It is the duty of the state to organise, coordinate and subsidise a unified,
decentralised social security system in accordance with, and with the partici-
pation of, the trade union associations and other working class organisations

Extracts from 1976 Constitution of the Portuguese Republic; 10 April 1976

The Social Welfare System before 1974

In 1970, three-quarters of the active population were wage or salary-earners.
More than two-thirds of the industrial workers were in factories employing
more than 20 people. Santos *et al.* (1976) report that there was an expansion
of the working class (understood here to be production workers in
industry) in the period from 1950 to 1970, from 768,000 to 1,020,000 and
that was in the midst of an out-and-out labour drain of the workforce, with
many migrating to destinations in the richer Western European countries.
In 1960, more than 40 per cent of Portuguese people were illiterate, 44
per cent had primary education, that is to say, they knew how to read and
write but had no secondary schooling and less than 1 per cent of the adult
population had higher education or had even completed higher secondary
education.[1]

The fall of the regime exposed a European colonial country with a
social structure that combined industrial development, a ruling class that
was making the first steps towards internationalisation[2] and a workforce
subjected to low salaries, ignorance and backwardness.

This was a country where 30 per cent of the population in the capital city
was illiterate, where there was no universal suffrage, no system of universal
social welfare, where going to the doctor required a paternalistic and
commercial relationship with charities controlled by the Catholic Church.
Cruz Oliveira, nominated as Minister of Health soon after 25 April, was
proud to have ended the dependence of hospitals on charities, the practices
of charging a fee for family members visiting relatives in the hospital and

the selling of blood for needy patients: 'Blood is not to be sold or bought, it's given!'[3]

Even considering countries such as Greece and Spain, Portugal had the lowest salaries in Europe.[4] One cannot understand the emergence of the welfare state in Portugal without understanding the key role of strike actions by workers in the conquest of political, social and cultural rights in the country.

Much of the welfare relied heavily upon charity, especially the Catholic Church. Social Security or the Social State was kept to the minimum in the New State and even in the 'New Spring', that is, in the days of Salazar's successor, Caetaeno, social insurance was merely a subsistence device. It did not provide for medicines and when it did start to contemplate them, it did not ensure any protection for maternity and, in the 1960s, the longest period of sickness it supported was 270 days. It was only after the 1950s that there was any assistance for hospitalised patients at all and, even then, it was only for those included in the assistance scheme; blood was bought and sold and the value of the assistance provided was pathetic, in those few cases where it actually existed. We can give just a few examples revealing that even authors like Manuel de Lucena, who considered that much progress had been achieved by the New State, does not deny that it was something that oscillated between destitution and 'Franciscan destitution'.[5] It might be remembered that the followers of Saint Francis of Assisi espoused poverty.

Researchers are unanimous in their opinion as to how poor and restricted the social insurance system was during the period of the New State.[6] Begging was legally a crime up until the end of the 1960s and a case for police intervention. Those who opposed the regime were deprived of their social benefits in addition to their political ones. All the other social welfare indicators, a question we have addressed in *Quem Paga o Estado Social em Portugal?* (Who pays for the Social State in Portugal?) – health, infant mortality, education, literacy training, leisure, life expectancy – were equal to those of the world's most backward and underdeveloped countries.[7]

As we have mentioned, the breadth of coverage and the amounts involved up until 1974, were always minuscule and derisory in all areas, but especially in the field of retirement. When one evaluates the history of Social Security, it is easy to appreciate qualitatively not only the poor outreach of social insurance, which clearly reveals how narrow its focus was, not only in terms of the number of people it embraced, which was far from universal then or at any other time prior to 1974, but in the value and effect of what beneficiaries received. In Portugal, up until 1974, we are talking about amounts well below the minimum needed for subsistence.[8]

The entire set of social expenditure of the State in Portugal in 1973 was a mere 4.4 per cent of the GNP, while at the same time in Great Britain, it was 13.9 per cent, in Italy 10.6 per cent and in Denmark 15.4 per cent.[9]

From 1926 to 1933, it seemed that there was a clear perception on the part of most sectors of the Portuguese bourgeoisie that the modernisation of capitalism and the accumulation of capital, mostly based on the colonial model, could not be achieved under a democratic regime because, as the twentieth century was well underway, the two processes were taking place at a time when there were new social subjects in existence, the industrial working class and middle sectors of society, demanding 'economic freedom', in addition to political freedom.

Concessions

There is an interconnection between the achievement of social rights and the development of worker control, which was becoming increasingly evident from February 1975 onwards. By then, basic trade union and democratic rights had been established and it seemed likely that elections would take place for the Constituent Assembly. Given the development and impending threat of workers' control, the government started to put into place a series of social measures designed to forestall this and which were intended to constitute the so-called Social State. Accordingly, one saw the allocation of resources to the State's social functions (education, health, social security, leisure, sports, public transport, subsidised incomes, etc.).

The military, in their endeavour to stabilise the State and halt the progress of the revolution, created the Council of the Revolution. This Council sought to ensure governability and stability within a state structure, thereby deflecting workers' disruption and threats to the control of the State. The burgeoning crisis and its other aspect, the increasing force of what was called *Poder Popular* (People's Power) meant that power itself was vacillating; employing consensus and concession more and more and coercion, less and less. The military made use of their prestige acquired through carrying out the coup against the regime. The parties acquired prestige because they had created a large apparatus with considerable influence in the social infrastructures. However, the threat of a revolution during that period was parried, above all, by giving way on social rights. After the demonstrations of 7 February 1975 and the placing of the chemical workers' union, which was led by the MRPP, under military law in the first quarter of 1975, and also the unsuccessful attempt to repress the strike in education (which had led to frequent scenes of violent combat between the extreme left and the Communist Party), and with the added 'trauma' of having Lisnave and TAP defying the control of the State, the powers backed down considerably in their use of repression and gave way on the level of social conquests which led to massive gains of labour over capital.

Let us look at three facets in turn: health, education and welfare benefits and then take an overview.

Health

Cruz Oliveira was a doctor and a major in the air force. He had joined the MFA right at the very beginning. He was designated to take charge of health, specifically, the unification of the health services under state administration:

> I looked at it this way; there was state-run medicine and private medicine. The state medicine was up to me, the private one, they could do what they liked, but I said let's get things straight! Those who want private medicine, go ahead but don't come back later, begging the State for help. While I was in the government, I nationalised by decree the hospitals of the Misericordia institutions (most of them run by the church) with the idea of bringing together all the health insurance companies, hospitals with all kinds of names, and health clinics, in a Single Health System.
>
> In Alondroal, everything was going smoothly – the doctors went to and from between the two sides, working half an hour here, a little bit there. When I arrived, I told them that now there was going to be just one service to serve the population as a whole. That seemed to go down reasonably well when up popped the administrator of the Misericordia Hospital, and, by the way, the Misericordia had good installations, and he said: 'I don't agree'. So I said to him 'Look, this is for the good of the country, from now on we are going to do things for everyone'. Well we had hit a stalemate. So I called my head of staff and another director and we discussed it 'So what are we going to do?' 'It's quite simple,' I said. I called the administrator and his assistants and said to him 'Please be so kind as to step into this room, administrator and I hope, sir, that you will think it over together with your assistants and that we can arrive at a satisfactory agreement. So, I am going to leave you in here and when you do arrive at a conclusion, knock on the door and I will open it'. Then I shut the door, locked it and went away. Well that was a pretty spectacular act and a lot of people came to the windows while I was out strolling around. But it didn't take very long. After a quarter of an hour

they knocked on the door and I opened it and they said 'Well, in view of the need to ... and so on and so forth ... alright', and that was how the integration of all the services was achieved!'[10]

The situation in the field of health, as ex-minister of health, Antonio Correia de Campos remembers, changed radically. In 1974, infant mortality was one and a half times that of Italy, two and half times that of France and almost four times that of Holland and Sweden; maternal mortality was double that of France, mortality from infectious diseases was 30 per cent higher than in Italy and three and a half times than that of Holland; life expectancy was seven years less than in Holland.'[11] After the changes that began to take place in the two-year period 1974–1975, Portugal came to have what was considered to be one of the best universal health systems in the world at the time and even occupied seventh position in the world ranking.

Article 64 of the Constitution 1976 states that every citizen has the right to health protection and the duty to defend and promote it. That right came into effect through the creation of a National Health Service offering universal, general and free health services. The article states that it is incumbent, principally on the State, to guarantee that all citizens, irrespective of their economic situations, shall have access to the prevention, curative and rehabilitation aspects of health care as well as to rational, efficient hospital and medical coverage throughout the country, which shall be ensured by the requirement that recently qualified doctors must serve one year in the field as a condition for embarking on a full medical career.

The ministerial dispatch published in the 29 July issue of the *Diário da República* (Official Gazette) and generally referred to as the Arnaut Dispatch actually anticipated a National Health Service as it opened access to Social-Medical Services for all citizens independently of their capacity to contribute. Act No. 56/79 dated 15 September created the National Health Service under the aegis of the Ministry of Social Affairs. Access was guaranteed to all citizens, irrespective of their economic and social situations, to foreigners in a regime of reciprocity, and to political refugees. As the Ministry of Health itself acknowledged, it was in 1974 that 'conditions were created',[12] which would enable that benefit to come into existence in 1979. Prior to 25 April, medical care depended on family solidarity, private institutions or on the social-medical services of the social insurance organisations to which access was highly restricted and unequal. As a result of the great struggles, in due course – many of them conducted by service users, nurses and doctors – the situation was radically altered.

Education

Already in May 1974, there had been massive demonstrations in favour of the abolition of examinations. The universities became a radicalised, politicised arena, swarming with Marxist ideas of various different schools. While it is true that the Communist Party had a greater presence in the factories, even though it had to grapple with the revolutionary factions, in many of the universities, it was the revolutionaries that had far greater influence than the Communist Party.

In the universities, plenaries with thousands of students multiplied, as did the purging of professors connected with the former fascist regime, all in a climate of permanent deliberation. It was in the area of education that the greatest numbers of staff closely identified with the former regime were purged. On 23 May 1974, a strike began in secondary education and on 25 May, around 10,000 students demonstrated in favour of abolishing examinations. As a result, the government was obliged to allow university entrance to all those students that had been approved, regardless of their final mark, which meant an increase that would double the number of university students. It went from 14,000 to 28,000.

This concession by the government gave rise to a technical problem; the universities would be accommodating twice as many students. The government, in spite of having agreed to the measure, insisted that there were not enough teachers or resources for that change.

The measure was a far greater problem for the Communist Party than for the government. It meant that there would be a massive influx of students to an environment that was already highly radicalised, in which groups of the extreme left were proliferating and over which the Communist Party did not have the degree of control that it was increasingly achieving in the workers' sectors. The 'leftist tendency' of the universities was undeniable. The argument of shortage of resources was hotly contested. To address the threat, in summer 1974, the Communist Party proposed measures that would prevent students getting access to the university or oblige them to leave temporarily. The party was tactically clever enough to create a campaign sympathetic to the values of those in the student sector. Hence, the *Serviço Cívico Estudantil* (Student Civic Service) came into being: the 'petit bourgeois students' would get to know and assist the people. The Student Civic Service was preceded in August 1974 by the *Campanha de Alfabetização e Educação Sanitária* (Literacy Campaign and Health Education), which established a presence in 100 locations and involved

10,000 students, doctors and nurses.[13] The Student Civic Service served the Communist Party policy well because it not only got the students away from a university climate which was highly permeated by the extreme left but it also supported a strengthening of the alliance with the MFA. The Communist Party had formulated its campaigns in an alliance with some of the MFA. Thus, it was by using the expedient of the Student Civic Service created in November 1974 that the Communist Party effectively took almost 20,000 students out of the universities in the two years of its existence (in the first year it was voluntary; in the second, obligatory).

For the União dos Estudantes Comunistas (Communist Students Union), the Civic Service programme was presented as way of connecting students to the people, to life and to reality became the 'great debate of the student movement'.[14] The Communist Student Union considered that there was scandalous 'overcrowding' in higher education and that those who from the far-left proposed setting up sheds and hiring more teachers 'do not want to study'.[15] In January, the Communist Student Union organised meetings in Lisbon, Porto and Coimbra in a bid to convince the students to adhere to the SCE. The SCE was specified as a prerequisite in the respective diploma, regulating and guaranteeing university entrance. The Student Civic Service wanted students to be integrated in the campaigns designed to make the MFA more dynamic. The Student Civic Service and Communist Student Union rebutted the criticism coming from the left-wing groups using these words:

> Prior to April 25, in the context of harsh fascist repression, the gentlemen of the left fought (verbally of course) for the connection of education to real life, to the reality of the workers. Now when we have the Civic Service, a profoundly progressive measure, here they are, roaring that the students are going to create added value for the capitalists; that the students are going to exacerbate unemployment, blah, blah, blah ....[16]

The government helped the Communist Student Union to implement the policy. Prime Minister Vasco Gonçalves made various speeches in which he called on the students to work: 'Students need to understand that they too should be workers just as much as the others and that it is the Portuguese people who pay for the universities.'[17]

The prime minister declared that he understood that young students could get carried away by 'illusory' attitudes but that he refused to accept a climate in which 'even the MFA is designated as fascist'.[18]

In February 1975 high school students rejected the administrative law approved by the government because they considered it to be anti-democratic. They also refused to participate in the SCE. They did not accept the proposal of minimum scores that must be attained to be exempted and they did not agree that the number of absences should be a criterion for elimination. On 17 February, a general strike began that rolled on into the month of March. On 1 March, the Minister of Education, Rodrigues de Carvalho, declared that the strike 'is of a political nature judging by the aspects that are being revealed in the midst of the confusion that reigns in higher secondary education'. On the same day, the Communist Party declared that 'the strike in education is reactionary'.[19] The high schools did not give in. The government adopted a policy of the 'carrot and stick'. On the one hand, it threatened to intervene in the schools with coercive measures but on the other it proposed to review teachers' pay criteria in an attempt to foil the unification of high school teachers and their students. In declarations approved by the Junta of National Salvation, the government announced that it was going to use coercive methods and close those schools in which the formal administrative bodies were not recognised, having been usurped by new administrative bodies democratically elected in the schools.[20] The Ministry of Education and Culture declared that: 'general assemblies of students cannot revoke Government decrees'.[21]

The Communist Party came out against the strike in education:

The schools that cost the country millions are there for learning and not to serve as the permanent stage for interminable discussions and assemblies coerced by provocateur groups, scuffles, aggressions and similar schemes. The situation in the technical schools frequented by worker-students is different from that in the universities where the vast majority of students are from the bourgeois classes, many of them bringing with them the mark of their origins in the form of their love of idleness and their parasitism.[22]

There were still, up until 25 April, elitist schools such as Lycées and private schools, where 'only the well-off could study there' according to the ordinary people, and there were almost no schools at all in the rural areas. Despite the obligatory nature of schooling from the age of six since 1965, in 1974 around 26 per cent of the population was illiterate, 85 per cent of children in the six to ten age group only completed the first four years of schooling and only 28 per cent of children in the 10 to 12 age group were enrolled in lower secondary education (fifth and sixth years of schooling).[23]

The revolution changed all that surprisingly quickly. Changes included curriculum contents in the school, working conditions for teachers and other school employees and study conditions for students. School transport networks were created, new schools, canteens and school residences were built, subsidies for poor students were fixed and school milk was distributed. The curricular offer was standardised for the 7th, 8th and 9th years of schooling, extinguishing the separate lines of technical, industrial, agricultural, commercial education and the education of the Lycées. In 1974–1975, the lay nature of education was re-established, the organisations *Mocidade Portuguesa* (Portuguese Youth) and *Mocidade Portuguesa Feminina* (Portuguese Female Youth) were abolished and students were no longer separated into classes by gender.

Again, in the administrative sphere, changes were introduced that would prevail unaltered right through to 2008. There was no longer a principal or director and the administrative bodies that ran the schools, the Conselho Diretivo and the Conselho Pedagógico (Board of Trustees and the Pedagogical Council) became democratic, that is, elected by their peers and the Pedagogical Council embraced representatives of the teachers, students, parents and those responsible for education as well as of others involved in the running of schools or the education process. Parents' and educators' associations were founded as well as students' associations, teachers' unions, and unions of non-teaching workers in education (some of them linked to civil service unions).

There were also changes in the higher education curricula and in the conditions of access to it. The universities came to enjoy pedagogical, financial and scientific autonomy and their internal bodies were also elected by peers. Among such bodies were those composed of representatives of the teaching staff, the non-teaching staff and the students. Education was free of charge.

Social Security

Another considerable victory, in 1974–1975, in terms of labour rights was the birth of Social Security. In 1974, the term changed from *previdência social* (social insurance) to *segurança social* (social security).

The force of the revolution created an integrated social security system which the entire population had access to; it increased the existing provisions and introduced a series of other reforms that reached out to the whole population. There were radical increases in pensions (see Figure 13.1) and the expansion of social security which, as the Constitution puts it: 'protects the citizens in sickness, old age and disability, widowhood, and orphanhood, as well as in unemployment and all situations where the means of subsistence or capacity for work are reduced or lacking.'[24]

Right away, in September 1974, a social pension for persons aged over 65 was established, as well as medical assistance in sickness and maternity, and a family allowance for the unemployed. The Ministry of Labour took on the responsibility for the Unemployment Fund.

Universal Social Security is based on the idea that those who don't earn a wage can still contribute to society, such as a peasant woman who educates her own children. Those with very low wages are exempt from making Social Security payments but still benefit from Universal Social Security because they are still considered to contribute to the collective wealth of the country through activities outside the workplace. On that basis, a system of non-contributable pensions was created.

The change of name from Insurance to Security is important insofar as it is the sign of a change in content. In Portugal, which until recently had one of the best health systems in the world and for many years an excellent public education service (today, we have more PhDs than there were qualified teachers in 1970), social security generally refers to two large areas. The first is retirement pay/pensions sustained by the contributions of workers or state-budgeted transfers in the case of non-contributable pensions and which were only possible because of an increase in the gross mass of wages generated. The second aspect is the so-called 'social action' policies, which seek to relieve poverty and involuntary unemployment.

A worker employed in the Candidinha Fashion Atelier tells how prior to 25 April 'we earned 70 to 80 escudos a day and we produced products in three days that were worth 30,000 to 40,000, so you can see the fortune they were making'.[25] Before 25 April, in the Atelier, the daily wage was 20 to 40 escudos for apprentices, 50 for assistants and 100 to 125 for top-class seamstresses. After 25 April, pay was fixed at 3,300 escudos a month and in May, it went up to 4,400 escudos a month.

Two essential interlaced ideas are associated within the Universal Social Security, that came into existence in 1974 and 1975. They are the process of the 'transferral' of capital income to labour, the most massive ever in contemporary Portugal, to the amount of an impressive 18 per cent (see Figure 13.1).

The second was the social and public commitment to universal benefits that put an end to discriminatory, discretionary and charity-based regimes and further broadened the scope of social protection, contemplating not only protection at the level of maintenance (education, health, pensions)

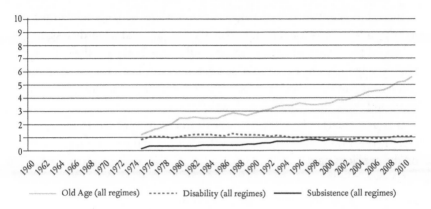

Figure 13.1 Benefits as a Percentage of the GNP

Source: Pordata.

and training of the workforce, but also at the levels of culture, sport and leisure.

The fundamental aspect for gaining an understanding of the birth of social security, without which it is impossible to understand the evolution of the social state in Portugal as a whole, is the increases in wages, that is, the transferral of part of the profit. In those years, the wage increases were achieved in various ways: direct increases of the wage or salary in cash, determining a minimum salary level (3,300 escudos in May 1974 and 4,000 escudos in May 1975), the right to benefits (such as unemployment, birth and maternity), free health and education services; price freezing; establishing a basic consumer 'shopping basket' which could be used to establish a price index. Considerable volumes of capital were transferred to salaries by other means such as nationalisations without any compensation, state intervention in decapitalised companies (more than 300 all told) and direct cuts in ultra-high salaries (freezing salaries of over 12,000 escudos in 1975).

The number of beneficiaries of the general regime and of the *Caixa Geral de Aposentações* (Civil Service Social Security Scheme, CGA) grew from 607,000 in 1973 to 943,000 escudos in 1975. In the CGA, the outlays rose from 7,700,000 in 1973 to 11,637,000 escudos in 1975. Revenues in the same period went from 4,185,000 to 8,293,000 escudos, that is to say, they almost doubled. The average contribution went from the equivalent of 9,200 escudos per user in 1973 to 17,100 escudos per user in 1975. The outlay for social security went from 4.5 per cent of the GNP in 1973 to 6.7 per cent in 1975. The average pension paid out by the social security system increased by 50 per cent in the period 1971 to 1975.[26]

It can be seen that the real value of direct wages actually fell from 1974 to 1975 due to inflation, among other factors, but that nevertheless, in the sphere of the State and Social Security – the social salary – the gains were readily apparent. Not only did salaries increase but also the disparities among salaries decreased; that is, the difference between those that gained more and those that gained less shrank.[27]

It is particularly clear how the transferral of income led to increases in benefit values as illustrated below by Table 13.1, and Figure 13.1, as shown on the previous page.

Table 13.1 Social Security Benefits: Total Outlay

Year	Total	Old Age (all regimes)	Type of Benefit Disability (all regimes)	Subsistence (all regimes)
1971	8,878.70			
1972	13,759.30			
1973	21,206.20			
1974	37,450.60			
1975	58,364.30	31,105.00	22,805.00	4,454.30
1976	90,437.00	46,488.00	33,284.80	10,664.30

Sources/Entities: IGFSS/MTSS.

Last update: 23 January 2013 (Amounts in thousands of Euros)

14
Scheming for Power

We must construct our own socialism. I give my whole-hearted support to these revolutionary councils.

Otelo de Carvalho[1]

This history focuses, above all, upon the democracy of those who met and organised in the factories, the neighbourhoods, the barracks and on the land. How were they going to be heard? What forms of representation would be suitable? Who would wield the power?

This chapter looks at some of the schemes that were generated, in attempts to harness and/or divert the democracy of the people. Immediately after 11 March, the MFA consolidated the power of its assembly of 240 delegates. These delegates could, in theory, hold any rank. All three wings of the armed forces were represented. The delegates elected the 'Supreme' Council of Revolution, which was responsible to the assembly and nobody else. This was an endeavour to reinforce the military powers of the MFA's upper echelons. Reluctantly, the MFA decided to honour its commitment to hold free elections on 25 April, one year after seizing power.

The CRTSMs

However, on the weekend before the Constituent Assembly elections, 660 people attended the founding conference of the *Conselhos Revolucionários de Trabalhadores, Soldados e Marinheiros* (Revolutionary Councils of Workers, Soldiers and Sailors, usually known as the CRTSMs).

This was the first attempt to unite workers with soldiers in a 'non-party' organisation. This disdain for party politics fitted with the military tradition of the MFA and its role of reflecting and mediating the different classes. Otelo was linked to the proposal; his hope was that a national network of councils would provide a support base. It included representatives (not delegates) from 161 workplaces such as Lisnave, Setenave, TAP, and, most significantly, 21 military units. There were a number of the soldiers in uniform.

The Revolutionary Councils of Workers, Soldiers and Sailors were promoted by the PRP-BR and they called for 'a revolutionary government without political parties'. Despite this, most people saw it as being a PRP creation. The military importance of this initiative must be underscored insofar as it reflected the attractiveness of the PRP-BR for some of the younger military personnel, among them Otelo Saraiva de Carvalho.'[2]

This was heralded by some, including Christopher Reed from *The Guardian*, as potentially the 'Birth of a Soviet'.[3] While the idea was bold, and in accordance with struggles from below from other epochs across the world. In practice, the CRTSMs were superficially very political, and deliberately disconnected itself from the day-to-day economic struggles. The focus was upon the threat from the right, the need to be prepared to take up arms and the need for revolution.

Having allowed elections, a number of the leading MFA individuals advocated their boycott, as did the PRP-BR (refer to MFA propaganda shown on page 206). The suggestion of boycotting the elections failed hopelessly and is evident by reminding ourselves that 91.73 per cent of the population turned out for the vote, which is, without question, the highest turnout for any free election in Western Europe since the First World War.[4]

The Elections

For the Right, the failure of the coups had made it clear that the strategy of military intervention and paternalist modernisation could not win. The alternative was to build a Western European-type social democracy within a parliamentary framework. The key to this strategy was the Socialist Party, which had been receiving support for some time from the USA and Europe. Social democracy was an unknown force in Portugal. In a study conducted by Gasper and Vitorino on the first free elections of 1975, the authors measured the amount of times each party used certain words.[5] They found that the word 'democracy' was among the most used. For the Confederation of Portuguese Industry (Confederação da Indústria Portuguesa, CIP), the main employers' organisation, democracy was a synonym for the maintenance of an employers' representative in nationalised companies along with representatives from the State and the trade unions.

The anniversary of the overthrow of the old regime, 25 April, was chosen for Portugal's first ever elections based on universal suffrage. Three weeks were allocated for electioneering, which was subject to intricate rules, including equal television time for all parties standing, regardless of size.[6] As parties were not allowed to flypost on top of one anothers' posters, it became necessary to carry longer and longer ladders to reach bits of unpostered wall. Interest was immense. Of the 6,176,559 enrolled electors, 5,666, 696 went to the polls – 91.73 per cent of the electorate.

The Socialist Party won 37.87 per cent of the vote, the PPD won 26.38 per cent, the Communist Party polled a meagre 12.53 per cent, plus the 4.12 per cent of its close ally the MDP. 'Socialism' was obviously extremely popular. The real victor was the Socialist Party; from just 200 members in April 1974, it had become the leading *parliamentary* party in Portugal under the banner of freedom of speech, democracy and a managed, modern economy. The very vagueness of its slogans for 'progress', 'democracy' and 'socialism' enabled it to appeal to broad sectors of the population including the less organised workers – those who fell outside the influence of the Intersindical and the Communist Party. The Socialist Party often appeared more left wing than the Communist Party. It had attacked the government's new labour laws in 1974 and tolerated its own left within the party. But it was also the party of the centre and the right – of the middle class. It sought to win back those sections of the state machine in the hands of the Communist Party and areas of society under control of the workers.

Portugal had had little experience of the betrayals of reformism in power. Reformist politicians posed as the champions of the interests of the workers. The 'brilliant' achievements of the struggle did not mean that Portuguese workers had bypassed reformism or were permanently immune from it. This is how Tony Cliff summed up the Socialist Party:

> At present the Socialist Party, as a petty bourgeois party par excellence, represents everything that is immature and confused in the masses' consciousness. Everybody who had not inherited from the period of fascism a clear political consciousness, i.e. belonged neither to the fascist right nor to the Communist Party nor the 'ultra-left' groups, now found himself ready to support the Socialist Party. This meant supporting the 25 April revolution without any further commitment: its banner is the simple one of 'pure democracy' – commitment to the revolution in general. [7]

At the time, those who were immersed in direct and revolutionary democracy were surprised by the outcome; it is hardly surprising so many people turned to the Socialist Party after 48 years without democracy. Above all, it had been the Socialist Party which had been talking about ballot-box democracy alongside socialism.

Even the PPD, the party of the centre-right, tried to fly socialist colours. In 1975, the PPD applied unsuccessfully to join the Socialist International. This was vetoed by the Socialist Party.

The newly elected Constituent Assembly was not a supreme body, merely an advisory body to the MFA, which still appointed the president. The subordination of the victors of the elections to the Armed Forces was to be a source of increasing tension. Within 24 hours, there was chanting at a Socialist Party victory demonstration of 'down with the MFA'. Over the next six months, the Socialist Party relentlessly pursued the interrelated themes of 'power to those elected', 'democracy', and 'freedom of speech'.

Finally, there is no mechanical connection between the force of a class and its electoral strength. Suffice it to say that 70,000 housewives in Beiras had far more electoral strength than 7,000 Lisnave workers, but workers and workers' actions determined such important things as – to give just one example – the failure to enforce the strike law at a national level, affecting almost all other workers in Portugal.

Power was divided between the State, the MFA and the places of production. The parties seeking to organise their structures and the debates in the Constituent Assembly were all veritable reflections of institutions in crisis. Here is one of many examples of the Parliament discourses:

Assembly President: Representative Manuel Alegre has the floor. I would ask you, Mr Representative, and everyone else, to be as brief as possible.

Representative Manuel Alegre (PS): Thank you Mr President but I relinquish the floor.

President: Representative Américo Duarte has the floor.

Representative Américo Duarte (UDP): I have two points to make. First I would like to make it very clear here why I left the chamber a short while ago. It was because of the reactionary words of Representative Arnaut; words that were supported by openly declared fascists present in this chamber and not in support of the MDP/CDE, offshoot of Mr Cunhal's party ...

Mr Manuel Gusmão (PCP): the Portuguese Communist Party!

Mr Dias Lourenço (PCP): That is an insult. The name of our party is the Portuguese Communist Party. We cannot accept that our party name should be insulted.

Assembly President: I would ask the speaker to modify his expressions and not use any that might be considered offensive.

The speaker: ... or that same party because my back is still smarting from the beating it got at the last plenary session of the metalworkers in the Sports Pavilion where the treachery of your gentlemen was clearly apparent and where your chiefs beat the workers attending it for not adhering to the treacherous line taken by those same parties.

A voice: Liar![8]

This is just a sample of the paralysis on the Constituent Assembly. Others were seeking other options, outside the assembly.

Committees for the Defence of the Revolution

The Communist Party responded to the CRTSMs with the CDRs (Committees for the Defence of the Revolution – Comités da Defesa da Revolucáo). These were supposed to be 'unitary, non-party entities to defend the ongoing revolutionary process' and were inspired by the Cuban experience with CDRs. In practice, they were fronts created by the Communist Party. They were also intended to steer the direction of workers' control towards forms of co-management shared by unions, workers and the government, or towards self-management under State intervention.

But the CDRs had little impact, perhaps only in the Lisbon Industrial Belt, in Marina Grande and in some zones of Alentejo. Their specific objectives were to support and connect with the MFA, defend the government's economic plan, back the Communist Party in its dispute with the revolutionaries and to fight against 'divisive and provocative manoeuvres'. Among their formal objectives were the 'permanent vigilance over the revolutionary process' in order to avoid 'fascism and reaction' and to maintain surveillance of the companies.

The CDRs sought to ensure that the workers, both men and women, in partnership with the military, backed the Communist Party 'front' strategy and blocked any impediments to the Battle for Production in the factories, whether they stemmed from workers' control or from economic sabotage and disinvestment of the companies. The committees were mobilised in the campaigns to support Vasco Gonçalves and in creating pressure for the formation of the Fifth Provisional Government with a political equilibrium similar to that of the Fourth Provisional Government before it was dismembered. Considering that the Communist Party strategy was never based on workers taking up arms for the fight but instead on reinforcing the unions and state apparatuses, the CDRs were never of great importance.

Apart from addressing the dispute, with the Socialist Party and with those officers influenced by the PRP, it was essentially designed to avoid any national-level coordination of dual power.

The Pontinha Popular Assembly

The Pontinha Popular Assembly was a prototype of a model that was often cited in the debates within the MFA and was held up as a living example of an alternative form of power. The beauty was that its origins did not come from the political parties, unlike the CRTMs and CDRs.

The Pontinha barracks was the nerve centre of the assembly, home to a regiment of engineers. These barracks had been the command headquarters for the 25 April coup. At Pontinha, officers sympathetic to MES, and attached to the Fifth Division, played a crucial part.

Paul Sweezy visited the barracks in June 1975. He reported:

it was an outstanding rather than a typical unit. About 700 soldiers live in or are attached to the barracks. Most of the noncoms and privates are mechanically trained, and workers by background. The officers for the most part are graduates in engineering from civilian schools, politically aware and open to ideas. After the end of the fighting in Africa a great deal of equipment was sent back to Portugal, and much of the necessary repair work was done in the Regiment's shops. On September 28th the soldiers went out on the barricades with the workers. The defeat of the attempted coup opened the way for political and cultural activity by the soldiers.[9]

The soldiers and officers formed direct links with the local population: building roads, bridges and repairing houses with military equipment refurbished by their mechanics. The regiment was interested in making links with all the workers' commissions and residents' commissions to form a more concrete link, which was not tied to a direct political superstructure. After 11 March, meetings between workers and soldiers became far more organised. MES was keen to be able to match the rival CRTSM and CDR schemes with what appeared to be a practical example of a workers' council, one built not by a political party, but by an amalgam of grass-roots forces with left activists in the military. One of the officers, Abegao, outlined the reasons for the assembly:

Hitherto all the work had been done with the workers' commissions and residents' commissions on a one to one basis. The general idea of creating the Popular Assembly was to create an institution, if you can call it so, which could co-ordinate and direct the priorities. This was seen as being better than having discussions on a one to one basis, for example between the barracks and a CM. The idea was to further the process and to gather all the interested parts of the zone, all the workers' commissions, all the residents' commissions and define those priorities with all the people interested. The dynamics of the process was profound. The whole process of creating the Popular Assembly was based on cultural work in which everyone took part and everyone was involved. In other regiments, other assemblies, the political dominance of (sections of the) left and the struggles were directed towards political lines of the parties. The work was specific because it was an engineering regiment. The idea of this project was based, but not mechanically, upon China. China with Gramsci.[10]

Following several months of planning, the first assembly was held on 29 June. It took place in the indoor sports hall belonging to the regiment. The hall was packed. Some 17 factories and 30 local residents' organisations were represented. Conscious of their role, only two formal representatives of the military, elected at mass meetings of the barracks, were permitted. Also, few soldiers were directly involved in the assembly as most went back to their homes at the weekend. Voting was to be 'by arm in the air' so that all could see how the various bodies felt. The assembly defined its main tasks as the organisation of defence in the event of an offensive from the right, and the strengthening of links between the soldiers and workers.

We will revisit the residents' commissions and ways of linking with other organisations when we look at the Fifth Provisional Government and the role of the Popular Assemblies and also much later, when we look, in particular, at the Setúbal Comité de Luta.

Officers on the Side of the Workers?

There was some talk of refusing to hand over power, as well as talk of a benevolent dictatorship. Another idea was that the MFA should become an actual political party. Given the options that presented themselves, the game of balancing – of making concessions to both sides – became more and more risky to play. There was a vacillation and shuffling of schemes.

Ramiro Correia, the head of the Fifth Division (which had been created by the Council of the Revolution to raise 'political awareness'; in effect, it was the propaganda wing of the MFA), prided himself on his revolutionary ideology. At the MFA assembly on 26 May, he expressed once again his preference for banning parties and placing the MFA above them. The proposal was again rebuffed but the feeling of the need to be non-party, or above parties, remained. All the time, the debate about the form of 'revolutionary councils' was raging and the crisis of government was gathering speed. A split was occurring within the MFA but those on the left, such as the Fifth Division officers, were open-minded. They were prepared to participate in CDR and CRTSM discussions.

The press reported a showpiece joint venture – a meeting that took place on 11 June 1975 in Monsanto, an air force base on the outskirts of Lisbon. The air force was the least radical wing of the armed forces, which made the meeting especially significant. Benjamin Formigo, a military correspondent for *Expresso*, wrote a full-page report titled: 'FIRST JOINT DISCUSSION ABOUT REVOLUTIONARY COUNCILS'.[11]

In attendance were officers, sergeants and troops of the three branches of the armed forces and workers from various enterprises such as Lisnave, Setenave, Siderurgia and Marinha Grande. This was the first such meeting in a barracks.

It started with 'clarifications' by workers of *República* on the current state of their dispute. (The dispute at *República* newspaper became world famous. This is covered in more depth in Chapter 16, on the Hot Summer.)

Sobral Costra (an independent leftist from the MFA) opened the meeting by saying:

> The theme to be discussed in this assembly today is one of the projects to link the Povo/MFA, namely, the one which is referred to as the Revolutionary Councils.
>
> Captain João Freire spoke about the links of the CRTSMs with the PRP-BR. It was the view of the PRP that: 'It was time to pass to a new phase, a phase in which it is possible to have autonomous councils … The MFA itself believed that the way was not socialising but socialist … it was urgent to create an organisation of workers which could make socialism a reality.'[12]

Manuel Crespo from the CRTSMs spoke on the importance of a meeting inside a barracks. He also stressed that the Revolutionary Council of the

MFA recognised that not it, itself, but the working masses were the motor of the revolution.

A Captain Luz (close to MES) spoke on behalf of the Fifth Division army section, which was one of the organising sources of the meeting. Carlos Antunes spoke as a member of the PRP and talked about Otelo putting COPCON to serve the working classes. There was a section on residents' struggles introduced by a Setúbal resident. The meeting lasted more than five hours. 'In conclusion Sobral Costa talked about the importance of the meeting, and the unity which was such a feature of the meeting.'[13]

In the shifting and juggling that was taking place Otelo, the commander of COPCON, increasingly came to favour the CRTSMs proposal. He said in a radio interview:

> I see no danger at all in these congresses or councils. I consider them, like neighbourhood committees, to be the essence of the Portuguese Revolution. I consider them similar to the Russian Soviets of 1917 ... the anarcho-syndicalists are very humorous when they write slogans on the walls such as 'A Portuguesa so temos cozido'. (The only Portuguese thing we have is 'cozido' – cozido being a popular dish of boiled potatoes, vegetable, pork, beef and sausage meat.) It's true enough. We must construct our own socialism. I give my whole-hearted support to these revolutionary councils.[14]

Otelo needed a base, an army in addition to the army. The CRTSMs, although barely in existence, were all that he could have. The CRTSMs project was resuscitated. Christopher Reed, a reporter for *The Guardian*, had been covering the CRTSMs and its intertwining with COPCON. He wrote: 'Now the PRP claims to have embryo or fully-fledged councils in 250 companies, supported from all 50 units in COPCON including commanders.'[15]

The project was approved by general assemblies of workers at the two bastions of revolutionary workers, namely, Lisnave and Setenave. In both, the assemblies were addressed by a member of the MFA as well as by a CRTSMs speaker. But in other perhaps less 'revolutionary' factories the proposals were not adopted. At the airport, an assembly of the workers turned the project down. There were discussions at IBM, at Sorefame (an enormous engineering complex), Massa and the Che Guevara commune based in a former luxury hotel. In a few places, provisional committees were formed but as they were not properly elected, they were not very different in form from the self-appointed CDRs. At the Siderurgia steel works, the Revolutionary Council project was amalgamated with the Councils for the Defence of the Revolution. Nevertheless, the amalgamation did not smooth over the antagonism between the Communist Party and the PRP.

The CRTSMs called a demonstration for 17 June. This demonstration, of some 30,000 people, was politically one of the most radical since 25 April, as it challenged all the political parties and their associated institution, the Constituent Assembly. Slogans in support of the MFA were conspicuously absent.

The demonstration was intrinsically linked to the defence of Rádio Renascença and *República*, both under workers' control and both under attack from the right. For several days, Rádio Renascença prepared for the demonstration and regularly devoted time to a phone-in. Some of the workers interviewed clearly recall it as the Renascença demonstration and not that of the CRTSMs.

The main slogans were 'For a revolutionary non-party government' and 'For a Socialist Revolution'. On the day of the demonstration, a third slogan was added: 'Immediate dissolution of the Constituent Assembly!' The demonstration itself was preceded by a street-wide banner, proclaiming '*Fora com a canalha: O poder a quem trabalha!*' (Out with the scum: Power to those who work!)

Carlos was involved with its organisation. He vividly describes the dependence of militants upon Otelo:

> When I got to the Marques Pombal, that is where the demonstration was to gather, nobody there was certain whether the Lisnave workers would actually turn up. And then they did come up the street. It was quite a sight, the sun glinting on their helmets, they were like an army, marching in groups of seven, very tightly organised.
>
> They had been in a sense conned because – and this I got from a PRP militant who worked at Lisnave later on – they had been promised that Otelo would be at the demonstration and Otelo did not turn up. They were crying out for him. When negotiations took place, it was always the demonstrators that suffered the most. Time was passing by and things were not moving and people did not know what was going on and there were rumours 'he is coming', 'he is coming', 'he is in jail', rumours of this and that. In the end we found out that Otelo was just at a mighty nice dinner somewhere with a Bulgarian military attaché or somebody like that. The Lisnave workers went there partly because of that (promise of Otelo being there).[16]

The CRTSMs were superficially very political, claiming to be 'the first soviet of revolutionary Portugal', but they were anti-party and called for 'a revolutionary government without political parties'. This disdain for party politics meant that this somewhat slight organisation, with relatively few roots in the workplaces, had a significant influence with some officers and helped shape events.

Povo–MFA Pact

Twenty-four hours after the CRTSMs demonstration, the Revolutionary Council of the MFA declared that the 'MFA rejects the dictatorship of the proletariat supported by its armed militia since it does not fit into its pluralistic concept, already defined, of the Portuguese revolution.' Within days, the General Assembly of the MFA narrowly approved the *Documento Guia*, – guidelines for the alliance between the people and the MFA – otherwise known as the MFA–Povo Pact, which managed to unify momentarily the Communist Party, the Fifth Division officers around MES, COPCON and some of the supporters of the CRTSMs. Presented to the MFA Assembly on 8 July 1975, this project had been planned since May 1975 and called for grass-roots assemblies of workers and residents to be controlled by the MFA. Its aim was to set up a parallel authority to the State and parliamentary system. The organisations of *Poder Popular* would be integrated into the popular assemblies, and all of this would be under the protective umbrella of the MFA. The Pontinha Assembly, which we referred to earlier in this chapter, was often cited as a living example. By 8 July, the date that the Povo–MFA Pact was signed, Pontinha had held two meetings.

The adoption of the Povo–MFA Pact, together with the continued incapability of the government to ensure the return of *República* and Rádio Renascença (where mass demonstrations had forced the MFA to veto a government decision to return the station to the church, and to allowing the workers to retain control), prompted Soares and the Socialist Party, on 10 July 1975, to formally abandon the Fourth Provisional Government. This was also depriving the Socialist Party of its main newspaper and led to many heated arguments around the right to publish and freedom of speech. This was very significant, given that the Socialist Party had been prohibited before 25 April. The latter accused the Communist Party of attempting to establish a dictatorial domination of the communication media.

This was another aspect of the attempt to circumvent the dual power at the work-place level (workers' control) and at the neighbourhood level. The creation of the Revolutionary Council was another attempt to to divert grass-roots power; it tried to promote confidence in the State, and the need for the Battle for Production.

Documento Guia

The *Documento Guia*, popularised by the MFA and Communist Party with the euphemism of the 'institutionalisation' of the People–MFA alliance, called for a cross-party organisation in which the MFA and other organs of the state apparatus would 'support' the popular assemblies and the Revolutionary Council as the 'highest body of national sovereignty',[17] assigning, therefore, the highest power to the MFA leadership, which did not emerge from the workers' representative bodies. For this reason, I do not agree with Maria Inácia Rezola, when she argues that the *Documento Guia Povo–MFA* was a project of 'popular and direct democracy',[18] since it placed, or tried to place, the workers and all of the bodies of popular power under the control of the MFA and particularly the Revolutionary Council.

Álvaro Cunhal, in his assessment 20 years later of the military left, has a different opinion about the *Documento Guia Povo–MFA* and considers it to be a form of the controlling labour and the funnelling the energies of the grass-roots movements:

> The *Documento* reflects the influence of petit-bourgeois radicalism over the military Left, which, at this point in the crisis, is in growing alliance with pseudo-revolutionary elements. The principles displayed in the document constitute an attempt to submit the workers' and popular movements to the MFA and to the officers in general, who would define which are the unified representative structures and would recognize them officially.[19]

I believe, because in the context of the Portuguese Revolution, with the crisis in the army, it was in principle a less ambitious project – probably rooted in a certain flirtation of the MFA with the theories known at the time as 'third-worldist', that is, the idea of a nationalist bourgeoisie or petit-bourgeoisie with a certain degree of independence from the central powers.

When it was proposed, the *Documento Guia Povo–MFA* was defended by the Communist Party as the 'organic achievement of the People–MFA alliance'.[20] And this was necessary for them, for at least three reasons: first, the unions didn't fully play this role, especially since 'assemblyism' had become widespread after February 1975; second, there was a dispute between the Communist Party and Socialist Party and the far-left over the leadership of the unions and the workers' commissions; finally, the possibility of the coalition's collapse and of open confrontation with the Socialist Party made the Communist Party attempt to mobilise its base, which would require greater control:

> The revolutionary organisations, the popular masses have proven to be conscious of such a need as they proceed to create residents' committees and other unified organisations from below, as they proceed towards forms of coordination between residents' committees in the same zone ... as they establish contacts between residents' and workers' committees, as they develop contacts between some committees and the Armed Forces Movement.[21]

The declaration of the Political Commission of the Central Committee of the Communist Party concerning the MFA 8 July assembly did not hide the fact that the *Documento Guia* sought the 'institutionalisation of the popular movement', putting an end to the 'artificial escalation of conflicts'.[22] Giving some revolutionary phraseology to the document, the Communist Party even made a call to respect the non-partisan nature of the popular structures,[23] seeking to avoid conflict between the parties, thus guaranteeing their submission to the MFA:

> It is particularly important to value the popular movement and the plan to institutionalise it ... Certain gatherings and demonstrations of employers planned for the coming days, which the organisers intend to give a counter-revolutionary direction, the artificial escalation of conflicts, the launching and relaunching of strikes that are inappropriate for the situation or lack a reasonable cause, clandestine agitation, the climate of disrespect for the democratic order that some are trying to foment in certain sectors, continue to require the people's vigilance and the readiness of the masses to defend the gains of the revolution under any circumstances, in close alliance with the MFA.[24]

The Popular Assemblies

The idea of popular assemblies was widespread in the movement. Could they take root and blossom? On 16 July, there was a large demonstration in support of popular power – specifically popular assemblies. (The photo on page 4 is from this demonstration.) MES was very influential in the organisation. Many hitched rides on friendly tanks supplied by RALIS – the first time tanks were seen in demonstrations other than on May Day and 25 April. In support of the same idea, there was a demonstration two days later in Porto. *Voz Do Povo* claimed that: 'more than 20,000 workers expressed their determination'.[25]

Immediately after the pact was approved, another group of organisations clustered near RALIS, convened the Marvila Popular Assembly, which they had been preparing since before the pact. Marvila is the area around the airport. The assembly met on 13 July and, among other organisations, 23 workers' commissions were represented.[26] Its scope, typical for a popular assembly, included the following points:

5 The Marvila Popular Assembly represents the class aspirations and organisations of the workers.

6 The Marvila Popular Assembly should progressively replace the organs of the state apparatus already decrepit and inefficient, taking into its own hands the power to legislate at a local level, over all the problems which affect the workers.

One of its first tasks was to elect a provisional secretariat, whose names were to be made public, with the exception of those from the RALIS barracks. Much of the projected programme was taken up 'detecting the existing problems in the workplaces and the localities'.

At the same time, one week after the Povo–MFA Pact, an assembly was convoked in the north of Lisbon, called 'Our Lady of Fátima' ('Nossa Senhora de Fátima'), which was the name of the area. One of its leading activists, who was also a member of MES, said:

It kept the name of the municipality which tells us something and was set up a week after the Povo–MFA Pact. We still had the local representatives from the junta. There were two military units in the area but we never went into the barracks. Between 200–400 people came to the meetings, and about 25 different workers' commissions sent delegates. We divided into groups around the issues of workplaces, housing, education, crèches and infant schools.[27]

In Setúbal, despite the planning meeting on 4 July and the blessing of the Povo–MFA Pact, it was not until 25 July that the first assembly was convened. This was called the committee of popular organisations – COPS. There were innumerable fierce debates about which bodies had the right to be represented and the role of political parties. The meeting on 25 July, which consisted of 300 people but without military representation, debated the CRTSMs and CDR proposals and allowed participation from these two organisations, but without voting rights. COPS decided in principle to elect committees of armed vigilantes.[28] The biggest meeting was on 6 August, where 50 workers' commissions and 30 residents' bodies met with members of the MFA.

The assemblies did not meet only in the larger towns. *República* carried a short report on a planning meeting in a village called Palmela, on the northern outskirts of Setúbal.[29] Palmela could only boast two medium-sized firms (Control Data and Cometna, which employed 600 and 530 workers respectively). Most other work in the area, such as wine production, tomato canning and meat production, was linked to the agricultural sector. It was reported that the residents' commissions of Quinta do Anjo and Cabanas (in the council of Palmela) had an emergency meeting with 25 people present. This meeting unanimously approved the COPCON document and proposed to call a popular assembly on 22 July. The preliminary meeting had already received messages of support for the COPCON document from the workers of the Arsenal do Alfeite and the leadership of the Merchant Seamen's Union.[30] A delegation from the British-based solidarity organisation the PWCC (Portuguese Workers' Co-Ordinating Committee) decided to visit an assembly. The MP Audrey Wise wrote up a detailed and graphic account of a fairly typical meeting.

We went along to a meeting at Palmela, a village about 20 miles south of Lisbon. About 200 people were present, probably a quarter of them women. The meeting was held in a place used as a semi open-air cinema. There were light-weight walls, and a metal framework roof covered with thickly growing plants, the framework being used to support lighting.

A neighbourhood committee had sprung up and been in operation for some weeks, and this meeting was an attempt to broaden and formalise it. In his opening remarks the man chairing the meeting stressed 'the need for people to talk freely and say what was in their minds.' He emphasised that everybody in the village had had the opportunity to come, and he again stressed the need for people to say what they really meant, and to help to solve the problems of the neighbourhood. He continued 'The Armed Forces Movement (MFA) is deeply involved in these attempts to build direct democracy or "popular power". Its General Assembly carried a decision in its favour on July 8th, and it was this which really sparked off the alarm of the right-wing in Portugal. Nothing is more dangerous to the right-wing than people asserting themselves and attempting to come to their own decisions, and MFA commitment to direct democracy is of tremendous importance.' The member of the MFA at this meeting said 'Is it not the workers who create the wealth of a country? When the workers have control of the wealth they produce then we will have the Socialist Revolution. "People's power" is democracy for all those who have nothing and have everything to gain. The right to health, the right to housing, the right to education. It is not enough to elect the neighbourhood committee and think they will solve the problems for you. It is necessary for people themselves to co-operate in solving problems. The functions of Workers' Committees and Neighbourhood Committees are complementary. People must not think in terms of each one for himself but must think collectively for the benefit of the group. Each one for himself is a relic of the dark 50 years of fascism.'[31]

Audrey Wise concluded: 'the meeting had been a fascinating experience, a situation where reform and revolution were not alternatives but were actually part of the same process, Democracy was struggling into being in this village, and it was a rare treat to be able to witness it.'[32]

The persistence of the problem of housing, of decent housing, would multiply the conflicts. And the *Documento Guia* did not achieve its central goals because one of its legs – the MFA – would soon split into pieces, taking with it the Povo–MFA Pact, that is, the project of a strongly regulated capitalist State. The State could not establish an equilibrium between sections of classes and could not avoid an insurrectionary shift of power towards the workers and their representative bodies. We have seen from just glimpsing at the above examples that the assemblies were autonomous, although at times influenced by the MFA and at others by elements from the political parties. The question of alternative power often came up, not always, and not succinctly, but nevertheless the assemblies, and similar coordination, went beyond the comfortable pyramid that had been imagined in the *Documento Guia*.[33]

15

The Land for its Workers:
Agrarian Reform

Comrades, let us work the land together. And why? To make it more productive.[1]

Rural worker, September 1975

Portugal witnessed 'the largest popular land seizures in European history'.[2] That impacted upon the revolution and that is why this chapter is being written.

Geography and Land Ownership

The occupations took place mainly in the southern half of Portugal, in the Alentejo – the area 'beyond the Tejo'. But before we get embroiled in the occupations, we need to look at the geography. Here is a succinct overview:

A useful categorization divides the mainland into three distinct topographical and climatic zones: the south (the Alentejo and the Algarve), the centre (the Ribatejo and Oeste), and the north (the Entre Douro e Minho, the Trás-os-Montes, the Beira Litoral, and the Beja Interior).

The north is mountainous, with a rainy, moderately cool climate. This zone contains about 2 million hectares of cultivated land and is dominated by small-scale, intensive agriculture. High population density, particularly in the northwest, has contributed to a pattern of tiny, fragmented farms that produce mainly for family consumption interspersed with larger and often mechanized farms that specialize in commercial production of a variety of crops. On the average, northern levels of technology and labor productivity are among the lowest in Western Europe. Extreme underemployment of agricultural workers accounts for the north being the principal and enduring source of Portuguese emigrant labor.

The centre is a diverse zone that includes rolling hills suitable primarily for tree crops, poor dryland soils, and the fertile alluvial soils of the banks of the Rio Tejo (Tagus River in English). A variety of crops are grown on the productive areas under irrigation: grains, mainly wheat and corn, oil seeds (including sunflowers), and irrigated rice. Farms located in the Rio Tejo Valley typically are 100 hectares in size.

The south is dominated by the Alentejo, a vast, rolling plain with a hot, arid climate. The Alentejo occupies an area of approximately 2.6 million hectares, about 30 percent of the total area of mainland Portugal, and produces about 75 percent of the country's wheat. Although much of the area is classified as arable land, poor soils dominate most of the area, and consequently yields of dryland crops and pasture are low by West European standards. The Alentejo is also known for its large stands of cork oak and its olive groves. The Algarve, less than a third the area of the Alentejo, occupies the extreme southern part of Portugal. This dryland area is characterized by smallholdings where animal grazing and fishing are the principal occupations of the inhabitants.[3]

The cleavage between those areas in which rural wage-labourers predominate and those in which peasant farmers are in the majority helps explain both the advances and counter-revolution, which came to a head on November 1975.

There was a strong regional difference in ownership. The North had some modern commercial vineyards, producing world famous wines and port. Nevertheless, the overwhelming majority of holdings in the North were extremely small. They belonged to smallholders or were farmed by individual tenants – a very conservative mix. Some were obliged to work part-time on other farms. As we saw in Chapter 2, many members of families of smallholders migrated to the cities or emigrated abroad. The women often remained behind to till the land. Large parts were still extremely underdeveloped. Some of the remote mountain villages in the Tras os Montes had only recently started using money as a medium of exchange. Peasants still wore leather around their feet instead of shoes. Famine was not a thing of the past.

The southern half of Portugal was dominated by large estates of the landed elite, called the *latifúndia*. Five per cent of landowners possessed 85 per cent of the land.[4] The land was used to grow olives, cork, cereal crops and breed livestock. Owners of the estates, the *latifúndia*, depended upon seasonal labour. The elite employed large numbers during peak growing time but for the rest of the time the labourers would be unemployed, or might work on the estates for one or two days a week. Very few were 'peasants'; they did not own land.

The agricultural population declined considerably during the 1960s, as a result of emigration and industrialisation, and saw chronic unemployment (seasonal employment).

Over the previous decades, notably in 1962, the land workers organised around the issue of contracts, albeit seasonal, coupled with wanting to cultivate fallow land. Historically, the Communist Party had strong roots with agrarian wage earners either because of the tradition of underground resistance, or because industrialisation in the 1960s had forced many of the farm workers to go to industrial belts of the cities, as industrial proletarians, where they connected with the party. These issues of contracts gathered momentum in the following months of autumn 1974. The agitation was led by unions.

After 25 April, a frenzy of activity was seen on the land vastly surpassing the struggles of 1962.[5] The initial policy of the State – at a time without a Ministry of Agriculture but with only one secretariat, headed by Esteves Belo – was to seek to maximise profits from the fields.[6] But social conflict broke out in the Alentejo: conflicts, including strikes by the workers and economic skullduggery by the *latifúndia* led the State to intervene and introduce various legislations, which were approved in October and November, but mainly through the Law-Decree 660/74 of 25 November 1974. This partially protected employment for the workers. According to Constantine Piçarra, this led to the growing awareness that agrarian reform would be the only way to ensure stability in employment. This was also the conclusion of Oliveira Baptista: 'Situations related to unemployment, often associated with poor land use, with wages in arrears or attempts at disinvestment, are at the root of the occupations.'[7] Clearly, the legislation was insufficient: according to António Barreto, the first land occupation took place in November 1974.

The Communist Party was the dominant party in the Alentejo and Ribatejo fields. Although António Barreto, citing the study of José Pacheco Pereira *Os Conflates Sociais nos Campos do Sul de Portugal* (*Social Conflicts in the Southern Fields of Portugal*) (1983), argues that the Communist Party influence had diminished in the Alentejo by 25 April,[8] it is a fact that the far-left, or the Socialist Party, never managed to counterbalance the influence of the Communist Party in the Alentejo as they did in industrial enterprises and in the service sector of the large urban centres. Barreto points out reasons why the Communist Party regained influence in the southern fields, such as the capacity for organisation, use of language and recruitment techniques, the predominance of the rural proletariat in the region, employing full-time workers, the collaboration of the MFA and the support of the Ministry of Agriculture and the Ministry of Labour.[9]

Because of the worsening employment in the cities, people were returning to the land, and many had been involved in collective experiences, through organising in the workplaces and these were not, in general, linked to the Communist Party. We have already shown how the Communist Party distanced itself from the autonomous developments in the workplaces.[10]

The Occupations Start

The unions did not take the lead in the actual occupation of the land. The collectivisation was driven by desperate land workers and inspired by what was happening elsewhere. The occupations, comprising 25 per cent of Portugal's arable land, were in essence autonomous. 'There was never talk of dividing up the land'.[11] According to António Barreto, the first land occupation took place in November 1974 and the pace was sporadic. But by February, there were already seven times more occupied lands than in January.[12] The occupations welled up in autumn 1975, often with the tacit or active support of the army. By then, the rural unions and the Communist Party had changed tack and supported them. Although 25 November spelled the end of any further occupations, it took much longer for the counter-revolution to reverse the agrarian reform movement.

There were major challenges confronting agrarian reform – the majority of these arising at the end of 1975 with a lack of access to finance. Nevertheless, the scale of the agrarian reform that took place in Portugal was unprecedented and needs to be remembered. Agrarian reform resulted in the farming of thousands of hectares of previously uncultivated land, the maximisation of employment and increased production. Profits declined with the implementation of these policies, but not so the wealth produced by workers engaged in cooperative and collective units of production.

Between 1975–1976, the number of permanent jobs increased from 11,100 to 44,100 and the number of seasonal positions increased from 10,600 to 27,800. In terms of dryland crops, the area of cultivation grew from 85,000 hectares[13] before land occupation to 255,000 hectares. Irrigation increased from 7,000 hectares to 16,000 hectares. With the help from government funds, and also the Communist Bloc, the number of tractors increased from 2,630 to 4,150 and that of harvesting machinery from 960 to 1720.[14]

Some Accounts

A group of rural workers from the parish of Cabecao, part of the municipality of Mora in the centre of the Alentejo, was interviewed for the television news, as part of a campaign of the Institute of Agrarian Reform, which had been founded to legalise and manage the struggles in the countryside and the application of rural policy:

> A man named Lopes Aleixo employed people working on his property whom he hadn't paid for three weeks, and we thought of occupying that property in addition to two others. We thought it through and carried out this occupation.
>
> Journalist: But, it seems, this occupation would be also motivated by a certain abandonment and neglect ...
>
> Rural worker: One was caused by the workers having walked there and not receiving payment, and another was due to the land being abandoned. Practically abandoned.[15]

The worker admits that the occupations could have been carried out more calmly, 'to see what's there', who 'goes there to work', to form a 'commission of workers to justify what properties should be occupied'.

It could not have been calmer. The Institute of Agrarian Reform was created – with real concern for legality – and governments supported and legalised what was done by the people, starting with small and medium renters of machines that had debts to banks and needed to have the machines to work the earth to pay them back; and then agricultural workers, who had no job but wanted to work. These last were the ones who would turn out to be the 'main protagonists'.[16]

In June 1975, a Portuguese public television report covered the occupation of Quinta da Verge, in Unhais da Serra, near Covilhã. At the time, nothing was known of the owner's whereabouts; he 'being absent, the brother was connected to the 11 March [conspiracy], but it was not known if he was in Madrid, or Brazil'.

The farm had 5,000 hectares, two-thirds pinewood, 75,000 apple trees, which produced 500 tons per year, 15,000 peach trees and 2,500 cherry trees, boasted a dam of its own, a large quantity of potatoes and 'was crossed by a river where Mrs Garrett (wife of the owner) and their friends would entertain themselves with fishing during leisure hours.'

The journalist interviewed a shepherd of the farm. Dressed in traditional garb, a large cloak, he related that: 'he never had a day of rest in his life', he comes home to eat at sunset every day to 'sleep at the feet of the cattle'.

Journalist: What was your salary when Mr Garrett was here:

— It was two contos and 500 reis.

— And then?

— Then went to six contos and 600 reis with benefits.

— Benefits?

— Yes, the house, 5 litres of olive oil and a bit of land to cultivate.

'Who pays you and what do you receive now in the absence of the owner?'

—Just the commission of the workers.[17]

The theme of agrarian reform has brought together the largest number of studies on the Portuguese Revolution. Works have been published on the geography, chronology and the extent of agrarian reform policy. All of these studies directly refer to the policy of the Communist Party, the organisation that claimed to lead the agrarian reform process. I have already referred to the works of Oliveira Baptista,[18] an agronomist and Minister of Agriculture of the Fourth and Fifth Provisional Governments in 1975; António Barreto, a sociologist and Minister of Agriculture of the First Constitutional Government (Socialist Party), responsible for the so-called 'Lei Barreto', (Barreto Law),[19] which began the process of dismantling agrarian reform, and the work of Constantino Piçarra,[20] which studies the reform in the district of Beja, where most of the occupation of lands occurred in 1974–1975.

Summer 1975

The tensions on the land spilled over into the rest of society. For example, on 25 July, a People's Court convened in Tomar freed the rural labourer José Diogo, who had killed his employer in 1974 and it condemned, posthumously, the landowner Columbano Libano Monteiro.

The workers established agricultural cooperatives, often named after political events and characters. The 'Soldado Luís' cooperative was named after the soldier killed on 11 March at RAL-1 barracks (see the photo on the next page). The most inspiring of the changes was the transformation of the traditional peasant women. Often illiterate, dressed in black from head to foot, they did much of the back-breaking labour. Now, they not only ensured that they were paid regular wages – at almost the same rate as men – but also that they played an active part in the management of the cooperative.[21]

In Couco, a small town inland from Lisbon with a tradition of rebellion against the Salazar regime, a protest for agrarian reform was being prepared, one of the several to take place in summer 1975, to press the Fifth Provisional Government to approve the credit that would be used to pay salaries – this measure would later be ratified by the Sixth Government, by a minister of the Socialist Party. Before the protest broke out, there was intense discussion about the pressing issues including access to a river, the opening of a road and use of machinery. The debate was interrupted by a worker seated on a tractor wearing a beret, mobilising people to start the demonstration: 'Comrades, let us work the land together. And why? To make it more productive. So that the money yielded from the harvests is for agriculture and not to be squandered! ... Let us begin our march. At your posts!'[22]

The first week of August witnessed a new wave of farm occupations in Serpa and Moura, in the Beja district, many of them to prevent the sale of livestock, agricultural machinery and 'acts of economic sabotage'. On 13 August, the Lobeira estate in Montemor-o-Novo, belonging to the Vácas

Photo 4   Funeral procession of Soldier Luís, killed during the attempted coup of 11 March 1975. (Jose Reis)

de Carvalho family, was occupied. On 20 August, the farms of Castros, Xévora, Poços de Cima, Ronquilha, Vale de Albuquerque, Poço de Baixo, Salvador, Mourinha and Serrinha in Campo Maior were occupied by rural workers and small farmers. A series of events were held in September, always with the same aim: to press for credit to ensure wages.

Such demonstrations and occupations generated a disruptive effect involving other workers and sectors in the chain of events. For example, on 25 October 1975, about 20 workers of the Marquesa Cooperative in Azambuja occupied the lands of Bafôa and Queijeira, properties of the Duke of Lafões, leased for 800,000 escudos to the SUGAL tomato concentrate factory. In the following weeks, up to 600 workers came and gave a hand harvesting the tomatoes.

Photo 5   Agricultural workers from the farm 'Os Machados' outside the Ministry of Agriculture in Lisbon complaining to a representative of the Ministry. (Jose Reis)

September 1975

On 29 September, the government changed tack, thus beginning what, for Piçarra, would be the third and final phase of land occupations in the southern fields and, most importantly, included the bulk of the land that would be occupied during this period.

On September 6, 1975, the Fifth Provisional Government fell, followed by the Sixth, led by Admiral Pinheiro de Azevedo. At this juncture, and because political changes at the state level were not indifferent to the future of agrarian reform, agricultural unions immediately reinforced the pressure on the government of the rural workers' social movement, demanding financial support for new units, particularly for the payment of wages. This power struggle between the unions and the government gave way to the Decree-Law no. 541-B/75 of September 27, promulgating the elimination of obstacles in accessing credit by UCPs [units of collective production] and cooperatives. On September 29, emergency agricultural credit was extended to farms managed by the workers and to be used for the payment of ... the wages of workers in the new production units from October, 1975 to the end of the year, peaking in October ... Hence the credit paid the salaries of the rural workers of 693,743 hectares of land, representing 59.9 per cent of all occupations carried out in 1975.[23]

Table 15.1   Movement of Land Occupations in the Fields of the South in 1975

Phases of the movement of occupations	Beja (1) Area (ha)	Évora (2) Area (ha)	Portalegre (2) Area (ha)	Alentejo Total Area (ha)	ZIRA[24] (2) Area (ha)
Phase 1 From 31 July 1975	30,783	53,461	40,144	124,338 (12.7%)	156,353 (13.5%)
Phase 2 From 1 August 1975 to 30 September 1975	53,915	213,098	9,910	276,923 (28.1%)	309,338 (26.6%)
Phase 3 From 1 October 1975 to 31 December 1975	233,420	164,232	183,857	581,509 (59.2%)	696,743 (59.9%)
Total	318,118	430,791	233,911	982,820 (100%)	1,162,434 (100%)

Source: Constantino Piçarra, *As Ocupações de Terras no Distrito de Beja, 1974–1975* (Coimbra: Almedina, 2008); Afonso Barros, *Do Latifúndio à Reforma Agrária: o caso de uma freguesia do Baixo Alentejo* (Lisbon: Fundação Calouste Gulbenkian, 1986).

The Influence of the Communist Party

Until the first two months of 1975, the policy of the Communist Party was to intervene in terms of the appropriate means of land usage, but without questioning the details of its ownership. As such, it failed to distinguish itself from the policy of the other members of the government, since the government had also put into practice measures, as observed Oliveira Baptista, 'which linked the right to exploit the land (and not its property!) to its good use.'[25] But in February, at the First Conference of Agricultural Workers of the South held in Évora, the party decisively assumed the struggle for agrarian reform and the defence of land occupation, with the following statement: 'The land obtained ... must be delivered to Agricultural Workers Unions or Small Farmers Leagues, to be utilized under a regime of cooperative production, or else to be utilized directly by the State.'[26]

The fact is that the occupations were not led, in the first place, by the Communist Party. They were in essence autonomous; they came about from below and were initiated by the labourers themselves.

As time went on, the Communist Party regained ground and was perceived to be the dominant force in the Agrarian Reform movement. Constantine Piçarra suggests three conclusions. The first is that the Communist Party responded politically to the process of land occupation once already in progress, to direct the process. The second is that the main demand of the agricultural workers – to have guaranteed employment 12 months a year – could only be ensured by the realisation of the agrarian reform.[27] The third was a reform proposal that gradually excluded the free association of small landowners in cooperatives during the first half of 1975 and proposed, as an alternative to expropriating land, that they be managed by state holdings, the Collective Units of Production.[28] This was the *Rumo à Vitória* (*Path to Victory*) policy, which had been promoted by the Communist Party. This policy was ratified only after October 1975, thus already in the midst of the revolutionary crisis and at the moment when two-thirds of all occupations of the revolutionary process were underway.

A Lasting Impact?

The impact of the process was brief. This was because the counter-revolution resulted in a shift away from this by government forces, and also because of the re-emergence of conventional market forces:

> The economy of collective and cooperative units was immersed in the market and the various units of production encountered distinct conditions of production – the quality of soils, types of cultivation (irrigated or dry), plantations, improvements, land improvements, equipment, constructions, machines. These inequalities of condition led to a marked differentiation between the units in relation to the economic results obtained.[29]

The agrarian policies remained in the hands of governors, who blocked their financing and their production remained always subject to the market. This quickly led to a series of problems: conflicts within cooperatives (according to Oliveira Baptista, exacerbated by the egalitarian wave that defended equal wages for all), and the absence of employment (later managed by the Unemployment Fund). The decline was inevitable by the late 1970s.

Nevertheless, during these two years, a new concept of the land arose to provoke an about-turn in agrarian policies and an unusual change took place, inducing the poor, the extremely impoverished and salaried agricultural earners to embrace wholeheartedly the cause of 'the land for its workers'. People have not changed the land in a lasting way, but the struggle for land has changed the people. These, who constituted the ranks of agrarian reform, the poor, often illiterate, were forced to act decisively, 'to take their lives in their own hands', just as those who travelled from Lisbon to the Alentejo to help in agrarian reform, and those who came from abroad, imbued with the romanticism of the Carnation Revolution, were forever changed.

Furthermore, the rural proletariat came into Lisbon and their presence, for example, on the truly gigantic demonstration organised by the workers' commissions of Lisbon on 16 November, packed in open-sided lorries and hanging onto tractors, including old women dressed in the traditional black and many young children, was extremely important. It provided a retort to the threat by the peasants and farmers in the North, who threatened to cut off food supplies to the 'red commune' of Lisbon.

The Backlash in the Rural North

Up till now, we haven't dwelled on the politics of the peasants and small farmers in the North – deliberately, because I have wanted to focus upon the rural proletariat.

Land reform, which didn't apply to holdings less than 500 hectares, or 50 hectares of irrigated land, scarcely touched those in the North. The endless media talk of a new life in Portugal contrasted starkly with the continuing grind of existence in the backward regions. The focus of governments was on the agrarian reform and collectivisation, not on the traditional aspirations of peasants, who wanted to own their own land, not to farm it communally. Talk of agrarian reform frightened the small farm owners into thinking their holdings would be expropriated.

This fear was to be greatly fuelled by the Catholic Church and led to the burning down of Communist Party offices, and even of shootings, in summer 1975. This process is described in more detail in the next chapter.

16

The 'Hot Summer' of 1975 and the Fifth Government's Frail Governance

Let us examine our own case for example: unconditional supporters of the MFA (and not rarely insulted for that), as time went by we came to realise that the very MFA had entered into a kind of binary fission so that whereas formerly there was one, we began to see two, three, even four... [1]

José Saramago, October 1975

This chapter covers summer 1975, commencing with collapse of the Fourth Provisional Government and ending with the collapse of the Fifth Provisional Government, which had hardly functioned as a government.

The country was becoming increasingly divided: in the north and centre between the communists and the church, in the south between the *latifúndia* and land-workers and in the towns and cities between waged labour and owners. The Socialist Party knew that the Constituent Assembly elections outcomes, although favourable to the party, were not enough to defeat the workers' control movement, which had spread since February in the public sector, education, hospitals, banks and the insurance sector. To use a metaphor: to defeat this army, the Socialists needed another army. The victory at the elections was insufficient. They made an agreement with the Catholic Church to mobilise against the leaderships of unions and left parties, mainly the Communist Party. The only organisation capable of mobilising the troops on behalf of the reaction was the church.

The main conflicts of this hot summer took place at the *República*, Rádio Renascença and land disputes in the North. After this moment, the Socialist Party was no longer alone, but in a clear alliance with the church, the upper hierarchy of the armed forces and the moderates in the MFA, which came to be known as the 'Group of Nine'. Simultaneously and in response, there was a febrile atmosphere everywhere and huge and repeated demonstrations in support of the revolution took place. All this meant that the Fifth Provisional Government, headed by Vasco Gonçalves was stillborn.

On 10 July 1975, the Socialist Party decided to formally abandon the Fourth Provisional Government. On 17 July, there was a huge political rally of the Socialist Party at the Fonte Luminosa in Lisbon at which Mário Soares spoke, openly attacking the Provisional Government and threatening to 'paralyse the country'.

República

The official reason the Socialist Party presented for leaving the government was the differences concerning the *República* daily paper, which had been taken over by the workers. Mário Soares called the *República* 'the last voice of Freedom', and asked the MFA to close down the paper and dismiss the 'Communist' printers. He said that it was necessary to 'take the paper away from Cunhal',[2] generally accusing the Communist Party of attempting to establish a dictatorial domination of the communication media. The burgeoning weight of the Communist Party in innumerable state structures and the direct control or strong political influence that it wielded at the time over most of the daily newspapers was very apparent.

The truth was somewhat different in this instance, and it is worth unpacking, because it is a vivid example of how the evolution of worker control in just one workplace led to disarray and prompted the semi-collapse of the power of the State.

República had been published as a daily since 1911, as an independent republican paper, and had survived through the years of repression and censorship. It was never an official Socialist Party paper, nonetheless, after the elections of April 1975, it campaigned fiercely against the MFA and the Gonçalves government. It was then that the printers of the paper refused to set type, accusing the editors of supporting the counter-revolution. On 20 June, the MFA dispatched a COPCON unit to return the paper back to its owners, insisting there were no sackings of the printers. The owner refused to conform and then shut down and abandoned the paper, which was subsequently taken over by the workers.

There were only two communists among the 30 on the elected workers' commission, which in turn represented 194 printers on the shop floor. The workers were fiercely autonomous and made it absolutely clear that they were independent of political parties. The workers' statement of aims (24 May) declared:

República will not henceforth belong to any party. All the progressive parties will be given identical treatment, depending only on the importance of events.

Photo 6   Workers in *República*, who had taken over their newspaper.
(Wendy Plimley)

Far from ordering the seizures of *República* and Rádio Renascença – as
the American press unanimously reported – the Communist Party actually
opposed the workers, knowing that the furor could serve as a pretext for
rightist agitation against the Gonçalves cabinet.[3]

Melo Antunes, in a conversation with the British prime minister,
stated that: 'the communists were actually taken over by the workers
themselves, who moved even farther to the left. That, he considered, was
due to the fact that the Maoists, in spite of their "bourgeois origins and
university educations" had managed to penetrate the workers [movement]
profoundly.'[4]

The pretext for withdrawing from government was actually founded on a
real situation: their need to thwart workers' control. The socialist leadership
accused the Communist Party of attempting to impose a communist dictatorship in Portugal and proclaimed its own role as a leadership capable of
retrieving freedom from the clutches of collectivist ideology, union control,
anti-clericalism and dictatorship of the communication media.[5] In that way,
it sought to gain the support of the middle classes. This resignation – on
10 July, was the very day *República* re-opened under the control of the
workers – leading to the formation of yet another provisional government,
the Fifth Provisional, headed by General Vasco Gonçalves and consisting
predominantly of communists and fellow-travellers. This was the first

provisional government that did not include the Socialist Party or the conservative PPD (Partido Popular Democrático).

The Catholic Church

Though Portugal was a nominally Catholic country, in order to understand the organisation behind the backlash against the revolution, it is necessary to focus upon the Church:

The practice of religion in Portugal showed striking regional differences. Even in the early 1990s, 60 to 70 per cent of the population in the traditionally Roman Catholic north regularly attended religious services, compared with 10 to 15 per cent in the historically anticlerical south. In the greater Lisbon area, about 30 per cent were regular churchgoers.

The traditional importance of Roman Catholicism in the lives of the Portuguese was evident in the physical organisation of almost every village in Portugal. The village churches were usually in prominent locations, either on the main square or on a hilltop overlooking the villages. Many of the churches and chapels were built in the sixteenth century at the height of Portugal's colonial expansion and were often decorated with wood and gold leaf from the conquests. In recent decades, however, they were often in disrepair, for there were not enough priests to tend them. Many were used only rarely to honour the patron saints of the villages. ... the celebration of saints' days and religious festivals were popular [in the rural areas].[6]

Fear of collectivisation and the failure of agricultural policy played into the hands of the Catholic Church, which over the early summer played a leading role in mobilising the small farmers.

The Archbishop of Braga famously equated the communists with Satan:

We are called upon to fight for God or against Him. To draw back would be betrayal. And betrayal would be death![7]

At a rally on 10 August 1975, just two days after the official formation of the Fifth Provisional Government, tens of thousands heard his scathing attack on the communists and immediately assaulted the Communist Party headquarters. When party militants inside refused to surrender, shots were fired and troops were called in to quell the crowd. But the gathering maintained the siege overnight and ultimately broke through the line of troops, drove the party members out, and burned the headquarters down. Some thirty people were injured.[8]

This same archbishop regularly supplied funds and premises to far-right organisations.[9]

On Sunday 13 July, the Church organised a rally in Aveiro, a coastal town, against the takeover of Rádio Renascença. This led to the burning down of the Communist Party headquarters in Aveiro – the Bishop of that diocese who is also the President of the Episcopal Conference, called for similar actions everywhere. 'The example of Aveiro,' he said, 'must be repeated in the North, in the South, all over.'[10] Some 60 offices were ransacked and burnt down, mainly of the Communist Party but also some trade union centres and offices of the revolutionary left. Hence, we had what was called 'the Hot Summer of 1975'.

The demonstrations, which provided the cover for these incendiary acts, were usually organised in the same way. They were called anonymously but announced from the pulpits by the priests. They concentrated on the rural population by leading many peasants to believe that not only were their small plots being threatened by the revolution, but also their religion. And they were brought by fleets of rented buses to the Episcopal cities where the demonstrations took place. The bishops participated in the actions and one of the central demands was for the return of *Renascença* 'stolen by the Communists'.

At around the same time as the *República* revolt, the Catholic radio station, Rádio Renascença, was being taken over by the workers. The station had been used to broadcast 'reactionary diatribes' against the revolution. This incensed the station's employees. Unlike the case of the newspaper *República*, which was not owned by the Socialist Party, the radio station was the property of the Catholic Church. The takeover, and the lack of action by the MFA, came to be portrayed as an anti-religious assault on the church.

The Catholic Church launched a 'holy crusade' against the Communist Party, which was accused of being responsible for the Rádio Renascença takeover. A massive campaign of incitation to violence followed. Bishops and priests worked closely with the rightist political leaders of the Social Democratic Centre (CDS) and the Popular Democratic Party (PPD).[11]

The retreat from the colonies meant that half a million bitterly disillusioned *retornados* had to be resettled and re-integrated into a population of 9 million. Many settled in the centre and the North, already traditionally conservative areas.

The structuring of the anti-communist terrorism was based on four components: the support of the church hierarchy, which had its epicentre in the episcopate of Braga; technical, operational and economic support

Photo 7   Special English solidarity issue of *República*,
published under workers' control.

from Spain, which also provided an escape route; the collaboration of
sectors of the military that were against the events of 25 April; and lastly,
the agreement of the political forces from socialists to right-wingers that
prevailed in the country's northern and central districts.

The Working Class Resists

As the struggles over 'religious rights' fomented, so did class struggles.
Looking at the strikes and the workers and social movement activities, we
can see a country paralysed by social upheaval. Hundreds of demonstrations took place in July and August in support of the revolution. On 14 July
alone, there were reports of more than a dozen large-scale demonstrations
in the cities. There was a big one in Lisbon in support of Rádio Renascença.
There was also in Lisbon an Intersindical demonstration in support of the

MFA. In front of the courts in Setúbal, there was a demonstration calling for the annulment of the sentence of a tenant who had killed his landlord. The demonstration in Beja called out by the Sindicato dos Trabalhadores Agricolas do Distrito de Beja (Beja District Agricultural Workers Union) was in support of the *Documento Guia, Povo–MFA*.

The grass-roots boycotting of railway fare increases continued and a strike of Lisbon metro workers began. In Porto, on 16 July, there was a people's demonstration called out by the residents' committees 'for the right to work, for housing, for the dissolution of the Constituent Assembly and for a non-party revolutionary government of the workers'. In Lisbon, on 16 July, there was a unitary demonstration for people's power demanding the 'dissolution of the Constituent Assembly' and 'worker's control'. Organisations that adhered to it included the UDP, CMLP, CRTSM, MES, ORPC (M-L) and PRP-BR. For the first time, hundreds of uniformed soldiers equipped with armoured vehicles took part.

On 17 July, the União dos Sindicatos dos Portos (Dockers Unions Federation) called for a general strike starting at 5pm the next day. In Lisbon again, on 1 August, there was a demonstration of the Secretariado Nacional (Provisorio) das Comissões de Trabalhadores (Provisional National Secretariat of Workers Commissions). Furthermore the occupation of houses, land and workplaces continued. The strikes went on and on.

In Chapter 15, on the agrarian struggles, we saw how, on 25 July, a People's Court freed rural labourer José Diogo who had killed his employer in 1974 and that this court also remarkably condemned the landowner, posthumously. What sort of State was this where one of its absolute pillars, the Judiciary, the one least susceptible to social transformations, could see its decisions overturned by a grass-roots group making a judgement contrary to the one determined by the State Courts?

Residents and others were inspired by the movement. Here is a typical speech, this one by a resident on the COPCON demonstration:

Comrades, the reign of capitalist exploitation, intensified by the fascist governments of Salazar and Caetano, threw the working class and the peasants into miserable conditions of life as seen in the shanty towns. Fighting against this exploitation alone and unorganised the struggles are not successful. The workers saw the necessity of forming workers' commissions in the factories, and residents' commissions in the shanty towns and poor areas that could represent and defend their interests. These commissions, which at first worked only at neighbourhood or factory level, were isolated in their fight for rent reductions, for the elimination of the hut dwellings, for decent housing, for the 'saneomento' of the fascists from the factories, for the increase of wages, etc. They realised that they were fighting the same struggle everywhere – the struggle to end the exploitation that was oppressing all.[12]

The emphasis is on 'real' democracy and collective control by the working class. (We will, for the moment, ignore the stress on this being an anti-fascist battle and how this obscured the threat from social democracy and reformism.)

The Fifth Government

Against the background of growing polarisation, the embryonic Fifth Provisional Government was hopeless and helpless. In the negotiations to form a new government, the Prime Minster Vasco Gonçalves did his best to ensure breadth of representation, but to no avail. This was the first provisional government that did not include the Socialist Party or the conservative PPD (Partido Popular Democrático).

On 25 July 1975, an assembly of the MFA approved a proposal for the constitution of a triumvirate made up of Costa Gomes (the president), Vasco Gonçalves and Otelo Saraiva de Carvalho as a means to put an end to the crisis. The Communist Party supported the decision and made it clear that the 'main enemy' continued to be the 'reaction' and that solutions needed to be found that would make them 'respect the democratic order'.[13]

On 4 August 1975 it was the turn of Otelo, who supported the COPCON project and was working in close alignment with some of the far-left, to reject the notion of a 'strong' government headed by Vasco Gonçalves.[14]

As this government was not supported by the Socialists or the Communists or the PPD, it was already devoid of the social conditions to actually be able to govern. The Fifth Provisional Government finally took office on 8 August. It comprised members of the military, independents and members of the MDP/CDE. The Prime Minister Vasco Gonçalves declared that he was not exactly 'clinging on to the post'.[15] Vasco Gonçalves was perceived as having moved close to the Communist Party, but now he wanted to create a bit more distance believing that a project *a la* Nasser was feasible for Portugal. He was a military figure who believed he had fulfilled his duty in having headed a government so that the country would not become totally paralysed.[16]

On taking office, Vasco Gonçalves appealed for reconciliation and the unity of the armed forces,[17] but at the same time, President Costa Gomes refers to a 'transitory'[18] solution. It was a government mainly supported by the military left and a significant portion of the far-left. Crucially, the government did not have the support of any of the major electoral parties. The Socialist Party was hostile. It didn't want a Communist Party 'fellow traveller' heading the government. It wanted power, which it felt was its right, empowered by its victory in the election for the Constituent Assembly. That day, after assuming power, on 9 August, the *Jornal Novo* published a note by Mário Soares demanding the dismissal of Vasco Gonçalves.[19]

Several currents could be seen within the MFA. These differences were to be critical. On the very day that the government was launched, a moderate group of military officers close to the PS, the Group of Nine, issued a manifesto.[20] The leader of the group was Melo Antunes, who had resigned as Minister of Foreign Affairs in June. Their document declared their refusal to accept 'a socialist model for society of the kind in force in eastern Europe' and furthermore, that they rejected 'the social-democratic model prevailing in Western Europe'. Instead, they advocated non-aligned socialism along the lines of Scandinavian social democracy. The document was published in a special edition of the *Jornal Novo* and became known as 'The Document of the Nine'. Those who signed were expelled from the Council of the Revolution, the governing body of the MFA.

Another group, around Otelo and influenced by the PRP-BR, MES and the UDP, issued on 12 August what was to be known as the COPCON document. This was firmly committed to development of the workers' and residents' movements. It criticised both the Group of Nine and those who had drawn close to the PCP and singled out Prime Minister Gonçalves for his links to the communists. On 20 August, in Lisbon, there was a demonstration in support of the COPCON 'anti-fascist and anti-imperialist document' that brought out more than 100,000 workers, operators, soldiers and sailors, demanding the immediate dissolution of the Constituent Assembly and the development of bodies reflecting the will of the people. It was called for and supported by workers' and residents' committees and the UDP, FSP, LCI, LUAR, MES, ORPC (M-L) and the PRP-BR.

Otelo still had a great deal of influence, both within the military and also within the workers' movement. He was loved but also known as having a mercurial personality and could be rather erratic and even volatile.

Right from the day that the Fifth Provisional Government took office, the Communist Party's support had been evasive, even though Vasco Gonçalves was said to be close to the Communists. *Avante!* had never run any front-page material explicitly supporting the Fifth Provisional

Government or Vasco Gonçalves but it published a special issue (on 11 August 1975) questioning that very government. The party, from that juncture was developing a rupture with the military left, which it did not have control over and which it seriously mistrusted.[21]

The communication issued by the political sub-committee of the Communist Party's Central Committee[22] on 8 August 1975 emphasised the urgent need to fill the political vacuum 'to avoid paralysing the State machinery' and that is why it tentatively supported the Fifth Provisional Government. It also criticised the Socialist Party for having abandoned the government coalition and left the question of recomposing the government open, to allow for 'widening the social and political base of support for its authority'. The communication defended the idea of a swift resolution for the divisions within the MFA and stressed the commonalties that existed between the MFA and the government. Yet the 11 August special issue of *Avante!* published extracts from the report by communist leader, Álvaro Cunhal, to the Central Committee, which questions the viability of The Fifth Provisional Government[23] and he did his best to persuade the party that the Group of Nine was a force that could be rejuvenated by a revolutionary process',[24] yet announcing that it was not going to support the military and there was still a risk that the military sector would turn against the party:

> The military left became greatly encouraged (unfoundedly, in our opinion) by the Directorate's decision that the signatories of the Melo Antunes Document should be removed from the Revolutionary Council … If the problem was already serious in the political sphere it was made even worse by the internal situation of the MFA where the Group of Nine is in conflict with the military left wing and there is another leftist anarchistic sector that makes the unity of the progressive forces increasingly difficult to attain. That means a hypothesis, the need for which cannot be confirmed, but a hypothesis of building certain bridges with forces or elements which today are situated in a sector that would be against the process; that is, in the civil and military spheres. It also so happens, that a certain part of the military which we can consider to be progressive has turned against the party or has left the party in isolation.[25]

These differences in effect signalled both the end of the Fifth Provisional Government and, ultimately, the MFA.

It must not be forgotten that when the Communist Party found itself isolated it was facing a massive physical onslaught in the towns and villages in the north and parts of the centre of the country. (The main topics in the *Avante!* editions of 7 and 14 August were all about defending the party from the attacks it was experiencing on its offices.) The government's only remaining allies were factions the Communist Party did not trust or did not control, which included the left-wing sectors of the military and part of the far-left, who called for an end to the Constituent Assembly and for the people to take up arms and to prepare for what would be a civil war. According to them, the first shots, the first roll of the drums were fired by the right-wing groups in the violence that marked the 'Hot Summer'. Accompanying the political crisis, were the break-ups of alliances in the heart of the MFA, and they proved to be irrevocable.

The Communist Party reaffirmed that it was prepared to fight for 'socialism' and for 'the liberties' that had been gained. Unlike the communications issued in late June and early July[26] in which it had threatened to marginalise the Socialist Party, the Communist Party was now ready to review the composition of the Government without any conditions.[27]

In Álvaro Cunhal's report to the Central Committee, it is easy to see that the party considered the crisis potentially turning into a full-blown civil war; the Communist Party did not want an armed conflict in any circumstances. Cunhal declared that the crisis affected all levels of society; it was a political, economic, military and social crisis and it also affected the decolonisation process (the civil war in Angola). The Communist Party leader stated that the priority was to create a political solution that would, in essence, restore the coalition with the major political parties and its close coordination with the MFA. He called on the militants to put aside 'sectarianism' and 'distinguish the main enemy', the 'fascist and fascist-forming forces' from those 'forces that were hesitant about the revolution process and the pathway to socialism'. The conditions for a new government must be, in first place, to keep the Communist Party in a government coalition and at the same time to put an end to the violence directed at the Communist Party. The report argued that there could not be a democratic regime without purging of the state apparatus (in the courts and diplomatic sectors and others) and the formation of a new government must be efficient and operational. Among the other urgent tasks it identified was an austerity policy, control of the deficit, a solution for the crises in the industrial sectors, development of the Battle for Production, restrictions on imports, and increased exports. The report also defended the nationalisation process and the agrarian reform. In the international field, it proposed maintaining good relations with the Common Market countries and Spain and with the third world countries, respecting those international treaties to which Portugal was a signatory.

In regard to decolonisation, the Communist Party wanted a government that would contribute to solving the situation in Angola by supporting the MPLA.

It warned against manipulations by the extreme left vanguard:

On the pretext of respecting the will of the masses, base-ism and democrat-ism, the subjection of decisions made by the vanguard to manipulate voting seeks to disorganise and eventually liquidate the vanguard itself. That situation is generalised and is just as valid for the workers' and people's vanguards as for that of the military ... All revolutions experience a process that is irregular and full of accidents. Flexibility and the capacity to re-examine and rectify, the courage to be self-critical ... are essential conditions for a policy to be truly revolutionary.

The report declared that the Communist Party was ready to examine the situation and forms of cooperation with all those that are for the revolutionary process and willing to cooperate with the communists. In regard to those basic conditions, it said 'we make no discriminations whatever.'[28] Cunhal admitted, in the document, that the military question had yet to be resolved, that the Fifth Provisional Government was a Government flawed from the inception and that it would weaken the Communist Party:

The entire scheme of the conservative and reactionary forces was to show this government as being a government of the communists, not supported by the military, and then let it fall afterwards. The failure of the government would be seen as the failure of the Communist Party, which would be dragged down in that defeat and suffer all its consequences.[29]

That document omitted the parts where Álvaro Cunhal declared that he already expected the government[30] to fall and acknowledged the enfeeblement of the MFA: 'The Constitution of the Directorate means that at this very moment the MFA is decapitating itself; that it no longer has a homogeneous leadership ...'.[31]

In the political rallies during the two weeks that followed the constitution of the Fifth Government, the Communist Party declared that it 'supported and would continue to support the Fifth Government'.[32]

The Communist Party, through the Intersindical called for a symbolic strike of half an hour on 19 August to protest against the 'scaling up of reactionary violence and in favour of a democratic and revolutionary authority'.

The party took part in demonstrations in support of the Government and of Vasco Gonçalves. Actually, the Government's strongest support came from certain sectors of the far-left.

But bets were being hedged. On 10 August, Cunhal called on the Central Committee to give the executive bodies space in which to decide 'and preserve a margin of initiative, including in the negotiations' in the case of an eventual military takeover coming from the moderate sectors of the MFA and the Socialist Party or of a situation in which that sector gained the political initiative.[33]

Cunhal declared that a coalition government of the MFA and the main political parties was precisely the one considered to be the alliance best adapted to the correlation and configuration of the class forces in play.[34] He went even further and stated that it was possible to combine the documents

Photo 8   Published by the 'cultural dynamisation wing' of the MFA, this children's comic book explains why people should not vote

proposed by the various military factions. The pressure upon Gonçalves, the Communist Party, and within the MFA was immense.

Then, on 25 August the backbone of radical support within the MFA began to buckle. The Fifth Division (the propaganda arm of the MFA), after a flurry of contradictory and inflammatory statements, was summarily suspended and COPCON troops moved in to take over its offices. Otelo was 'trimming his sails' as he detected the wind of opinion within the MFA changing direction.[35]

FUP – The United Popular Front

The growing isolation of the Communist Party from the MFA factions, in the North, and from many rank-and-file militants, presented it with innumerable problems. It was partly to protect itself that the party initiated a united front – Frente de Unidade Popular (FUP) with six groups of the far-left. *O Século*, a daily paper influenced by the Communist Party, produced a special midday edition on Monday, 25 August, to welcome the establishment of the front as a historic occasion. Another enormous demonstration, although with fewer soldiers, was held on 27 August.

There was seen as a tremendous turn to the left by the PCP. The gyrations towards FUP must have caused some bewilderment among the Communist Party rank and file, whose leader had only recently been stressing the Battle for Production. Their confusion was quickly resolved. Within 24 hours of the 27 August demonstration, the Communist Party withdrew from the front and called for a reconciliation with the Socialist Party and the formation of a coalition government.

Carlos Brito, at that time, the Communist Party's parliamentary leader and a member of the political committee, mentioned in his recent book of memoirs the great unease within the Communist Party caused by the participation in the FUP. He tells how he represented the Communist Party at the FUP meeting, having been assigned the task by 'comrade Álvaro' and that he left the meeting 'with the feeling that he had done his duty'. However, on the following morning when he met Cunhal, the latter's opinion was quite different. 'What he told me in effect was that I had involved the party in a political commitment with leftism that went against the line approved by the Central Committee and that I had seriously jeopardised the bridges they were attempting to construct in regard to the Nine.'[36]

Responding to the criticism coming from its own left wing, the Communist Party issued a further statement in which it alleged that there was a need to conduct 'a negotiation with the adversaries'[37] and it rebutted the criticism coming from the Frente de Unidade Popular (People's Unity Front, FUP) by stating that the Communist Party left open the possibility of sporadically collaborating with those organisations in the future but at the same time, accused them of carrying out an old left wing project that consisted of 'growing at the expense of the Communist Party'.[38]

On 29 August, Vasco Gonçalves resigned as prime minister.[39] He was succeeded by 57-year-old Admiral Pinheiro de Azevedo, a member of Spínola's original junta and widely regarded as a left-winger though of a more pragmatic nature than Gonçalves and not firmly allied to the Communist Party.[40]

At a press conference held at 11pm on the night of 29 August, Álvaro Cunhal said that he was willing to meet with the Socialist Party, the Group of Nine and the COPCON to seek for a governable solution.

It is not quite clear what the relations between key military personnel and the Communist Party were. This has meant that it is difficult to explain the differences with the factions of the MFA. The relations between the military and the Communist Party were not harmonious. We do know, however, that the Fifth Provisional Government fell without any great show of resistance on the part of its members or of Vasco Gonçalves, who supported the policy of the Communist Party, and we also know that the fall of the Fifth Provisional Government exacerbated the tension between the left-wing sectors of the military and the Communist Party.

Photo 9   People's United Front (FUP) demonstration, 27 August 1975. (Wendy Plimley)

The Communist Party's policy in the eyes of the sectors that made up the FUP provoked an intense polemic. On 1 September 1975, the well-known writer José Saramago published an article entitled *Intervalo para Acusar* (A Pause to Accuse) in which he wrote 'if the Communist Party forms a left-wing front and then three days later appeals for negotiations in which God and the Devil are included – how can we, from now on, define strategy and tactics?'[41]

Perhaps it would be more accurate to say that the Communist Party's loss of control over the political situation occurred, not when the Communist Party constituted the FUP but instead, when it broke off with it and simultaneously supported the Pinheiro de Azevedo government, mobilised in favour of the Vasco Gonçalves Government and against 'imperialism and social-democracy'. The most important challenge the Communist Party had to face was to justify its withdrawal of support for the military left: 'Let us examine our own case for example: as unconditional supporters of the MFA (and not rarely insulted for that), as time went by we came to realise that the very MFA had entered into a kind of binary fission so that whereas formerly there was one, we began to see two, three, even four...'.[42]

In spite of no longer being able to enjoy the support of the military left or at least a part of it, the Communist Party wanted to retain room for maneuvering in the negotiations around the formation of the Sixth Provisional Government and in the political and institutional design of the future regime.

FUR – the Revolutionary United Front

On 2 September 1975, the FUP transformed itself into the Frente de Unidade Revolucionária (Revolutionary United Front, FUR) and the FSP, LCI, LUAR, MDP/CDE, MES, PRP were part of it.[43] FUR was to provide some cover, some unification, for the increasingly beleaguered left. Its manifesto defended the arming of people's grass-roots organisations in self-defence, the right of soldiers and sailors to hold meetings, purging and repression of fascists, nationalisations of big industrial and agricultural corporations with no compensation, placing them under workers' control, the fight for worker control and full employment, Portugal's withdrawal from NATO and the extinction of the Iberian Pact, support for the MPLA, the dissolution of the Constituent Assembly and the constitution of a Government of Revolutionary Unity.[44]

With rare exceptions,[45] the far-left had supported the Fifth Provisional Government in view of its pro-socialist and anti-fascist policy and that had led to a very unusual situation. The Fifth Provisional Government was indeed fragile but it was the one that had experienced the least opposition from the revolutionary left, which focused on the anti-revolutionary attacks it viewed as being a fascist threat. It was a government that gave way to pressures from the grass-roots political front. The support was as great as the disillusion and rupture that followed. When the Communist Party allowed the Fifth Provisional Government to fall, the revolutionary left turned its attention to its roots, to the *Poder Popular* (Popular Power) movement.

Robinson's research of Popular Assemblies tells that us throughout this period there were many meetings with delegates from residents' commissions and workers' commissions and/or soldiers from local barracks. It may be that they chose not to call themselves 'popular assemblies'. This may be because the organisation dealt with a specific issue or because the participants decided not to call themselves popular assemblies for ideological reasons. There were at least 38 popular assemblies, and the attendance at these meetings, certainly the inaugural meetings, was in the hundreds. Some withered away but many continued to meet up till 25 November.[46]

As we have seen, the crumbling of the Fifth Provisional Government didn't weaken the struggles. Both the neighbourhood/housing struggles and the process of dual power in the barracks developed with the crisis of the State, which was accentuated by a semi-paralysed government.

The communist-influenced Fifth Provisional Government, without the Socialist Party and PPD and with many stalwarts of the MFA suspended from the Council of Revolution, resigned on 19 September. We will see in the next but one chapter, how a divided MFA, coupled with a hostile attitude by the main political parties, helped unleash a seemingly uncontrollable situation in the barracks. The revolutionary crisis opens up on another front.

Soldier Luis Agricultural co-operative: Forward with Agrarian reform

Revolutionary Unity Front, showing the six parties (FSP, LCI, LUAR, MDP/CDE, MES, PRP)

PRP sticker declaring 'Unite, Organise and Arm: The Revolution Will Triumph'

Radio Renascença: towards the final victory

Photo 10   Examples of stickers produced by worker, grassroots and revolutionary organisations in order to publicise their causes.

17

Spain and Other 'Links in the Chain'

'Portugal, the weakest link in the capitalist chain in Europe can become the launching pad for the socialist revolution in the whole of the continent'
Tony Cliff, Portugal at the Crossroads[1]

This chapter focuses in the main upon the links with Spain, and then broadens out to look at links with the British and international left, albeit only briefly.

Burning the Spanish embassy

On the 27th of September 1975 three daily newspapers, *Diário Popular*, *Diário de Lisboa* and República had the same the front-page headline – *'Franco Assassin'*[2]

On that day students and far-left militants assaulted and burned the Spanish embassy in Lisbon and the Spanish consulates in Porto and Setúbal, in reaction to the execution of five anti-Franco militants. Popular support was so high for this that the MFA decided not to intervene. This stance was the result of a strong democratic consciousness that condemned the death penalty and grew out of the mobilisations that had multiplied during August and September culminating with the attacks on the embassies and consulates on 27 September. *Diário Popular* wrote:

> As a protest against the shooting of five Spanish antifascists, the consulate of Spain (in Setúbal) was attacked around 3 in the morning, with the assailants burning various documents in the street ...
> At about 4.30am, when the Embassy (in Lisbon) had already been taken over by assailants for two hours, a command force headed by an official by the name of Apollinaris arrived with several armoured cars.
> Suddenly, when hundreds of people who had not even realised that the military force had arrived, shots were fired. Effectively, the 'commandos'

released several bursts into the air for a few minutes in order to disperse the protesters.

With the shooting, the protestors fled in all directions while others sought shelter behind fire trucks and private cars. Soon, however, hundreds of people who had withdrawn, regrouped around the 'commando' forces shouting anti-Franco slogans while others succeeded, after some time, in beginning a dialogue with the soldiers.[3]

The demonstration and the attacks, seen from the diplomatic point of view, constituted 'the most serious incident between Spain and Portugal'.[4] They were a popular expression of the international movement against Franco. They were strongly supported and a source of joy for the radical left in Spain.

Differences in the Histories

Naturally, there had always been close contact between the populations of Spain and Portugal.

If it is true that Portugal and Spain had, during part of the twentieth century, very similar dictatorial regimes[5] – the only times in his entire life that Salazar left Portugal was to visit Franco – it is also indisputable that the dynamics of the prolonged Spanish Civil War and the rapid defeat of the attempted insurrectionary general strike of 1934 in Portugal shaped the movements in the two countries quite differently.

The defeat of the Republican side in the Spanish Civil War was an enormous defeat for the progressive left, one of the worst of the twentieth century.[6] There were hundreds of thousands of dead and exiles in a war that lasted three years. The defeat of the Portuguese labour movement was slower and more erosive, beginning at the hands of the Republican regime in 1910 and ending in 1934 when the New State brutally repressed, with relative ease, the insurrectionary uprising in the traditional glassmaking town of Marinha Grande, in the centre of the country. A situation of civil war never arose in Portugal. As Paloma Aguilar shows, the legacy of the brutality of the civil war severely curtailed sectors of the anti-Francoist opposition.[7]

Communist militants were the main targets of repression by Salazar's political police – as Irene Pimental's investigations have shown[8] – with the torture, murder and dozens of years in prison for the main leaders. But the Portuguese labour, peasant and popular movements did not experience the massacres that took place in Spain in the 1930s.

Many of the Spanish leaders of the PCE (Spanish Communist Party) – together with prominent Republicans, socialists, intellectuals, and writers – chose France as the place of their long exile. Paris would also be the host of some Portuguese intellectuals, but, after the Second World War, most of the exiled Communist cadres went to the Soviet Union and its satellite republics such as the Czech Republic and the German Democratic Republic. The tradition of intellectual and cultural formation of the leading cadres of the two parties – parties, it should be recalled, who resisted in harsh clandestine conditions under dictatorial regimes – was distinct with the PCP more attached to Moscow than the PCE. The question of party financing involved aspects that we still do not know well, but everything indicates that the PCP was much more dependent on the funding of the International Soviet apparatus than the PCE, which had earlier established close relations with the leaderships of the French and Italian communist parties. These parties already had a long tradition of occupying posts in the French and Italian state apparatuses – via elections – which guaranteed them some autonomy, including financial autonomy from the USSR. On the other hand, it is important to remember that Eurocommunism developed after the Portuguese Revolution, particularly from 1975 in Italy, and not before that.

The differences between the political history of PCP, directed by Álvaro Cunhal, and the PCE, led by Santiago Carrillo, are indelibly etched by historical events in the two Iberian countries throughout the twentieth century. We see two parties with histories, tactics and policies sometimes substantially different, but we cannot reduce these differences to a somewhat simplistic analysis that combines the PCP of Álvaro Cunhal to Leninist tactics and the PCE to Eurocommunist reformism.[9]

In Portugal, the state crisis was deeper than in Spain because it stemmed from the very mainstay of the State, the armed forces and their defeat in the colonial war.[10] This meant that in Portugal democratic freedom was immediately established: freedom of expression, assembly, association as well as the legalisation of political parties, elections forecast for the Constituent Assembly, the end of the political police and the end of censorship. This process was immediate and accompanied by a social mobilisation without precedent in the history of the country: less than a month after the fall of the regime, the Communist Party shared office, along with the Socialist Party and the PPD to form the First Provisional Government, breaking an almost 30-year taboo of Communists in Western governments.

The Portuguese Revolution invited a kind of revolutionary tourism, of passionate people eager to have a close look at the country where in the university, in the factory meetings, in the fields, among the poorest people, words like freedom and socialism were heard with an intense joy – scenes which were well described, photographed and filmed during these months.[11] A Spanish lawyer from *Iberia* was fired from his job. The reason was that he had spent 'holidays in Portugal to celebrate May 1'.[12] Indeed, it was next door, in Spain, that the Carnation Revolution produced its first seeds.

We know it was not only this lawyer who travelled to Portugal. Spaniards came to Portugal to see freedom, buy banned books, participate in demonstrations and celebrate the revolution. Students from Spain organised 'recreational and political' tours whose exclusive objective was to witness the Carnation Revolution.

Members of the *Partido Socialista Obrero Español* (PSOE – the Spanish Socialist Workers' Party), were photographed by the *Diário de Lisboa* when they came to Portugal to celebrate May Day in 1974, with a large sign, 'Health and Freedom for the Portuguese People'. They sang in the streets of Lisbon 'Portugal today, Spain tomorrow'.[13] A few months later, these words gained strength in Spain when participants in the student movements, the *vecinos* [neighbourhood] committees[14] and general strikes in the Basque Country sang the Portuguese revolutionary song *'Grândola Vila Morena'*, with Spanish pronunciation. Posters, murals and stickers against the Franco dictatorship were sent from Portugal, mainly organised by the fraternal parties of the extreme left (Maoists, guerrilla groups and Trotskyists, among others). A sticker with the image of Guernica was signed by several political organisations with the slogan 'Solidarity with the Spanish Peoples' Struggle' and circulated through the country. Another sticker referred to the first unitary conference between PSAN (National Liberation Socialist Party), ETA (Basque Land and Freedom), UPG (Union of the People of Galego) and various groups in Portugal – the FSP, LUAR, MES, and others. Another sticker in red with a photograph of Garmendia and Otaeguy (the last political prisoners executed, by garrote, by the Franco regime in 1975) says 'The People Set You Free!'. In another, a Nazi cross is drenched in blood.[15]

Students

In February 1975, Spanish students massively mobilised for a 'day of action and struggle' and the police were unable to thwart them despite their brutality and hundreds of arrests.

In celebration of the eve of the first anniversary of the Carnation Revolution in April 1975, the university students in Seville organised a celebration. They filled the old Tobacco Factory and the bar of the Sciences

Faculty with posters depicting the fall of Marcelo Caetano. The police followed them closely and started to pull down the posters.

Yet an immense number of students were mobilised. They made flags and bought hundreds of red carnations, and the historian Alberto Carrillo-Linares tells us:

> In the first minutes of daylight on 25 April it was clear that it would not just be any other day: the central university building awoke decorated with communist, Republican and Portuguese flags, which had been placed by a small group of students from various parties who had hidden inside the enclosure. When the doors of the other centres opened, they were also soon adorned with various flags, converting the university into a kind of student occupation.[16]
>
> The police response was immediate. With the use of unprecedented force and full equipment, the 'riot' police invaded and dissolved the assembly. Police were surprised by the number of students and professors 'sporting red carnations.[17]

Connections

The special correspondent of the *Diário de Lisboa* in Spain, Fernando Assis Pacheco, noted on 25 July 1974, that: 'A new factor animates Spanish political life. These are the neighbourhood committees, [similar to the ones in Portugal] that have increasingly formed almost everywhere and whose visible target is to train left cadres.' They are in neighbourhoods like Leganes, Villaverde, Alcobendas, located in the working-class belt of Madrid, and as Assis Pacheco described, were 'very politicised'.

Eleven months after 25 April 1974, the PSOE in Spain was partly legitimised in March 1975: still illegal, it was nevertheless now able to use its symbols and flags in the street.[18] The first time that the Spanish Government used a computer was in 1975 to construct a database of all soldiers in the União Militar Democracia (Democratic Military Union, UMD), a group of about 200 army officers and sergeants, with a minor influence in the Civil Guard, who had organised a programme directly inspired by the MFA, the movement of intermediate officers who had organised the coup against the dictatorship of Salazar.

Following the coup attempt of 11 March 1975, Spínola exiled himself to Spain, a country that served as the support base for the Exército de Libertação Português (Portuguese Liberation Army, ELP), an ultra-reactionary

Portuguese militia. In October 1975, Morocco expelled the Spanish Army of the Sahara (until then Spanish territory) and the Spanish rulers were incapable of mobilising its army in defence.

The influence of Portugal on Spain could also be seen in social and cultural events such as Portuguese book fairs, organised in Spain in several cities, or in the pilgrimage of Spaniards to Lisbon, who queued up to see the famous scene of sodomy between Marlon Brando and Maria Schneider in Bertolucci's *Last Tango in Paris*, a film banned in Spain. The influence of Spain on Portugal could also be seen in the dozens of posters that the Portuguese extreme left painted in solidarity with Spanish political prisoners.

Trade Unions

In this turbulent process, a fragile movement of solidarity arose between Spanish and Portuguese unions. Two national union confederations, including the most consolidated and still clandestine CCOO (Confederación Sindical de Comisiones Obreras – Union Confederation of Workers' Commissions), in Spain and the growing and now legal Intersindical in Portugal exchanging verbose telegrams of institutional solidarity.

One of the developments in Spain that had most impact on the trade union movement in Portugal was the 'Process 1001' of 1973 that condemned the clandestine leaders of CCOO to heavy prison sentences. The leadership had been arrested on 24 June 1972 in the Oblate Convent Pozuelo de Alarcón in Madrid where they were meeting. One of them, Marcelino Camacho, was sentenced to 20 years in prison (released in 1976, he would direct the CCOO until 1987).

On 27 November 1974, the Intersindical demanded the 'immediate release' of the imprisoned Spanish unionists. In Portugal, it distributed a statement about the persecution of Spanish unionists, demanding 'better conditions of life, for freedom, for democracy'.[19] The Federation of Unions of Porto organised a protest at the Spanish Embassy in Lisbon. The Bank workers' union sent a telegram to Arias Navarro on 21 November 1974, demanding the release of 16 trade unionists whose judgement would be on the 28 November. Later the Metalworkers' Union of the District of Porto demanded the annulment of the sentence.

The echoes of solidarity reached the Francoist prisons: six renown trade union prisoners in Spain wrote to the Intersindical in May 1975, thanking them for the solidarity shown to 'workers from the brother country':

From the Carabanchel prison, where we have been almost 3 years, we want to send this greeting of thanks and solidarity. It is recognition for your valuable contribution to the very broad international support for us, which helped to prevent the dictatorship to condemn us for the monstrous penalties that the Special Public Order Court had decreed in the first instance ... We are convinced that the Portuguese and Spanish working class, their respective peoples, with many roots and common feelings, will march increasingly more united on the path to freedom and socialism.[20]

The text was signed by Marcelino Camacho, Julian-Muñiz Zapico, Eduardo Sabol, Nicolas Sartorius and Fernando Soto, and also by Garcia Salve held in Zamora prison. International pressure from various countries led the regime to modify the sentences to a maximum of six years. King Juan Carlos was forced to pardon the defendants on 25 November 1975, five days after Franco's death.

The World Trade Union Conference in Solidarity with the Workers and Peoples of Chile scheduled to be held in Lisbon was cancelled due to 'various difficulties'. In my opinion, this was related to the TAP (aviation) strike and the demonstrations of Lisnave workers against the Second Provisional Government, and internal tensions within the Intersindical. Regretting the postponement of the conference, the Delegación Exterior de Comisiones Obreras (Foreign Delegation of the Workers' Commissions, Spain) would write to Intersindical: 'Your victory is our victory [A reference to the defeated 28 September 1974 coup] and represents an invaluable help for us. Its impact in Spain will be as important as that of April'.[21] Pedro Cristobal from the CCOO would travel to Lisbon on 4 November to schedule the dates of a future meeting. On the Portuguese side, Augusto Silva represented the international contacts of Intersindical. Consultation of the archives leads us to conclude that these contacts did not go beyond the institutional diplomatic field or the mere solidarity greetings read at the start of congresses or meetings. Strangely, the conference scheduled between the two confederations, which would also be repeatedly delayed, did not in fact focus on the process of overthrowing dictatorships by social mobilisations in the Iberian Peninsula, but on Chile. What greater solidarity could be given to Chile than overcoming capitalism in a corner of Western Europe?[22]

On 4 June 1974, the cover of Mundo Obrero featured an interview with Carrillo on the Portuguese situation. His citation was instructive: 'Even if some people have said Spain should avoid being "Portugalised", it seems to me that the "Portugalisation" of Spain is inevitable'.

The political advisor to the Spanish embassy that had been burnt down, José Antonio de Yturriaga Barberan, said in a 2009 interview that it was 'Impossible to separate governmental instability in Portugal from the events in Spain'. Recalling the moment of the attacks, he said that it showed the 'weaknesses of the Portuguese government and the growing international isolation of Franco'.[23]

In fact, the weakness of the state in Portugal and the fragility of the regime in Spain were interrelated. After the optimism with which, in general, almost all sectors in Spanish politics received the election results in April 1975, the discussion would centre on the evolution of the Fourth and Fifth Provisional Governments and divisions within the MFA from August onwards.

It seemed obvious, writes Carrillo-Linares, that the Portuguese Revolution would have a domino effect in the entire Mediterranean. This is also the historical thesis formulated by Cesar Oliveira, among others, on the impossibility of two very different regimes coexisting for a long time in the Iberian Peninsula.[24] Francoist Spain could not remain glued to a 'red' Portugal.

In Spain, the end of Francoism resulted from a negotiation in which it is clear now that the workers' and social movements[25] (including the Portuguese Revolution itself) played an indisputable role. Yet the Spanish regime did not suffer the convulsions of the Portuguese state.

Britain's 'Oldest Ally'[26]

Let us now switch to Britain.

It was said that Portugal was Britain's 'oldest ally'. Britain had strong historical ties to Portugal, dating back 500 years. In 1970, 25 per cent of all foreign investment in Portugal was British. Ted Heath's Conservative government was content to let the Southern African wars continue in order to protect British investments and thereby the Portuguese were propped up in their African escapades. In general, the British establishment kept rather quiet about their link with this archaic and brutal dictatorship, although there was a lot of coverage in the British Press of the Carnation Revolution, the focus was more on the overthrow of the regime, and the adventures of the young captains, than on the workers' movement and the international ramifications. The latter dimension was explored by those on the far-left, in particular by the International Socialists (IS) forerunners of today's Socialist Workers' Party (SWP).

According to McGrogan, the IS were: 'the most energetic of the British revolutionary left ... the IS had arguably the most important organisation at this point, with an estimated 4000 members and their weekly *Socialist Worker* print run of over 30,000.'[27]

Tony Cliff, the founder of the International Socialists, argued that 'Portugal, the weakest link in the capitalist chain in Europe can become the launching pad for the socialist revolution in the whole of the continent'.[28] He saw the PRP as 'an authentic revolutionary Marxist organisation' making a real effort to transform itself into a workers' party, which was playing a positive role in the various workers' struggles.

In the first instance, the IS central committee dispatched two experienced comrades, to survey the situation and make connections. As time went on more and more comrades went over, to see what was happening and to make links. By summer 1975, the IS were organising large group visits, including block bookings on planes and comrades being put up at the Hotel Ambassador, which was under workers' control and which gave a discount to revolutionaries. This is how the English editor of this book first became involved, in the late summer.[29] There were about 150 comrades (and friends) behind the IS banner on the COPCON demonstration on 20 August.

Furthermore, the IS was arranging meetings and tours in the UK, for example, by two soldiers and a young PRP militant from the Lisnave

Photo 11   Portuguese soldiers reading *Socialist Worker*, the paper of the International Socialists (UK). (*Socialist Worker*)

shipyards. A leading PRP member José Sousa, known as Crac, came and spoke at the annual IS conference in spring 1975.[30] There was a colourful solidarity demonstration in central London on 20 September 1975 called by the Portuguese Workers Coordinating Committee in which the IS were heavily involved. According to *Socialist Worker*, 6,000 people joined in.

Very considerable resources were invested in writing about the events. Tony Cliff wrote 'Portugal at the Crossroads', which appeared as a pamphlet and was rapidly translated into Portuguese and eight other languages. The aim was to tell the world, to try to influence things internationally, and even influence the PRP. Several thousand copies in Portuguese were sent to Portugal for distribution, almost all the leading bookshops in Lisbon took copies, and were also sold by comrades on demonstrations. But there was not an adequate distribution infrastructure and many copies were left unsold.

This account of the left's involvement has focused on the major player, the IS. However, there was an important non-aligned support group, the Portuguese Workers Coordinating Committee – the PWCC. It would be churlish not to mention that other sections of the British left were also highly motivated. Big Flame published useful materials. McGrogan tells how one British Trotskyist group, the International Marxist group – IMG – 'confidently proclaimed the Carnation Revolution the "foundation stone of the United Socialist States of Europe',[31] and that: 'In October 1975 the internal bulletin of the FI [Fourth International] wrote of a very favourable situation for revolutionaries (namely, the LCI LCI – Liga Comunista Internacionalista: Internationalist Communist League) "giving them extraordinary opportunities to spread their ideas among the radicalizing layers of workers" (Fourth International Internal Discussion Bulletin 1975)'.[32]

However, the IS were much larger than the IMG. And the PRP was much larger than the LCI. By October, the IS had decided that they needed a better intervention in Portugal. While leading comrades had gone over for visits and talks with the PRP, the visits had been short and what was needed was a more consistent intervention.[33]

Differences with the PRP emerged. Their emphasis was on the armed struggle, and the machinations within the army. The PRP's traditions were those of a clandestine guerrilla group, preoccupied with the military and the seizure of power, substituting itself (or COPCON) for the class. There was very little emphasis on membership and building its own organisation and not enough focus on the workplaces. The IS argued that the PRP should produce a daily newspaper. As time progressed the IS became increasingly anxious about time running out, and the threat of counter-revolution.

It tried to sharpen its intervention in Lisbon and pulled two full-time organisers out of their districts and based them in Lisbon.

By 25 November, the IS had a cell of 5 or 6 comrades operating in Lisbon, and one of them, Robin Doughty, was living in the Barreiro *sede*, on the other side of the Tagus estuary, a ferry ride from Lisbon and did a lot of good work fostering fraternal relations.

The 25 November coup sent the revolutionary left in Portugal into a tailspin. As you will read, officers in the army were arrested, rebel units were disbanded and many members of the PRP went underground. But within days, the IS had written, in English and translated in a rush from English to Portuguese 'The Lessons of 25 November' by Cliff and Chris Harman.[34] This was on sale within a week.[35]

McGrogan wrote: 'Overall although it is unlikely that the IS influenced the PRP much, despite their best efforts to bond through discussion, financial donation and solidarity networking back in the UK.'[36]

The World Watches … and Hopes

The global left, from social democracy to the communist parties, to groups to the left of these, trade unions, human rights groups, progressive sectors of the Church, and democrats and republicans saw in Portugal an alternative to the blood baths carried out under the boots of the Latin American and Asian military dictatorships. Only seven months after the bloody 11 September 1973 events in Chile, one people in Europe was actually winning. And it was in Portugal!

Although this chapter has focused on Spain, and the intervention by some of the far-left from the UK, remember revolutionaries worldwide were galvanised.

Indeed, for sections of the European radical left, the Carnation Revolution was perceived as the latest in a line of workers' movements that had begun in France during May 1968 with student riots and a nationwide general strike. There followed the Italian 'hot autumn' of 1969, strike waves in Germany and Britain in the early 1970s, and the struggle against military rule in Greece in 1973–1974. It was a period of popular resistance to the established order(s) that swept through Europe and culminated in a full-blooded revolutionary situation in Portugal. Furthermore, the revolution lifted the mood of despondency on the global Left, following the right-wing military coup of September 1973 in Chile, where a socialist government had been violently overthrown, its supporters rounded up, tortured and murdered in their thousands. 'After half a century during which Portugal had suddenly seemed largely irrelevant to the outside world, suddenly the most convoluted dispute of that nation's smallest political faction became a weighty matter of absorbing interest to Paris, London and New York.'[37]

The drawing, included here, by João Abel Manta who had become the MFA's official artist, was commissioned for the MFA Fifth Division's 'cultural dynamisation' campaign. The drawing shows a crowd of eager observers from the past including Karl Marx and Bertrand Russell, pencils in hand, eagerly staring at a map of Portugal drawn on a blackboard.[38] Leading figures from far-left groups from other parts of the world – such as Ernest Mandel from the Fourth International, the Brazilian Maoist Diógenes Arruda Câmara and the Argentinean Trotskyists Nahuel Moreno and Aldo Casas came and visited and influenced the direction of development of the embryonic revolutionary groups.

It is thought that: 'By the end of the revolutionary process, "10,000 foreign Marxists, Maoists and Third Worldists" were said to have been in Portugal.'[39]

Furthermore, Portuguese revolutionaries who had been in exile were very affected by what they learnt and saw while in exile. And non-partisan support groups performed a valuable role in reporting and publishing documents from those halcyon days. There are many examples of visits and giving money from the far-left, from many different countries.

It remains that before 25 November the possibility of a red Mediterranean was obvious. Troops in other European countries were becoming restless. In Italy, more than 1,000 soldiers, wearing uniforms and handkerchief masks, took part in a demonstration in support of Portuguese workers and soldiers. Many argue that the Portuguese experience could not have sparked off an

Figure 17.1 'A difficult problem', 1975. By João Abel Manta.

international revolution. With hindsight, such a conflagration now appears improbable. However, it has to be remembered that events in Portugal did not occur in isolation. They occurred because Portugal could not continue to exist in isolation!

18

The Crisis

It was exactly during this period that power was fully disintegrating and was being influenced by the demonstrations in the streets ... The SUV was another step in the revolutionary escalation, an obvious attempt to Sovietize the Army, which would naturally proceed toward the destruction of the military establishment, to build a new power upon its base.[1]

Mário Soares, leader of the Socialist Party

Revolt in the Ranks

On 7 September, just two days after the MFA forced the resignation of Vasco Gonçalves, a group of embattled soldiers (who remained anonymous) gave a press conference announcing the creation of the SUV (*Soldados Unidos Vencerão* – Soldiers United for Victory), a soldiers' rank and file organisation. These corresponded to workers' and residents' commissions insofar as they were organised from below. They were against the imposition of commands from the MFA and for the 'destruction of the bourgeois army'.[2] The SUVs – whose story remains to be written – went on to conduct demonstrations, sometimes with thousands of soldiers, many of them sporting beards in a visible symbol of the hierarchical crisis. Its founding manifesto advocated fighting for democratisation of the barracks (which included 'holding plenary sessions of soldiers whenever we want'); fighting for the constitution of 'elected organs of power for the uniformed workers in the quarters to be revocable at any moment by a plenary of soldiers;' expulsion of reactionary officers; same food as the officers, protected against military oversight; and for 'the preparation of conditions that would permit the destruction of the bourgeois Army and the creation of the armed wing, the Power of the Workers, a People's Revolutionary Army'.[3]

The 8246 Company of the Regiment of Military Police refused to embark to Angola on that same day. On 8 September, the Council of the Revolution met and resolved to act with disciplinary measures against the Military Police.

On 9 September, in response to the 'undermining of military discipline and obedience,' the Council of the Revolution, already empowered by their alignment of the Socialist Party and the Group of Nine, published a law which sought to prohibit the media from 'disseminating reports and news, etc. on the events or positions of military units'.[4] Known as the 'Law of Military Censorship', it would never be put into practice simply because newspapers, radio and television refused to comply. It would be repealed after two weeks.

On 10 September, 1,000 G3 automatic rifles were rerouted from an arms warehouse in Beirolas to the PRP/BR. Amongst and around the PRP there was much talk about the need for an insurrection.[5] On 13 September 1975, Eurico Corvacho, a 'Gonzalez' military man, was replaced by Pires Veloso in command of the Northern Military Region, provoking a general reaction of the soldiers and of the parties on the left that led to a mobilisation on the streets for the readmission of Eurico Corvacho.

On 21 September, 1,500 uniformed soldiers under the direction of the SUV, together with 10,000 civilians, paraded at a demonstration in Porto against the government and the generals Fabio and Charais, who they accused of trying to end the revolution. Also on that day, bombs exploded in the mess hall of the General Staff of the Armed Forces, where Prime Minister Pinheiro de Azevedo was sleeping.

On 24 September, staff of the General Armed Forces met to deal with the crisis of 'the disciplinary issues in general and in particular the SUVs, and the lack of personnel with sufficient competence to neutralise the small groups that have formed within the armed forces'.[6]

On 25 September, in Lisbon, a demonstration of the SUV took place, calling for the release of two soldiers who had been arrested for distributing SUV literature. This was the largest demonstration of soldiers ever in Portugal. Jornal Novo, quoted by Inácia Rezola, thus describes the demonstration: 'Supported by the FUR and many committees of residents and workers in the Lisbon region, thousands of soldiers marched through the city. The protesters took over 30 buses, crossed the river, and released soldiers (from the left) who had been detained in Trafaria.'[7]

Before morning, the authorities conceded and announced that the soldiers would be released. They also decided to re-establish the MFA infrastructure at the level of military units and regions in order to avoid 'creating parallel organisations within the barracks'.[8]

The SUVs were of particular importance during the crisis because, as mentioned above, they were diametrically opposed to the MFA, insofar as they advocated direct democracy through the creation of commissions of soldiers.

The SUV has nothing to do with the MFA, its structures or its internal struggles. The SUV did not intend to carry out a 'turn to the left' for the MFA, nor would it 'place military revolutionaries on the Council of the Revolution'. The SUV set out to fight side by side with all the workers, to prepare the conditions for the destruction of the bourgeois army and the creation of the power of the workers' armed forces, the Popular Revolutionary Army.[9]

They argued that the ADUs (Assemblies of Democratic Units) were not democratic and were under the control of the MFA – and their dynamics of

Figure 18.1 SUV leaflet. Source: Author's personal archive.

growth. However, despite the formal alignment, it appears that, in practice, the ADUs constituted areas of contention, even rebellion within the Armed Forces. I say this somewhat tentatively because there has not been much research on the ADUs.

The SUVs had no illusions in the ADUs, as they were 'collaborative organs of soldiers (uniformed workers) within the military hierarchy (uniformed bourgeoisie)'.[10] The stipulations that the ADUs must consist of 50 per cent soldiers, would be 'a rock in the officers' boot,'[11] therefore the SUVs would operate within the ADUs where they existed. But, in general, the SUVs' position was to break with the ADUs and instead focus on joining the committees of workers and residents, and to build soldiers' commissions to be 'elected and revocable at all times'.[12]

Soon, similar organisations would appear or re-emerge: the ARPE led by the Communist Party, the RPAC led by the MRPP, and the Organisation of Soldiers and Sailors under the leadership of the UDP, a coalition of Maoist groups. The SUVs would remain the biggest rank and file organisation and most important of these.

Soares later told Maria João Avilez that: 'It was exactly during this period that power was fully disintegrating and was being influenced by the demonstrations in the streets ... The SUV was another step in the revolutionary escalation, an obvious attempt to Sovietize the Army, which would naturally proceed toward the destruction of the military establishment, to build a new power upon its base.'[13]

O Expresso, describing a meeting of the Council of the Revolution on 25 September 1975, where the military situation was being discussed, wrote: 'a very simple political test has been proposed: find out how many notable personalities of the MFA feel safe walking the street in Rossio.'[14]

The MFA was no longer able to act as the authoritative disciplinary body. This impacted upon the lower ranks, namely soldiers, throughout the army; in other words, reached beyond the organisation of ADUs and SUVS. Major Tomé of the Military Police recalled that commissions of de facto soldiers came into being in force after the split of the MFA and that: 'commissions of soldiers were the revolutionary nucleus within the squad, even within the left squadron'.[15]

Faced with the conflict within the Armed Forces, the Council of the Revolution decided to try a series of measures, as mentioned, primarily in the form of military reorganisation linked to the various sectors of the left, attempting to rebuild the military hierarchy. Hence, it decided to accommodate some of the demands of the Armed Forces, to dissolve the Military Police Regiment, and to create a Military Intervention Group (AMI), which would be a disciplinary force composed of operational forces of the three branches of the Armed Forces capable of responding to what they might consider a challenge to 'national tranquility'. It was an 'attempt to resolve the question of authority'.[16]

The Sixth Provisional Government

The Sixth Provisional Government officially came into power on 19 September. None of the party leaders had seats. Pinheiro de Azevedo continued as prime minister. The government, with five members of the Socialist Party, three from the PPD and a single Communist Party minister, had in its hands 'a seemingly uncontrollable country'. The history of the period would refer to this duality of powers as 'military indiscipline' or a 'politico-military crisis'. These are superficial concepts, insufficient to specify the historical essence of the process. As we have just seen, orders from the Armed Forces were questioned by many military units.

This challenging of military authority, which is the essence of a process of democratisation, only had the support of a few dozen MFA officers. One of them, António Pessoa, pointed out that this reaction originated mainly from the 'dissolution of the military units' carried out by the Council of the Revolution after Tancos.[17]

On 5 September 1975, the Assembly of the MFA met at the School of Engineering in Tancos. Its hands were full dealing with, for example, the process of decolonisation in Angola and Timor and regulations dealing regimental protocol. The main business was the restructuring of the Council of the Revolution in favour of the supporters of the Group of Nine.

The Council of Revolution could not restore the legitimacy of the State. In addition to the crisis in the MFA and the duality of powers in the military, the Sixth Provisional Government experienced strong social dissent. Soldiers demonstrated, there were widespread land occupations, an attack on the prime minister, and radio and television broadcasters were shut down. The government became paralysed. Almost daily, rumours and threats of a *coup d'état* covered the front pages of newspapers, occasioning a 'coup psychosis'. The preponderance of left and right military intrigues was particularly numbing. Rumours of impending coups became an endemic feature of political life. [18]

The Government would respond classically, combining consensus with coercion. On the one hand, dozens of left-wing militants were rounded up, the new internal disciplinary group (AMI) covering all three armed forces was constituted, and there was an attempt to steer the media toward the side of repression; on the side of consensus-building money was released to pay wages to agricultural workers involved in agrarian reforms, and the most of the demands of the disabled veterans of the Armed Forces were conceded. But this would not be enough to stop the revolutionary crisis.

Radio and Television

The control of the media was critical. Rádio Renascença, an organ of the Catholic Church, had been occupied in May 1975 by its workers on the revolutionary left who broadcasted a programme for months on end 'at the service of the working class and working people'. The Sixth Provisional Government of Pinheiro de Azevedo, much pressured by the Patriarchate of Lisbon, tried to silence the station. On 29 September, Pinheiro de Azevedo ordered the occupation of the television and radio broadcasters, arguing that: 'it was to avoid declaring a state of siege', which, in his opinion, 'was what the *de facto* situation demanded'.

The conflict was not extinguished. A representative of the *Emissora Nacional* (State Radio), was questioned by a television journalist on the national news about government accusations of manipulating the information and responded by saying: 'the workers of the national broadcasting services are fighting so that the control over what happens in the station is exercised by the workers themselves through their organs of popular will, a workers' commission.'[19]

Demonstrators surrounded the *Emissora Nacional* facilities and reoccupied them:

> Considering the ambiguous nature of the communiqué justifying the occupation of the National broadcasting Service, as well as the other radio stations and the RTP; considering the pure and simple silence of the organs of national information and what great mobilising power these can bring to the victory and progress of the Portuguese Revolution; considering that such a measure dictated in defence of pluralism began by establishing censorship and monopolizing information; and considering that such an occupation could conceal another goal such as silencing the voices of revolution, the workers of the *Emissora Nacional* studios, paratroopers and disabled Armed Forces veterans currently occupying the National Broadcasting studios, we have decided first to suspend transmission of the communiqué and to return to normal programming, agreeing not to disseminate news or information of an alarmist nature

given the difficult moment that our country is going through; and to support any eventual decisions made on information provided that establishes clearly and unequivocally the purposes of defending the interests of the working class.[20]

The unresolved struggle over Rádio Renascença epitomised the powerlessness of the ruling government and demonstrated how moods and energies shifted quickly. COPCON had been instructed to occupy the radio station. After a demonstration by workers, Otelo Carvalho, in tears, ordered his troops to withdraw. Within six hours, the radio was re-occupied by the commandos under Colonel Jaime Neves.

On 1 October, army officials surrounded the Rádio Renascença Buraca premises in Lisbon, and the PSP riot police remained watchful at the site. There followed protests against the government's decision and on 21 October an enormous demonstration, followed by a temporary encampment set up in front of the broadcasters, organised by commissions of soldiers, residents and workers, forced the commandos to withdraw. The radio started transmissions again.

The government was almost powerless. Its only resort was dynamite. On 7 November, its saboteurs, under the protective cover of the supposedly loyal 'and backward' paratroopers, blew up the station's transmitters.

A communiqué from the Coordinating Committee of Rádio Renascença Workers condemned the attitude of the Council of the Revolution and the Provisional Government, as an act of struggle 'against socialism'.

Setúbal Comité de Luta

The Setúbal Comité de Luta (Committee of Struggle) was formed in reaction to the attempt by the Sixth Provisional Government, on 29 September, to close down all the radio stations including, in particular, Rádio Renascença. At this moment, a number of the popular assemblies were attempting to reconstitute themselves, placing less reliance on the leadership of the now hopelessly divided MFA. Organisations linking workers' commissions and residents' commissions emerged, which did not always call themselves Popular Assemblies.[21]

It was no accident that the Comité de Luta saw itself, not as a popular assembly, but a committee of struggle. Representatives from the barracks with others from residents' commissions and workers' commissions met on the night of 30 September and decided to formally launch the Comité. The assembly meetings became an alternative forum for democracy, from below. The very fact of its existence changed local political complexion. It was a source of authority and power, which rank-and-file workers could refer to.

It was one of the few organisations which forced the Communist Party to become involved in an arena where the revolutionaries set the pace. 'It created a space for discussion between far-left and Communist Party militants. People close to the PCP but without party membership were present so the party activists had to be there too' [22]

The committee helped organise and coordinate a number of practical actions concerning ordinary matters and also at the same time challenged the very authority of the State. Here is but one example, told through the eyes of FUR.

On 20 October 1975, the FUR held a press conference – which was aired on the National News of the RTP – in which it refused to recognise the verdict of the state justice in relation to protests against a PPD rally leading to the repression and consequent death of a worker. The FUR noted that the capacity to judge the case rested with the Setúbal Committee of Struggle, which brought together the commissions of the workers, residents and soldiers. Henrique Costa read the communiqué on air:

The FUR in Setúbal strongly condemns the communiqué and conclusions drawn from a report produced by the General Staff of the Armed Forces regarding the events of 7 March in Setúbal. At this time of aggravated political, economic and military crisis in which imperialist forces are launching an assault on lost ground, with the formation of the AMI, the attempt to marginalise the organs popular power, the boycott and closure of the organs of information to the service of the working class, the repression of autonomous organisation of the soldiers, the arrest of revolutionary soldiers, the reorganisation of the left, the establishment of the terrorist dictatorship of the bourgeoisie over the workers, we finally have the report, the false inquiry into the events of 7 March in Setúbal, which is nothing more than the attempt by the right-wing forces under the General Staff of the Armed Forces to carry out repressive measures against revolutionary organisations and the growing organisation of workers and soldiers in Setúbal ...

It is effectively public knowledge that the murderous shots came from a machine gun installed on the first floor of the PSP squad, which shot not only those who peacefully protested to repudiate the PSP's brutality at the Naval Pavilion, but also shot people coming out of a movie theater in front of the station. It is also public knowledge that the commitment of

Major Passos, PSD commander, the civil governor of Setúbal, Mr Fuzeta da Ponte, set the trap in conjunction with the PPD, the PSP (Public Security Police) forces of Setúbal and Almada. In this sense, the FUR of Setúbal gives full support to the constitution of a popular commission of inquiry, for the proposal presented in the Setúbal Struggle Committee, coordinating body of the committees of workers, residents and soldiers. Those responsible for the death of the worker, João Manuel, and the dozens of wounded will not go unpunished.[23]

At one time the Comité de Luta discussed whether it should organise an insurrection and decided not to do so, not because it could not, but because there was no existing national network of similar organisations.[24]

Later we will see how the Comité responded to 25 November. It was broader than most workers' councils insofar as it linked workers, neighbourhood activists, and soldiers. Sometimes this worked very well and other times there were issues – as to be expected.[25]

I agree with Robinson when he suggests that although this was more than a collection of workers' commissions – in other words, it included residents' and soldiers' commission – it remains that the Comité de Luta was the most extraordinary example of a workers' council to have emerged in Europe since the workers' councils in Hungary 1956.

Escalation on Many Fronts

There had never been so many demonstrations in Portugal – many bringing together tens or hundreds of thousands of workers – as between September and November 1975. Some of these would be in favour of the Sixth Government; the overwhelming majority against. Because the media was focused primarily on the capital and to a lesser extent on the other industrial cities, many popular demonstrations and protests away from these areas were not mentioned. Furthermore, there has been a lack of studies of what happened in the outlying areas during the revolution. But power is measured in terms of social force, the number of soldiers in a war and not by the number of press reports.[26]

At the time, Tony Cliff wrote:

A revolutionary situation exists in Portugal, a situation of fragmentation of power – leading to powerlessness. It cannot continue for long. Either the crisis will be resolved by the working class or by the forces of reaction. Such situations are the supreme test of parties, programmes, policies. In the last resort, all the political tendencies in the working-class movement are to be judged by their willingness and their ability to lead the working class forward to power in the time of crisis – or by their contribution to its defeat. Today Portugal is the touchstone for organisations claiming to be socialist or communist.[27]

The agrarian reform demonstrations – many with tractors and open back lorries crossing into Lisbon – took place in September until the beginning of October, to press for the approval of credit for wages. In Torres Vedras, on 11 October for example, a crowd shouted 'Soldiers and sailors forever, always on the side of the people!'[28] Speeches were made by the commission of residents of what was called 'neighbourhood number three'.

On 14 October, there was a large demonstration in Oeiras, in support of Major Correia Borrego, commander of the Costal Artillery Regiment (RAC), who had been purged. On that day, also, a demonstration in Carnaxide of Philips workers brought together thousands. There, residents' commissions from Porto Salvo shouted, 'Reactionaries out of the barracks now', 'Popular Power!'[29]

As we have seen, on 27 September, the Spanish embassy and consulates were assaulted and burnt down by far-left demonstrators against the Franco regimes' sentencing to death of five Basque nationalists.

Overnight, from 21 to 22 September, the wounded from the armed forces, who had not seen their demands for compensation and care satisfied, occupied the 25 April bridge, which connects the Tagus estuary down river from Lisbon. RTP showed an unusual scene on the news from the bridge. In the early morning, with an intense sunlight, viewers saw an attractive, long-haired toll collector standing at her work station laughing boisterously at every passing car without requiring them to pay the toll, while a surreal scene unfolded beside her: a man in a wheelchair – a disabled veteran of the Armed Forces – gesturing and directing the traffic with a superb and determined air. Shortly thereafter, the disabled veterans headed to Afonso de Albunique Square, in front of the Belem Palace, the home of the President of the Republic. Here, too, they interposed themselves and blocked the flow of cars and public transport. In an interview, later that day with RTP, one of the members of the association stated that the occupations at the end of the day were only lifted because there were assurances from the Provisional Government and the Council of Revolution that their demands had been met.[30]

In November 1975, SUVs were organised in Oporto, Lisbon, Coimbra, Évora, Portalegre and Beja. However, the movement was uneven, and considerably weaker outside the main industrial centres. Some of the SUV groups melted away – faded away. The general strike in support of the radio stations did not gather much support. The right wing was gaining ground in the army.

Reports of the residents' committees show at the neighbourhood level that they became a social force, with the State unable to intervene or attenuate the conflicts. Although it never formally existed, there were references to the 'Lisbon Commune' referring to the loose coalition of Popular Assemblies and 'soviet barracks'. Of course, there was the Setúbal Committee of Struggle – uniting workers', residents' and soldiers commissions – with all of their limitations and disputes over political orientation, expressed this duality of power. Pinheiro de Azevedo, Prime Minister of the Sixth Government, appeared on television on 13 October 1975, to say that he recognised the 'generous revolutionary impetus', but that the attacks on private property demanded 'the response of the majority of the population'.[31]

The Portuguese Communist Party was making headway. It had grown from about 2,000 to more than 100,000 militants. We believe that among the many factors that explain this growth and the confidence that its leadership received was, first of all, the fact that the Portuguese Communist Party was the party of resistance to the dictatorship, which had suffered the most in the prisons of the Estado Novo, a fact that the party legitimately claims throughout the revolution.

When the revolution began, the other organisations are in a very embryonic state.[32]

The bakers dispute surfaced in October and it was to have enormous reverberations. 'We want to sleep next to our wives! We want to sleep next to our wives!' shouted the protesting bakers. On 14 October 1975, a communiqué from the Union of Workers of the Baking and Foodstuffs Industries justified the abolition of night-shift labour for the advantages which would follow from 'improving the quality and frequency of fresh bread to large daily meals' and also for the satisfaction of 'an old claim of the class' of bakers to 'live a normal life'.[33]

The next day, bakers' delegates and union leaders met with the minister and the Secretary of State for Labour to present the motion to abolish night work in the sector. Bakers' demonstrations continued for weeks and reached a crescendo in November.

When Prime Minister Pinheiro de Azevedo declared that the government went on strike because the whole country was on strike, he was confronted on television, about whether the bakers' demonstration had also bothered him, he paused and with a playful air, scratched his chin and pursed his lips, saying:

'I'm tired of these games! I've already been kidnapped twice. I don't like it. It's annoying!'

'Was there anything particular that made you take that position yesterday afternoon?' asked a journalist.

'Yesterday afternoon? No, I don't remember anything like that ...'

'Could it be the demonstration of the bakers?' the journalist inquired.

'No, no, no. The demonstration of the bakers. Look ... I guess, maybe. Perhaps the frequency of the demonstrations did raise an issue in the subconscious of the ministers ... You're right! But look, I didn't even think of the demonstration of the bakers!'[34]

However, it wasn't the bakers' demonstration that led Pinheiro de Azevedo to declare the suspension of the government. Almost every action seemed to call into question who has the power.

There were also unexpected strikes, such as that of the cleaning services in Lisbon, which on 22 November 1975, two days after the government itself went on strike, left Lisbon full of trash. A bookstore strike was planned and took place on 25 November.

Near the very beginning of this book we told you about Pinheiro de Azevedo, and how in his direct and indiscrete style, decided to suspend government functions on 20 November 1975 and he said: 'The situation, as far as I know, remains the same: first, they hold plenaries and then they carry out their orders!'[35] He went on to say that the Government cannot ensure security 'to continue to govern, requiring guarantees of military support'.

This was undoubtedly foreshadowing of the counter-revolutionary coup that was being hatched. On that same day, on 20 November 1975, Otelo Saraiva de Carvalho resigned the command of the Military Region of Lisbon and was replaced by Vasco Lourenço. Also, on that day there was the threat of transferring the Constituent Assembly to Oporto.

On 21 November, in a TLP plenary, a member of the workers' commission read a statement before a crowded room in total silence:

What is happening in relation to the restructuring of the TLP is as follows: workers have been suspended for about ten months by the current administration and the workers' committee has decided to call a plenary session for the workers to solve the problem, and not the administration which, by the way, has proven incapable of solving it until now. Under the bourgeois laws, workers on probation or suspension could only be so for three months. However, there are already ten months in which this case has dragged on. Following a true path that we consider one of popular power, we issued this call for a plenary and the workers, after a broad, democratic discussion of the subject, and having listened to the various points of view, regardless of their political ideology and their party affiliation, have decided by a vast majority what to do with these suspended elements and it will be in accord with our law and not with a bourgeois law, or a law of the current government or any other governments that may exist thereafter.[36]

This chapter has underplayed the impact and inter-relationship with the struggles in the colonies. Portugal had to accommodate between 500,000 and one million refugees from Africa. On 11 November 1975, during several popular demonstrations in Defence of the MPLA, the high commissioner, Leonel Cardoso, transferred Portuguese sovereignty to the Angolan State.

Construction Workers

The State's ultimate source of power at the institutional level – that of the MFA – had been split, opening a space for the questioning of power in the barracks by rank-and-file soldiers. To affirm that the commissions of soldiers, whether clandestine or not, organised or not, had little power is to misunderstand the alarms that sounded in all the offices of the country and which Pinheiro de Azevedo captured with his irritation when he said: 'first, they [the soldiers] held plenaries, then they carried out their orders!'.[37] But the straw that broke the camel's back was the construction workers' strike, which we referred to in the opening pages of this book. Let us tell you more about it now.

On 12 November 1975, there was a large demonstration of construction workers, some tens of thousands, near the Palace of São Bento, in Lisbon, where the Constituent Assembly was meeting. The siege lasted for two days. The demonstration, which began by concentrating on the demands of the construction sector and was radicalised by the refusal of the Ministry of Labour to receive the workers, rapidly became a mobilisation against the Sixth Government. This showed the power of the workers, who laid siege to the Constituent Assembly meeting place and trapped the deputies inside. The Communist Party participated in the demonstration with caution.[38] It strongly opposed the siege. A communiqué issued on 13 November stated:

> The PCP considers that the events unfolded around the Palace of S. Bento during the great demonstration and concentration therein are the responsibility of the Ministry of Labour and Government. For a long time, the workers were entertained with false promises ... Supporting the demonstration and the concentration of S. Bento, the PCP disagrees, however, with the kidnapping of the deputies of the Constituent Assembly and the prime minister. ... kidnapping is not a form of struggle that favours the workers.[39]

The far-left enthusiastically supported the siege of the Constituent Assembly. The images on national TV show the besieged Parliament in one corner and the Military Police and construction workers are seen together, laughing and sharing roast chicken. The siege took form as an outdoor encampment, despite the cold November weather. Several bonfires were lit and, on the ground, glowing coals were used to bake sardines. Cigarettes and bottles of red wine circulated. One of the workers huddled around a fire reading the book *Karate and Zen*. Most of the workers wore their construction helmets throughout the siege. The claims and declarations spread throughout São Bento on banners reading 'Peasants and sailors, we shall win', 'We have come to stay', 'Vertical collective agreement', 'Unemployment no. Right to work, yes', 'Away with Marcelo Curto and his supporters', 'Out with Tomas Rosa', 'Down with the AMI'.

After two days, when the deputies were released, most of them left on foot, through a long, bustling corridor of workers, journalists and military personnel. Most of them went out with their heads low, but those of the Communist Party and the UDP were cheered amidst shouts and applause.

The Sixth Provisional Government was paralysed. The siege was inadmissible, said Pinheiro de Azevedo. That was when, in his characteristic tone, he reported being 'tired of being kidnapped', and suspended the Government.

Workers' Committees and the Industrial Belt of Lisbon

The Communist Party was now preoccupied with what it considered to be 'militant sectarianism' – it was said 'in a certain spirit of the sect'[40] – both in relation to workers' commissions and to certain professional sectors such as employers and employees. Indeed, this sectarianism had been generated by the opposition of the party to the commissions of workers at the beginning of the revolution, but the leadership of the Communist Party now shows, as I have described, a clear desire to change this policy and win the leadership of the commissions of workers. The Communist Party felt that part of its base, real and potential, was being eroded, towards either the Socialist Party or the far-left. In this sense, it proposed an 'internal battle against sectarianism', and the pages of its organisational bulletins often emphasise this point.[41]

This concern is accompanied by a very realistic analysis of the party's relationship with the labour movement, which is not welcomed in the pages of *Avante!* but regarded with serenity in *O Militante*, which argues that, despite the great achievements of the trade union movement, there are difficulties that are reflected in the electoral results in the workplace. These difficulties are amplified here:

'A great sectarianism, demonstrated in the workings of trade unions characterised by a closed work'; 'The fair position of Inter-union and unions, not to support certain strikes and other struggles citing unrealistic claims ... led Inter and the unions to a certain degree of defensiveness in the initiative, not always responding to concerns over workers' 'rights'; the withdrawal of unions from federative structures, but also from grass-roots structures; bureaucratic methods of work; lack of staff; the anti-communist campaign and even to the 'incomprehension of certain organisations, of distinguished leaders and other trade union activists of the workers' commissions in opposition to these unitary structures, which have been detrimental to the unity of the workers.'[42]

The most important of all the coordinating bodies to emerge in summer 1975, eventually was the Workers Committees of the Industrial Belt of Lisbon – Cintura Indústria de Lisboa – CIL for short. This coordinated all the workers' commissions of the Lisbon Industrial Belt and turned out to be highly important in the 1975 summer and autumn mobilisations insofar as it brought together 200 or 300 workers commissions of the Portuguese capital and was destined to inspire similar structures in Setúbal, Porto and Braga in the months that followed. Although there was a considerable presence of Communist Party members in its leadership, at the time, the CIL was not a monolithic structure run by that Party. The CIL enjoyed the support of practically all the parties to the left of the Socialist Party and organised demonstrations, protests, including stoppages in workplaces to have meetings. It organised the great demonstration, of perhaps 300,000 people, in the *Terreiro do Paço* on 16 November 1975. The paper *Avante!* told us the manifestation was: a 'sea of people, working people' that 'flooded' Lisbon, in a demonstration of unity to halt the 'road to reaction'. The newspaper lists the various commissions of workers present, left-wing military units such as Ralis and the Military Police, and highlights the 'presence of SUVs and progressive officers in the great unitary journey alongside the people'. The message of the demonstration is to force the Government to agree to negotiate the position of the PCP in the Government and in the Council of the Revolution: 'We do not come here to "assault power", but we want to transform power ... to ensure the defence and triumph of our revolution, aimed at socialism.'[43]

When the CIL met for the first time formally to constitute itself in Barreiro on 8 November, the Communist Party advocated a policy of maintaining production, which would be verified by production control commissions, representing 'all the most important sectors of the company'. At the congress, bearing in mind that, at the time there were 322,000 workers unemployed, almost ten times the number registered on 25 April 1974, the Communist Party declared that 'the way to address the unemployment crisis was not cutting down on working hours' but instead, ensuring better organisation of the workers, nationalisation of overseas trade and 'taking maximum advantage of production capacity'.[44] Questions of workers' control and the national coordination of the workers' commissions were two of the items that divided opinions among the commissions represented there.

Finally, the Communist Party declared that it was completely against the creation of a national body to coordinate workers' commissions, arguing that the latter should play the role of injecting dynamism into grass-roots assemblies but: 'we perceive that the creation of a definitive institutionalised superior body of the workers' commissions would bring with it the danger of dispersing efforts and diverting the workers' commissions from their fundamental objectives'.[45]

Government prepares for the coup

On 13 October 1975, Admiral José Pinheiro de Azevedo, in an interview with the US-based magazine *Time*, stated that 'we only have another month of this' before we put Portugal in order again. The Sixth Provisional Government was the one that found it most difficult to govern, insofar as this crisis of the State coincided with the strengthening processes of housing occupations and residents' committees, far beyond just the questions relating to neighbourhood management. On 20 November, when Azevedo declared the government strike and spoke of his being kidnapped, he also said ominously that there would be a coup against the revolution.

Part of that interview was cut and is now available in the public domain:

Journalist: What are the minimum conditions of government?

Pinheiro de Azevedo: Oh, well, I'm sorry, but this really is part of the commitment between the Sixth Government, with myself and the President of the Republic. It stands, without a doubt, by the military force in Lisbon and in some focal points.[46]

On the same day, Costa Gomes made a public speech asking the population not to resist an eventual coup:

My dear friends and comrades. In the first place, I want to thank you for this great demonstration of support that you have tried to bring me. I know perfectly well the individual and collective sacrifices that you have made to be present here at this event since 2.30 in the afternoon. I wish to assure you that, as you know, my presence was delayed for two reasons: first, because I was presiding over the Council of the Revolution which was analysing the current political moment. Secondly, because I wanted to express to your leaders that I am not in agreement with the various demonstrations characterised by a pressure that doesn't conform to national principles ... Although I am perhaps the person who best knows the genesis, and the effects of a calamity such as civil war, I will by all means possible avoid this calamity for my people (applause, shouts of 'No to civil war! No to civil war!').

Civil war only brings misfortune, ruin, hatred and sacrifices to those who have endured for 13 years an unjust colonial war. With 30,000 wounded and countless dead because of this wicked war, we have finally had enough.

By no means would anyone affirm that civil war solves political, social, and military problems. I know full well that we are very far from achieving the political stability that allows us to govern without overcoming obstacles and with tranquillity to quickly achieve the goals that the revolution of April 25 proposed, which is that of a country wherein reigns a socialism based on justice and equality of all men before the law and not on the exploitation of man by man.

... I must tell you that I understand that in this extraordinarily acute emergency in which we find ourselves, that we need all Portuguese of good will to join hands and fight together to face the increscent danger that courts a reaction from the right that could usher us into a regime similar to the one in Chile.[47]

On 20 November, a 'Manifesto' drawn up by 'Revolutionary Officers' was presented. It was time to 'fight for the revolution', they said. In the days that followed, there were general meetings between the signatories and plenaries of the workers' committees of Lisnave, Sorefame, EUROFIL, Lusalite, Baptista Russo, SIPE and Setenave, to discuss the Manifesto. The SUVs signed off on the manifesto, as did some of the far-left.

On 21 November 1975, 170 recruits made an historic pledge of allegiance, in which they vowed fidelity 'to the working class' in a ceremony presided over by general Carlos Fabião. A delegation of paratroopers and the Coordinating Committee of the Committees of Workers and Residents of the RALIS Zone were present. On the same day, the provisional secretariat of the Workers' Committees of the Industrial Belt of Lisbon (CIL) called for a two-hour partial strike on 24 November, from 4–6pm, to promote the 'formation of a People's Power'. The leadership of the Journalists' Union, which was driven by the MRPP and the Socialist Party, was stopped by a majority of the members in a general plenary for 'not having effectively opposed the offensive that the bourgeoisie and its lackey Almeida Santos have led against the media workers.'

The reader will recall that the paratroopers at Tancos were indirectly involved in the dynamiting of Rádio Renascença; they thought they were providing protection and that 'the orders came from the left'. This betrayal so shocked them that they were to revolt within weeks. The 1,600 previously loyal paratroopers from Tancos now rebelled against their officers and forced 123 of the 150 officers to walk out.

The allegation was frequently made that the paratroopers were preparing a left-wing coup; it should be stressed that the paratroopers had prepared no command nor had they prepared or centralised any plans.

They were demanding to be placed under the overall command of Otelo and COPCON. In response, a coup was set in motion planning to end the ongoing revolutionary process, and, in the words of Manuela Cruzeiro, to replace it with an 'ongoing constitutional process'.[48]

25 November

The pretext for carrying out the coup of 25 November and the outcome that the Group of Nine intended to affect, under Costa Gomes, was 'the capture of the paratroopers banner' by paramilitary actions.'[49]

The coup's civil direction was headed up by the Socialist Party and the Church, and militarily, by the Group of Nine – and it remains unknown what other parties were involved – as had been the case since at least August 1975.[50] Behind the scenes, preparations were now being made for a decisive move against radical sections of the troops. On the evening of 24 November, Rio Maior farmers cut the access roads to Lisbon in coordination with 'moderate' military personnel. The coup began on 25 November 1975.

The coup was ignited by the paratroopers occupying several air bases in an attempt to receive support from COPCON. The occupations of the paratroopers was a reaction to repeated provocations made throughout November by orders from military personnel assigned to the Group of Nine, who first ordered the unit to be decommissioned, then froze their salaries, and finally ordered the cutting of the supply of food and electricity to Tancos air base. The coup was headed by Ramalho Eanes, with the operational command of Jaime Neves and Pires Veloso, with a 'very small military force' based at the commando barracks at Amadora.[51] Carlos Fabião, the Chief of Staff of the Army, Soares and others had rejected the idea of an overtly counter-revolutionary coup. They were not inspired by the example of Chile. A state of emergency was declared and the anti-revolution operation centre set in motion. In effect, the operations centre used only 200 people as its task force, including the highly 'professional' commandos led by the notorious Colonel Jaime Neves, and some officers who had been sacked by their underlings from other units.

The 'moderates' moved into action. They sought to avoid a potentially bloody confrontation and even they must have been surprised at the ease with which they succeeded. They were not sure that the commandos would leave the barracks – let alone fight. Once on the road confidence grew as one by one the rebel units collapsed. Three soldiers from the Military Police were killed. The officer networks 'on the side of the people' failed to act. This collapse led to confusion of the 'Popular Power' forces. Much more than on 12 March, people were confused, and demobilised. For example, just before midnight on 25 November, several hundred working-class people gathered on one of the approach roads leading to the military police barracks. There was a discussion with a bus driver. Should they turn his bus over? It would help to make a good barricade. On the other hand, perhaps, the military police wanted to take to the roads. Nobody seemed to know. Nothing was done.[52]

On the previous day, the Lisbon ferries and many factories had emergency meetings and stoppages lasting two hours in order to discuss the threat from the right. On 25 November,

People stopped working – but there was no organised strike. Many did not go to work, others went in, saw nothing was happening so came into town. Some went asking for machine guns in front of the barracks; there were assemblies in factories but no-one knew what to do.

All the revolutionary groupings were taken completely unawares by the speed of the events. None were involved in instigating a military response. Workers would have resisted and possibly defeated any conservative forces outside the MFA. The popular movement was looking for an external enemy, not one within the MFA. The radical soldiers and their friends on the revolutionary left were isolated. In the preceding weeks the Communist Party had turned left, once again, in order to retain its political support and to buttress its position within the unstable Sixth Provisional Government. On 24 November it called a two-hour general strike against the threat from the right, with limited success. The

Photo 12   November 1975, left-wing paras weep with disappointment as they surrender to the commandos, the men who made the coup for the right-wing. (*Big Flame*)

sergeants of the paratroopers and some of the officers who planned the resistance to the removal of Otelo were encouraged and influenced by the PCP.[53]

A couple of days later my editor interviewed a revolutionary:

Above all what characterises the events of 25 November is the lack of any serious organisation of the revolutionary soldiers when it came to the crunch.

Too much trust was put in revolutionary officers and no real structure of organisation of the rank and file existed able to lead at the testing time.

There was no co-ordination, no real co-ordination ... the so-called revolutionary units because they were caught in a totally defensive position, discussing and so forth. Inside the barracks they did not take a single initiative. Yet they were exposed to the extent that they never pledged themselves to the military commanders and did not follow this or that order.

No one offered resistance (to the commandos). There were only a few shots in the case of the military police. And even there the top commander of the military police opened the door to them. He surrendered himself after a little shooting – and not from the other side.

One of the military police, a soldier, told me how annoying it was for these soldiers who were seemingly prepared and organised for a socialist insurrection. As soon as the two commanders – Tome and Andrade disappeared – one surrendered, the other was captured – they didn't know what to do. There wasn't anyone to give orders. Although the soldiers were refusing military discipline, they didn't know how to operate in any other way.

The so-called revolutionary officers are finished.[54,55]

We cannot be conclusive about the nature of the agreement between the Communist Party and the Group of Nine. Nuno Brederode Santos confirms that his house was the scene of a meeting between Álvaro Cunhal and Melo Antunes on the eve of 25 November. Cunhal did not deny or confirm the meeting and Melo Antunes confirms that there was such a meeting, but denied that 'any agreement, any business, resulted'. We know that Melo Antunes went on to television, in the early hours of 26 November, to reject any kind of crackdown on the Communist Party. On 25 November, as soon as the coup is launched, the Communist Party mobilised the workers' cells of several companies dominated by them, including the National

Broadcasting station and the RTP, and places the Committees of Defence of the Revolution (CDRs) of the Lisbon Region on alert. According to Robinson 'by the afternoon of the 25th it became apparent that the party sharply altered tack. It used its main agencies, the Intersindical and the Cintura Industrial de Lisboa, to do so. Officials and activists in the engineering union offices who were organising overnight occupations and strikes changed their tune at 6 o'clock on the Tuesday evening when the message from headquarters got through. Other unions got the message later. One of the workers at the Ministry of Social Communications recalls witnessing union officials backdating the call for a retreat from 26 to 25 November. The Communist Party give orders for the demobilisation of the civil actions conducted by Intersindical, which was, in the words of Manuela Cruzeiro,[56] 'the real blow to the kidneys'. And, finally, they do not allow the departure of the marines, led by the party. The Communist Party refuses to distribute weapons to hundreds or thousands of militants and sympathisers who requested them from Communist Party headquarters and military units.

The fact that Communist Party leader Álvaro Cunhal, on behalf of the Communist Party – agreed not to resist on 25 November weighs heavily on the party that had a heroic role against the dictatorship.

The Portuguese Communist Party was prepared to abandon its radical army supporters (and a great many others) in exchange for a continued stake in government. The military left had become a burden on the Communist Party because its performance undermined the balance of power with the Nine and peaceful coexistence agreements between the USA, Western Europe and the USSR. Some 200 soldiers and officers, plus a handful of building workers, were arrested.

The counter-revolution had begun.

The days after 25 November

On 26 November, Ernesto Melo Antunes goes to television to say that the Communist Party is indispensable to build the Portuguese democracy and, against the Socialist Party and sectors to the right, refuses to proscribe the party, which remains as a member of the Sixth Provisional Government. In the field of those who directed the coup there was, it seems, a political wing that wanted to isolate the Communist Party and a military wing that, perhaps because it recognised the political and military weight of the Communist Party, found it better to negotiate with it and find a political solution which includes the Communist party in the frame.

Although sections were exhausted, the movement was still enormous and it was by no means spent. The resistance by groups of building workers gives some indication of how the working class could have exerted its not inconsiderable forces. These workers, using walkie-talkies, commandeered enormous earth-movers and concrete-mixers in order to block the advance of the commandos. In Setúbal, they contacted the *Comité de Luta* and asked them to set up blockades around the city. The committee set up a clandestine radio, which operated for a few days. The town hall had been occupied. Isabel Guerra from the *Comité* said:

> We tried to contact all the organisations including the unions and cultural organisations. We called a rally outside the barracks. All the time we were connected with the principal barracks in Lisbon and other cities. The problem of 25th of November was that neither the unions nor the workers' commissions controlled by the PCP were interested in what was going on – they said so – they did not mobilise. Many people were influenced by them. In the regiment the soldiers took arms from a captain and controlled the situation as long as they could. After a certain time they couldn't do so any longer ...
>
> What 25th of November did show was that the Committee of Struggle could function in time of crisis. But the problem was much more complex. Even today I would like to know what actually happened then. What was clear even then was that the PCP did sabotage the movement. We called the *sindicatos* and they said 'No, nothing is going on'. In the big enterprises, like Setenave, the worker's commission which was PCP controlled, said 'No we haven't heard anything, everything is all right'.[57]

The economic and social struggles were to continue, in all sorts of ways. The occupations of the land ceased. There was an enormous retreat in urban struggles. Yet, the right to housing would be written into the social pact – the Constitution approved this in 1976 – under the ambit of social rights (on the same level as the right to health, education, social security, and the environment and quality of life). However, this would be the right that was least implemented. There was never a change to the Land Law to prevent the total private acquisition of surplus value[58] and the post-25 April era did not eradicate most of the slums made of shacks, a question that would only be 'solved' by the explosion of real estate speculation and credit during the 1990s.

Cunhal, the leader of the communists, acknowledges deep changes after 25 November and defends the opportunity to restore the alliance strategy with the Group of 9 and the Socialist Party. He affirms that, having annihilated the military left, this policy of alliances has become much easier: 'Paradoxical as it may seem, the defeat of the military left, the tragic teachings it brings, and the immediate dangers it raises create new conditions for the unity of forces interested in safeguarding liberties, democracy and revolution.'[59]

The 25th of November was the turning point. The change was abrupt – similar to the change described by George Orwell in Barcelona in 1936 where the 'startling change in the atmosphere' is something, which is 'difficult to conceive unless you actually experience it'. The 25th of November was the beginning of the counter-revolution.

19
Democracy and Revolution:
The Meaning of the Carnation Revolution

Nationalising the companies alone won't solve the workers' problems!
Therefore, it's fundamental for the workers to fight to effectively win political
power.

CUF Worker[1]

The Peoples History of the Carnation Revolution

There has been much debate about the nature of the Carnation Revolution.
The focus has predominantly been on the role of the parties, and the
MFA, often resorting to interviews with military and civil leaders of the
revolution.[2] Interviews and archives are indispensable for an understanding
of the Portuguese Revolution. But the predominance of works that centre
on political agendas and having as their main source the political protagonists themselves (causing a boom in oral histories of state leaders, parties,
associations, schools, etc.) has been at the expense of studies that deal with
social classes.

One could attribute the fact to the perennial problem of sources, which
always bears mention when it comes to analysing the history of the working
and popular classes. Carlo Ginzburg, for example, begins his '*O Queijo
e os Vermes*' (The Cheese and the Worms), noting that 'the scarcity of
testimony describing the behavior and attitudes of the lower classes of the
past is certainly the first – but not the only – obstacle into which historical
works of the genre collide.'[3] The first characteristic of a revolutionary
situation is the social participation of millions of people far removed from
politics, and not used to the luxury of keeping a record of their participation. Hence, there is a scarcity of sources which is difficult to overcome.
It is not, however, impossible. Leon Trotsky, in *The History of the Russian
Revolution*, rightly refers to the obligation of historians to overcome the
partial scarcity of sources: 'The difficulties encountered in studying the
changes in the consciousness of the masses in the epoch of revolution are

quite evident. The oppressed classes make history in the factories, in their quarters, in the fields, and in the city, in the streets. They do not, however, have the chance to put down what they do in writing.'[4]

Ultimately, it is from the fragments and the 'random' notes the masses happen to produce, Trotsky says, 'that revolutionary leaders adapt their tactics. But the ephemeral flotsam from the turmoil creates problems for the historian.'[5]

It is not only a matter of its sources, but to have historians available to work on a given object, as Eric Hobsbawm wrote in his essay 'History from the Ground Up': 'Many sources for the history of popular movements were only recognized as such because someone asked a question and then searched desperately for some way – any way – to answer it. We cannot be positivists, believing that questions and answers arise naturally from material study.'[6]

Fortunately, during the revolution and shortly afterwards, studies were being carried out which focused on the Portuguese labour movement and the history of classes and their leadership. The research by Chip Dows,[7] Santos *et al.*,[8] John Hammond,[9] Loren Goldner,[10] and Peter Robinson[11], among others, is still indispensable.

Building a competent, rigorous historiography capable of withstanding the pressures of political power implies much more than a debate on terminology. It will involve, among other things, the rejection of postmodern philosophical theories that decontextualise history itself to the advantage of a more fragmented view of social science; and will require a renewed return to social history and the centrality of social conflicts to explain the historical process. It will involve a broad survey of labour conflicts during the revolution and, finally, a preparedness to explore the threats to power from revolutionary quarters. For example, it is impossible to understand the entire coup of 11 March 1975, without a survey of the factories and companies of the country where in fact a process of workers' control was developing.

A historiographical approach that favours social struggles is indispensable for understanding a revolutionary situation, a step in the direction of changing the questions from the outset. We need to comprehend the Portuguese Revolution from the perspective of researching the social history of the labour movement, in the words of Chris Harman,[12] this is to study the backbone, the skeleton.

By not doing so, history will become reduced to a struggle of political leadership – political parties, trade union organisations, management, ruling elites – that act independently of their social base and class of origin.

This is what Hobsbawm warned us against. It is an option that promotes the admission of the relative autonomy of theory, that is, the assumption that documents do not 'speak for themselves', as the positivists once intended, and as today, somehow, postmodern theories posit, by hiding themselves in undifferentiation of the explanatory causes of historical process. In other words, the historian leads with a theory to verify whether it is confirmed by reality and seeks to explain this reality by stratifying, in a history under construction, the factors that contributed to a given event.

The role of the reformists/reformers, in the classic sense of the term (nationalisation, agrarian reform, wage improvement), gained a revolutionary dimension because they were at times able to encompass the labour movement, while not agreeing with the tactics (strikes, occupations of land and factories). Understanding the revolution, from the historiographical point of view, implies refocusing it on its real dimension, that is, recovering, investigating, knowing and cataloging social conflicts. And to highlight as protagonists the *social subjects* (classes, their fractions and in particular the autonomous workers', residents', agricultural workers' and, at some point, soldiers' organisations), as an alternative to an approach that looks at history through the prism of *representative subjects* (elites), consequently ignoring the notion of collective composition arising from social conflict.

A good example of the focus upon the dramatic events is the coup attempt of 11 March. The 11 March did not begin the revolution, a theory propagated by the Communist Party, which combined the concept of revolution to its moments of power in the state apparatus. The 11 March is the fruit of the radicalisation of the revolution under workers' control. Conventional narratives over-focus upon the twists and turns of the six provisional governments and the danger is that they neglect the grass roots organisations. The revolution is unbroken by the loss of state control, whether it is more controlled by the Communist Party or the Socialist Party and the fractions of the MFA. The weakening of the State and the MFA accelerates the revolution, accelerates the posing of an alternative power.

We believe that social changes are at the root of governmental ruptures and the inability to produce institutional and political agreements, which are made impossible to achieve by the very dynamics of social movement, and not the other way around. If our analysis is social and has as its central axis the relation between workers' and popular power – whether organised or not – and the State, the periodisation of the revolution undergoes some changes vis-à-vis the classical periodisation proposed so far, centred above all on the changes of provisional governments and *coups d'état*. Here is my overview focusing on the relation of social forces:

a) Between April 1974 and September 1975 the revolution was marked, after the inaugural coup, by a period in which social struggles were determined both in the metropolis and in the colonies by demonstrations and strikes or the refusal to act. (Troops in the colonies were demoralised by war and the MFA opposition to prolonging the conflict.) This finally led to the fall of Spinola in September 1974, reinforcing the populist front in the Government and strengthening the ranks of the Communist Party and the MFA and also further empowered the movement from below. This period is marked, from a social point of view, by the achievement of the democratic forces – ensured just a few days after the coup – and by the continuation of a social mobilisation in which strikes are the decisive form of struggle, as well as the beginning of the struggle against lay-offs.

b) Between September 1974 and February 1975, a second period was marked by the fight against lay-offs leading to the generalised occupation of companies and the reinforcement of the commissions of workers as organs of power parallel to that of the State. We have already noted the emergence of the inter-empresas, which pulled together many factories in the Lisbon region, and challenged the State, and demonstrated the potential of an alternative power, a dual power. This was most spectacular in the run-up and around the demonstration of 7 February, which was against unemployment and the presence of NATO, and it created a schism between the MFA and the Provisional Government, and also where rank and file solders were won over to the support for demonstrating workers. The occupation of factories and enterprises forced the State to mobilise capital to maintain production. The economic crisis deepened.

c) From February 1975 to September 1975 began the period of worker control. The Socialist Party would attempt, by self-management and emphasising electoral legitimacy (elections for trade unions, autarchies, the legitimacy of the Constituent Assembly), to subvert the control of the operation; the far-left, for the most part, would support workers' control; the Communist Party would seek to contain the workers' control through the nationalisation of companies. All government parties would try to put an end to the workers' control of the politics of production. They were unable to do so and in August, the government breakdown was formalised. Operational control would be marked by the birth of embryonic structures of regional and national coordination of workers' and popular power bodies. The first of these had been the Inter-Empresas, then we had, for example, the CRTSMs, the national co-ordination of metalworking workers' commissions and the Popular Assemblies.

There was a parallel issue of the role of the armed forces and the relationship with popular power. Significant sections of the extreme left explored this vigorously in partnership with officers in the MFA who had been both radicalised by the grass roots movements and were simultaneously disillusioned with the established political parties. This culminated in the MFA *Documento Guia Povo* – (the People's Guide Document). The Communist Party welcomed this as a way of funneling the energies, as part of an enlarged state apparatus.

d) From September 1975 to November 1975, a revolutionary crisis, known as the 'political-military crisis', that is, the historical period during revolutions in which there is either a displacement of the State under the aegis of the workers or a coup thwarting the revolution. These periods are marked by the refusal of the bourgeoisie to accept expropriation and which leads to start a civil war. In this period, the State could not govern, institutional power, such as control of the media, banks, the army, local government and the legal system, was challenged at all levels because all measures by the State were prevented by strikes, protests, occupations (Ponte 25 de Abril, the siege of São Bento, and the radio transmitters, etc.).[13] We consider the revolutionary crisis to have begun only in September 1975, to the extent to which the MFA crisis, which began in early summer, resulted only in September in the spread of the duality of powers in the Armed Forces. The Socialist Party was, along with the right and the Group of Nine, determined to end the process by a coup. The military left, supported by a generalised duality of powers within the barracks, reflected the general 'mobilisation of society, but neither the military left nor the workers' or popular power were centralised at the national level resist the coup. The revolution was defeated. The only structure with national power refused and did not resist, namely the Intersindical.

The revolution, Portugal's historic adventure of 1974–1975, was not completed in its insurrectional moment, in the 'final assault' on the power of the State, which led some to question whether there had been a revolution at all – a theoretically fragile argument in which the victory or defeat of a revolutionary process does not imply that this process did not exist.[14] Curiously, it was a revolution that threatened economic power much more than that of the State.[15]

The counter-revolutionary coup of 25 November 1975 did not come from the boots of a military dictatorship; it had deep roots within the MFA, which gave it some credibility. The thesis – that of the democratic reaction – as articulated by the historian Valério Arcary, is the one that accords with empirical evidence, in my opinion.

The coup restored discipline in the armed forces, ensured the stability of institutions, maintaining the rule of law, a parliament, free elections, and the rights and freedoms of citizens. Representative democracy, for us, was not the boundary of the revolution, but a break with the revolution. It was a face of capitalist modernisation. Every revolutionary process is a tragic refutation of the gradualist thesis that diminishes the importance of rupture, of insurrection, in the strategy of the anti-capitalist struggle. The modernisation perspective views the Portuguese Revolution as a long process of extending democracy, of the accumulation of forces and rights and the convincing of or neutralisation of social enemies without the maximum severity of the assault on power, is not based upon what happened.[16]

Revolution Against the 'Chaos'

In May 1975, Gabriel García Márquez arrived in Lisbon, a city famous for its restaurants, where delicious rice is eaten with chicken blood, and where the waiters wonder aloud: 'would it be fair to accept a tip?'[17]

The writer was speechless, but one didn't have to be a stranger to be surprised. Nobody living in Portugal could have imagined what was going to take place in that corner of Western Europe between 1974 and 1975.

For many, then, it was not clear that 25 November had meant a social upheaval – also because it was not an immediate change. In other words, the cleansing of the far-left in the Armed Forces was just the beginning of a long process of counter-revolution that took years to consolidate in the factories and neighbourhoods. Although the mood changed the situation of the workers, who had been living under the direct management of workplaces and housing and even workers' control, did not simply change 'from one day to the next'.

Even in April 1976, a group of journalists walked through the nation's factories and asked people 'what do you think of socialism'?[18] How could a Western European country, from within NATO, that had been under a 48-year dictatorship, where unions and political organisations were banned, within a two-year period come to be discussing between workers, intellectuals, and women who spent the entire day in factories, the question 'what do you think of socialism?' Indeed Phil Mailer told us how, within days of the 25 April coup: 'People are discussing the situation in France, England, Argentina and Brazil as if they'd been professors of politics all their lives.'[19]

The uniqueness of the Portuguese Revolution is also this: its impact had been so profound as to see a victorious revolution, although without a seizure of power, and a displacement of the State under the aegis of the workers – which now, for the first time in Portuguese history, witnessed a national discussion of the possibility of a transition from the capitalist mode of production to a socialist mode of production.

The counter-revolution, like the revolution, was a process, recalled historian Valério Arcary in his analysis of the history of revolutions. For this reason, in 1976 and 1977, the transition to socialism in Portugal was still being discussed as an ongoing and pressing issue in the factories and academy.

The exact moment in which this situation changed, in which the 'transition to socialism' became a chimera unrelated with the reality of common sense giving way to a marginal project, turning into a means for the consolidation of the democratic liberal regime, is still a subject of controversy. Arcary places this change in the gradual transfer of structural funds and adhesion of the Country to the then European Community.[20] I locate the axis of this change, this moment of consolidation of the counter-revolution, at the birth of social conciliation in 1986,[21] which I classify as the end of the social pact born of the revolution and embodied in the 1976 Constitution. Both moments are most likely the result of the same movement, although other factors may have contributed to it, but I believe that the defeat of the Lisnave workers and the union negotiations was particularly significant. This led to increasing division of labour facing insecurity, moving in and out of precarious work that gives little meaning to their lives on one hand, and the maintaining of 'acquired rights', outweighing the transfer of rights, on the other, took some time to make themselves felt.

To be sure, the consolidation of the democratic regime and the virtual collapse of the groups to the left of the Portuguese Communist Party, had a substantial impact on the discussion of the revolution. Academics stopped analysing a Revolution in itself and began to analyse it from the perspective of consolidation of the liberal democratic regime. Thus, the Portuguese Revolution was submerged by the memory of the victors, who obscured the Revolution in a vague notion of 'chaos' and attempted to erect the theory of the transition from dictatorship to representative democracy without considering the revolutionary forces. This phenomenon was revealed in the very abandonment of the concept of *revolution* and in the adoption of the concept of *transition to democracy*.[22]

The 25 April is, we argue, the period of greatest democracy in the history of Portugal – due to the extent and breadth of citizens' power – and this period was defeated not by a dictatorial coup but by a counter-revolutionary process whose turning point was the constitution of a representative democratic regime. We will then provide a periodisation of the revolution centred on the existence of a duality of powers – with an alternative power present in workplaces, housing and finally barracks – as opposed to a periodisation that has hitherto privileged as chronological beacons a succession of coups and changes to the government.

A loose selection of facts – dissociated from its general social context and without any hierarchy in the selection – allows commentators like Rui Ramos to emphasise violence in the narrative, which, by all means, and in comparison with other revolutionary processes, was scarce in Portugal during the revolution (although it was not lacking on the other side of the revolution, in the colonies).

Ramos highlights left-wing violence.[23] In summary, here are the characteristics of violence in the Portuguese Revolution:

1. A virtual absence of violence, in the metropolis, due precisely to the crisis of the Army.

2. The violence exerted was often carried out on workers, repression of strikes, in the arrest of militants such as the MRPP and AOC after 11 March 1975 and a small right-wing party, the Partido Democracia Cristã.

3. Dozens 'fled' from prison, witnessing the complacency of the authorities, and most suffered no significant penalty.

4. A revolution in which most of the serious violence was marked, during the Hot Summer, by the violence of the right, by the complicit silence of the Socialist Party and the Church, against the unions and the leftist parties. There followed another provisional government, the Sixth, heralded by acts such as the bombing of Rádio Renascença's headquarters and the creation of the AMI, a special force of repression.

5. Finally, there was little violence in the absence of judgement for most of the New State regime, many of whom, including generals with a criminal role in the war, were faced with 'early compulsory retirement'. Unlike some left-wing and far-left military personnel, they were to be granted amnesty.

In relative terms, the violence of 1974 and 1975 was predominantly from the side of the right and the Socialist Party, the Group of Nine, and the Church coalition.[24]

The violence that existed in 1974–1975, however limited in scope, targeted the left more than the right.[25]

There was political use of the state apparatus by the Socialist Party and the Communist Party against each other, depending on the relation of forces – this does not of itself define whether a regime is dictatorial or a representative democracy. There was no stable state power, much less a dictatorial power: all freedoms were widely assured as never before in the history of Portugal. As a final note, it is curious that the word 'chaos' is used to describe the revolution, but no equivalent expression is used to speak of a regime involved in a colonial war with low wages, widespread misery, underdeveloped health standards, police politics, and censorship, that it had forced a million and a half of people to emigrate. Is that, 'order'?

The most repressive moment of the whole revolution was the coup that initiated the counter-revolution, which gave rise to the arrest, during several months, of more than 100 officers.

The narrative of 'chaos' has no historical density. It is part of a theoretical framework that tries to associate the 'PREC' (the ongoing revolutionary process) with a time of disorder and repression, a framework that can only be built through the elimination of facts. The story of a people who organise themselves in committees of workers, dwellers, soldiers and the deep basic democracy that led Prime Minister Pinheiro de Azevedo, before the coup of 25 November, to desperately say that everything had come to pass 'by plenary' is replaced by a story of great military figures blamed for manipulating an entire people who are not the historical subjects of their own lives. Never in Portugal did so many people decide so much as in those days of the revolution. It was the most democratic period of our history.

The Popular or Representative Democracy?

Real democracy began on 25 April 1974 and not on 25 April 1975. It began with endless hours of meetings where ordinary people intervened on labour, and production issues, housing and management and voted by show of hands in committees with representatives who were revocable at any time, if they disrespected the results of the plenários that enjoyed wide participation. Never before had so many people decided their own futures as in 1974 and 1975.

The masses at first – we use the concept of masses in the sense that they are not organised groups with a political program, hence in this concept, of course, a disoriented, disruptive mass – evolve into basic structures, commissions, associations, parties or trade unions.

The strikes and occupations registered in this period arose mainly from plenários (disparagingly classified in Portuguese as *selvagens* – 'savages'–

although such a term has been 'cleansed' by academic studies). They crystallised, as we have seen, from democratic assemblies of workers and were directed, in most cases, by workers' commissions. They were convened on the margins of the Communist and Socialist parties (both formed part of the government) as well as from the trade unions, which were only formed from this point on. Some of the strikes occurred in sectors where during the dictatorship workers had already been mobilised – transport, electronics, insurance, fishing – but the act of striking became such a current and common phenomenon in Portuguese society that it affected all sectors at the national level. Some of these strikes had a qualitative importance because they paralysed key economic sectors of the country such as urban transport and bread strikes in May 1974 or the CTT strike which brought together 35,000 workers despite the opposition a union led by the Communist Party that ended up being defeated by police intervention ordered by the Provisional Government.

The 25 April is, we argue, the period of greatest democracy in the history of Portugal – due to the extent and breadth of citizens' power.

The striking feature of social and workers' movements in the Portuguese Revolution is not their number, which, is of course, relevant, but their dynamics. Suddenly, this dynamic permitted the questioning of the foundations of the industrial hierarchy, going beyond the appearance of freedom in the sphere of the circulation of capital and dragging down the productive mechanisms of the capitalist mode of production.

On the other hand, there are those who argue for 'representative' democracy, and we have briefly surveyed their arguments already. For them the elections for the Constituent Assembly, tellingly one year after the overthrow of the New State, on 25 April 1975 was a milestone. The left dismissed this as another mask of capitalism but under-estimated its ability to attract and absorb sections of the working class. Militants had not been schooled in the fight against reformists on the day-to-day issues, in the workplaces, the unions and through the ballot boxes.

Despite the urging by MFA to spoil the ballots, and the CRTMs conference the weekend before, telling people that real democracy lay in Portuguese Soviets, 91.73 per cent of the electorate voted. In hindsight, it is hardly surprising so many people voted after nearly 50 years of dictatorship. The Socialist Party attracted millions of votes of ordinary people by appealing to socialism, freedom, personal liberty, a desire for a proper parliamentary system and the orderly management by the State of the economy.

In September 1975, Soares explained to *The Times* that his programme 'was not meant to correct the most unjust aspects of capitalism but to destroy capitalism'.[26] Many workers lacked the experience and judgement to prove otherwise. The 'brilliant' achievements of the struggle did not mean that Portuguese workers had bypassed a faith in reformism or were permanently immune from it.

The movement was still young, people were picking and choosing their options. Communist Party militants in the workplaces could still support the workers' commissions when their party did not. Others would have supported the PCP in workplace struggles and voted for the Socialist Party in the elections for the Constituent Assembly. In reality, if there is such a thing as a 'typical' pattern of consciousness, that pattern is deeply uneven and contradictory; because conflict is experienced as uneven, discontinuous and partial, and its organisational expressions normally reflect this. Reformist organisations captured some contradictory patterns of consciousness and struggle.

The behaviour of both the Socialist Party and the Communist Party was necessarily different in some respects from the general pattern of behaviour of similar parties in Western Europe. Despite using a similar vocabulary of 'democracy and socialism', there was a sharp distinction between the two parties. Nevertheless, it remains true that all the major political parties preferred 'representative democracy, where they could be represented, to direct democracy.[27]

Revolution or Transition to Democracy?

On the bicentenary of the French Revolution, a polemic marked world historiography. In the debate, François Furet, in *Pensando a Revoluçao Francesa* (*Thinking the French Revolution*),[28] characterised the revolution of 1789 as an 'historical accident' and tried to distinguish the process begun in 1789 from later revolutions, especially the Russian Revolution of 1917. On the other side of the controversy, Eric Hobsbawm published a series of essays, collected in *Echoes of Marseillaise*,[29] where he argued that Furet's position, and that of the other historians who shared his view, resulted from revisionist ideological pressures and not from a renewed investigation of the French Revolution.[30]

Ever since 25 November, there have been discussions and theorising around about how to characterise the change of regime.[31] The polemic, however, burst into flames in Portugal, on no less occasion than the 30th Anniversary of the Portuguese Revolution, in April 2004. In the wake of the selection of the official commemorative poster for the celebration with the inscription 'April is Evolution', an argument broke out on the front pages of the newspapers over the meaning of the Portuguese Revolution. The debate quickly focused on the question of what should be emphasised in Portugal after the end of the dictatorship: the revolution, or the evolution of the country in the post-revolutionary period?

António Costa Pinto, at the time commissioner for the celebrations of the 30th anniversary of 25 April, wrote in the heat of the moment:

> In the customarily tepid landscape of historical celebrations, some dimensions of the celebrations of the 30th anniversary of April 25 provoked at least debate as an interesting feature. Nostalgic troglodytes, with the exception of the few defenders of history at the service of the 'revolution today and forever', had little visibility. ... Celebrating the 30 years of evolution for democracy and development that followed the Revolution of 1974 did not please part of the left, which is natural. They found the sight of the right-centre Carnations commemorating 25 April disagreeable.[32]

The historian Fernando Rosas criticised António Costa Pinto for comments he considered 'pseudoscientific': 'April was not an evolution because the Portuguese ... were historically incapable of carrying out a process of transition, that is, of carrying out, from the regime itself, an endogenous and sustained process of reform.'[33]

Other social scientists, such as António Borges Coelho, Manuel Villaverde Cabral and Luís Salgado de Matos, became involved.[34]

For the past two decades or so, Furet's theses have inspired a series of academic papers that, like Furet, explore points of continuity between the old and the new regimes, pointing out the ways in which revolutionary processes are mutable in the regime changes from dictatorship to democracy. They associate the concept of representative democracy (liberal, Western, or bourgeois are concepts used by historians to conceptualise this type of regime) as the only regime form that would oppose 'authoritarianism'. So often liberal democracy forgets the adjective and is simply referred to in this condition as 'democracy', with the authors focusing their debate on the quality and coverage of it, type and actors of that democracy, always in opposition to dictatorships, and never in relation to types of regimes.

Within this broad area of theoretical influence there are nuances, but all ignore what is the qualitative leap of revolutionary processes: water does not transform from ice to vapour without melting and boiling, as a dialectical historian would say; a political scientist inspired by the theories of the *transitology* might say water passes from ice to steam without boiling.

The controversy in Portugal did not move immediately from the pages of the newspapers to the spaces of academic reflection. Today, the term 'revolution' coexists in the academy to refer to the same period, with terms such as 'transition', 'democratisation' or 'democratic normalisation', without rigorously theorising the way the debate began in 2004. More recently, in Spain, political science has adopted the term 'transition by rupture' as opposed to 'agreed transition'.

Social scientists and historians of Marxist inspiration who studied the Portuguese Revolution, such as Loren Goldner, Valerio Arcay or John Hammond (all already referred to), do not question the terms revolution and counter-revolution. They ask whether it was a revolutionary or pre-revolutionary situation and examine the degree of its radicalisation. Even outside the field of Marxism many works have maintained the use of the concepts, revolution and counter-revolution, as in the studies of Boaventura Sousa Santos and Medeiros Ferreira. [35] João Medina and Fernando Rosas clearly identify the Revolution in (1974–1975) as the period of transition to democracy, which began in 1976. Other authors use the terms revolution and transition indiscriminately. [36] It is in the field of political science that we see studies that tend to use the concept of 'transition' exclusively for the change of regime that took place in Portugal, with the works of Philippe Schmitter and António Costa Pin as notable influences. [37]

The theoretical debate between Portuguese historians and social scientists is often neglected. Terminological uncertainty has epistemological consequences. In other words this impacts upon the nature of knowledge, justification and the rationality of belief. The controversy is inescapable.

There are associated terms such as 'transition to democracy' and 'transition by breakdown', which we cannot explore in depth in this study. Carlos Taibo sums it up well when he writes that 'much of the transitional literature' is not limited to analysing transitions, but 'adds to them a desired final destination: democracy'. [38]

Democracy, as it was consolidated in Portugal, was the result of class struggle, of the revolution and of the counter-revolution, but it was not an inevitable result, which can legitimately be deduced from the studies that analyse the transitions to democracy in Southern Europe. One could consider, in the case of Portugal, the factors that favoured the consolidation of liberal democracy – its geographical location in Western Europe context within the sphere of NATO influence; the weight of the Portuguese middle classes; the quality of the leadership of the counter-revolution, which rested on great political leaders like Mário Soares and Álvaro Cunhal, etc. Liberal democracy was not, it cannot be said to be, inevitable.

The new is born from the old. But it must be remembered that the Portuguese Revolution was not the 'accident' that gave rise to liberal democracy. The liberal democratic regime is based on two radically distinct assumptions of the revolutionary period: representative (and not direct) democracy and respect for private ownership of the means of production.

The term transition is ultimately unfit because it explains the 'how'– a negotiation between 'elites', that is, agreement between leaders of the conflicting classes – without telling 'why' this came about, which ultimately cedes the grounds of such negotiation to the individual will of the leaders.

In conclusion, there is a tendency within the fields of historical and political research to consider the Portuguese Revolution as a 'disease', a 'pathology', which arises at a moment already ripe for the transition of the country towards democratisation, that is to say, it tends to dominate a view that the Revolution disrupted, as if unintentionally, a transition of modernisation that was already in progress, that would have allowed for change and, at the same time, the stability of the State. The use of the concept of 'transition' is not, in this case, an unconscious choice, because the concept itself brings with it a teleological view of society. It is like arguing 'everything happens for a reason'. In this case, the rationale is the concept of democracy and the democratic regime is seen as the end of history. It is also this ideological worldview that justifies the way in which some works on the Portuguese Revolution, which were not anchored in the theories of transition and based on a rigorous historical survey, have been uninhibited in branding the Revolution as a pathology, such as the work in *Portugal em Transe* by José Medeiros Ferreira[39] or *Os Dias Loucos do PREC*, by journalists José Pedro Castanheira and Adelino Gomes.[40]

A 'Peaceful' Model of Counter-Revolution

Historically there have been various configurations of revolutions and various forms of counter-revolution. The example of Chile was still fresh.

It skewed the movement, which was dominated by the threat of fascism, and polarised the struggle as being between barbarism and socialism. However, because of the strength of the movement and the unreliability of the armed forces it was not an attractive proposition.

Just as a revolution is an historical process not limited to a military coup or the barracks, the counter-revolution is not a historical process that can be summed up in a violent coup that establishes dictatorship.

Indeed, from the experience of restraining the Portuguese Revolution by peaceful and democratic means, applied preventively in Spain with great success, there arose a laboratory of counter-revolutionary processes that have nothing to do with the Chilean model (a counter-revolutionary coup made under the heel of a bloody military dictatorship).

This 'peaceful' model of counter-revolution (now framed by the teleological concept of 'transitions to democracy') would be adopted by the USA for its foreign policy, in the 'Carter doctrine', and later applied to Latin America with the progressive replacement of dictatorships by the democratically affiliated regimes.[41] In essence, the idea was to defeat revolutionary processes through elections; liberal democracy is preferable to dictatorial regimes.

Such a model focuses on the idea of putting an end to revolutions or avoiding them entirely by creating an electoral social base within the framework of a representative democratic regime, that is, a transition to a liberal democracy that avoids revolutionary ruptures.

What Sort of Revolution?

In his analysis of the Russian Revolution, Trotsky highlighted three elements that constitute a revolutionary situation: the emergence of millions of mobilised workers, the attraction of the middle sectors of society to the organisations and methods of struggle of the working class and a national crisis (later Trotsky adds to this definition the existence of a revolutionary party).[42] In short, a revolutionary situation would be a political process characterised by the emergence of vast sectors of the population (workers and the middle classes) that change the relation of forces between social classes, in a context of national crisis (decadence). Valerius Arcady, whose writings also inspired this work, in his research on the revolutions of the twentieth century, proposed the distinction of two types of revolutions, political revolutions and social revolutions. In the former, political power changes; in the latter, economic power changes hands, that is, private property is questioned. By analogy with the Russian Revolution, he classifies these political revolutions as 'February revolutions', and social revolutions, 'October revolutions'. According to this criterion, most revolutions of the twentieth century, the century in which there were more revolutions than ever before in the history of humanity, are political revolutions, objectively anti-capitalist, that stayed in the 'February' phase, that is, they did not question private ownership of the means of production. The Portuguese Revolution is exactly one of the exceptions which evolved into the situation of a revolutionary 'October'. The struggle in the workplaces led to control in the workplaces, and also, for that matter, in the neighbourhoods. However, workers' control was not possible without the struggle being carried into other sectors, the capitalist system, such as the means of communication, the banks, the armed forces, the education system and the State. In effect, Portugal became October. But the revolutionaries were not able to seize the State, and the final stage of the revolution was not achieved. The fall of the regime on 25 April was the inaugural act of a political stage incomparably deeper in popular radicalisation – a revolutionary situation during which the experience of self-organisations was constructed.

Independently of the regimes in force during the 19 months of 1974–1975, the Revolution took a course, which influenced and was influenced by regimes, yet remained an independent course, driven by the bodies of 'popular power'. The State did not impose itself, as there was no 'stability', it had to negotiate systematically with these organisations, *de facto* or not, until May 1975, and from there coordinated regionally or by sectors. Thus, it is conceptually more accurate to consider that direct democracy is the daughter of revolution and representative democracy is the daughter of the counter-revolution. Often this assertion meets immediate criticism, which alleges its espousal of a more ideological than a historical view. It is an unjust attack because the other view, which omits or devalues the existence of a duality of powers, is much more targeted by the ideological pressures of a country that has not yet settled accounts – and therefore has more difficulties in making history – with its past.

Charles Tilly, recalling the difficulty that all revolutionary processes pose to a unified theory or definition common to each moment of social transformation, and the variability of factors that characterise a revolutionary situation, chose as the central defining element of revolutions the duality of powers[43] – which we consider to be a central criterion for the definition of a revolutionary process in its various dimensions – the presence of an alternative power, whether organic or inorganic, embryonic or organised, or even nationally coordinated and organised. Tilly's work attached much importance to the relationship between revolutions and macrostructural factors.[44] Perry Anderson, for his part, emphasises the speed of social transformation in the revolutionary processes, as opposed to the reform processes, on the one hand, and its objectives on the other: 'an episode of convulsive political transformation, compressed in time and in the objective, which has a definite beginning – when the old state apparatus is still intact – and a clear end in sight, when this apparatus is broken and the new one is erected in its place. In a process of transition to socialism this new state, in order to be 'truly transitional', must implement its own dissolution.[45] Eric Hobsbawm stresses, among other factors, the 'presence of mass mobilisation' and the degree of uncertainty of these processes, concluding that we must not neglect 'the context of uncontrollable forces' governing revolutionary processes.[46]

In 1974–1975, the State was always, even in crisis, a capitalist state (there was never a socialist state in Portugal, but a state in crisis marked by the existence of parallel powers in 1974–1975). There were various factions represented around the Sixth Provisional Government and by 25 November, sections of the bourgeoisie were sufficiently united to lead the State in the coup against grass-roots democracy. There was an alternative. We can certainly see that the Sixth Provisional Government was both paralysed and threatened by an alternative type of power, a dual power. But the workers' movement was never strong enough, coordinated sufficiently, at the national level. The leading workers' organisations, such as the Communist Party and the Intersindical, were not prepared to take on the State. There was no equivalent of the Bolsheviks and the equivalent of a national Soviet system. There had been many moments where collectively the movement from below challenged the State, but in the end, it was not enough.

There is still intense controversy today around 25 November – and some of what happened is still hidden from history. However, it is indisputable that this day marked the beginning of the end of the revolution and the consolidation of what António de Sousa Franco, economist and social scientist, has called the 'democratic counter-revolution'[47] and which, because of the ideological strength of the victors, is today dubbed 'democratic normalisation'.

But the defeat, even the collapse of the movement, must not be used to mask the fact that rapidly groups of workers and residents, students and later soldiers had organised, turning into the centre of the revolution. These actors determined the course of the crisis of State and of accumulation, which resulted not only in the increase of political rights, but in the greatest erosion of capital ever, leaving behind what remains the greatest increase in labour income over capital gains ever witnessed in the history of Portugal. They went from being the equivalent, in 1973, of 50 per cent of GDP for work (salary and social contributions) and 50 per cent for capital (interest, profit and rent) to almost 70 per cent for work and 30 per cent for capital in 1975. This transfer owes itself to social struggles in the form of interventions in de-capitalised enterprises, direct increases in wages, increases in social wages, and income subsidised housing, the freezing of prices, etc.

20

In Celebration

The bloody defeat in Chile on 11 September 1973 – only seven months before the Portuguese Revolution broke out – has been carefully used, in the struggle over memory, to render forgotten a partially victorious revolution in a European country, within the NATO sphere, which took 19 months to defeat. And it was not defeated in the end by resorting to violence and coercion, but instead by consensus and with very large social reforms won by the working class. Why then is Chile in 1973 much better known and studied than Portugal in 1975?

The Portuguese Revolution was a social explosion that US president Gerald Ford considered capable of transforming the entire Mediterranean into a 'red sea' and causing the downfall of all of the regimes of southern Europe like dominos.[1] We can argue today that it began a wave of resistance in southern Europe that delayed the implementation of neoliberal plans attempted from 1973–1975 until the crisis period of 1981–1984. Measures which survived include the nationalisation without compensation of banks and large companies, the birth of the welfare state and social security, the agrarian reform of large estates in the south of the country and the worker management of 300 companies. These measures were not realised by state decree or by governmental action, as some have tried to frame them, but from below, through people assembling and organising. The workers in the banks stopped the flight of capital, before they were nationalised. It was the strikes in the major companies that forced salary increases and price freezes; hospitals and schools were occupied and democratically run; public transport was under the control of workers and users, who decided to extend this to peripheral areas and to reduce fares; thousands of empty houses and apartments were occupied by residents (usually through residents' commissions and often with the help of soldiers), the land was occupied in the south and centre by agricultural workers,[2] which more than tripled productivity and employment. In other words, it was not only the results but the entirely democratic way in which they were achieved in this 'new country', to use film-maker Sérgio Tréfaut's fitting term,[3] which makes the Portuguese Revolution an extraordinary case study of 'change from below'.

Furthermore, this was in the midst of an international crisis, the so-called 'oil crisis' of 1973, which caused a dramatic fall in Portuguese GDP. Economic growth fell from 10.78 per cent in 1972 to 4.92 per cent in 1973 and 2.91 per cent in 1974 to -5.10 per cent in 1975. The 1973–1975 crisis precipitated falling investment that in turn led to a drastic increase in redundancies. During the revolution, the unemployment rate doubled between 1974 and 1975 from 2.1 to 4 per cent, and the reaction to redundancies – the occupation of factories and companies – would be one of the factors that explains the existence and development of workers' control during the revolution, and is perhaps the most significant reason for the progressive expansion of social rights in 1974–1975.[4]

As Marx argued and the twentieth century confirmed, there are no revolutions without crises (in this sense they are an opportunity), but there are crises without revolutions, and economic collapses without political responses. 1974 was another story.

In a way, through being an urban European revolution in a society where the role of industry and services was already greater than that of the majority of twentieth-century revolutions (which, by contrast, came from a peasant base and were supported by military parties), the Portuguese Revolution can be seen not only as the last revolution of the century to put into question the private ownership of the means of production, but arguably also belongs to the twenty-first century. The majority of the social conflicts of the revolution were carried out by industrial workers with 19 per cent of labour struggle taking place in the textile industry, 15 per cent in machining and metalwork, 9 per cent in construction and public works, and 7 per cent in the chemicals and food industries. These struggles were waged especially by the proletariat of the large industrial belts (Porto, Lisbon and Setúbal), with a particular focus on Lisbon, where 43 per cent of labour conflicts occurred.

The Carnation Revolution was the last European revolution to call into question private property of the means of production. This has resulted in the transfer, according to official data, of 18 per cent of capital, to the right to work, wages above the bread-line (above 'work to survive'), equal and universal access to education, health and social security. It was also the last revolution where workers' control was developed extensively. There was even a wide discussion and confrontation between self-management (workers being 'owners' of the factory) and workers' control (the total questioning of production and the refusal to 'manage capitalist anarchy'). Self-management dominated in small companies that had not been capitalised and nationalised. The extension of the division of society into social classes and the consciousness of this division in 1974 and 1975, has a historical dimension. The interconnections between the workers in the uniforms of the armed forces and the workers in work clothes was unparalleled, nothing like it had been seen in Europe since just after the World War, and it terrified the rich and the mighty. It is one of the special moments of workers demonstrating what power they had in the history of this country, moments which workers can be proud to be workers.

The Carnation Revolution is one of the outstanding revolutions of the twentieth century: because the spread of the forms of power (commissions of workers, residents, soldiers, the equivalent of councils, elected from the base, in plenary and with representatives who can be recalled at any time) which threatened the regimes, and their assumptions of authority. The grass-roots democracy that was in force, and centred on places of work and housing, allowed something like 3 million people to decide, not by putting a vote through a ballot box every four years, but day by day, on how society was to produce, and be managed. Never have so many people decided so much in Portugal as between 1974 and 1975. This is the legacy of the revolution. As we have seen this was to be defeated with a *coup d'état* on 25 November 1975 which, in turn, instituted a representative democracy within the framework of capitalism, which inevitably eroded social rights.

It is one of the most important revolutions of the entire twentieth century: by the extension of duality powers (committees of workers, residents, soldiers). It is, from the point of view of the parallel to the State, of a historical process that bears many similarities to the German revolution after the First World War,' Italy through two years in 1919–1920 (known as the 'biennio rosso'), with the 1956 Hungarian revolution and with the Chilean experience in the early 1970s. It is also, and this is another important characteristic, a revolution in the metropolis that happens by virtue of anti-colonial revolutions (colonial war) in the Portuguese colonies. It's a social revolution, which becomes a democratic revolution. I also propose the hypothesis that there was worker control in the Portuguese Revolution and that this process was distinguished from self-management; the thesis that nationalisations were to circumvent labour control; the hypothesis that the Fourth Government falls due to the workers' control and that I extend to the whole book, that is, the idea that it is the social movements that lead to changes of Government and not the other way around.

What began on 25 April – a classic *coup d'*état – unleashed a social revolution in terms of ways of meeting and organising (threatening and resulting in changes in the relations of production). In a few days or weeks, it was practically assured that the political regime of dictatorship would be replaced by a more benevolent regime, one which would allow, inadvertently perhaps, the working class and the popular and student sectors to enter (without fear), onto the stage of history. Soon these actors would jump ahead of this army and would lead the revolution from the front, leaving the MFA behind, trying to recompose the State. The Carnation Revolution, which cannot be summed as the day of the coup, 25 April (as recently has been done, pressing only to celebrate the day of the coup and not the whole process), but as a historical process of almost two years, is the most democratic moment in the history of Portugal. Never have so many people helped shape their future in Portugal as between 1974 and 1975. The defeat of the revolution put an end to fundamental democracy, particularly in the barracks, factories, companies, schools and neighbourhoods. There's nothing unusual about this. But it may be that Portugal is the first example of the success of a defeating revolution by replacing it with establishment of a 'representative' democratic regime.

Representative democracy had to defeat grass-roots democracy. In 1974–1975, while in special moments unions represented their memberships, they were also a buffer, one which became a channel for owners and their allies, committed to rebuilding the State, and opposing, with internal tensions, bodies of that challenged the power, namely, the committees of workers, residents and soldiers. I advance the thesis that the duality of powers was not only embryonic – there was coordination in the most important sectors, at the regional and sector level and the bourgeoisie could not rely on 'their' press, the army, the education system, and municipal government and the State. This is what led the bourgeoisie and its social allies to prepare for the coup of 25 November 1975.

Today this revolutionary past – when the poorest, most fragile, often illiterate, have dared to take life in their hands – is a kind of historical nightmare of the current Portuguese ruling classes. So much so that the insistence remains that in the 40 years of the revolution, only the 25 April should be celebrated, forgetting that this day was the first of the historically more surprising 19 months of Portugal's history.

And, next to Vietnam, Portugal was the country that was most covered by the international press at the time because the images of people in the shanty towns smiling with open arms alongside bearded and cheerful young soldiers filled the people of Spain, Greece and Brazil with hope. For almost everyone, the colonial war was suddenly forgotten, almost forgiven, and the Portuguese Revolution became the revolution of the metropolis, 'without deaths', of hope.

They witnessed the joy of the majority of those who lived here. One of the characteristics of the photos of the Portuguese Revolution is that people are almost always smiling. It was not by chance that Chico Buarque sang: 'I know you are partying, man'.[6]

Chronology

Editor's note: The Portuguese edition provided a very detailed and invaluable chronology focusing upon workplaces and the strikes. Unfortunately, for reasons of space, we are unable include the detail here. For those who wish to look further the full translation of the chronology has been translated and can be accessed online.

Raquel Varela identified five waves of strikes of the revolution between 25 April 1974 and 25 November 1975. A summary of this has been incorporated in the chronology.

1974

25 April   The MFA coup. Occupation of key installations including broad-casting stations, Lisbon Airport and the Army headquarters. The headquarters of the PIDE/DGS (secret police) was surrounded, then taken over. Thousands of people spill out onto the streets in support of the soldiers.

26 April   The Junta for National Salvation (JSN) set up. Spínola announces MFA programme on television. Street demonstrations demand the release of political prisoners, the first of which were released from Caxias prison.

27 April   Presentation of the MFA Programme.

28 April   Residents of Boavista in Lisbon occupy vacant houses. Occupation of the Bus Drivers' Union and in Porto, the Union of Office Workers and the Bakers' Union.

29 April   The Bankworkers' Union blocks the exit of capital from banks, organising pickets at entrances.

Strike Wave 1

This started immediately after the coup and continued into June. Strikes and factory occupations affects all sections of industry, including some of the largest Portuguese companies, such as Lisnave, Timex and CTT. Most of the demands involved wage increases, minimum wages (usually a monthly minimum wage in excess of 6,000 escudos), and a limited working week, 13 and 14 month wages, sanitations – that is, the firing of bosses and in 40 per cent of the cases, control over the company. Furthermore, many uninhabited houses were occupied.

1 May   Massive demonstration in Lisbon with participation of around 500,000 people. Large demonstrations, in the major cities and all over the country.

2 May	Occupation of vacant houses in the districts of Fundação Salazar and Casalinho da Ajuda, Lisbon.
9 May	Occupation of Timex.
10 May	Beginning of a strike by Timex workers. Lisnave workers began an unsuccessful strike to purge management.
14 May	Censorship abolished.
15 May	Spínola officially proclaimed President. General assembly of Timex workers accepts the proposal of the JSN to dismiss the directors, thus ending the strike.
16 May	Formation of First Provisional Government under Prime Minister Palma Carlos. At ministerial level, this includes the Socialist Party, the Communists, the MDP/CDE and the PPD.
Mid-May	Neighbourhood commissions are formed in many shanty towns and on public housing estates. Domestic servants start a union. Strikes in high schools.
19 May	The JSN legalises housing occupations and prohibits new ones.
25 May	Police use water-cannon against left-wing demonstrators calling for the release of the Cuban guerrilla Captain Peralta. Rádio Renascença censured for reporting this news.
26 May	Minimum salary established at 3,300 escudos.
29 May	Strike by workers at the Ponte 25 de Abril and fares go uncollected. University entrance exams are abolished for all students.
7 June	Saldanha Sanches (MRPP leader) imprisoned for calling on troops to desert. Demonstration for his release.
10 June	Right-wing demonstration in Lisbon to support a federalist solution for the colonies. Demonstration in Lisbon to support the MFA.
12 June	Workers at Sogantal, a textile factory in Montijo, occupy the company and start selling their products directly, supported by a demonstration of thousands.
14 June	Riots by common-law prisoners who want civil rights.
17 June	Postal strike by 35,000 CTT workers for a guaranteed work week, vacation and overtime pay and the purging of fascists. Denounced by the Communist Party. The strike ends on 20 June when Spínola threatens a military intervention.
21 June	Demonstration of 20,000 people to liberalise the Civil Code in favour of divorce.
23 June	Formation of the Association of Disabled People from the Armed Forces – with an estimated 30,000 people – accompanied by declarations against the colonial wars.
8 July	Formation of COPCON (Continental Operational Command) headed by Otelo de Carvalho. Meeting of Catholics in Braga against an archbishop connected to the dictatorship.

9 July	Collapse of First Provisional Government. President Palma Carlos resigns two days later.
18 July	Second Provisional Government takes office. Vasco Gonçalves is Prime Minister. Two military cadets who refused orders against the CTT strike are arrested.
23 July	Military junta for Angola imposed by the Portuguese, with Admiral Rosa Coutinho as governor. White riots in Mozambique against independence.
25 July	Demonstrations in Lisbon and Porto against the colonial war. Workers at Sogantal (occupied for three months), supported by around 2,000 Montijo residents, prevent the removal of equipment from the factory in the early hours.
27 July	Spínola recognises the right of the colonies to independence.
28 July	Plenary at TAP with around 4,000 workers is surrounded by the military. Workers' vote for the continuation of the strike

Strike Wave 2

A new period of strikes emerged at the end of August 1974. It arose from a combination of political and economic factors, including the victory represented by the approval of the law of independence of the colonies and the concomitant weakening of the State leaders. The deepening economic crisis resulted in dozens of employers responding with lay-offs, and the closing of factories and businesses. This period is especially significant not only for the sheer number of strikes, but also by the political impact of three strikes in particular, those at TAP, the *Jornal do Comércio* and Lisnave. The frustrated government attempted to prohibit strikes through an extremely restrictive law. The period was accompanied by the widespread occupation of vacant housing stock belonging to local government.

27 August	Strike by TAP workers. The army surrounds the *Jornal do Comércio* occupied by workers.
28 August	The Provisional Government introduces an anti-strike law limiting the right to strike. Military occupies TAP and threatens to arrest striking workers.
31 August	Creation of the SAAL, a government housing agency, to intervene in social housing.
4 September	General strike of every newspaper in solidarity with the strike of fellow journalists at the *Jornal do Comércio*.
10 September	Independence of Guinea-Bissau. Speech by Spínola against 'anarchy'. He calls on the 'silent majority' for their support. Nationalisation of the central banks (Banco de Portugal, Banco de Angola, Banco Nacional Ultramarino).
12 September	About 7,000 Lisnave workers march into Lisbon in forbidden demonstration against the anti-strike law. Military forces are

withdrawn, after being asked to repress the protesters. Law passed to control the rents on new housing and giving landlords 120 days to rent their properties or turn them over to the government to rent.

23 September   TAP maintenance workers organise a total strike calling for the end of the military occupation.

26 September   Prime Minister Vasco Gonçalves publicly insulted by President Spínola at rally in Lisbon.

27 September   The government authorises a demonstration by the 'silent majority' against the 'revolution'. Communist Party activists and those from the far-left set up roadblocks at gateways into Lisbon from the North, to prevent the entrance of right-wing activists into the city

28 September   Workers' Commissions and revolutionary organisations organise a counter-demonstration with about 40,000 people, aiming to confront and dismantle the demonstration by the 'silent majority'. Barricades go up around Portugal to stop the right-wing demonstration. Soldiers replace civilians in the roadblocks. This mobilisation was an extraordinary success and led to the immediate defeat of the coup. About 100 participants of the 'silent majority' 'uprising' were detained by the military.

29 September   President Spínola resigns.

30 September   Third Provisional Government formed (Socialist Party, Communist Party and PPD) with Vasco Gonçalves as prime minister and Costa Gomes as president. A demonstration of around 100,000 people in Lisbon expressed support for President Costa Gomes and the MFA.

October   Chemical workers union comes out against Communist Party control of Intersindical. Factories are occupied and products sold on the streets.

21 October   7th Congress of the Communist Party declares it no longer supports the call for the 'dictatorship of the proletariat'.

25 October   After a fraudulent bankruptcy was triggered by the Sousa Abreu employer (textile firm in Braga) the workers took over the management.

4 November   Meeting of CDS youth section broken up by MRPP demonstrators. Police fire into crowd. One dead, 16 wounded.

11 November   Law decreeing 45-hour week for agricultural workers. Introduction of the Student Civic Service, a compulsory gap year undertaking, before the going onto higher education.

In December and January there was a comparative lull in strikes, which may be explained by, amongst other factors, the growing influence of the MFA in the government and the political alliance between the Communist Party and the MFA in controlling workers' demands, managed through the Ministry of Labour, in coordination with Intersindical. Strikes and occupations took on a more defensive nature, for example in construction, steel, and textiles, as owners cut back on work, laid off workers, and refused to pay the decreed December bonus.

6 December   First plenary of the MFA Coordinating Committee.
7 December   The government decides to pay the 13th-month allowance to state pensioners.
13 December   The United States grants a financial loan to the Portuguese government for an economic support plan for the country.
15 December   First Congress of the Socialist Party.

1975

January

Early in 1975, several hundred fishermen from the Pedroso and Carvalhos zone (Vila Nova de Gaia) went on strike. Around 1,300 workers of the Grão-Para company continue to occupy their workplaces to assure jobs and the payment of salaries. They demanded the nationalisation of the firm.

The civil construction and winery workers at Xavier de Lima decided to sell 800,000 litres of wine to buy construction material, thus permitting the civil construction workers to continue working and enabling the payment of salaries to the remaining workers of the group.

Inhabitants of many of the poor districts of Lisbon decided to occupy vacant, finished or nearly finished houses. They organised an inter-commission of 30 residents' organisations.

The first land occupation had taken place in November 1974 and the pace was sporadic. In January there was a flurry of meetings of agricultural workers, demanding better working conditions, a minimum wage and equal pay for equal work. In Ribatejo and Alentejo, rural workers began a wave of land occupations. The Union of Rural Workers decided not to take part in the occupations.

13 January   MFA Coordinating Commission announces its support for *unicidade*, that is, that each trade would be represented by one union and that there would be one legally recognised central trade union federation.
14 January   Gigantic Intersindical demonstration in favour of *unicidade*.
16 January   Socialist Party demonstration in Lisbon against *unicidade*.
18 January   A meeting of 800 army officers asserts that the MFA will advance the revolutionary process.
19 January   Plenary of 1,000 rural workers union of the District of Santarem to discuss agrarian reform, dismissals and the collective work agreement.

20 January	The principle of *unicidade* supported legally.
26 January	Rally of the CDS in Porto closed by counter-demonstration and the armed forces have to intervene to rescue the CDS supporters.
27 January	An Inter-Empresas meeting, attended by delegates from 37 workers' commissions, finalises the organisation for the demonstration of 7 February.
30 January	In Lisbon, a demonstration took place of the Applied Magnetics workers demanding their right to work. The factory had been closed in August 1974, leaving 640 workers unemployed and with insufficient compensation.

Strike Wave 3

A new strike wave emerged from February 1975 onwards, reflecting the radicalisation of the revolution. This period is marked by struggles against unemployment, for example at IBM, Applied Magnetics and MESSA, accompanied by the development of organs of dual power (at this stage mainly workers' and residents' commissions). The demand for nationalisation of the financial system is led by the bank workers. This last demand was also taken up by workers in the largest companies, including the gigantic CUF conglomeration. Particularly noteworthy were the strikes in TAP, in chemical companies and a general strike in the high schools that continued for nearly a month. The conflict at Rádio Renascença, with successive shutdowns and occupations by the workers, also began in this period.

Occupation of vacant private housing took place around the country as the 120-day notice, set on 12 September, expired. Occupations of agricultural land escalated and by February there were already seven times more occupied lands than in January.

2 February	Recognition of the right of divorce. National meeting of workers' commissions organised by the Communist Party. In Beja, a demonstration of about 20,000 rural workers, organised by the union, calls for the expropriation of landowners and collectivisation of land.
5 February	The Lisbon civil governor prohibited public demonstrations from 7 to 12 February, in order to prevent the workers' demonstration against unemployment planned for 7 February.
7 February	Demonstration by Inter-Empresas, against NATO visit and rising unemployment. Massive participation, despite prohibition by government and condemnation by the Communist Party and the Intersindical.
9 February	Strike at Rádio Renascença: the transmission of the daily rosary and the Sunday Mass was assured.
21 February	Melo Antunes' Plan for Economic and Social Policy is published.

March 1975	Housing and land occupations continue.
7 March	PPD rally in Setúbal ends after a counter-demonstration is attacked by the police and one person killed and many wounded. Local police force shut down by COPCON.
11 March	Abortive right-wing coup by Spinolist officers. RAL-1 barracks bombed. Intense popular mobilisation (concentrations, vigils, occupations, barricades, etc.). Spínola and other officers flee to Spain. End of Third Provisional Government. During the night of 11 to 12 March, the MFA assembly expelled the Spinolist officers involved in the coup, and reinforced its powers. In Marinha Grande, delegates from three factories presented a motion to create a Revolutionary Workers' Council.
12 March	Rádio Renascença returns to the air under workers' control. The JSN was abolished and the MFA expanded its assembly to 240 members, and set-up the Council of the Revolution with 25 members. The Council promptly introduces a major nationalisation programme (banks, insurance companies, transportation, etc.). All over the country, there were demonstrations in support of the MFA.
After 11 March	The failed coup precipitated another wave of occupations of abandoned companies and houses. Also, most of the far-left groups occupied buildings and turned them into their '*sedes*' (headquarters).
26 March	Fourth Provisional Government takes office.
31 March	Unemployment benefit introduced.
2 April	Beginning of 25 April election campaign.
11 April	Signing of the pact between the MFA and the political parties.
14 April	Legalisation of occupied housing.
15 April	Nationalisation of electricity, transport, oil and gas. Agrarian Reform announced; some price freezes.
19 April	First conference of the CRTSMs (the Revolutionary Councils of Workers, Soldiers and Sailors), which set itself up as the alternative to the elections and the political parties and called for a boycott of the forthcoming election. The workers' committee occupied the headquarters of the CUF group.
25 April	First free elections for nearly 50 years: 93 per cent turnout. This was to elect the Provisional Constituent Assembly, the primary purpose of which was to draft a new constitution.
1 May	Massive May Day celebrations and demonstrations all over the country.

Strike Wave 4

A fourth period of strikes emerged between May and July 1975, highlighted especially by demands for workers' control of factories and businesses.

Workers' strikes included: Torres Sado workers in Setúbal, the ITT-Rabor workers (manufacturer of electricity items), and of 1,300 workers of Fábrica de Tecidos Lionesa in Leca do Bailio. Workplace occupations included the premises of Alfredo Gonçalves Silva (a rug manufacturer company) in Viana do Castelo, workers of União Metalúrgica Bandeira & Irmão in Vila Nova de Gaia and the Sociedade de Fiação de Vizela (SOFIL) in S. Martinho do Campo.

5 May	A plenary meeting of the municipal workers of Porto decided on a strike (of about 3,500 workers) to correct 'serious wage injustices'. About 15,000 chemical workers in the North decided to strike since the employers unilaterally stopped negotiations for a collective contract.
10 May	Three-day strike by 50,000 hotel and restaurant workers to 'force employers to comply with the pay scales negotiated in the collective agreement'. The strike of chemical workers, led by the Socialist Party and the MRPP, was declared illegal by the Ministry of Labour.
11 May	General strike of the First Division football players.
12 May	Civil war starts in Angola.
17 May	In Lisbon, a demonstration took place to reject Decree 198 A-75, which condemned the occupation of houses, allowing the residents to be expelled, as well as the imprisonment of the future occupiers.
18 May	EFACEC/INEL workers occupied the company, refusing to release a commercial director until a janitorial maid would be reinstated.
19 May	*República* newspaper occupied by its workers. who accused the Editor, Raul Rego, of having turned the newspaper into a Socialist Party organ. Socialist Party condemns this.
20 May	*República* evacuated by the military.
26 May	MFA Assembly pledges support for Vasco Gonçalves and discusses various 'popular power' proposals.
28 May	Some 400 Maoists (MRPP) arrested by COPCON.
June 1975	Numerous housing occupations in response to the Decree 198-A75 that threatened the eviction of every family occupying the premises.
2 June	First meeting of Constituent Assembly.
8 June	MFA Assembly discusses '*Guiding document on Popular Power*'.
13 June	Nationalisation of rail and road transport.
17 June	Militant CRTSM demonstration calls for the downfall of the Provisional Government. COPCON and the workers' committee reopen the *República* premises. COPCON occupies Rádio Renascença.

18 June	Demonstration against decision to hand Rádio Renascença back to the Catholic Church.
21 June	MFA publish 'Political Action Plan' (PAP).
25 June	Mozambique becomes independent.
29 June	First meeting of the Pontinha Popular Assembly.
30 June	89 former PIDE/DGS agents escaped from Alcoentre, 17 were recaptured in the first hours by civilians and COPCON.
July 1975	Land occupations continue. Large demonstrations in the North against the MFA and the Provisional Government, strongly influenced by the Catholic Church. It was estimated that, just in this month, 86 violent actions occurred against the headquarters of parties to the left of Socialist Party. The Socialist Party organises massive demonstrations, the largest at Fonte Luminosa, in response to the situation of the newspaper *República*. The PPD followed suit.
2–5 July	Strike wave hits main service industries: Hotels, CTT, TLP and TAP. Chemical workers strike in the North.
4 July	Vast demonstrations in support of struggles at *República* and Rádio Renascença. In Lisbon, around 40,000 people in a demonstration called by the Siderurgia steelworkers supported by UDP, PRP-BR and MES (which Communist Party and Intersindical opposed) to demand the trial of the PIDE and support the struggle of the Rádio Renascença and *República* workers.
7–9 July	General Assembly of MFA institutionalises the Povo–MFA Pact.
10 July	First issue of *República* under workers' control. Socialist Party withdraws from the coalition government.
12 July	Around 5,000 TAP workers suspend their strike.
13 July	Beginning of violent actions against the headquarters of political parties and left organisations, recorded with higher intensity in the north and centre of the country.
15 July	Demonstration in Lisbon to support the Socialist Party secretariat. It demanded the resignation of Vasco Gonçalves.
16 July	Tanks and armed soldiers support a demonstration in Lisbon called by Inter-Comissoes (federation of shanty town neighbourhood committees). Collapse of Fourth Provisional Government.
18 July	Demonstration in Porto in support of the Povo-MFA Pact. Socialist Party supporters stopped from assembling in Lisbon, nevertheless, a number of Socialist Party demonstrations take place around the country that weekend, against the Povo-MFA pact and the *República* takeover.
21 July	Fifth Division (the MFA's propaganda arm) reiterates its support for Vasco Gonçalves.
25 July	Costa Gomes warns that 'revolution is taking place at too fast a pace'. A 'troika', that is, a three-part directorate, comprising

Costa Gomes, Vasco Gonçalves and Otelo de Carvalho is set up by the MFA assembly. It never functioned.

August 1975	The land occupations continue in the south and centre of the country.
4 August	Demonstrations in Coimbra and Braga to support the Catholic Church.
7 August	Publication of the '*Document of the Nine*'.
8 August	Vasco Gonçalves forms the Fifth Provisional Government, supported by Communist Party and MDP.
10 August	Melo Antunes and supporters withdraw from the Council of Revolution. Demonstration in Braga to support the Catholic Church ended up with the assault to the Communist Party, MDP/CDE and union offices.
12 August	Socialist Party demonstration in Evora in front of the headquarters to support Brigadier Pezarat Correia, one of the signatories of the Document of the Nine. Beginning of a wave of occupations of agricultural undertakings in the district of Beja, many of them to prevent the sale of cattle, agricultural machinery and acts of economic sabotage. The Council of Ministers decided to nationalise the CUF Group.
13 August	COPCON document attacks Fifth Provisional Government and calls for strengthening of organs of 'popular power'.
20 August	Massive demonstration, of more than 100,000 workers, soldiers and sailors, in support of COPCON document in Lisbon, demanding immediate dissolution of the Constituent Assembly to be replaced by the agencies of the popular will, such as the Popular Assemblies. It was convoked by workers' and residents' committees, trade unions, UDP, FSP, LCI, LUAR, MES, ORPC (M-L) and PRP-BR.
25 August	The Communist Party forms an alliance with left-wing groups (FUP – the Popular United Front).
27 August	Another massive demonstration in Lisbon, with around 130,000 people, in support of FUP demands. Thousands of people participate in a Socialist Party demonstration in Porto against Vasco Gonçalves and the Fifth Provisional Government, the Fifth Division and Communist Party. COPCON forces occupy the Lisbon premises of the Fifth Division, as it was said to be 'remotely controlled' by the Communist Party. The operation was commanded by Colonel Jaime Neves.
28 August	PCP leaves FUP, which now becomes the Revolutionary United Front (FUR).
30 August	Vasco Gonçalves resigns as prime minister. Negotiations take place to form the Sixth Provisional Government. Occupation of radio and television broadcasting companies.
31 August	South Africa invades Southern Angola.

Strike Wave 5

In the period of the Fifth Provisional Government in August 1975, there was a slight decrease in the number of strikes, which is perhaps explained by the support given to the Provisional Government by the Communist Party and sectors of the extreme left.

The wave of strikes and conflicts from September 1975 extends unstoppably until the counter-revolutionary coup of 25 November 1975. There was a dramatic rise in land occupations. The strikes in the metalworker and bakery sectors were particularly noteworthy but, the most significant would be the strike of about 100,000 civil construction workers accompanied by a siege of nearly three days of the Constituent Assembly.

September 1975	Housing and land occupations intensify.
1 September	Law against workplace lay-offs takes effect.
5 September	MFA convokes its assembly at Tancos – the Army and Air Force do not attend and forces the resignation of Vasco Gonçalves, the Chief of Staff.
5 September	In Lisbon, demonstration in defence of Basque patriots who had been sentenced to the death penalty.
8 September	SUV movement (Soldiers United Will Win) issues its first communiqué. A company of Military Police refuses to go to Angola.
10 September	SUV demonstration in Porto; with the presence of 40,000 protesters, including 2,000 soldiers and a RALIS delegation. ITT announces it is withdrawing financially from Portugal. Re-integration into the MFA Revolutionary Council of those suspended on 29 August.
11 September	SUV demonstration in Lisbon. Gonçalvists expelled from the Council of Revolution.
13 September	Military police demonstrate against being sent to Angola.
18 September	Large number of land occupations. Unitary demonstration organised by the workers' and residents' committee of the Lisbon industrial belt in defence of nationalisations, the agrarian reform and the advancement of the revolution.
19 September	Sixth Provisional Government takes office; this includes the PPD, the Socialist Party and the Communist Party.
20 September	Disabled ex-servicemen occupy the toll-bridge over the Tagus estuary and collect money in support of *República*.
20 September	Demonstration in Lisbon for fair war pensions by the disabled ex-servicemen.
22 September	Demonstration in Funchal of the civil construction workers. The struggle of the disabled ex-servicemen continues with roadblocks

	next to Belém and occupying radio stations and disrupting the Estoril rail line.
25 September	SUV (Soldiers United Will Win) demonstration in Lisbon, commandeering many buses, going on to free two militants from military prison in Trafaria.
26 September	The MRPP dominated National Congress of Factory Committees meets in Covilha. The MFA Council of the Revolution creates the AMI – Military Intervention Grouping – intended to mediate in public order cases and to replace of COPCON.
27 September	The Spanish embassy in Lisbon is burnt down.
28 September	Symbolic demonstration of the Disabled People of the Armed Forces Association, who left their prostheses and wheel chairs at the door of the Amadora Command Regiment.
29 September	Radio and television stations occupied by the military. Rádio Renascença silenced.
30 September	Formation in Setúbal of the Comité de Luta, attended by 500 people.
October 1975	Around 118,000 hectares of land occupied in the district of Beja.
2 October	Demonstration in Porto to support Admiral Pinheiro de Azevedo and the Sixth Provisory Provisional Government, organised by the PPD and attended by around 100,000 people.
4 October	First plenary of the Lisbon housing occupiers organised by the Secretariat of the Autonomous Revolutionary Committees of Residents and Occupiers (CRAMO).
7 October	Occupation in Porto of RASP military base in protest against purging of leftist soldiers and officers. General strike of about a quarter of a million metallurgical workers all over the country.
8 October	Demonstration for popular power promoted by the Amadora Popular Assembly (in Lisbon).
9 October	Creation of AMI – elite military intervention force for use against 'disorder'. SUV demonstration in Coimbra. Popular demonstration to support the Military Police organised by committees of residents.
11 October	Demonstration of civil construction workers (more than 100,00) who had declared a strike a few days prior demanding better salaries.
16 October	Large demonstration in Setúbal organised by the Comité de Luta.
21 October	Popular Power demonstration forces the re-opening Rádio Renascença.
22 October	Agrarian Reform Centre in Alcacer de Sal destroyed by a bomb. Revolutionary Brigades (the BR in PRP/BR) go underground.
23 October	Large gathering in the Rossio square, Lisbon, of workers, soldiers and sailors struggling for the advancement of Popular

Assemblies. Supported by hundreds of workers' and residents' committees and other organisations of popular power from within the capital.

24 October   Beginning of bakery workers' strikes.

November 1975

5 November   Demonstration of SUV in Lisbon. Demonstration in Lisbon to protest against the State Secretary of Information, accused of being connected with the former regime.

7 November   Rádio Renascença blown up by a unit of paratroopers.

8 November   Inaugural conference of Cintura Industrial de Lisboa (CIL). 124 workers' commissions represented.

9 November   Large Socialist Party-PPD demonstration in support of Sixth Provisional Government, supported by the PPM and Communist Party (M-L). Paratroopers repudiate their dynamiting of Rádio Renascença and demand that they be placed under the command of Otelo de Carvalho.

10 November   123 officers resign from the Tancos regiment.

11 November   Independence of Angola. Demonstration of civil construction workers in Lisbon of about 100,000 protesters and in Porto and other cities.

12 November   Construction workers' strike and go on to besiege the Constituent Assembly for two days, until demands are met.

15 November   RALIS soldiers break the military rule when taking the oath to the Portuguese flag, instead performing it with clenched fists in support of the revolution.

16 November   Enormous demonstration of at least 200,000 people in Lisbon, against the Sixth Provisional Government. Demonstration in Lisbon organised by the Provisional Secretariat of the Workers' Committees of the Lisbon Industrial Belt (CIL).

19 November   1,200 paratroopers, suspended from Tancos, occupy the base.

20 November   Sixth Provisional Government goes on strike, demanding that the armed forces guarantee its ability to function. Demonstration in Belém (Lisbon) against the Sixth Provisory Provisional Government organised by the CIL and supported by Intersindical, Communist Party and FUR. Otelo removed as head of Lisbon Military Region.

21 November   Franco dies. Military aircraft and air force officers shifted to deactivated NATO base.

24 November   Two-hour strike, co-ordinated by CIL and supported by Intersindical, in a number of Lisbon and Setúbal factories, protesting against alterations in the command of the Lisbon Limitary Region.

25 November   The occupation of air bases by paratroopers, demanding removal of Air Force Chief of Staff and others is used as pretext for a

	military coup led by a force of two hundred commandos, led by Colonel Jaime Neves. 'State of Siege' proclaimed. Imprisonment of insurgent militaries who had occupied the Monsanto Base.
26 November	Commandos force the surrender of Military Police, after three people are killed. COPCON abolished.
28 November	Generals Carlos Fabião and Otelo de Carvalho were dismissed from their positions. General Antonio Ramalho Eanes was appointed as the new head of the army. State takeover of remaining newspapers and radio stations in Lisbon.
28 November	The Sixth Provisional Government resumed its functions, promising the right to return the expropriated land to the landowners. The publication of nationalised newspapers suspended.
December 1975	East Timor invaded by Indonesia. Arms searches in homes, factories, cooperatives, union headquarters; none were found. Some foreigners expelled. Purges in the military.
21 December	Demonstration in Porto for the release of those taken prisoner on 25 November.
22 December	*República* stops publishing and is given to the Socialist Party.
28 December	Rádio Renascença given back to the Catholic Church.

Notes

1. Introduction

1. A song by the Portuguese singer and poet Sérgio Godinho.
2. On the concept of who lives from work, see Ricardo Antunes, *Os Sentidos do Trabalho* (Coimbra: Almedina, 2013).
3. Maria de Lurdes Santos, Marinús Pires de Lima and Vítor Matias Ferreira, *O 25 de Abril e as Lutas Sociais nas Empresas* (Porto: Afrontamento, 1976), 3 vols.
4. The PPD was founded in May 1974 and was the most established party of the centre/right. It had ministers in every Provisional Government, except the Fifth Provisional Government. Its leader was Francisco Sá Carneiro.
5. The PS was re-formed in 1973 and led by Mario Soares.
6. The PCP was founded in 1921.
7. Zinn Howard, *A People's History of the United States* (New York: HarperCollins, 1999).
8. Chris Harman, *A People's History of the World* (London: Bookmarks, 1999).

2. The Seeds of Change

1. Actually, the full quote reads:

   Men make their own history, but they do not make it as they please; they do not make it under self-selected circumstances, but under circumstances existing already, given and transmitted from the past. The tradition of all dead generations weighs like a nightmare on the brains of the living.

   Karl Marx, 'The Eighteenth Brumaire of Louis Bonaparte' (1852), www.marxists. org/archive/marx/works/1852/18th-brumaire/cho1.htm.
2. Valério Arcary, *Quando o Futuro era Agora: Trinta Anos da Revolucao Portuguesa* (São Paulo: Xamã, 2004), no. 11, 71–92.
3. Scenes from the film, *The Class Struggle in Portugal*, directed by Robert Kramer, 1977.
4. RTP Archives, 1975, www.youtube.com/watch?v=6DB42QUJYSM (accessed 19 January 2015).
5. Refer to the song 'Tanto Mar' by Chico Buarque from 1975. The Brazilian military dictatorship governed the country from 1 April 1964 to March 1985.
6. Henrique Pinto Rema, *História das Missões Católicas da Guiné* (Braga: Editorial Franciscana, 1982), 856, cited in Dalila Mateus, 'Conflitos Sociais na Base da Eclosão das Guerras Coloniais', in Joana Dias Pereira, Raquel Varela and Ricardo

Noronha (eds), *Greves e Conflitos Sociais em Portugal no Século XX* (Lisbon: Colibri, 2012), 180.

7. Basil Davidson, *Révolution en Afrique: la Libération de la Guinée Portugaise* (Paris: Éditions du Seuil, 1969), 36–37, cited in Mateus, 'Conflitos Sociais na Base da Eclosão das Guerras Coloniais', 181.

8. The Makonde is a Bantu ethnic group living in south-east Tanzania and north-east Mozambique, especially in the Mueda plateau.

9. Mateus, 'Conflitos Sociais na Base das Guerras Coloniais', 183.

10. Mateus, 'Conflitos Sociais na Base das Guerras Coloniais', 69.

11. Aida Freudenthal, 'A Baixa de Cassange: Algodão e Revolta', *Revista Internacional de Estudos Africanos* 18–22 (1995–1999): 260.

12. Freudenthal, 'A Baixa de Cassange: Algodão e Revolta', 263.

13. Mateus, 'Conflitos Sociais na Base das Guerras Coloniais', 185.

14. 'Forced Labour System in Portuguese Africa', Reuters, 25 October, s/d, *Anticolonialismo Internacional, 1961–1963*, CIDAC, H34-5.

15. Dalila Cabrita Mateus, *A PIDE/DGS e a Guerra Colonial* (Lisbon: Terramar, 2004), 396.

16. 'New State' was the name used to describe the dictatorial regime in Portugal from 1933–1974. It was ruled from 1933 to 1968 by Antonio de Oliveira Salazar and from 1968 to 1974 by Marcelo Caetano.

17. Davidson is cited in Perry Anderson, 'Portugal and the End of Ultra-Colonialism, 2', *New Left Review* 1(16) (July–August 1962), https://newleftreview.org/I/16/perry-anderson-portugal-and-the-end-of-ultra-colonialism-part-2, 96.

18. Karl Marx, *Capital: A Critique of Political Economy*, Vol. 1 (London: Penguin Books, 2011).

19. Felipe Demier, *O Longo Bonapartismo Brasileiro (1930–1964): um ensaio de interpretação histórica* (Rio de Janeiro: Mauad, 2013).

20. Estado-Maior do Exército/Comissão para o Estudo das Campanhas de África in *Resenha histórico-militar das Campanhas de África (1961–1974)*, 5 vols (Lisbon: Estado-Maior do Exército, 1988). This is covered in more detail in Chapter 5.

21. *República*, 26 April 1974.

22. Karl Marx, *O Capital* (São Paulo: Boitempo Editorial, 2011).

23. Adapted from David Little, 'Primitive Accumulation', *Understanding Society*, 29 March 2009, https://understandingsociety.blogspot.co.uk/2009/03/primitive-accumulation.html.

24. Editor's note: It may be that Salazar collapsed in the bathroom but those who handled the news thought it would be ignoble to say so.

25. António Barreto, 'Mudança Social em Portugal: 1960–2000', in António Costa Pinto (ed.), *Portugal Contemporâneo* (Lisbon: D. Quixote, 2005).

26. Dalila Cabrita Mateus, *A PIDE/DGS e a Guerra Colonial* (Lisbon: Terramar, 2004).

27. Editorial, Especial 25 de Abril, *Visão* magazine, 15 April 2004, 1.

28. Osvaldo Coggiola and José Martins, *Dinâmicas da Globalização: Mercado Mundial e Ciclos Económicos, 1970–2005* (São Paulo: Instituto Rosa Luxemburgo, 2006), 69.

29. Michel Beaud, *História do Capitalismo* (Lisbon: Teorema, 1992), 260.
30. Coggiola and Martins, *Dinâmicas da Globalização*, 69.
31. Beaud, *História do Capitalismo*, 260.
32. In the survey I organised with Alejandro Lora and Joana Alcântara, we recorded hundreds of meetings in the first week after the coup, but it was based solely on the principal newspapers, leaving out various other regions of the country and probably hundreds or thousands more small companies.

3. 25 April 1974: 'The People are no Longer Afraid'

1. *Os Comunicados do 25 de Abril. CD25A.* In http://www1.ci.uc.pt/cd25a/wikka.php?wakka=mfa1 (accessed 7 March 2012).
2. The Marines and the Paratroopers did not adhere to the coup, but refused to act against the MFA. The Air Force was neutral, yet a group of its officers took part in the occupation of operations of the Radio Club. Vítor Crespo, a Lieutenant Commander in the Navy, tried until the last minute to convince the Marines to join the coup.
3. 'Long night' was the metaphor used by the writer and revolutionary Victor Serge to describe German fascism and the Second World War.
4. Grandola is a small town in the Alentejo region. *Grândola, Vila Morena* can be translated as meaning the sun-baked or swarthy town of Grandola.
5. Luís Leiria, '25 de Abril: a guerra para conseguir a paz', in António Simões do Paço, *Os Anos de Salazar*, Vol. 30 (Lisbon: Planeta DeAgostini, 2008), 21.
6. Leon Trotsky, *História da Revolução Russa*, Vol. 1 (Lisbon: Versus, 1988), 74–75.
7. 'France is boring' was an expression that became famous from an article titled, 'Quand la France s'ennuie ...' by the Editor-in-Chief, Pierre Viansson-Ponté in *Le Monde*, 15 March 1968.
8. Leiria, '25 de Abril: a guerra para conseguir a paz'.
9. Leiria, '25 de Abril: a guerra para conseguir a paz', 24–25.
10. *Os Comunicados do 25 de Abril. CD25A.*
11. *Os Comunicados do 25 de Abril. CD25A.*
12. *Os Comunicados do 25 de Abril. CD25A.*
13. Leiria, '25 de Abril: a guerra para conseguir a paz', 27.
14. *República*, 26 April 1974, 10.
15. 'Quartel do Carmo', 25 April 1974, RTP Archive.
16. The year 1640 was when Portugal seceded from the Spanish empire.
17. 'Quartel do Carmo', 25 April 1974, RTP Archive.
18. 'Quartel do Carmo', 25 April 1974, RTP Archive.
19. Diego Cerezales, *Portugal à Corunhada: Protesto Popular e Ordem Pública nos séculos XIX e XX* (Lisbon: Tinta-da-china, 2011), 338.
20. *República*, 26 April 1974, 15.
21. *República*, 26 April 1974, 15.
22. *República*, 26 April 1974, 16.
23. *Diário de Lisboa*, 3 May 1974, 15.

24. *Diário Popular*, 3 May 1974.
25. *Diário Popular*, 3 May 1974.
26. *República*, 26 April 1974, 14.
27. *Diário de Lisboa*, 2 May 1974, 13.
28. Cerezales, *Portugal à Coronhada*.
29. *Diário Popular*, 2 May 1974, 28.
30. Raquel Varela, *A História do PCP na Revolução dos Cravo*s (Lisbon: Bertrand Editora, 2011).
31. The phrase 'festival of the oppressed' was used to describe the euphoria during the weeks of the Paris Commune in 1871.
32. Originally reported in *Diário de Lisboa*, 28 May 1974, cited by Phil Mailer, *Portugal: The Impossible Revolution?* (London: Solidarity, 1977), 80.
33. Sophia de Mello Breyner Andresen (1919–2004), translated by Richard Zenith from *O Nome Das Coisas* in *Log Book: Selected Poems (Aspects of Portugal)* (Manchester: Carcanet Press, 1997).
34. *Diário Popular*, 11 May 1974, 1.
35. Sunday Times Insight Team, *Portugal: The Year of the Captains*, The Sunday Times (London: Andre Deutsch, 1975).
36. Mailer, *Portugal: The Impossible Revolution?*, 85.
37. A reference to the title of the book by Diego Palácios Cerezales, *O poder caiu na rua: Crise de estado e acções colectivas na revolução portuguesa* (Lisbon: Imprensa de Ciências Sociais, 2003).
38. *Diário Popular*, 26 April 1974.
39. *Diário Popular*, 11 May 1974.
40. Interview with Cruz Oliveira by the author, 24 July 2012, Lisbon.
41. *Diário Popular*, 11 May 1974.
42. Charles Downs, *Revolution at the Grass Roots: Community Organisations in the Portuguese Revolution* (Albany, NY: SUNY, 1990). Note that this book has been published in Portuguese, where he uses the name Chip Dows.
43. Varela, *A História do PCP na Revolução dos Cravos*.
44. Pereira de Moura, leader of the MDP/CDE.
45. Victor Wengorovius, founder of the MES (Movement of the Socialist Left).
46. Interview with Cruz Oliveira by the author, 24 July 2012, Lisbon.
47. *Diário Popular*, 3 May 1974, 19.
48. Ana Mónica Fonseca, 'Apoio da social-democracia alemã à democratização portuguesa (1974–1976)', *Ler História* 63 (Lisbon: ISCTE-IUL, 2012): 93–108.
49. *Diário Popular*, 2 May 1974.
50. António Medeiros Ferreira, 'Portugal em Transe (1974–1985)', in José Mattoso (ed.), *História de Portugal* (Lisbon: Círculo de Leitores, 1993).
51. *República*, 2 May 1974.
52. Fonseca, 'Apoio da social-democracia alemã à democratização portuguesa (1974–1976)'.
53. *Diário de Notícias*, 3 May 1974.
54. *Diário de Notícias*, 3 May 1974.
55. *Diário de Notícias*, 3 May 1974.

56. *Diário de Lisboa*, 2 May 1974.

57. *As Armas e o Povo* (*The Arms and the People*), interview with Glauber Rocha, in Outro País, de Sérgio Tréfaut, Videos Published, *25 de Abril, 20 Anos, 2004*.

58. *As Armas e o Povo*, interview with Glauber Rocha.

4. Who Governs?

1. *Diário de Lisboa*, 2 May 1974.

2. Sheila Cohen, 'Workers' Councils: The Red Mole of Revolution', in Immanuel Ness and Dario Azzellini (eds) *Ours to Master and to Own: Workers' Control from the Commune to the Present* (Chicago, IL: Haymarket, 2011).

3. José Pires, *O Povo em Acção: Greves e o 25 de Abril* (Lisbon: Edições Base, 1978), 66.

4. Various names were given to such organisations such as Workers' Commissions, Pro-Union Commission and Workers' Defence Commissions.

5. *Jornal de Greve dos Trabalhadores da Efacec-Inel* (suspensa), Lisbon, 26 August 1974, 21.

6. Marcel van der Linden, *Workers of the World: Essays toward a Global Labor History* (Leiden: Brill, 2008).

7. Maria de Lurdes Santos, Marinús Pires de Lima, and Vítor Matias Ferreira, *O 25 de Abril e as Lutas Sociais nas Empresas* (Porto: Afrontamento, 1976), Vol. 1.

8. Parkin interviewed in 2014 by Manus McGrogan, 'Rendezvous with a Revolution: British Socialists in Portugal 1974–5', *Interventions* 19(5) (2017): 646–665.

9. In Portugal, and for that matter Brazil, the custom was that those on a permanent contract were paid for 13 and 14 months each year.

10. Maria Luísa Cristovam, *Conflitos de Trabalho em 1979: Breve Análise Sociológica* (Lisbon: Ministério do Trabalho, 1982), 74.

11. Cristovam, *Conflitos de Trabalho em 1979*, 76.

12. Interview with Joaquim Aguiar by Raquel Varela and Jorge Fontes, 11 December 2012, Lisbon.

13. *Luta Popular*, May 2012. Due to a damaged copy, I was not able to specify the exact date of the Assembly.

14. 'Caderno reivindicativo dos trabalhadores da Timex Portugal', in Maria de Lurdes Santos, Marinús Pires de Lima and Vítor Matias Ferreira, *O 25 de Abril e as Lutas Sociais nas Empresas* (Porto: Afrontamento, 1976), 3 vols, 161–164.

15. Sunday Times Insight Team, *Insight on Portugal: The Year of the Captains*, (London: Andre Deutsch, 1975), 152.

16. 'Cerco aos TLP', 1974, RTP Archive, www.youtube.com/watch?v=d4m-SP--gyYw&list=PLEF504D728EFCCA3C (accessed 10 January 2013).

17. José Pires, *O Povo em Acção: Greves e o 25 de Abril* (Lisbon: Edições Base, 1978), 72.

18. Bob Light, 'Portugal 1974–5', *International Socialism*, 142, 25 April 2014, http://isj.org.uk/portugal-1974-5/.

19. *Diário Popular*, 14 May 1974, 23.

20. *Diário Popular*, 14 May 1974, 23.

21. *Diário Popular*, 14 May 1974, 2.

22. *Diário Popular*, 14 May 1974, 23.

23. António Costa Pinto, 'Saneamentos Políticos e Movimentos Radicais de Direita na Transição para a Democracia, 1974–1976', in Fernando Rosas (ed.), *Portugal e a Transição para a Democracia* (Lisbon: Edições Colibri/IHC, 1999), 32.

24. *República*, 4 May 1974.

25. *Diário de Lisboa*, 23 May 1974.

26. *Diário Popular*, 4 May 1974.

27. *Diário de Lisboa*, 12 May 1974.

28. *Diário Popular*, 4 May 1974.

29. *Diário de Lisboa*, 12 May 1974.

30. *República*, 4 May 1974.

31. António Costa Pinto, 'Saneamentos Políticos e Movimentos Radicais de Direita na Transição para a Democracia, 1974–1976'.

32. *Diário Popular*, 4 May 1974.

33. *Cerco aos TLP*, 1974, RTP Archive, www.youtube.com/watch?v=d4mSP--gyYw&list=PLEF504D728EFCCA3C (accessed 10 January 2013).

34. *Diário de Notícias* and *República*, 2 and 3 May 1974.

35. Such as the *Mundo Desportivo*, *Editorial Notícias*, *Vida Rural* and *Anuário Comercial de Portugal*.

36. *Diário Popular*, 5 May 1974.

37. *Diário Popular*, 5 May 1974.

38. *Diário Popular*, 5 May 1974.

39. The soldiers' commissions didn't emerge until autumn 1975.

40. *Diário de Lisboa*, 20 May 1974.

41. *Diário Popular*, 11 May 1974.

42. *Diário Popular*, 10 May 1974.

43. Raquel Varela, *A História do PCP na Revolução dos Cravos* (Lisbon: Bertrand Editora, 2011).

44. Francisco Rodrigues (ed.), *O Futuro era Agora* (Lisbon: Dinossauro, 1994).

45. *Diário Popular*, 17 May 1974.

46. Correios, Telégrafos e Telefones (Post, Telegraph and Telephone), a state-owned company.

47. José Pires, *O Povo em Acção: Greves e o 25 de Abril* (Lisbon: Edições Base, 1978), 87–89.

48. Bob Light is cited in Chris Harman, *The Fire Last Time: 1968 and After* (London: Bookmarks, 1988), 274.

49. Peter Robinson, *Portugal 1974–1975: The Forgotten Dream* (London: Socialist History Society, 1999).

50. Rafael Durán Muñoz, *Contención y Transgresión: Las Movilizaciones Sociales y el Estado en las Transiciones Española y Portuguesa* (Madrid: CPPC, 2000).

5. The Anti-Colonial Movements and the Myth of a 'Bloodless Revolution'

1. Raquel Varela, 'Oficiais milicianos optam pela deserção', in António Simões do Paço (ed.), *Os Anos de Salazar* (Lisbon: Planeta DeAgostini, 2008), Vol. 26, 60–69.
2. Phil Mailer, *Portugal: The Impossible Revolution?* (London: Solidarity, 1977), 82.
3. Mailer, *Portugal: The Impossible Revolution?*, says the demonstration was organised by MES.
4. *Diário Popular*, 26 May 1974.
5. Aniceto Afonso and Carlos de Matos Gomes, *A Guerra Colonial* (Lisbon: Editorial Notícias, 2000).
6. Afonso and Gomes, *A Guerra Colonial*, 526–533. Others have suggested more, and earlier in this book, I referred to 9,000 deaths of Portuguese military.
7. António Costa Pinto, *O Fim do Império Português* (Lisbon: Livros Horizonte, 2001), 52–53.
8. Ruth Leger Sivard, *World Military and Social Expenditures 1987–88*, 12th edn (Washington, DC: World Priorities, 1987).
9. Luis Graça, Editorial, *Revista Portuguesa de Saúde Pública* 29 (January 2011).
10. John P. Cann, *Counterinsurgency in Africa: The Portuguese Way of War, 1961–1974* (Westport, CT: Greenwood Press, 1997), 106; and Pinto, *O Fim do Império Português*, 52.
11. Dalila Cabrita Mateus, *A PIDE-DGS e a Guerra Colonial* (Lisbon: Terramar, 2004).
12. IAB/TT, The PIDE archives, cited in Mateus, *A PIDE/DGS e a Guerra Colonial*, 196.
13. *Diário Popular*, 29 May 1974.
14. *Diário Popular*, 15 May 1974.
15. *Diário Popular*, 17 May 1974.
16. *Diário Popular*, 29 May 1974.
17. Dalila Cabrita Mateus, *Memórias do Colonialismo e da Guerra* (Porto: Edições Asa, 2006), 150.
18. Estado-Mayr do Exército/Comissão para o Estudo das Campanhas de África, *Resenha histórico-militar das Campanhas de África (1961–1974)*, 5 vols (Lisbon: Estado-Maior do Exército, 1988).
19. Rui Bebiano, 'As Esquerdas e a Oposição à Guerra Colonial', in *A Guerra do Ultramar: Realidade e Ficção. Atas do II Congresso sobre a Guerra Colonial* (Lisbon: Editorial Notícias – Universidade Aberta, 2002), 293–313.
20. Bebiano, 'As Esquerdas e a Oposição à Guerra Colonial', 293–313.
21. From the LP *Meu País (My Country)*, 1970.
22. Interview by the author with Fernando Cardeira, 12 January 2008.
23. Interview by the author with Fernando Cardeira, 12 January 2008.
24. Curso de Oficiais Milicianos (Militia Officials Course).
25. Curso de Sargentos Milicianos (Militia Sergeants Course).
26. Varela, 'Oficiais milicianos optam pela deserção'.

27. Varela, 'Oficiais milicianos optam pela deserção'.

28. See Peter Robinson, 'Portugal 1974–75: Soldiers on the Side of the People', in Mike Gonzalez and Houman Barekat (eds), *Arms and the People: Popular Movements and the Military from the Paris Commune to the Arab Spring* (London: Pluto Press, 2013).

29. António de Spínola, *Portugal e o Futuro* (Lisbon: Arcádia, 1974).

30. Kenneth Maxwell, *The Making of Portuguese Democracy* (Cambridge: Cambridge University Press, 1995).

31. Maxwell, *The Making of Portuguese Democracy*.

32. According to Wikipedi (28 April 2018) Ruy Luís Gomes (5 December 1905, Porto–27 October 1984) was a Portuguese mathematician and founder of the Abel Salazar Biomedical Sciences Institute. He was one of 'the great intellectual figures' during the twentieth century in Portugal.

33. *Diário Popular*, 30 July 1974.

34. *Diário de Lisboa*, 3 May 1974.

6. Strikes and their Reverberations

1. From the 'Workers of Lisnave to the Population', Statement of Lisnave Workers, in Maria de Lurdes Santos, Marinús Pires de Lima and Vítor Matias Ferreira, *O 25 de Abril e as Lutas Sociais nas Empresas* (Porto: Afrontamento, 1976), Vol. 2, 110–112.

2. Maria de Lurdes Santos, Marinús Pires de Lima and Vítor Matias Ferreira, *O 25 de Abril e as Lutas Sociais nas Empresas* (Porto: Afrontamento, 1976), 3 vols.

3. *Diário de Lisboa*, 27 May 1974.

4. *Avante!*, 7 June 1974.

5. Phil Mailer, *Portugal: The Impossible Revolution?* (London: Solidarity, 1977). Editor's note: Mailer is a libertarian, who argues on principle against all parties and trade unions.

6. *Avante!*, 3 July 1974.

7. *Avante!*, 31 May 1974.

8. José Valente, 'O Movimento Operario e Sindical (1970–1976): entre o Corporativismo e a Unicidade', in J.M. Brandao Brito (ed.), *O País em Revolução* (Lisbon: Editorial Notícias, 2001), 241.

9. Intersindical Nacional, *Projeto de Restruturacao Sindical*, July 1974, cited in Miguel Pérez, *Contra a Exploracao Capitalista. Comissoes de Trabalhadores e Luta Operaria na Revolucao Portuguesa (1974–75)*, Masters dissertation in History of Nineteenth and Twentieth Centuries, Faculty of Social Sciences and Humanities, Universidade Nova de Lisboa, August 2008, 48.

10. The economic crisis hit the national ruling class, causing internal divisions and making the war effort unviable. The war consumed 40 per cent of state expenses (and 8 per cent of the GNP). The number of unemployed went from 40,000 in April 1974 to 320,000 in November 1975. Eugénio Rosa, *A Economia Portuguesa em Números* (Lisbon: Moraes Editora, 1975).

11. Interview by Peter Robinson with Fernanda, 30 April 1984 in *Workers' Councils in Portugal 1974–1975*, MPhil, 1989.

12. Interview by Peter Robinson with Artur Palácio, 2 August 1982 in *Workers' Councils in Portugal 1974–1975*, MPhil, 1989.

13. José Pires, *O Povo em Acção: Greves e o 25 de Abril* (Lisbon: Edições Base, 1978), 183.

14. *Diário Popular*, 27 August 1974, 17.

15. Law of Strikes, 27 August 1974.

16. In 1977, a new Law of Strikes came into effect, repealing the legislation passed during the revolution. The 1977 Strike Law was still much less restrictive than the law passed in August 1974. But it has to be remembered that the 1974 law could never be implemented, because of the balance of forces.

17. *Dos Operários da Lisnave à População*, Comunicado dos Trabalhadores da Lisnave, 11 September 1974, in Maria de Lurdes Santos, Marinús Pires de Lima and Vítor Matias Ferreira, *O 25 de Abril e as Lutas Sociais nas Empresas* (Porto: Afrontamento, 1976), 110–112.

18. *Revolução*, no. 13, 21 September 1974.

19. *Revolução*, no. 13, 21 September 1974. See also Pérez, *Contra a Exploracao Capitalista*.

20. Published in the first issue of Causa Operario, a Marxist-Leninist paper, September 1974; see Peter Robinson, in *Workers' Councils in Portugal, 1974–1975*.

21. Pires, *O Povo em Acção*, 191.

22. Pires, *O Povo em Acção*, 193.

23. Pires, *O Povo em Acção*, 195.

24. Pires, *O Povo em Acção*, 208.

25. Pires, *O Povo em Acção*, 210.

26. *Revolução*, 7 September 1974.

27. *Diário Popular*, 15 September 1974.

28. Interview by Peter Robinson with Fátima Patriarca, 1 September 1980 in *Workers' Councils in Portugal, 1974–1975*.

29. Pérez, *O Povo em Acção*, 121.

30. Kenneth Maxwell, *The Making of Portuguese Democracy* (Cambridge: Cambridge University Press, 1995), 80.

31. Here I have borrowed heavily from Peter Robinson, *Portugal 1974–1975: The Forgotten Dream* (London: Socialist History Society, 1999).

7. Self-Management and the Struggle Against Redundancies

1. Television programme, *Temas e Problemas*, 30 July 1975, RTP Archive.

2. José da Silva Lopes, *A Economia Portuguesa desde 1960* (Lisbon: Gradiva, 1999).

3. Lopes, *A Economia Portuguesa desde 1960*.

4. Parkin interview in Manus McGrogan, 'Rendezvous with a Revolution: British Socialists in Portugal 1974–5', *Interventions* 19(5) (2017): 646–665.

5. Ocupacao de empresa, www.youtube.com/watch?v=UPjDrLMeo5U (accessed 23 September 2013).

6. Miguel Pérez, 'A mobilizacao operaria anticapitalista na Revolucao de 1974–75', I Congresso de Historia do Movimento Operario e dos Movimentos Sociais, 15–17 March 2013, Lisbon, FCSH-UNL, 6.

7. See the chapter by Nancy Bermao, 'Worker Management in Industry', in Lawrence S. Graham and Douglas L. Wheeler (eds), *In Search of Modern Portugal: The Revolution and Its Consequences* (Madison, WI: University of Wisconsin Press, 1983).

8. Television programme, *Artes e Oficios*, 5 November 1975, RTP Archive.

9. *Artes e Oficios*, 5 November 1975, RTP Archive.

10. GIS stands for Gabinete Investegao Social, an institute which carries out social research.

11. Pérez, 'A mobilizacao operaria anticapitalista na Revolucao de 1974–75', 6.

12. Sogantal journal, late September 1974, translated and published in *Radical America* (November–December 1975).

13. Pérez, 'A mobilizacao operaria anticapitalista na Revolucao de 1974–75'.

14. Pérez, 'A mobilizacao operaria anticapitalista na Revolucao de 1974–75'.

15. Pérez, 'A mobilizacao operaria anticapitalista na Revolucao de 1974–75'.

16. Television programme, *Temas e Problemas*, 30 July 1975, RTP Archive.

17. *Temas e Problemas*, 30 July 1975, RTP Archive.

18. *Temas e Problemas*, 30 July 1975, RTP Archive.

19. *Temas e Problemas*, 30 July 1975, RTP Archive.

20. *Temas e Problemas*, 30 July 1975, RTP Archive.

21. Francisco Rodrigues (ed.), *O Futuro Era Agora* (Lisbon: Dinossauro, 1994), 91.

22. Jean-Paul Sartre, *História*, April 2004, n.p.

23. Editor's note: The struggle by French workers at the Lip watch factory in Besançon in the 1970s was an exception. The workers raised money by selling the appropriated watches. Well-attended assemblies were held daily and the workers campaign was very well known at the time. However, it was not, as Charles Piaget, the leading militant in the action, claimed, 'the beginning of a socialist society'. See Mitchell Abidor's *May Made Me* (London: Pluto, 2018).

24. *Diário de Notícias*, 3 May 2013.

25. Rodrigues, *O Futuro era Agora*, 91.

26. Tony Cliff and Robin Peterson, 'Portugal: The Last 3 Months', *International Socialism* 87 (March–April 1976): 10–19.

27. *Temas e Problemas*, 30 July 1975, RTP Archive.

28. Rodrigues, *O Futuro era Agora*, 91.

29. Comissão Coordenadora das Empresas em Autogestao, Diogo Duarte, Luís Ferreira, Nelson Trindade, Vasco Corregedor da Fonseca, *A Realidade da Autogestão em Portugal* (Lisbon: Perspectivas & Realidades, 1981), 151.

30. José da Silva Lopes, *A Economia Portuguesa desde 1960* (Lisbon: Gradiva, 1999).

31. Comissão Coordenadora das Empresas em Autogestão, n.d. – the Coordinating Committee of Self-Managed Companies.

32. Raquel Varela, *A História do PCP na Revolução dos Cravos* (Lisbon: Bertrand Editora, 2011).
33. *Esquerda Socialista*, 14 January 1975.
34. Cliff and Peterson, 'Portugal: The Last 3 Months'.
35. Bermao, 'Worker Management in Industry'.
36. Bermao, 'Worker Management in Industry'.

8. *Women in a Democracy are not Mere Decoration: Social Reproduction and Private Life in the Revolution*

1. Marco Gomes, 'O Lado Feminino da Revolucao dos Cravos', *Storia e Futuro* 25, February 2011, http://storiaefuturo.eu/lado-feminino-revolucao-dos-cravos/.
2. Movimento Democrático de Mulheres (MDM).
3. Movimento de Libertação da Mulher (MLM).
4. União das Mulheres Antifascistas e Revolucionárias (UMAR).
5. Manuela Tavares, *Movimentos de Mulheres em Portugal, décadas de 70 e 80* (Lisbon: Livros Horizonte, 2000), 55.
6. Salazar, 'Discursos Políticos', cited in Julieta de Almeida Rodrigues, 'Continuidade e mudança nos papéis das mulheres urbanas portuguesas: emergência de novas estruturas familiares', *Análise Social* 19(77–79), (1983): 909–938.
7. Demographic Census, Instituto Nacional de Estatistica, 1971.
8. Gomes, 'O Lado Feminino da Revolucao dos Cravos'.
9. Ana Nunes de Almeida, Maria das Dores Guerreiro, Cristina Lobo, Anália Torres and Karin Wall, 'Relações familiares: mudança e diversidade', in José Manuel Leite Viegas and António Firmino da Costa (eds), *Portugal, Que Modernidade?* (Oeiras: Celta Editora 1998), 48; statistics in summary, DETEFP.
10. Rodrigues cited in 'Continuidade e mudança nos papéis das mulheres urbanas portuguesas'.
11. For further information on women's organisations in the New State, see Irene Flunser Pimentel, *História das Organizações Femininas no Estado Novo* (Lisbon: Círculo de Leitores, 2000).
12. *Diário Popular*, 7 June 1974.
13. *Diário Popular*, 19 May 1974.
14. Departamento de Mulheres da UDP, *Movimentos de Mulheres*, Roteiro Cronológico 70–90. 2000.
15. Departamento de Mulheres da UDP, *Movimentos de Mulheres*, Roteiro Cronológico 70–90. 2000.
16. RTP Archive, 11 June 1975.
17. RTP Archive, 11 June 1975.
18. RTP Archive, 11 June 1975.
16. RTP Archive, 11 June 1975.
17. RTP Archive, 11 June 1975.
18. RTP Archive, 11 June 1975.
19. RTP Archive, 11 June 1975.

20. RTP Archive, 11 June 1975.
21. RTP Archive, 11 June 1975.
22. RTP Archive, 11 June 1975.
23. RTP Archive, 11 June 1975.
24. *Diário Popular*, 19 May 1975.
25. Karin Wall, 'A Intervencao do Estado: Politicas publicas de familia', in José Mattoso (ed.), *História da Vida Privada: Os Nossos Dias* (Lisbon: Círculo de Leitores, 1993), 351.
26. Wall, 'A Intervencao do Estado', 354.
27. Teresa Libano Monteiro, 'Janelas entreabertas: os valores, as normas', in José Mattoso (ed.), *História da Vida Privada: Os Nossos Dias* (Lisbon: Círculo de Leitores, 1993), 320.
28. Cited in Adelino Gomes and José Pedro Castanheira, *Os Dias Loucos do PREC* (Lisbon: Expresso-Publico, 2006), 107.
29. 'Teresa Torga', by Zeca Afonso, album *Com as Minhas Tamanquinhas*, 1976.

9. Artists and the Revolution

1. *Diário de Notícias*, 3 March 2013.
2. The Barcelos Rooster – symbolising honesty, integrity, trust and honour – is considered to be the unofficial symbol of Portugal.
3. José Marques, *As Paredes em Liberdade* (Lisbon: Teorema, 1974).
4. Taken from the Foreword of *As Paredes na revolução*, with photographs by Sérgio Guimarães (Lisbon: Mil Dias, 1978).
5. Phil Mailer wrote an article called 'Murals of the Carnation Revolution', which was published in the April 2104 issue of the arts magazine *Signal*, published by PM Press.
6. José Mário Mascarenhas (ed.), *A Cor de Abril* (Lisbon: Câmara Municipal de Lisboa, 2004).
7. Mailer, 'Murals of the Carnation Revolution'.
8. Photographs by Sérgio Guimarães, *As paredes na revolução*. This book is now on the web: https://issuu.com/ucd25/docs/grafitisgnet_nregeb0004.pdf.
9. Nuno Chuva Vasco, *Os ultimos 50 anos da pintura e escultura portuguesa do século XX* (Figueira da Foz, Chuva Vasco, 2005), www.chuvavasco.com/50anos.pdf.
10. *Diário de Notícias*, 3 May 2013.
11. *25 de Abril 30 Anos 100 Cartazes*, (Lisbon: Diário de Notícias, 2004), 20.
12. *25 de Abril 30 Anos 100 Cartazes*, 17–21.
13. Mascarenhas, *A Cor de Abril*.
14. José Gualberto de Almeida Freitas, *A Guerra dos Cartazes* (Guimarães: LembrAbril, 2009). See also AAVV, *25 de Abril 30 Anos 100 Cartazes*.
15. The text was signed by Alexandre Babo, Baptista Bastos, Sophia de Mello Breyner, Mário Castrim, Ferreira de Castro, Mário Dionisio, Fernando Namora, Álvaro Guerra, José Cardoso Pires, Luís de Sttau Monteiro, Fernando Assis Pacheco and many others.

16. *Diário de Lisboa*, 2 May 1974.

17. *Diário de Notícias*, Lisbon, 2 May 1974.

18. *Alternativa*, issues 40, 41 and 42, published 30 June, and 7 and 14 July 1975.

19. *Diário de Notícias*, 3 May 2013.

20. Monteiro has been described as a writer, novelist and playwright, a man to whom 'the only sacred thing was to be free as the wind'.

21. *Diário de Notícias*, 3 May 2013.

22. *Diário de Notícias*, 3 May 2013.

23. *Diário de Notícias*, 3 May 2013.

24. *Diário de Notícias*, 3 May 2013.

25. Flamarion Maués, 'A edicao politica em Portugal: Do combate a ditadura a Revolucao dos Cravos', *Literatura e Autoritarismo* (May 2012), 313.

26. Vera Borges, *O Mundo do Teatro em Portugal: profissão de actor, organizações e mercado de trabalho* (Lisbon: Imprensa de Ciências Sociais, 2007).

27. Micael de Oliveira, *Para uma Cartografia da Criacao Dramatica Portuguesa Contemporanea (1974–2004), Os Autores Portugueses do Teatro Independente: Repertorios e Canones*, Masters dissertation, Estudos Artisticos, Faculdade de Letras da Universidade de Coimbra, 2010.

28. Mascarenhas, *A Cor de Abril*, 7.

29. Eduardo M. Raposo, *O Canto e o cante: a alma do povo* (Lisbon: Público, 2005), 1020.

10. Workers' Commissions and Unions

1. See the compilation of strike bulletins, written by workers from Efacec-Inel, 39–42.

2. Interview by Peter Robinson, with TAP worker on 5 August 1982 in *Workers' Councils in Portugal, 1974–1975*, MPhil, 1989.

3. 'A Proposito das Manobras da NATO: Comunicado do CC do PCP, 4 February 1975', *Avante!*, Series 7, 6 February 1974, 3.

4. Derived from the article from the French weekly *Libération*, which was republished in 'Portugal a Blaze of Freedom' (London: Big Flame, June 1975).

5. Miguel Pérez, *Contra a Exploracao Capitalista: Comissoes de Trabalhadores e Luta Operaria na Revolucao Portuguesa (1974–75)*, Masters dissertation in History of Nineteenth and Twentieth Centuries, Faculty of Social Sciences and Humanities, Universidade Nova de Lisboa, August 2008, 139.

6. Interview by Peter Robinson with Palácio on 2 August 1982, *Workers' Councils in Portugal 1974–1975*, MPhil, 1989.

7. Sheila Cohen, 'Workers' Councils: The Red Mole of Revolution', in Immanuel Ness and Dario Azzellini (eds), *Ours to Master and to Own: Workers' Control from the Commune to the Present* (Chicago, IL: Haymarket, 2011).
Editor's note: Workers' Councils appeared in the twentieth century as Soviets, in Russia in 1905 and 1917; in Germany in 1919, 1920 and 1923; in Italy 1919 and 1920; in Canton in 1925; in Barcelona in 1936; in Hungary in 1956; and in

Czechoslovakia in 1968. In the 1970s, the cordones emerged in Chile and the shoras in Iran. The Polish inter-factory strike committees and Solidarnosc itself were also expressions of this type of movement.

8. Maurice Brinton, *Os Bolcheviques e o Controlo Operário* (Porto: Afrontamento, 1975), cited in John L. Hammond, 'Worker Control in Portugal: The Revolution and Today', *Economic and Industrial Democracy* 2(4) (December 1981): 413–453.

9. *Diário Popular*, 8 February 1975.

10. Editor's note: The PRP were the other side of the coin: they downplayed the party in the name of the councils. They went as far as saying that the party must dissolve itself – commit suicide – at the moment when the class has taken power.

11. Interview with Eduardo Pires conducted by Raquel Varela and Jorge Fontes, 26 November 2012.

12. Pérez, 'Contra a Exploracao Capitalista', 143.

13. Even today in Portugal, at the demonstrations of the CGTP (the successor to the Intersindical), the phrase 'CGTP, union unity!' is shouted.

14. *Alavanca*, 16 December 1974 and 24 January 1975.

15. 'Documento de Orientacao e Accao', *Avante!*, 31 July 1975.

16. 'Grande Jornada de Unidade dos Trabalhadores Portugueses', *Avante!*, Series 7, 31 July 1975, 6.

17. 'I Conferencia Nacional Unitaria de Trabalhadores', *Avante!*, Series 7, 6 February 1975, 4.

18. *Avante!*, 6 February 1975.

19. Interview with Eduardo Pires conducted by Raquel Varela and Jorge Fontes, 26 November 2012.

20. Editor's note: The anti-fascist dimension of the popular power movement was extremely potent. Opponents were readily labelled as being fascists, or neo-fascists, or social fascists. And others on the left talked about the authoritarian threat from the right.

    This stress on the overthrow of fascism and counter-revolution, such as the possible Chileanisation of Portugal, blurred the distinction between fascism and capitalism, resulting in an underestimation of the capacity of capitalism to modernise and reform, using the tools of social democracy.

21. Interview with Lisnave workers, 2 August 1982, *Workers' Councils in Portugal 1974–1975* (1999), MPhil, Centre for Sociology and Social Research, Open University, http://oro.open.ac.uk/19940/1/pdf115.pdf.

22. Interview by Peter Robinson with Carlos Nunes, 4 June 1984, *Workers' Councils in Portugal 1974–1975*.

23. Pérez, 'Contra a Exploracao Capitalista', 47.

24. Álvaro Cunhal, *A Crise Político-Militar. Discursos Políticos 5* (Lisbon: Edições Avante!,1976), 347, quoted by Miguel Pérez, 'Comissões de trabalhadores', in *Dicionário de História de Portugal: o 25 de Abril* (Porto: Figueirinhas, 2016).

25. Pérez, 'Contra a Exploracao Capitalista'.

    Editor's note: My estimate of 2,500 workers commissions was taken from an internal Ministry of Labour document, in my possession.

26. 'O processo revolucionário e a batalha da produção', *Avante!*, Series 7, 22 May 1975, 1 and 4.

27. Philippe Schmitter, *Portugal: Do Autoritarismo à Democracia* (Lisbon: ICS, 1999), 219.

28. *O Militante*, 4 August 1975.

11. 'Here is the Nursery' – Urban Struggles and Residents' Commissions

1. *Revolução*, 16 May 1975.
2. João Castro Caldas, *Terra e Trabalho* (Oeiras: Celta, 2001).
3. Noticiário Nacional, 9 September 1975, RTP Archive.
4. Miguel Pérez, 'Comissoes de moradores', in *Dicionário Histórico do 25 de Abril* (Porto: Figueirinhas, 2017).
5. (Zoning Law) *Lei dos Loteamentos* (D.L. 46 673), 1965.
6. José Carlos Guinote, 'Urbanismo e corrupcao: as mais-valias e o desenvolvimento urbano', *Le Monde Diplomatique*, Portuguese edition, 6 August 2008.
7. Chip Dows, *Os Moradores à Conquista da Cidade* (Lisbon: Armazém das Letras, 1978), 46.
8. *Esquerda Socialista*, 1 April 1975.
9. Noticiário Nacional, 9 September 1975, RTP Archive.
10. Charles Downs, 'Residents' Commissions and Urban Struggles in Revolutionary Portugal', in Lawrence S. Graham and Douglas L. Wheeler (eds), *In Search of Modern Portugal: The Revolution and Its Consequences* (Madison, WI: University of Wisconsin Press, 1983), 163.
11. Pérez, 'Comissoes de moradores'.
12. On the dispute between the PS and PCP in municipal politics, see Raquel Varela, *A História do PCP na Revolução dos Cravos* (Lisbon: Bertrand Editora, 2011).
13. Pérez, 'Comissoes de moradores'.
14. Downs, 'Residents' Commissions and Urban Struggles in Revolutionary Portugal'.
15. Pedro Ramos Pinto, 'Urban Social Movements and the Transition to Democracy in Portugal, 1974–1976', *The Historical Journal* 51(4) (2008): 1025–1046.
16. Pérez, 'Comissoes de moradores'.
17. *Diário Popular*, 14 November 1974.
18. For more on SAAL, see José Manuel Bandeirinha, *O Processo SAAL e a Arquitectura no 25 de Abril* (Coimbra: University of Coimbra, 2007).
19. Nuno Portas, 'O Processo SAAL: entre o Estado e o Poder Local', *Revista Crítica de Ciências Sociais* 18, 19, 20 (February 1986): 635–644.
20. Portas, 'O Processo SAAL: entre o Estado e o Poder Local', 639.
21. Portas, 'O Processo SAAL: entre o Estado e o Poder Local', 635–644.
22. Helena Vilaça (1994). 'As Associaçõs de Moradores enquanto Aspecto Particular do Associativismo urbano e da Participação social', Sociologue Revista da Faculdade de Letras da Universidade do Porto, no. 4.
23. Dows, *Os Moradores à Conquista da Cidade*.
24. *Diário Popular*, 29 March 1975.
25. Dows, *Os Moradores à Conquista da Cidade*, 47.
26. Dows, *Os Moradores à Conquista da Cidade*.

27. Dows, *Os Moradores à Conquista da Cidade*, 48.
28. Dows, *Os Moradores à Conquista da Cidade*, 47.
29. Dows, 'Residents' Commissions and Urban Struggles in Revolutionary Portugal', 23.
30. *Las Revoluciones Europeas, 1492–1992* (Barcelona: Critica, 1995), 26–27.
31. Noticiário Nacional, 9 September 1975, RTP Archive.
32. Maria Inácia Rezola, *Os Militares na Revolução de Abril: O Conselho da Revolução e a Transição para a Democracia em Portugal* (Lisbon: Campo da Comunicação, 2006), 275.
33. Noticiário Nacional, 9 September 1975, RTP Archive.
34. Dows, *Os Moradores à Conquista da Cidade*, 170.

12. Workers' Control, 11 March and Nationalisations

1. Fátima Patriarca, 'Controlo Operário em Portugal (I)', *Análise Social* 12(3) (1976): 765–816.
2. Eugénio Rosa, *A Economia Portuguesa em Números* (Lisbon: Moraes Editora, 1975).
3. Rafael Durán Muñoz, *Contención y Transgresión: Las Movilizaciones Sociales y el Estado en las Transiciones Española y Portuguesa* (Madrid: CPPC, 2000).
4. Chip Dows, *Os Moradores à Conquista da Cidade* (Lisbon: Armazém das Letras, 1978).
5. The soldiers' commissions began to develop in September 1975.
6. *República*, 5 March 1975.
7. 'Surto Grevista', *Diário de Lisboa*, 5 May 1975, 1. 'A TAP disse não à greve', *Diário de Lisboa*, 6 May 1975, 1.
8. *Ocupação da SAPEC*, Noticiário Nacional, 30 June 1975, RTP Archive.
9. *Ocupação da SAPEC*, Noticiário Nacional, 30 June 1975, RTP Archive.
10. *Ocupação da SAPEC*, Noticiário Nacional, 30 June 1975, RTP Archive.
11. FIL programme: 'Que futuro?', RTP, 1 July 1975, RTP Archive.
12. FIL programme: 'Que futuro?', RTP, 1 July 1975, RTP Archive.
13. FIL programme: 'Que futuro?', RTP, 1 July 1975, RTP Archive.
14. Comissão Coordenadora das Empresas em Autogestão, Diogo Duarte, Luís Ferreira, Nelson Trindade, Vasco Corregedor da Fonseca, *A Realidade da Autogestão em Portugal* (Lisbon: Perspectivas & Realidades, 1981).
15. Patriarca, 'Controlo Operário em Portugal (I)', 765–816.
16. Patriarca, 'Controlo Operário em Portugal (I)', 1056–1057.
17. Patriarca, 'Controlo Operário em Portugal (I)', 765–816.
18. Patriarca, 'Controlo Operário em Portugal (I)', 1056–1057.
19. Noticiário Nacional, 7 September 1975, RTP Archive.
20. Raquel Varela, *A História do PCP na Revolução dos Cravos* (Lisbon: Bertrand Editora, 2011).
21. Paulo Spriano, *The Occupation of the Factories in Italy 1920* (London: Pluto Press, 1975), 72.

22. *Avante!*, 22 May 1975.

23. *Avante!*, 22 May 1975.

24. *Avante!*, 3 July 1975.

25. *Diário de Lisboa*, 12 May 1975.

26. *Avante!*, 26 July 1975.

27. *Diário de Lisboa*, 9 May 1975.

28. Speech by Vasco Gonçalves on May Day 1975, http://www1.ci.uc.pt/cd25a/ wikka.-hp?wakka=poderpolo1 (accessed 14 July 2009).

29. Ministry of Labour Document cited in Patriarca, 'Controlo Operário em Portugal (I)', 765–816.

30. Ministry of Labour Document cited in Patriarca, 'Controlo Operário em Portugal (I)', 765–816.

31. *Avante!*, 3 July 1975.

32. *Diário de Lisboa*, 12 May 1975.

33. *Diário de Lisboa*, 9 May 1975, 1; May Day 1975 speech of Vasco Gonçalves, http://www1.ci.uc.pt/cd25a//wikka.php?wakka=poderpolo1 (accessed on 14 July 2009).

34. Patriarca, 'Controlo Operário em Portugal (I)', 769–770.

35. António Medeiros Ferreira, 'Portugal em Transe (1974–1985)', in José Mattoso (ed.), *História de Portugal* (Lisbon: Círculo de Leitores, 1993), 114.

36. *Diário Popular*, 15 March 1975.

37. The Bonapartist Party, which advanced the claims of the Napoleon Bonaparte family, believed in an autocratic but benevolent government engineered by members of the military with the assumed consent of the people.

38. José da Silva Lopes, *A Economia Portuguesa desde 1960* (Lisbon: Gradiva, 1999), 310.

39. Lopes, *A Economia Portuguesa desde 1960*, 314–315.

40. Ferreira cited in Medeiros, 'Portugal em Transe (1974–1985)', 116.

41. Lopes, *A Economia Portuguesa desde 1960*, 316.

42. Lopes, *A Economia Portuguesa desde 1960*, 320.

43. Patriarca, 'Controlo Operário em Portugal (I)', 765–816.

13. *The Birth of the Welfare State*

1. António Barreto, 'Mudança Social em Portugal: 1960–2000', in António Costa Pinto (ed.), *Portugal Contemporâneo* (Lisbon: Dom Quixote, 2005), 137–162.

2. Lisnave, for example, belonged to the powerful Companhia União Fabril (CUF), which was founded in the 1960s by Portuguese, Swedish and Dutch capital.

3. Interview by the author, 24 February 2012.

4. António Barreto and Clara Valadas Preto, *Portugal 1960/1995: Indicadores Sociais* (Lisbon: ICS and Público, 1996).

5. Manuel de Lucena, 'Previdência Social', in António Barreto and Maria Filomena Mónica (eds), *Dicionário de História de Portugal* (Porto: Figueirinhas, 2000), Vol. 9, 160.

6. Lucena, 'Previdência Social',152–167; Irene Flunser Pimentel, 'A assistência social e familiar do Estado Novo nos anos 30 e 40', *Análise Social* 34(151–152), (1999): 477–508; Luís Capucha, 'Assistência Social', in Maria Filomena Mónica and António Barreto (eds), *Dicionário de História de Portugal* (Porto: Figueirinhas, 1999), Vol. 7, 137.

7. Raquel Varela *A História do PCP na Revolução dos Cravos* (Lisbon: Bertrand Editora, 2011), 71–108.

8. Pimentel, 'A assistência social e familiar do Estado Novo nos anos 30 e 40'.

9. Bernardete Maria Fonseca, *Ideologia ou Economia? Evolução da Proteção no Desemprego em Portugal*, Masters Thesis, Universidade de Aveiro, 2008, 87.

10. Interview with Cruz Oliveira conducted by the author on 24 June 2012, in Lisbon.

11. António Correia de Campos, 'Saúde Pública', in António Barreto and Maria Filomena Mónica (eds), *Dicionário de História de Portugal* (Porto: Figueirinhas, 2000), Vol. 9, 405.

12. Historia do Servico Nacional de Saude, Ministerio da Saude, www.portaldasaude. pt/portal/conteudos/a+saude+em+portugal/servico+nacional+de+saude/ historia+do+--sns/historiadosns.htm (accessed 15 May 2012).

13. Cronologia Pulsar da Revolução, 1974–1975, Centro de Documentação, 25 April.

14. 'O Servico Cívico em Questão', in *UEC*, no. 12, 2nd series

15. 'O Servico Cívico em Questão', in *UEC*, no. 12, 2nd series

16. 'Os esquerdistas e a resposta dos trabalhadores', in *UEC*, no. 12, 2nd series, 4.

17. Vasco Gonçalves, *Discursos, Conferências, Entrevistas* (Lisbon: Seara Nova, 1977), 103–104.

18. Gonçalves, *Discursos, Conferências, Entrevistas*, 103–104.

19. *República*, 1 March 1975.

20. *República*, 3 March 1975.

21. *República*, 5 March 1975.

22. Speech at the I Encontro Nacional da Uniao da Juventude Comunista, 9 March 1975, in Álvaro Cunhal, *Discursos Políticos (3)* (Lisbon: Edições Avante!, 1975), 148.

23. Raquel Varela and Sandra Duarte, 'Paixão pela educação ... privada. Educação e terceira via em Portugal: da revolução dos cravos aos nossos dias', in Vera Peroni (ed.), *Redefinições das fronteiras entre o público e o privado: implicações para a democratização da educação* (Brasília: Liber livro editora, 2013), 120–140.

24. Constitution of the Portuguese Republic, Art. 63, 1976.

25. RTP Archives, 1975.

26. Date accessed: 16 March 2013.

27. Manuela Silva, 'A repartição do rendimento em Portugal no pos-25 de Abril 74', *Revista Crítica de Ciências Sociais* 15–17 (May 1985), 271.

14. Scheming for Power

1. RTP interview quoted by Phil Mailer, *Portugal: The Impossible Revolution?* (London: Solidarity, 1977), 254.

2. Miguel Pérez, 'Conselhos Revolucionários de Trabalhadores, Soldados e Marin-heiros', in *Dicionário de História da Revolução* (Porto: Figueirinhas, 2017).

3. Christopher Reed, *The Guardian*, 21 April 1975.

4. Editor's note: I am reminded by Lenin's criticisms of the German Communists in 1919, as written in his pamphlet, '"Left-Wing" Communism: An Infantile Disorder'; 'The error consisted in their denial of the need to take part in the reactionary bourgeois parliaments and in the reactionary trade unions'. It just so happens that the CRTSMs had a similar disdain for getting involved in the trade union movement.

5. Jorge Gaspar and Nuno Vitorino, *As Eleições de 25 de Abril: Geografia e Imagem dos partidos* (Lisbon: Livros Horizonte, 1976).

6. Editors' note: Hence parties to the left of the Communist Party, which eventually won less than 8 per cent of the vote, had more than 50 per cent of the television air time assigned to them for political broadcasting.

7. Tony Cliff, 'Portugal at the Crossroads', *International Socialism* (first series) 81/82, Special Issue (September 1975). Cliff then goes on to say:

> What characterises the petty bourgeoisie, however, is their fear and mistrust of the masses, and their cringing before the rich and mighty. A long time ago Engels explained the role of petty bourgeois democracy in a letter to Bebel (11 December 1884) on 'pure democracy': ... when the moment of revolution comes, acquires a temporary importance ... as the final sheet-anchor of the whole bourgeois and even feudal economy ... Thus between March and September 1848 the whole feudal-bureaucratic mass strengthened the liberals in order to hold down the revolutionary masses.

8. *Diário da Assembleia Constituinte*, 15 July 1975.

9. Paul M. Sweezy, 'Class Struggles in Portugal: Part I', *Monthly Review* 27(4) (September 1975): 1–26.

10. Interview by Peter Robinson with Jorge Abegao on 5 May 1984, in *Workers' Councils in Portugal 1974–1975*, MPhil, 1989.

11. *Expresso*, 13 June 1975, cited in Peter Robinson's *Workers' Councils in Portugal 1974–1975*, MPhil, 1989.

12. *Expresso*, 13 June 1975.

13. *Expresso*, 13 June 1975.

14. RTP interview, quoted by Mailer, *Portugal: The Impossible Revolution?*, 254.

15. *The Guardian*, 19 June 1975.

16. Interview by Peter Robinson with Afonso da Sousa, 31 August 1980, in *Workers' Councils in Portugal 1974–1975*, MPhil, 1989.

17. Orlando Neves (ed.), *Textos Históricos da Revolução* (Lisbon: Diabril, 1976), 50–51, cited by Maria Inácia Rezola *Os Militares na Revolução de Abril: O Conselho da Revolução e a Transição para a Democracia em Portugal* (Lisbon: Campo da Comunicação, 2006), 276.

18. Rezola, *Os Militares na Revolução de Abril*, 277.

19. Álvaro Cunhal, *A Revolução Portuguesa: Passado e Futuro* (Lisbon: Edições Avante!, 1994), 177.

20. 'Nota sobre a assembleia do MFA de 8 July', in *Documentos do CC do PCP, julho/dezembro de 1975* (Lisbon: Edições Avante!, 1976).
21. 'Com o PCP pela Unidade Popular Rumo ao Socialismo', *Avante!*, Series 7, 3 July 1975, 4.
22. 'Nota sobre a assembleia do MFA de 8 July', 24–27.
23. 'Nota sobre a assembleia do MFA de 8 July', 24–27.
24. 'Nota sobre a assembleia do MFA de 8 July', 24–27.
25. *Voz Do Povo*, 25 July 1975.
26. MFA Bulletin, 14 July 1975, 4.
27. Interview by Peter Robinson with an activist from the assembly, and a member of MES, February 1976, in *Workers' Councils in Portugal 1974–1975*, MPhil, 1989.
28. *Capital*, 26 July 1975.
29. *República*, 16 July 1975.
30. *República*, 16 August 1975.
31. Audrey Wise, *Eyewitness in Revolutionary Portugal* (Nottingham: Bertrand Russell Peace Foundation for Spokesman Books, 1975).
32. Wise, *Eyewitness in Revolutionary Portugal*.
33. Most of the section on Popular Assemblies has been derived from Peter Robinson's chapter on the Popular Assembles, taken from his MPhil thesis.

15. The Land for its Workers: Agrarian Reform

1. Noticiário Nacional, 7 September 1975, RTP Archive.
2. Nancy Bermeo, *The Revolution within the Revolution: Workers Control in Rural Portugal* (Princeton, NJ: Princeton University Press, 1986), 4.
3. Eric Solsten (ed.), *Portugal: A Country Study* (Washington, DC: GPO for the Library of Congress, 1993).
4. António Barreto, *Anatomia de uma Revolução: A Reforma Agrária em Portugal, Europa–America* (Lisbon: Europa-América, 1987), 45.
5. Barreto, *Anatomia de uma Revolução*.
6. Constantino Piçarra, *As Ocupações de Terras no Distrito de Beja, 1974–1975*, (Coimbra: Almedina, 2008).
7. Oliveira Baptista, *Portugal 1975: Os Campos* (Porto: Afrontamento, 1978), 25.
8. Barreto, *Anatomia de uma Revolução*, 178.
9. Barreto, *Anatomia de uma Revolução*, 43.
10. Bermeo, *The Revolution within the Revolution*, 4.
11. Phil Mailer, *Portugal: The Impossible Revolution?* (London: Solidarity, 1977), 258.
12. Mailer, *Portugal: The Impossible Revolution?*, 215.
13. One hectare equals 2.47 acres.
14. Oliveira Baptista, 'O 25 de Abril, a sociedade rural e a questão da terra', in J.M. Brandão Brito, *O País em Revolução* (Lisbon: Editorial Notícias, 2001), 183–184.
15. Noticiário Nacional, 27 May 1975, RTP Archive.
16. João Castro Caldas, *Terra e Trabalho* (Oeiras: Celta, 2001), 133.
17. *Ocupacao da Quinta da Vargem*, 24 June 1975, RTP Archive.

18. Oliveira Baptista, *Portugal 1975: Os Campos* (Porto: Afrontamento, 1978).
19. The Law No. 77/77 of 29 September, adopted on 10 August 1977 with the support of the Socialist Party, the PPD and the CDS and with the votes of the Communist Party and the UDP.
20. Piçarra, *As Ocupações de Terras no Distrito de Beja, 1974–1975.*
21. Peter Robinson, *Portugal 1974–1975: The Forgotten Dream* (London: Socialist History Society, 1999).
22. Noticiário Nacional, 7 September 1975, RTP Archive.
23. Constantino Piçarra, 'A Reforma Agraria no Sul de Portugal (1975)', in Raquel Varela (ed.), *Revolução ou Transição? História e Memória da Revolução dos Cravos* (Lisbon: Bertrand, 2012), 86–87.
24. Zona Intervenção da Reforma Agrária (Intervention Area of Land Reform).
25. Baptista, *Portugal 1975*, 9.
26. *I Conferencia de Trabalhadores Agricolas do Sul*, 9 February 1975, in *O PCP e a Luta pela Reforma Agrária. Cadernos do PCP 7* (Lisbon: Edições Avante!, 1975), 154.
27. Piçarra, 'A Reforma Agraria no Sul de Portugal (1975)', 184.
28. Constantino Piçarra (ed.), *Campos do Sul: Memória de uma Revolução* (Lisbon: IHC, 2009), 17.
29. Baptista, 'O 25 de Abril, a sociedade rural e a questão da terra', 188–189.

16. The 'Hot Summer' of 1975 and the Fifth Government's Frail Governance

1. José Saramago, 'A Distancia como Politica, 8 October 1975', in José Saramago, *Os Apontamentos* (Lisbon: Caminho, 1990), 314.
2. Gil Green, *Portugal's Revolution* (New York: International Publishers, 1976), 64.
3. See the report in the Harvard Crimson, 17 September 1975, www.thecrimson.com/article/1975/9/17/the-real-threat-in-portugal-pbobn/.
4. Records of the Prime Minister's Office: Correspondence and Papers PREM 16/602 Visit to UK by Portuguese Foreign Minister, Major Melo Antunes: meeting with Prime Minister on 27 June 1975. Records of the Prime Ministers. Date: 1975. Source: The Catalogue of the National Archives.
5. Mário Soares interview, *Diário de Lisboa*, 7 May 1975, 1.
6. Eric Solsten (ed.) *Portugal: A Country Study* (Washington, DC: GPO for the Library of Congress, 1993).
7. Richard Robinson, *Contemporary Portugal: A History* (London: George Allen & Unwin, 1979).
8. John L. Hammond, *Building Popular Power: Workers' and Neighbourhood Movements in the Portuguese Revolution* (New York: Monthly Review Press, 1988), 212.
9. Günter Wallraff, *The Undesirable Journalist* (London: Pluto Press, 1978), 13–14.
10. Green, *Portugal's Revolution*, 67.

11. See Green, *Portugal's Revolution*, 66–67; and Hammond, *Building Popular Power*, 211–212.
12. *República*, 21 January 1975, cited by Robinson in *Workers' Councils in Portugal 1974–1975*, MPhil, 1989.
13. 'Nota da Comissão Politica, 27 July 1975', *Avante!*, Series 7, 31 July 1975, 4.
14. 'Cronologia Pulsar da Revolução, julho 1975', Centro de Documentação 25 de Abril, http://www1.ci.uc.pt/cd25a/wikka.php?wakka=PulsarJulho75 (accessed on 12 November 2009).
15. Vasco Gonçalves, *Discursos, Conferências, Entrevistas* (Lisbon: Seara Nova, 1977), 377.
16. Maria Manuela Cruzeiro, *25 de Novembro: Quantos Golpes Afinal?*. Comunicação apresentada no Colóquio sobre o 25 de Novembro, realizado no Museu Republica e Resistencia, 2005. In http://www1.ci.uc.pt/cd25a/wikka.php?wakka=th10 (accessed on 28 November 2010).
17. Gonçalves, *Discursos, Conferências, Entrevistas*, 357–359.
18. Maria Inácia Rezola, *Os Militares na Revolução de Abril: O Conselho da Revolução e a Transição para a Democracia em Portugal* (Lisbon: Campo da Comunicacao, 2006), 347.
19. Rezola, *Os Militares na Revolução de Abril*.
20. Namely, Melo Antunes, Vasco Lourenço, Sousa e Castro, Vitor Alves, Pezarat Correia, Franco Charais, Canto e Castro, Costa Neves and Vítor Crespo.
21. Álvaro Cunhal, *Do 25 de Novembro às Eleições para a Assembleia Constituinte. Discursos Políticos 6* (Lisbon: Edições Avante!, 1976), 9–35.
22. 'Comunicado sobre a formação do Fifth Governo Provisorio', Comissão Politica do CC do PCP, 8 August 1975. In *Documentos Políticos do CC do PCP*. Vol. 3, July–December 1975 (London: Avante, 1976), 70–74.
23. Álvaro Cunhal, *A Crise Político-Militar. Discursos Políticos 5* (Lisbon: Edições Avante!, 1976), 139.
24. Cunhal, *A Crise Político-Militar*, 162.
25. Cunhal, *A Crise Político-Militar*, 127–166.
26. Cunhal, *A Crise Político-Militar*, 94–95.
27. 'Comunicado sobre a formação do V Governo Provisório'.
28. *Avante!*, 11 August 1975.
29. Cunhal, *A Crise Político-Militar*, 139.
30. 'Intervenção na reunião plenária do Comitê Central do PCP', 10 August 1975, in Cunhal, *A Crise Político-Militar*, 127–166.
31. 'Intervenção na reunião plenária do Comitê Central do PCP'.
32. Cunhal, *A Crise Político-Militar*, 189. See Évora, 24 August 1975.
33. Cunhal, *A Crise Político-Militar*, 156–157.
34. 'Declaração sobre a crise politica atual, August 20, 1975', in Documentos Políticos do Comité Central do PCP, Vol. 3, July–December 1975 (Lisbon: Edições Avante, 1976), 87–98.
35. Sunday Times Insight Team, *Portugal: The Year of the Captains* (London: Andre Deutsch, 1975), 264.

36. Carlos Brito, Álvaro Cunhal, Os Sete Fôlegos do Combatente, Memórias (Lisbon: Edições Nelson de Matos, 2010), 176–177.

37. *Avante!*, 7 August 1975, 4.

38. *Avante!*, 7 August 1975, 4.

39. Vasco Gonçalves was appointed as the general Chief of Staff but not long after expelled from the Council of the Revolution as this body became more moderate.

40. Sunday Times Insight Team, *Portugal: The Year of the Captains*.

41. Saramago, 'A Distancia como Politica, 8 October 1975', 311.

42. Saramago, 'A Distancia como Politica, 8 October 1975', 314.

43. 'FUR, por uma Frente de Unidade Revolucionária', http://arquivo.sinbad.ua.pt/Cartazes/2005000411 (accessed 14 January 2013).

44. 'FUR, por uma Frente de Unidade Revolucionária'.

45. Parties such as the Trotskyist PRT (Partido Revolucionário dos Trabalhadores) and the Maoist MRPP.

46. See Peter Robinson's chapter on *Popular Assemblies* in his thesis on *Workers' Councils in Portugal 1974–1975*, MPhil, 1989.

17. Spain and Other 'Links in the Chain'

1. Tony Cliff, 'Portugal at the Crossroads: The Collapse of the Fascist Regime', *International Socialism* (first series) 81–82, Special Issue, September 1975.

2. The reference to the identical front-page headlines of the various newspapers is to be found in *Diário Popular*, 27 September 1975.

3. *Diário Popular*, 27 September 1975.

4. Josep Sánchez Cervelló, *A Revolução Portuguesa e a sua Influência na Transição Espanhola (1961–1976)* (Lisbon: Assirio e Alvim, 1993), 353.

5. Juan Carlos Jiménez Redondo, *Franco e Salazar: As Relações Luso-Espanholas durante a Guerra fria* (Lisbon: Assírio e Alvim, 1996).

6. Paul Preston, *Franco: A Biography* (London: HarperCollins, 1993).

7. Paloma Aguilar, *Memoria y Olvido de la Guerra Civil Española* (Madrid: Alianza Editorial, 1996).

8. Irene Flunser Pimentel, *História da PIDE* (Lisbon: Círculo de Leitores/Temas e Debates, 2007).

9. Maxwell also discusses how the 'the behaviour of the Portuguese communists alarmed communist Parties in France, Spain and Italy'; Kenneth Maxwell, *The Making of Portuguese Democracy* (Cambridge: Cambridge University Press, 1995), 133–134.

10. 'A La Intersindical Nacional Portuguesa, Carabanchel, Madrid, Marzo 1975'. Archivo de la Fundación 1.º de Mayo, Quota 191, File: Delegación Exterior de Comisiones Obreras.

11. With respect to the list of films and music related to the Carnation Revolution, see the collection by the newspaper *Público*, on the 30th anniversary celebration of 25 April 1974.

12. *Gaceta de Derecho Social*, nos 42–43, Ano IV, November–December 1974.

13. *Diário de Lisboa*, 3 May 1974.
14. Equivalent to the residents' commissions in Portugal.
15. Stickers from the Portuguese far-left. Private collection.
16. Alberto Carrillo-Linares, *Subversivos y Malditos en la Universidad de Sevilla (1965–1977)* (Seville: Centro de Estudios Andaluces, 2008), 500–506.
17. Carrillo-Linares, *Subversivos y Malditos en la Universidad de Sevilla (1965–1977)*.
18. Carrillo-Linares, *Subversivos y Malditos en la Universidad de Sevilla (1965–1977)*.
19. Archivo de la Fundación 1.º Mayo, 'Intersindical Nacional, Informação à Imprensa'. CECO, 191.
20. 'A La Intersindical Nacional Portuguesa, Carabanchel, Madrid, Marzo 1975', Archivode la Fundación 1.º de Mayo, Quota 191, File: Delegación Exterior de Comisiones Obreras.
21. Archivo de la Fundación 1.º de Mayo, Quota 191, File: Pasta Delegación Exterior de Comisiones Obreras, 8 October 1974.
22. In the event, the World Trade Union Conference in Solidarity with the Workers and Peoples of Chile was, since May 1974, scheduled for 11–15 September 1974 and was cancelled due to 'various difficulties'.
23. *Expresso*, 20 April 2009.
24. César Oliveira, *Cem Anos nas Relações Luso-Espanholas. Política e Economia* (Lisbon: Edições Cosmos, 1995).
25. Xavier Doménech Sampere, 'El Cambio Político (1962–1976): Materiales para una perspetiva desde abajo', *Historia del Presente. La sociedad Española durante el Segundo Franquismo*, Asociación Historiadores del Presente, UNED – Centro Asociado de Melilla, no. 1 (2002), 46.
26. Author's note: Please note that the remainder of this chapter has been written by my English editor, who was personally involved at the time.
27. Manus McGrogan, 'Rendezvous with a Revolution: British Socialists in Portugal 1974–5', *Interventions* 19(5) (2017): 646–665.
28. Cliff, 'Portugal at the Crossroads'.
29. Editor's note: This is how I first became involved. The day after I returned [in August 1975], we were on a demonstration of over 100,000 people organised by FUP. This is how I described it: 'The colour, the variety, the composition, it's like everything you dream about … how can you know what to expect when you're reaching into beauty and the unimaginable? We were going into the centre of a vortex.'
30. Editor's note: We were very, very excited, particularly as the PRP had a vision of revolutionary councils of soldiers, workers and sailors (CRTSMs) and we thought: 'Ah! This is the organisation for us. Look at them, they're young, they're vibrant, they're flexible and they've got this notion of soviets.'
31. Manus McGrogan, 'Portugal', *Red Weekly* 51, 9 May 1974.
32. McGrogan, 'Portugal', *Red Weekly* 51, 9 May 1974. Lack of space means we cannot cover the differences between the IMG and the IS.
33. Editor's note: The two organisers were Jimmy MacCullum from the Glasgow district and myself from the Manchester district.
34. McGrogan, 'Rendezvous with a Revolution: British Socialists in Portugal 1974–5'.

35. Editor's note: I remember selling it 'like hot cakes', for example, selling 60 copies in an hour at the Rossio Metro station.
36. McGrogan, 'Rendezvous with a Revolution: British Socialists in Portugal 1974–5'.
37. Kenneth Maxwell, *The Making of Portuguese Democracy* (Cambridge: Cambridge University Press, 1995), 135.
38. Maxwell, *The Making of Portuguese Democracy*.
39. McGrogan, 'Rendezvous with a Revolution: British Socialists in Portugal 1974–5'.

18. The Crisis

1. Maria João Avilez, *Soares: Ditadura e Revolução* (Lisbon: Público, 1996), 483.
2. *Os SUV em Luta: manifestos, entrevistas, comunicados* (Lisbon, 1975).
3. *Soldados Unidos Vencerão*, órgão central dos SUV, no. 1, 9 October 1975.
4. 'Cronologia Pulsar da Revolução', http://www1.ci.uc.pt/cd25a/wikka.php?wakka=PulsarSetembro75 (accessed 16 February 2011).
5. Editor's note: I will never forget how, in early October, one of the leading PRP comrades, a young Lisnave shipyard worker, telephoned from our house in Salford, Lancashire, and asked impatiently, over the international telephone lines 'Well, when is the coup?'. So much for 'The art of insurrection'!
6. Maria Inácia Rezola, *Os Militares na Revolução de Abril: O Conselho da Revolução e a Transição para a Democracia em Portugal* (Lisbon: Campo da Comunicação, 2006), 418.
7. Rezola, *Os Militares na Revolução de Abril*, 419.
8. Rezola, *Os Militares na Revolução de Abril*, 418.
9. *Os SUV em Luta*, 31.
10. *Os SUV em Luta*, 40.
11. Interview with a soldier from the Northern SUV, In *Os SUV em Luta*, 20–30.
12. Interview with a soldier from the Northern SUV.
13. Avilez, *Soares: Ditadura e Revolução*, 483.
14. Rezola, *Os Militares na Revolução de Abril*, 420.
15. Interview with Mario Tome and Francisco Barao da Cunha on 11 November 2011.
16. Rezola, *Os Militares na Revolução de Abril*, 421.
17. Interview with Antonio Pessoa on 29 November 2011.
18. Editor's note: I remember being told how in Barreiro, across the Tagus Estuary from Lisbon, the *bombeiros* (voluntary firemen) sounded the fire-bells at any sign of a 'putsch' and the population, often woken in the early hours of the morning, rushed into the streets only to discover the alarm was false.
19. Rezola, *Os Militares na Revolução de Abril*, 423.
20. Noticiário Nacional, 29 September 1975, RTP Archive.
21. Another example comes from Évora, where on 14 October, 34 of the residents' commissions met in order to build links with the soldiers' commissions, mainly by supporting the SUV-organised demonstration. This was attended by 20,000–30,000 people, including some 1,500 soldiers; *Poder Popular*, 23 October 1975.

22. Interview by Peter Robinson with Francisco Queroz, December 1979, in *Workers' Councils in Portugal 1974–1975*, MPhil, 1989.

23. Noticiário Nacional, 20 October 1975, RTP Archive.

24. Editors' note: When I interviewed Isobel Guerra, from the Setúbal Comité de Luta, she emphasised:

> The committee was more than a collection of political activists. It was a front united in common activities, despite political differences. It had a life like that of many other apartidaria organisations, which affected the ways that the parties intervened.
>
> Sometimes the slogans of the parties, the PRP included, did not coincide with the discussion. Sometimes the parties even spoke with a language, which made people laugh. It was really difficult for a party to control the process, including the PRP. The PRP was in a better position because it always defended the autonomous organisation, and did not mind if the organisation went in directions other than it wished.
>
> I think that what happened in Setúbal was very, very interesting. I learnt a lot. I learnt that people can organise and discuss together even when they have political differences. I remember one political discussion, prior to a demonstration organised by the PCP, MES, UDP, LCI, PRP and MRPP. It was decided that the slogans would be by consensus. They would never be voted on. They would talk until agreement was reached. And they did.

25. Refer to Charles Downs' PhD, *Community Organization, Political Change and Urban Policy: Portugal 1974–1976* (Berkeley, CA: University of California, 1980). This study has a great deal of valuable information about the relationship between the various organisations, in particular the residents' commissions, within Setúbal.

26. On 8 September, a 'popular power', protest by the far-left front, FUR, attracted 1,000 people in Setúbal with placards and banners from reading, for example, 'Soldiers and sailors forever, always on the side of the people and "control over production", from organisations such as the Residents' commission of the fishermen's district'.

27. Tony Cliff, 'Portugal at the Crossroads: The Collapse of the Fascist Regime', *International Socialism* (first series) 81–82 Special Issue, September 1975.

28. Noticiário Nacional, 11 October 1975, RTP Archive.

29. Noticiário Nacional, 14 October 1975, RTP Archive.

30. Noticiário Nacional da RTP, 23 September 1975, RTP Archive.

31. António Costa Pinto, 'Political Purges and State Crisis in Portugal's Transition to Democracy 1975–76', *Journal of Contemporary History* 43(2) (2008), 1036.

32. Editor's note: A great many were attracted to revolutionary ideas and the left parties. The UPD and PRP, among others, could organise meetings of thousands and even at times more than 10,000 people. So the left grew, unevenly, and often in relation to the success and failures of actions, alliance and strategies. At times, they were able to unite, and work together in the movement. These are important moments. However, all too often the left appeared fragmented. The PRP while

raising the important issues of armed power, and councils, was ultimately divisive. The UPD was hamstrung by its absurd idolisation of Albania. No group was able to emerge as the single pole of attraction.

33. 'Abril de novo: Memoria do PREC, da Extrema-Esquerda, da resistencia antis-salazarista, da I Republica e outras cronicas históricas', http://abril-de-novo. blogspot.pt.

34. 20 November 1975, RTP Archive.

35. RTP Archive, www.youtube.com/watch?v=6DB42QUJYSM (accessed 19 January 1975).

36. Noticiário Nacional, 21 November 1975, RTP Archive.

37. 20 November 1975, RTP Archive.

38. 'Trabalhadores da Construção civil em Luta', *Avante!*, Series 7, 13 November 1975, 2.

39. *Nota do PCP sobre a greve e a manifestação da construção civil*, 13 November 1975. Nota da Comissão Política do CC do PCP. In Documentos do PCP. Centro de Documentação 25 de Abril, Coimbra.

40. *O Militante*, 4 August 1975.

41. *O Militante*, October 1975.

42. *O Militante*, October 1975.

43. 'Na unidade os trabalhadores avançam', *Avante!*, Series 7, 20 November 1975, 6.

44. *Avante!*, Series 7, 13 November 1975, 5.

45. *Avante!*, Series 7, 13 November 1975, 5.

46. 20 November 1975, RTP Archive.

47. Noticiário Nacional, 20 November 1975, RTP Archive.

48. Maria Manuela Cruzeiro, *25 de Novembro: Quantos Golpes Afinal?*. Comunicação apresentada no Colóquio sobre o 25 de Novembro, realizado no Museu Republica e Resistencia, 2005. In http://www1.ci.uc.pt/cd25a/wikka.php?wakka=th10 (accessed 28 November 2010), 1.

49. Cruzeiro, *25 de Novembro*, 9.

50. Rezola, *Os Militares na Revolução de Abril*, 485.

51. Cruzeiro, *25 de Novembro*.

52. Peter Robinson, *Portugal 1974–1975: The Forgotten Dream* (London: Socialist History Society, 1999).

53. Robinson, *Portugal 1974–1975*.

54. This is included in Tony Cliff and Chris Harman, *Portugal: Lessons of the 25th of November*, 1975, Marxists Internet Archive, www.marxists.org/archive/cliff/works/1975/12/lessons.htm.

55. Editor's note: in *Workers Liberty*, 29 July 2014, Miguel Pérez, when interviewed said:

The whole Left in Portugal expected the Armed Forces Movement to protect the whole revolutionary movement from physical violence. But the left had no strategy – in particular, no military strategy – and the right did. The Communist Party had a strategy of 'legalising the revolution', or 'institutional-ising the revolution'. The Armed Forces Movement simply had no plan to fight the coup. The 25 November coup was carried out by 200 soldiers in Lisbon. The left [in the army], which numbered easily 1,500, did nothing.

56. Cruzeiro, *25 de Novembro*.

57. Peter Robinson, interview with Isabel Guerra, 4 June 1984, in *Workers' Councils in Portugal 1974–1975*, MPhil, 1989.

58. José Carlos Guinote, 'Urbanismo e corrupcao: as mais-valias e o desenvolvimento urbano', *Le Monde Diplomatique*, Portuguese edition, 6 August 2008.

59. Álvaro Cunhal, *Do 25 de Novembro às Eleições para a Assembleia Constituinte. Discursos Políticos 6* (Lisbon: Edições Avante!, 1976), 9–35.

19. Democracy and Revolution: The Meaning of the Carnation Revolution

1. 'A Procura do Socialismo II', RTP Archive, 21 April 1976.

2. Maria Inácia Rezola, *Os Militares na Revolução de Abril: O Conselho da Revolução e a Transição para a Democracia em Portugal* (Lisbon: Campo da Comunicação, 2006).

3. Carlo Ginzburg, *O Queijo e os Vermes* (São Paulo: Companhia das Letras, 2007), 11.

4. Leon Trotsky, *História da Revolução Russa* (Lisbon: Versus, 1988), Vol. 1, 15.

5. Leon Trotsky, *História da Revolução Russa* (Lisbon: Versus, 1988), Vol. 1, 15.

6. Eric Hobsbawm, *Sobre História* (São Paulo: Companhia das Letras, 1998), 220.

7. Chip Dows, *Os Moradores à Conquista da Cidade* (Lisbon: Armazém das Letras, 1978).

8. Maria de Lurdes Santos, Marinús Pires de Lima and Vítor Matias Ferreira, *O 25 de Abril e As Lutas Sociais nas Empresas* (Porto: Afrontamento, 1976).

9. John L. Hammond, 'Worker Control in Portugal: The Revolution and Today', *Economic and Industrial Democracy* 2(4) (December 1981): 413–453.

10. Loren Goldner, *Ubu Saved from Drowning: Class Struggle and Statist Containment in Portugal and Spain, 1974–1977* (Cambridge, MA: Queequeg Publications, 2000).

11. Peter F. Robinson, *Workers' Councils in Portugal 1974–1975*, MPhil thesis, Centre for Sociology & Social University (Open University, 1990).

12. Chris Harman, *A People's History of the World* (London: Bookmarks, 2002), iv.

13. Editor's note: The British Socialist Tony Cliff refers to 'dual powerless' and his comrade Chris Harman wrote about 'the fragmentation of power'; see Harman's book *The Fire Last Time: 1968 and After* (London: Bookmarks, 1988). John Hammond has a similar analysis. These are two ways of seeing the same phenomena, and Raquel Varela's central point is about the sources of grass-roots power. But there was no authority, such as a revolutionary party or a network of workers councils, that had the capacity to lead.

14. Valério Arcary, *Quando o Futuro era Agora: Trinta Anos da Revolucao Portuguesa*, no. 11 (São Paulo: Xamã, 2004), 71–92.

15. Arcary, *Quando o Futuro era Agora*, 71–92.

16. Arcary, *Quando o Futuro era Agora*, 92.

17. Gabriel García Márquez, *Diário de Notícias*, 3 May 2013.

18. 'A Procura do Socialismo II', RTP Archive, 21 April 1976.
19. Phil Mailer, *Portugal: The Impossible Revolution?* (London: Solidarity, 1977), 85.
20. Arcary, *Quando o Futuro era Agora*, 71–92.
21. Raquel Varela, *A História do PCP na Revolução dos Cravos* (Lisbon: Bertrand Editora, 2011), 71–108.
22. António Costa Pinto, 'Political Purges and State Crisis in Portugal's Transition to Democracy 1975–76', *Journal of Contemporary History* 43(2) (2008): 305–332.
23. Rui Ramos (ed.), *História de Portugal* (Lisbon: Esfera dos Livros, 2009), 728.
24. Diego Cerezales, *Portugal à Corunhada: Protesto Popular e Ordem Pública nos séculos XIX e XX* (Lisbon: Tinta-da-china, 2011).
25. Cerezales, *Portugal à Corunhada*.
26. *The Times*, 23 September 1975.
27. Editor's note: The Communist Party was less committed to parliament than its Eurocommunist allies. Unlike the Socialist Party and its communist counterparts in Europe, the Portuguese Communist Party was not preoccupied with the parliamentary road to socialism. It sought to consolidate its power, making maximum use of its connections within the armed forces and the existing state structure. Had it been sufficiently confident of its popular support, it may even have been prepared to organise a *coup d'état* like the one in Prague in 1948. That had been a classic instance, one of which Álvaro Cunhal was very aware, of a communist party coming to power after a period of coalition government.
28. Francois Furet, *Pensando a Revolução Francesa* (Rio de Janeiro: Editora Paz e Terra, 1989).
29. Eric Hobsbawm, *Ecos da Marselhesa* (São Paulo: Companhia das Letras, 1996).
30. Hobsbawm, *Ecos da Marselhesa*, 123.
31. See, for example, José de Medeiros Ferreira, '25 de Abril, uma Revolução?', in José Mattoso (ed.), *História de Portugal: Portugal em Transe* (Lisbon: Círculo de Leitores, 1993), 7–11, where he discusses the question in his text 'April 25, a revolution?'.
32. António Costa Pinto, 'Abril e o Futuro', *Diário de Notícias*, 28 April 2004.
33. Fernando Rosas, 'Abril e Revolucao', *Público*, 14 April 2004.
34. António Borges Coelho, 'Nos Trinta Anos da Revolucao de Abril', *Le Monde Diplomatique*, April 2004; Manuel Villaverde Cabral, 'O 25 de Abril em Retrospetiva', *Le Monde Diplomatique*, April 2004. See also Luís Salgado de Matos, 'O 25 de Abril e a Democracia', *Público*, 12 April 2004.
35. Boaventura Sousa Santos, 'A Crise e a Reconstituição do Estado em Portugal. 1974–1984', *Revista Crítica de Ciências Sociais* 14 (November 1984): 7–29. António Medeiros Ferreira, 'Portugal em Transe (1974–1985)', in José Mattoso (ed.), *História de Portugal* (Lisbon: Círculo de Leitores, 1993).
36. See Josep Sánchez Cervelló in *O processo democrático português 1974–75*. See also Rezola, *Os Militares na Revolução de Abril*; and Bernardino Gomes and Tiago Moreira de Sá, *Carlucci versus Kissinger*, trans. Susana Serras Pereira (Lanham, MD: Rowman & Littlefield, 2011).
37. Philippe Schmitter, *Portugal: Do Autoritarismo à Democracia* (Lisbon: ICS, 1999); and Pinto, 'Political Purges and State Crisis in Portugal's Transition to Democracy 1975–76', 305–332.

38. Carlos Taibo, 'Sovietólogos y Transicionólogos: una Relación Conflictiva'. *Las Transiciones en Europa Central y Oriental* (Madrid: Catarata, 1998), 12.

39. Ferreira, 'Portugal em Transe (1974–1985)'.

40. Adelino Gomes and José Pedro Castanheira, *Os Dias Loucos do PREC: do 11 de Março ao 25 de Novembro de 1975* (Lisbon: Expresso/Publico, 2006).

41. Encarnación Lemus, *En Hamelin … La Transición Española más allá de la Frontera* (Oviedo: Septem Ediciones, 2001).

42. Editor's note: Some of the far-left stressed the need for The Party. One problem was that they often had delusions of grandeur. On occasion the rhetoric espoused by the *grupusculos* was not in touch with reality. Yet, party militants managed to effectively organise around many issues and battled for and alongside working people. One or more sections of the revolutionary left were in the midst of virtually all the struggles and revolts mentioned so far. Often these militants played leading positions and of course it is difficult to say whether this was because the best and most aware militants happened to join political organisations or whether it was because they were in organisations which gave 'the lead' which made them the best militants.

43. Charles Tilly, *Las Revoluciones Europeas, 1492–1992* (Barcelona: Crítica, 1995), 26–27.

44. Tilly, *Las Revoluciones Europeas, 1492–1992*, 23.

45. Perry Anderson, 'Portugal and the End of Ultracolonialism: Part 1, 2 and 3', *New Left Review* 15–17 (1962), 112.

46. Eric Hobsbawm, *Ecos da Marselhesa* (São Paulo: Companhia das Letras, 1999), 8–9.

47. Antonio de Sousa Franco, 'A Economia', in Antonio Reis (ed.), *Portugal 20 Anos de Democracia* (Circulo de Leitores, 1994), 207.

20. In Celebration

1. *La Vanguardia* (Barcelona), 23 March 1975.

2. 1975–1976, as a result of the agrarian policies, which are known together as agrarian reform, the number of permanent jobs rose from 11,100 to 44,100; and the number of temporary jobs rose from 10,600 to 27,800. The area of cultivated dryland rose from 85,000 hectares before the land occupations to 255,000 after. Irrigated areas grew from 7,000 hectares to 16,000. The number of tractors rose from 2,630 to 4,150 and the number of harvesters rose from 960 to 1,720.

3. *Outro País*, Sérgio Tréfaut, Vídeos Público, 25 de Abril, 20 Anos, 2004; see also, Raquel Varela, 'The PCP in the Portuguese Revolution 1974–5: Crisis, State and Revolution', *International Socialist* 157, 9 January 2018, http://isj.org.uk/the-pcp-in-the-portuguese-revolution-1974-5-crisis-state-and-revolution/.

4. I analyse the impact of the cyclical crisis of 1973 in the Portuguese Revolution as well as the relationship between workers' control and social rights in Raquel Varela, *História do PCP na Revolução dos Cravos* (Lisbon: Bertrand, 2011).

5. See William A. Peltz, *A People's History of the German Revolution* (London: Pluto Press, 2018).

6. See 'Tanto Mar' by the famous Brazilian composer Chico Buarque, www.youtube.com/watch?v=ST30-i7cZJk.

Bibliography

Books Written by Raquel Varela

Varela, R. (2005) *Fernão de Magalhães*. Lisbon: Planeta DeAgostini.

Varela, R. (2006) *D. Pedro IV*. Lisbon: Planeta DeAgostini.

Varela, R. (2008) *Breve História da Europa*. Lisbon: Bertrand.

Varela, R. (2011) *História do PCP na Revolução dos Cravos*. Lisbon: Bertrand.

Varela, R. (2012) *25. Abril 1974: Die Nelkenrevolution. Das Ende der Diktatur in Portugal*. Berlin: Laika-Verlag.

Varela, R. (2012) *Quem Paga o Estado Social em Portugal?*, 3rd edn. Lisbon: Bertrand.

Varela, R. (ed.) (2013) *A Segurança Social é Sustentável. Trabalho, Estado e Segurança Social em Portugal*. Lisbon: Bertrand.

Varela, R. (2014) *História do Povo na Revolução Portuguesa (1974–1975)*. Lisbon: Bertrand.

Varela, R. (2015) *Para onde vai Portugal?* Lisbon: Bertrand.

Varela, R., Arcary, V. and Demier, F.A. (2015) *O Que é Uma Revolução? Teoria, História e Historiografia*. Lisbon: Colibri.

Varela, R. and Barbosa Pereira, L. (2017) *História do Povo de Loulé na Revolução Portuguesa (1974–1975)*. Lisbon: Editora Âncora.

Varela, R. and Barbosa Pereira, L. (2017) *História do Povo da Madeira no 25 de Abril*. Lisbon: Parsifal.

Varela, R., Barbosa Pereira, L. and Simões do Paço, A, (2017) *Sines na Revolução dos Cravos*. Lisbon: Colibri.

Varela, R. and Coimbra de Matos, A. (2016) *Do Medo à Esperança*. Lisbon: Bertrand.

Tese de doutoramento, História da Política do Partido Comunista Português na Revolução dos Cravos, Lisboa, ISCTE-IUL, 2010, ®versão eletrónica - ISBN 978-989-732-358-4

® versão impressa - ISBN 978-989-732-360-7 Disponível em http://hdl.handle.net/10071/7112

Books Edited and/or Contributed to by Raquel Varela

Mateus, J., Varela, R., Gaudêncio and S., (2017) *Roteiro da Revolução*. Lisbon: Parsifal.

Simões do Paço, A., Cancela, D., Tavares, M.A. and Varela, R. (2017) *Trabalho, Acumulação Capitalista e Regime Político no Portugal Contemporâneo*. Lisbon: Colibri.

Varela, R. (ed.) (2012) *Revolução ou Transição? História e Memória da Revolução dos Cravos* Lisbon: Bertrand.

Varela, R. *et al.* (2014) *Relações laborais em Portugal e no Mundo Lusófono. História e Demografia*. Lisbon: Colibri.

Varela, R. *et al.* (2015) *Actas do I Congresso de História do Movimento Operário em Portugal.* Lisbon: FCSH-UNL. Ebook open access in https://run.unl.pt/handle/10362/17159.

Varela, R. *et al.* (2015) *Trabalho, educação e conflitos sociais: Diálogos Brasil e Portugal.* São Paulo: Verona.

Varela, R., van der Linden, M. and Murphy, H. (2017) *Shipbuilding Labour Around the World: A Global Labour History.* Amsterdam: Chicago University Press. Ebook open access in http://press.uchicago.edu/ucp/books/book/distributed/S/bo23454408.html.

Varela, R., Noronha, R. and Dias Pereira, J. (2012) *Greves e Conflitos Sociais no Portugal Contemporâneo.* Lisbon: Edições Colibri.

Varela, R., Simões do Paço, A. and van der Velden, S. (2012) *Strikes and Social Conflicts. Towards a Global Labour History.* Lisbon: IASSC-IHC.

References and Further Reading

Abidor, M. (2018) *May Made Me.* London: Pluto.

Afonso, A. and Gomes, C.M. (2000) *A Guerra Colonial.* Lisbon: Editorial Notícias.

Aguilar, P. (1996) *Memoria y Olvido de la Guerra Civil Española.* Madrid: Alianza Editorial.

Almeida, A.N. de, Guerreiro, M.D., Lobo, C., Torres, A. and Wall, K. (1998) 'Relações familiares: mudança e diversidade'. In José Manuel Leite Viegas and António Firmino da Costa (eds), *Portugal, Que Modernidade?* Oeiras: Celta Editora.

Anderson, P. (1962) 'Portugal and the End of Ultra-Colonialism, 2'. *New Left Review* 1(16) (July–August).

Antunes, R. (2013) *Os Sentidos do Trabalho.* Coimbra: Almedina.

Arcary, V. (2004) *Quando o Futuro era Agora: Trinta Anos da Revolucao Portuguesa.* São Paulo: Xamã.

Avilez, M.J. (1996) *Soares: Ditadura e Revolução.* Lisbon: Público.

Bandeirinha, J.M. (2007) *O Processo SAAL e a Arquitectura no 25 de Abril.* Coimbra: University of Coimbra.

Baptista, O. (1978) *Portugal 1975: Os Campos.* Porto: Afrontamento.

Baptista, O. (2001) 'O 25 de Abril, a sociedade rural e a questão da terra'. In J.M. Brandão Brito, *O País em Revolução.* Lisbon: Editorial Notícias.

Barros, A. (1986) *Do Latifúndio à Reforma Agrária: o caso de uma freguesia do Baixo Alantejo.* Lisbon: Fundação Calouste Gulbenkian.

Barreto, A. (1987) *Anatomia de uma Revolução: A Reforma Agrária em Portugal, Europa–America.* Lisbon: Europa-América.

Barreto, A. (2005) 'Mudança Social em Portugal: 1960–2000'. In António Costa Pinto (ed.), *Portugal Contemporâneo.* Lisbon: D. Quixote.

Barreto, A. and Valadas Preto, C. (1996) *Portugal 1960/1995: Indicadores Sociais.* Lisbon: ICS and Público.

Beaud, M. (1992) *História do Capitalismo.* Lisbon: Teorema.

Bebiano, R. (2002) 'As Esquerdas e a Oposição à Guerra Colonial'. In *A Guerra do Ultramar: Realidade e Ficção. Atas do II Congresso sobre a Guerra Colonial.* Lisbon: Editorial Notícias – Universidade Aberta, 293–313.

Bermao, N. (1983) 'Worker Management in Industry'. In Lawrence S. Graham and Douglas L. Wheeler (eds), *In Search of Modern Portugal: The Revolution and Its Consequences.* Madison, WI: University of Wisconsin Press.

Bermeo, N. (1986) *The Revolution within the Revolution: Workers Control in Rural Portugal.* Princeton, NJ: Princeton University Press.

Borges, V. (2007) *O Mundo do Teatro em Portugal: profissão de actor, organizações e mercado de trabalho.* Lisbon: Imprensa de Ciências Sociais.

Breyner Andresen, S.M. (1997) *Log Book: Selected Poems (Aspects of Portugal)* trans. Richard Zenith. Manchester: Carcanet Press.

Brinton, M. (1975) *Os Bolcheviques e o Controlo Operário.* Porto: Afrontamento.

Brito, C. (2010) Álvaro Cunhal, Os Sete Fôlegos do Combatente, Memórias. Lisbon: Edições Nelson de Matos.

Caldas, J.C. (2001) *Terra e Trabalho.* Oeiras: Celta.

Campos, A.C. de (2000) 'Saúde Pública'. In António Barreto and Maria Filomena Mónica (eds), *Dicionário de História de Portugal,* Vol. 9. Porto: Figueirinhas.

Cann, J.P. (1997) *Counterinsurgency in Africa: The Portuguese Way of War, 1961–1974.* Westport, CT: Greenwood Press.

Capucha, L. (1999) 'Assistência Social'. In António Barreto and Maria Filomena Mónica (eds), *Dicionário de História de Portugal,* Vol. 7. Porto: Figueirinhas.

Carrillo-Linares, A. (2008) *Subversivos y Malditos en la Universidad de Sevilla (1965–1977).* Seville: Centro de Estudios Andaluces.

Cerezales, D. (2011) *Portugal à Corunhada: Protesto Popular e Ordem Pública nos séculos XIX e XX.* Lisbon: Tinta-da-china.

Cerezales, D.P. (2003) *O poder caiu na rua: Crise de estado e acções colectivas na revolução portuguesa.* Lisbon: Imprensa de Ciências Sociais.

Cervelló, J.S. (1993) *A Revolução Portuguesa e a sua Influência na Transição Espanhola (1961–1976).* Lisbon: Assirio e Alvim.

Chuva Vasco, N. (2005) *Os ultimos 50 anos da pintura e escultura portuguesa do século XX.* Figueira da Foz, Chuva Vasco.

Cliff, T. (1975) 'Portugal at the Crossroads: The Collapse of the Fascist Regime'. *International Socialism* 81–82, Special Issue, September, Marxists Internet Archive, www.marxists.org/archive/cliff/works/1975/portugal/2-collapse.htm.

Cliff, T. and Harman, C. (1975) *Portugal: Lessons of the 25th of November.* Marxists Internet Archive, www.marxists.org/archive/cliff/works/1975/12/lessons.htm.

Cliff, T. and Peterson, R. (1976) 'Portugal: The Last 3 Months'. *International Socialism* 87 (March–April).

Coggiola, O. and Martins, J. (2006) *Dinâmicas da Globalização: Mercado Mundial e Ciclos Económicos, 1970–2005.* São Paulo: Instituto Rosa Luxemburgo.

Cohen, S. (2011) 'Workers' Councils: The Red Mole of Revolution'. In Immanuel Ness and Dario Azzellini (eds), *Ours to Master and to Own: Workers' Control from the Commune to the Present.* Chicago, IL: Haymarket.

Comissão Coordenadora das Empresas em Autogestao, Duarte, D., Ferreira, L., Trindade, N. and Fonseca, V.C. de (1981) *A Realidade da Autogestão em Portugal*. Lisbon: Perspectivas & Realidades.

Cooke, S. (2014) *The Response of the Labour Government to the 'Revolution of Carnations' in Portugal, 1974–76*. PhD University College London, http://discovery.ucl.ac.uk/1452985/1/Simon_Cooke_-_PhD_-_November_2014.pdf.

Cristovam, M.L. (1982) *Conflitos de Trabalho em 1979: Breve Análise Sociológica*. Lisbon: Ministério do Trabalho.

Cunhal, A. (1975) *Discursos Políticos (3)*. Lisbon: Edições Avante!.

Cunhal, A. (1976) *A Crise Político-Militar. Discursos Políticos 5*. Lisbon: Edições Avante!.

Cunhal, A. (1976) *Do 25 de Novembro às Eleições para a Assembleia Constituinte. Discursos Políticos 6*. Lisbon: Edições Avante!.

Cunhal, A. (1994) *A Revolução Portuguesa: Passado e Futuro*. Lisbon: Edições Avante!.

Davidson, B. (1969) *Révolution en Afrique: la Libération de la Guinée Portugaise*. Paris: Éditions du Seuil.

Davidson, B. (1992) *The Black Man's Burden: Africa and the Curse of the Nation-State*. Times Books/Random House.

Doménech Sampere, X. (2002) 'El Cambio Político (1962–1976): Materiales para una perspetiva desde abajo'. *Historia del Presente: La sociedad Española durante el Segundo Franquismo*, Asociación Historiadores del Presente, UNED – Centro Asociado de Melilla, no. 1.

Demier, F. (2013) *O Longo Bonapartismo Brasileiro (1930–1964): um ensaio de interpretação histórica*. Rio de Janeiro: Mauad.

Dornbusch, R., Eckaus, R.S. and Taylor, L. (1976) *Analysis and Projections of Macroeconomic Conditions in Portugal*. Report from OCDE-sponsored mission to Portugal, 15–20 December 1975. Lisbon: MIT.

Downs, C. (1980) *Community Organization, Political Change and Urban Policy: Portugal 1974–1976*. PhD thesis, Berkeley, CA: University of California.

Downs, C. (1983) 'Residents' Commissions and Urban Struggles in Revolutionary Portugal'. In Lawrence S. Graham and Douglas L. Wheeler (eds), *In Search of Modern Portugal: The Revolution and Its Consequences*. Madison, WI: University of Wisconsin Press.

Downs, C. (1990) *Revolution at the Grass Roots: Community Organisations in the Portuguese Revolution*. Albany, NY: SUNY.

Dows, C. (1978) *Os Moradores à Conquista da Cidade*. Lisbon: Armazém das Letras.

Ferreira, A.M. (1993) 'Portugal em Transe (1974–1985)'. In José Mattoso (ed.), *História de Portugal*. Lisbon: Círculo de Leitores.

Ferreira, H.G. and Marshall, M.W. (1986) *Portugal's Revolution: Ten Years On*. Cambridge: Cambridge University Press.

Fonseca, A.M. (2010) 'Apoio da social-democracia alemã à democratização portuguesa (1974–1976)'. *Ler História* 63 (Lisbon: ISCTE-IUL): 93–108.

Fonseca, B.M. (2008) *Ideologia ou Economia? Evolução da Proteção no Desemprego em Portugal*. Masters Thesis, Universidade de Aveiro.

Freitas, J.G.A. (2009) *A Guerra dos Cartazes*. Guimarães: LembrAbril.

Freudenthal, A. (1995–1999) 'A Baixa de Cassange: Algodão e Revolta'. *Revista Internacional de Estudos Africanos* 18–22.

Furet, F. (1989) *Pensando a Revolução Francesa*. Rio de Janeiro: Editora Paz e Terra.

Gaspar, J. and Vitorino, N. (1976) *As Eleições de 25 de Abril: Geografia e Imagem dos partidos*. Lisbon: Livros Horizonte.

Goldner, L. (2000) *Ubu Saved from Drowning: Class Struggle and Statist Containment in Portugal and Spain, 1974–1977*. Cambridge, MA: Queequeg Publications.

Gomes, A. and Castanheira, J.P. (2006) *Os Dias Loucos do PREC*. Lisbon: Expresso-Publico.

Gomes, B. and Moreira de Sá, T. (2011) *Carlucci versus Kissinger*, trans. Susana Serras Pereira. Lanham, MD: Rowman & Littlefield.

Gomes, M. (2011) 'O Lado Feminino da Revolucao dos Cravos'. *Storia e Futuro* 25 (February).

Gonçalves, V. (1977) *Discursos, Conferências, Entrevistas*. Lisbon: Seara Nova.

Graham, L.S. and Wheeler, D.L. (1986) *In Search of Modern Portugal: The Revolution and Its Consequences*. Madison: WI: University of Wisconsin Press.

Green, Gill. (1976) *Portugal's Revolution*. New York: International Publishers.

Guimarães, S. (1978) *As Paredes na revolução*. Lisbon: Mil Dias.

Guinote, J.C. (2008) 'Urbanismo e corrupcao: as mais-valias e o desenvolvimento urbano'. *Le Monde Diplomatique*, Portuguese edition, 6 August.

Hammond, J.L. (1981) 'Worker Control in Portugal: The Revolution and Today'. *Economic and Industrial Democracy* 2(4) (December).

Hammond, J.L. (1988) *Building Popular Power: Workers' and Neighbourhood Movements in the Portuguese Revolution*. New York: Monthly Review Press.

Harman, C. (1974) 'Portugal: The First Six Months'. *International Socialism* 72 (October): 5-6, Marxists Internet Archive, www.marxists.org/archive/harman/1974/10/portugal.htm.

Harman, C. (1988) *The Fire Last Time: 1968 and After*. London: Bookmarks.

Harman, C. (1999) *A People's History of the World*. London: Bookmarks.

Hobsbawm, E. (1999) *Ecos da Marselhesa*. São Paulo: Companhia das Letras.

Howard, Z. (1999) *A People's History of the United States*. New York: HarperCollins.

International Socialism (1975) 'Portugal: The Views of a PRP Leader'. *International Socialism* 80 (July–August), Marxists Internet Archive, www.marxists.org/history/etol/newspape/isj/1975/no080/prp.htm.

Jiménez Redondo, J.C. (1996) *Franco e Salazar: As Relações Luso-Espanholas durante a Guerra fria*. Lisbon: Assírio e Alvim.

Leiria, L. (2008) '25 de Abril: a guerra para conseguir a paz'. In António Simões do Paço, *Os Anos de Salazar*, Vol. 30. Lisbon: Planeta DeAgostini.

Light, B. (2014) 'Portugal 1974–5'. *International Socialism*, 142, 25 April, http://isj.org.uk/portugal-1974-5/.

Linden, M. van der (2008) *Workers of the World: Essays toward a Global Labor History*. Leiden: Brill.

Little, D. (2009) 'Primitive Accumulation'. *Understanding Society*, 29 March.

Lomax, B. (1983) 'Ideology and Illusion in the Portuguese Revolution: The Role of the Left'. In Lawrence S. Graham and Douglas L. Wheeler (eds), *In Search of*

Modern Portugal: The Revolution and its Consequences. Madison, WI: University of Wisconsin Press.

Lopes, J.S. (1999) *A Economia Portuguesa desde 1960*. Lisbon: Gradiva.

Lucena, M. de (2000) 'Previdência Social'. In Maria Filomena Mónica and António Barreto (eds), *Dicionário de História de Portugal*, Vol. 9. Porto: Figueirinhas.

McGrogan, M. (2017) 'Rendezvous with a Revolution: British Socialists in Portugal 1974–5'. *Interventions* 19(5).

Mailer, P. (1977) *Portugal: The Impossible Revolution?* London: Solidarity.

Mailer, P. (2014) 'Murals of the Carnation Revolution'. *Signal* (April).

Marques, J. (1974) *As Paredes em Liberdade*. Lisbon: Teorema.

Marx, K. (2011) *Capital: A Critique of Political Economy*, Vol. 1. London: Penguin Books.

Marx, K. (2011) *O Capital*. São Paulo: Boitempo Editorial.

Mascarenhas, J.M. (ed.) (2004) *A Cor de Abril*. Lisbon: Câmara Municipal de Lisboa.

Mateus, D.C. (2004) *A PIDE/DGS e a Guerra Colonial*. Lisbon: Terramar, 2004.

Mateus, D.C. (2006) *Memórias do Colonialismo e da Guerra*. Porto: Edições Asa.

Mateus, D.C. (2012) 'Conflitos Sociais na Base da Eclosão das Guerras Coloniais'. In Joana Dias Pereira, Raquel Varela and Ricardo Noronha (eds), *Greves e Conflitos Sociais em Portugal no Século XX*. Lisbon: Colibri.

Maués, F. (2012) 'A edicao politica em Portugal: Do combate a ditadura a Revolucao dos Cravos'. *Literatura e Autoritarismo* (May).

Maxwell, K. (1995) *The Making of Portuguese Democracy*. Cambridge: Cambridge University Press.

Maxwell, K. (2009) 'Portugal: The Revolution of the Carnations, 1974–75'. In Adam Roberts and Timothy Garton Ash (eds), *Civil Resistance and Power Politics: The Experience of Non-Violent Action from Gandhi to the Present*. Oxford: Oxford University Press.

Monteiro, T.L. (1993) 'Janelas entreabertas: os valores, as normas'. In José Mattoso (ed.), *História da Vida Privada: Os Nossos Dias*. Lisbon: Círculo de Leitores.

Muñoz, R.D. (2000) *Contención y Transgresión: Las Movilizaciones Sociales y el Estado en las Transiciones Española y Portuguesa*. Madrid: CPPC.

Neves, O. (ed.) (1976) *Textos Históricos da Revolução*. Lisbon: Diabril.

Oliveira, C. (1995) *Cem Anos nas Relações Luso-Espanholas. Política e Economia*. Lisbon: Edições Cosmos.

Oliveira, M. de (2010) *Para uma Cartografia da Criacao Dramatica Portuguesa Contemporanea (1974–2004), Os Autores Portugueses do Teatro Independente: Repertorios e Canones*. Masters dissertation, Estudos Artisticos, Faculdade de Letras da Universidade de Coimbra.

Patriarca, F. (1976) 'Controlo Operário em Portugal (I)'. *Análise Social* 12(3).

Patriarca, F. (1976) 'Controlo Operário em Portugal (II)'. *Análise Social* 12(4).

Peltz, W.A. (2018) *A People's History of The German Revolution*. London: Pluto Press.

Pérez, M. (2008) *Contra a Exploracao Capitalista. Comissoes de Trabalhadores e Luta Operaria na Revolucao Portuguesa (1974–75)*. Masters dissertation in History of Nineteenth and Twentieth Centuries, Faculty of Social Sciences and Humanities, Universidade Nova de Lisboa, August.

Pérez, M. (2013) 'A mobilizacao operaria anticapitalista na Revolucao de 1974–75'. I Congresso de Historia do Movimento Operario e dos Movimentos Sociais, 15–17 March 2013, Lisbon, FCSH-UNL.

Pérez, M. (2016) 'Comissões de trabalhadores'. In *Dicionário de História de Portugal: o 25 de Abril*. Porto: Figueirinhas.

Pérez, M. (2017) 'Comissoes de moradores'. In *Dicionário Histórico do 25 de Abril*. Porto: Figueirinhas.

Piçarra, C. (2008) *As Ocupações de Terras no Distrito de Beja, 1974–1975*. Coimbra: Almedina.

Piçarra, C. (ed.) (2009) *Campos do Sul: Memória de uma Revolução*. Lisbon: IHC.

Piçarra, (2012) 'A Reforma Agraria no Sul de Portugal (1975)'. In Raquel Varela (ed.), *Revolução ou Transição? História e Memória da Revolução dos Cravos*. Lisbon: Bertrand.

Pimentel, I.F. (1999) 'A assistência social e familiar do Estado Novo nos anos 30 e 40'. *Análise Social* 34(151–152): 477–508.

Pimentel, I.F. (2000) *História das Organizações Femininas no Estado Novo*. Lisbon: Círculo de Leitores.

Pimentel, I.F. (2007) *História da PIDE*. Lisbon: Círculo de Leitores/Temas e Debates.

Pinto, A.C. (1999) 'Saneamentos Políticos e Movimentos Radicais de Direita na Transição para a Democracia, 1974–1976'. In Fernando Rosas (ed.), *Portugal e a Transição para a Democracia*. Lisbon: Edições Colibri/IHC.

Pinto, A.C. (2001) *O Fim do Império Português*. Lisbon: Livros Horizonte.

Pinto, A.C. (2008) 'Political Purges and State Crisis in Portugal's Transition to Democracy 1975–76'. *Journal of Contemporary History* 43(2): 305–332.

Pinto, P.R. (2008) 'Urban Social Movements and the Transition to Democracy in Portugal, 1974–1976'. *The Historical Journal* 51(4): 1025–1046.

Pinto Rema, H. (1982) *História das Missões Católicas da Guiné*. Braga: Editorial Franciscana.

Pires, J. (1978) *O Povo em Acção: Greves e o 25 de Abril*. Lisbon: Edições Base.

Porch, D. (1977) *The Portuguese Armed Forces and The Revolution*. London: Croom Helm.

Portas, N. (1986) 'O Processo SAAL: entre o Estado e o Poder Local'. *Revista Crítica de Ciências Sociais* 18, 19, 20 (February): 635–644.

Poulantzas, N. (1976) *The Crisis of the Dictatorships: Portugal, Greece and Spain*. London: New Left Books.

Preston, P. (1993) *Franco: A Biography*. London: HarperCollins.

Ramos, R. (ed.) (2009) *História de Portugal*. Lisbon: Esfera dos Livros.

Raposo, E.M. (2005) *O Canto e o cante: a alma do povo*. Lisbon: Público.

Rezola, M.I. (2006) *Os Militares na Revolução de Abril: O Conselho da Revolução e a Transição para a Democracia em Portugal*. Lisbon: Campo da Comunicação.

Robinson, P. (1979) 'Portugal 1974–5: Popular Power'. In Colin Barker (ed.), *Revolutionary Rehearsals*. London: Bookmarks.

Robinson, P. (1999) *Portugal 1974–1975: The Forgotten Dream*. London: Socialist History Society, www.socialisthistorysociety.co.uk/wp-content/uploads/2017/04/robport.pdf.

Robinson, P. (1990) *Workers' Councils in Portugal 1974–1975*. MPhil thesis, Centre for Sociology & Social University, Open University, http://oro.open.ac.uk/19940/1/pdf115.pdf.

Robinson, P. (2011) 'Workers' Councils in Portugal, 1974–1975'. In Immanuel Ness and Dario Azzellini (eds), *Ours to Master and to Own: Workers' Control from the Commune to the Present*. Chicago, IL: Haymarket.

Robinson, P. (2013) 'Portugal 1974–75: Soldiers on the Side of the People'. In Mike Gonzalez and Houman Barekat (eds), *Arms and the People: Popular Movements and the Military from the Paris Commune to the Arab Spring*. London: Pluto Press.

Robinson, R. (1979) *Contemporary Portugal: A History*. London: George Allen & Unwin.

Rodrigues, F. (ed.) (1994) *O Futuro era Agora*. Lisbon: Dinossauro.

Rodrigues, J.A. (1983) 'Continuidade e mudança nos papéis das mulheres urbanas portuguesas: emergência de novas estruturas familiares'. *Análise Social* 19(77–79): 909–938.

Rosa, E. (1975) *A Economia Portuguesa em Números*. Lisbon: Moraes Editora.

Santos, M.L., Pires de Lima, M. and Ferreira, V.M. (1976) *O 25 de Abril e as Lutas Sociais nas Empresas*. Porto: Afrontamento, 3 vols.

Saramago, J. (1990) 'A Distancia como Politica, 8 October 1975'. In José Saramago, *Os Apontamentos*. Lisbon: Caminho.

Schmitter, P. (1999) *Portugal: Do Autoritarismo à Democracia*. Lisbon: ICS.

Silva, M. (1985) 'A repartição do rendimento em Portugal no pos-25 de Abril 74'. *Revista Crítica de Ciências Sociais* 15–17 (May).

Sivard, R.L. (1987) *World Military and Social Expenditures 1987–88*, 12th edn. Washington, DC: World Priorities.

Spínola, A. de (1974) *Portugal e o Futuro*. Lisbon: Arcádia.

Spriano, P. (1975) *The Occupation of the Factories – Italy 1920*. London: Pluto Press.

Solsten, E. (ed.) (1993) *Portugal: A Country Study*. Washington, DC: GPO for the Library of Congress.

Sousa Franco, A. de (1994) 'A Economia'. In Antonio Reis (ed.), *Portugal 20 Anos de Democracia*. Circulo de Leitores.

Sousa Santos, B. (1984) 'A Crise e a Reconstituição do Estado em Portugal, 1974–1984'. *Revista Crítica de Ciências Sociais* 14 (November): 7–29.

Sunday Times Insight Team (1975) *Portugal: The Year of the Captains*. London: Andre Deutsch.

Sweezy, P.M. (1975) 'Class Struggles in Portugal: Part I'. *Monthly Review* 27(4) (September): 1–26.

Tavares, M. (2000) *Movimentos de Mulheres em Portugal, décadas de 70 e 80*. Lisbon: Livros Horizonte.

Tilly, C. (1995) *Las Revoluciones Europeas, 1492–1992* Barcelona: Critica.

Trotsky, L. *História da Revolução Russa*, Vol. 1. Lisbon: Versus.

Valente, J. (2001) 'O Movimento Operario e Sindical (1970–1976): entre o Corporativismo e a Unicidade'. In J.M. Brandao Brito (ed.), *O País em Revolução*. Lisbon: Editorial Noticias.

Varela, R. (2008) 'Oficiais milicianos optam pela deserção'. In António Simões do Paço (ed.), *Os Anos de Salazar*. Lisbon: Planeta DeAgostini, Vol. 26, 60–69.

Varela, R. (2011) *A História do PCP na Revolução dos Cravos*. Lisbon: Bertrand Editora.

Varela, R. (2018) 'The PCP in the Portuguese Revolution 1974–5: Crisis, State and Revolution'. *International Socialism* blog, 9 January, http://isj.org.uk/the-pcp-in-the-portuguese-revolution-1974-5-crisis-state-and-revolution/.

Varela, R. and Sandra Duarte, S. (2013) 'Paixão pela educação ... privada. Educação e terceira via em Portugal: da revolução dos cravos aos nossos dias'. In Vera Peroni (ed.), *Redefinições das fronteiras entre o público e o privado: implicações para a democratização da educação*. Brasília: Liber livro editora, 120–140.

Wall, K. (1993) 'A Intervencao do Estado: Politicas publicas de familia'. In José Mattoso (ed.), *História da Vida Privada: Os Nossos Dias*. Lisbon: Círculo de Leitores.

Wallraff, G. (1978) *The Undesirable Journalist*. London: Pluto Press.

Wise, A. (1975) *Eyewitness in Revolutionary Portugal*. Nottingham: Bertrand Russell Peace Foundation for Spokesman Books.

Index

About the Author

Raquel Varela is an historian whose areas of study are the Carnation Revolution, labour history and the welfare state. She is a researcher at the Institute of Contemporary History at the Universidade Nova de Lisboa where she coordinates the Study Group 'Labour and Social Conflict' and the International Institute of Social History, Amsterdam where she coordinates the *'In the Same Boat?'* project which covers International Shipbuilding and Ship Repair Workers around the World (1950–2010). She is also project coordinator of the History of Industrial Relations in the Portuguese speaking world. She has a PhD in Political and Institutional History from the ISCTE - University Institute Lisbon. She is currently president of the International Association of Strikes and Social Conflicts and co-editor of its scholarly journal, *Workers of the World: International Journal of Strikes and Social Conflicts*. She is vice-coordinator of the Study Network on Labour, the Labour Movement and Social Movements in Portugal.